Philosophy Through Film

Second Edition

Burton Porter
Western New England College

SLOAN
PUBLISHING

2009
SLOAN PUBLISHING
Cornwall-on-Hudson, NY 12520

Library-of-Congress Cataloging-in-Publication Data

Porter, Burton Frederick.
Philosophy Through Film / Burton Porter. -- 2nd ed.
p. cm.
Rev. ed. of: Philosophy through fiction and film, 2004.
Includes bibliographical references and index.
ISBN 978-1-59738-018-8 (alk. Paper)
1. Literature and morals. 2. Motion pictures--Moral and ethical aspects. I. Porter, Burton Frederick. Philosophy through fiction and film. II. Title.
PN49.P675 2009
791.43'68--dc22
2008011927

Cover photo: Still from *On the Waterfront*, reprinted with the
   permission of Sony Pictures Entertainment
Cover designer: Amy Rosen

© 2009
Sloan Publishing, LLC
220 Maple Road
Cornwall-on-Hudson, NY 12520

First edition published in 2004 by Pearson Education.

Printed in the United States of America

10 9 8 7 6 5 4 3 2 1

ISBN–13: 978-1-59738-018-8
ISBN–10: 1-59738-018-0

To my wife Barbara and my son Mark—
twin sources of warmth, stability, and sustenance,
and to those engaged, and reflective students
throughout the years who have had some of the
best of myself.

Contents

Preface

Philosophy Through Film was written to introduce students to philosophy by means of films as well as the systematic works of philosophers. The book therefore incorporates the perspectives of creative directors to express philosophic ideas as well as the major philosophers themselves. Through this two-dimensional approach, the student is better able to understand philosophy, for the concepts are presented in a more immediate and lively way, one that shows their various facets and appeal to different learning styles.

The works that are excerpted or summarized from moving pictures are grouped under the major branches of philosophy, each in a separate chapter. Substantial introductions describe each of the branches and critically evaluate the basic concepts and theories within them. At the end of each chapter an extensive bibliography is provided for further exploration; this should be especially valuable for identifying films that contain philosophic themes. A list of literary works is also provided that have strong philosophic ideas. As Santayana said, "All great literature is inherently philosophical."

The book therefore covers the major fields of philosophy, showing their exposition in philosophic works and their expression in film. The fields include epistemology or theory of knowledge; metaphysics, the study of the nature of reality; ethics, the evaluation of our life purpose, conduct, and character; philosophy of religion, the critical analysis of religious belief; and political philosophy, theories of the ideal state. In the case of films, synopses are provided that explain the philosophic points they express, intrinsically or overtly. Study questions follow each selection to further illustrate the philosophic concepts.

The principal of selection used is that of major philosophic works and high-quality films by world standards. As might be expected, employing this principle results in a diverse and multicultural group of selections from a variety of countries. The ancient, Medieval, modern, and contemporary world are all represented. The bibliographies contain an even broader array of works from North America, South America, Europe, Africa, and Asia.

To view philosophy through film can animate the ideas and place them within a human context. Philosophy and film often have similar concerns, so films can offer a unique and engaging introduction to philosophy, showing the basic issues of human life in a moving way. Because films are so prevalent today, resonating strongly with audiences, their inclusion makes the philosophic ideas more current, personal, and accessible. Most students will be more familiar with the films than with the philosophic works, and the expositions will show their philosophic meaning.

Students who read the headnotes and synopses of the films should then view the film itself (or re-view it) whenever possible. For the impact of seeing the film far exceeds that of the summary, just as the musical score is meant to be performed and the written play takes on depth when staged in a theater. Classes can watch a film together; individual students can screen DVDs in a viewing room in the library; or videotapes can be made available to be viewed at home. This is especially valuable for long films and when class time is better used for explication and discussion. Additional viewing assignments could also be valuable in understanding philosophy through film. Students could watch 2 or 3 outside films during the term, drawn from the bibliography or current releases, and report on the philosophic ideas they contain. These could be individual or group projects, for presentation in class or in written form.

Philosophy Through Film therefore offers an original approach to philosophy using film narratives along with standard philosophic works. The fundamental fields of philosophy are covered but in a fresh way, using a wide range of sources and a variety of viewpoints. As Thomas Mann wrote, "All subject matter is boring unless ideas shine through it." The films enrich the philosophic dialogue, linking traditional philosophy to our contemporary experience, while the philosophic works ground the issues, showing their deeper significance. The result is that philosophy comes alive as something vivid and compelling.

ACKNOWLEDGEMENTS

I wish to thank the editor of Sloan Publishing, Bill Webber, for his advice and assistance throughout this project; he is to be commended for his genuine commitment to educational publishing. I also wish to acknowledge the work of Ross Miller, the editor at Prentice Hall who guided the first version of this book to publication. Wendy Yurash, assistant editor, also deserves recognition for her keen mind and gentle hand.

During the process of bringing this book to fruition, the following individuals reviewed the manuscript and offered suggestions for its improvement: Scott D. Blackwell, Indiana University; Dan Flory, Montana State University; Richard Gilmore, Concordia College; Joseph H. Kupfer, Iowa State University; and Thomas E. Wartenberg, Mount Holyoke College. I am grateful for all of their ideas.

Burton F. Porter
Amherst, Massachusetts

Introduction:
The Basic Branches of
Philosophy

The field of philosophy can be divided into several branches, although how the division should be made is a matter of some dispute. For the nature of philosophy is itself a philosophic issue, so different philosophers divide the field in different ways depending upon their philosophies.

One common classification, however, is to recognize five distinct branches: *epistemology*, the study of how to gain reliable knowledge; *metaphysics*, which is concerned with what is ultimately real; *ethics*, dealing with worthwhile actions and goals in living; *logic*, or systematic, rigorous reasoning; and *aesthetics*, the search for standards in judging art.

In addition, philosophers will often include within the field the philosophic dimensions of other areas of knowledge. Thus we have the philosophy of politics, of science, of religion, of psychology, and so forth. (Sometimes aesthetics is categorized as the philosophy of art.) In each case the philosopher is interested in exploring the presuppositions, methods, relations, implications, and basic nature of the academic area. What assumptions lie behind the theory of natural rights or a paternalistic theory of government? What evidence does the scientist use as opposed to the religious believer? What are the implications of regarding people as rational beings or as stimulus-response mechanisms?

In this introductory textbook, we examine the basic branches of epistemology, metaphysics, and ethics. We also study the philosophy of religion and the political philosophy–two especially intriguing areas of philosophy.

I. Obtaining Reliable Knowledge: Epistemology

The main issue of epistemology is how to gain genuine knowledge. The epistemologist, as he or she is called, is not concerned with what we know but *how* we know, not what is real but the basis for asserting that something is real. In what way does knowledge differ from personal belief, or understanding from mere matters of opinion? How can we differentiate between certainties, guesses, hypotheses, convictions, and self-evident truths?

We all maintain that certain things exist such as the mountain we see in the distance, the person we touch, the sunset or rainbow that we find beautiful, and so forth, but such claims are based on some means of knowing that we trust. When we question whether that means does in fact disclose reality, then we are engaged in epistemological speculation.

The mountain appears small from a distance but huge if we have to climb it, and purple from far away but green with trees close up. Is the mountain small and purple or gigantic and green? We think we can touch other people but from the standpoint of physics that never occurs. It is only that an electrical repulsion is set up between the atoms in our fingers and the atoms in the other person's body. We never touch the person at all. Furthermore, the sun does not actually set, rather we view the earth turning, and the colors we admire in the rainbow are only the refraction and reflection of the sun's rays in drops of rain. We will never find the pot of gold because, as we approach the end of the rainbow, the color is no longer visible. Has it faded to nothing or was it nothing to begin with?

Considerations of this kind make us wonder what we truly know, and in our most skeptical moments, we question whether we are equipped to grasp reality at all. The Chinese philosopher Lao-tze once said "The other night I dreamt I was a butterfly flitting from flower to flower. Now I do not know if I was a man dreaming I was a butterfly or whether I am now a butterfly dreaming I am a man."

In this chapter we will address two epistemological questions: Can we distinguish between appearance and reality, and if knowledge is attainable, what means of knowing is the most reliable in understanding the world?

1.   APPEARANCE AND REALITY: IS THE WORLD THE WAY IT SEEMS?

The preliminary problem of epistemology lies in separating the way things seem from what they are. How can we gain access to the real world rather than experiencing illusions of the senses and delusions of the mind? We know the magician is tricking us but we would swear the woman was cut in half and that the rabbit came out of an empty hat. In the same way, we may be convinced that a table is solid and stationary whereas the physicist will tell us it consists mainly of space and of atoms in constant motion. A stick may look bent in water when in fact it is straight, and train tracks appear to come together in the distance even though parallel lines never meet. Sugar looks white to the naked eye but under a microscope it appears black. In all objects, the greater the magnification, the greater the difference with ordinary perception, so we are never sure at what distance the actual object is perceived.

Similarly, the telescope enables astronomers to understand that the earth is rotating on its axis, orbiting the sun, wheeling through the cosmos as part of the Milky Way galaxy, and moving outwards in the continuing expansion of the universe, like dots on an inflating balloon. We are constantly moving in four directions at once while not being aware of any motion at all. To take another example from astronomy, because of the enormous distances between the stars and the earth, starlight can take years to reach us—even traveling at a speed of 186,281 miles per second. This means that we do not see the stars as they are but as they were. In fact, some of the stars we think we now see may have disappeared by the time we see them, so that we are looking at a ghostly image of the past.

At the individual level, we never know whether other people experience the same world that we do. We are not sure that another person sees the same hue of red in the flower, tastes the same delicious or awful flavor, or has identical emotions of love, depression, contentment, or sympathy. Can we ever share our feelings with others or are we each trapped inside our skins, forever alone and confined to a private world? Perhaps the problem of communication stems from the fact that no two people experience the world the same way, so that when someone uses words such as beautiful, considerate, loyal, or democratic, they may mean very different things. Disputes over whether something is green or blue, may only indicate that people learned to use the words differently.

Aside from such considerations (what is sometimes called the "egocentric predicament"), we have an additional problem in interpreting someone else's behavior. We may not know whether another person can be trusted, whether they are being sincere or manipulative, and whether they are enjoying our company or only pretending to for some devious purpose. A boy whose friend passes him by without saying hello may ask himself "Did he deliberately ignore me or was he preoccupied with other things?" A girl in a romantic situation may wonder "Why did he say that he loves me?"

Even greater problems occur when people believe in the fantastic, uncanny, or bizarre, claiming to have special knowledge that goes beyond ordinary comprehension. Then we have enormous problems in separating what seems so to that person from what is so. For example, suppose someone maintains that déjà vu demonstrates we have all lived previous lives, that dreams are premonitions of disasters, maybe predestined disasters, or that the 22 tarot cards can be used for telling fortunes. Suppose people believe that there is a monster in Loch Ness, that ships disappear in the Bermuda Triangle, or Yetis (Abominable Snowmen) inhabit the Himalayas. How can such assertions be disproven? How can we separate superstition from religious beliefs that are also claimed to surpass all understanding?

To take Christianity, which is our dominant Western religion, we are asked to believe that Christ transformed water into wine, fed the multitude with a small number of loaves and fishes, healed the sick and disabled, cast out demons, raised the dead, and was himself resurrected. What reasons can be offered to accept such miracles—reasons that differentiate them from absurd or even dangerous beliefs? Are these events to be taken literally or are they important just to show how God works in the world?

Fairly recently the members of a religious cult called Heaven's Gate committed mass suicide. They were convinced that creatures of superior intelligence were waiting for them in rocket ships in the tail of Hale-Bopp comet. Prior to that, members of a cult in Guyana drank Kool Aid laced with poison on the orders of their leader, Jim Jones; 900 men, women, and children died. The epistemological question is how can we know when we are in receipt of divine revelation and when we are acting in a delusional or psychotic way?

2.   MODES OF KNOWING: PERCEIVING, REASONING, INTUITING

Not only is the epistemologist concerned with issues of appearance and reality but with finding the most trustworthy means of knowing.

   a. Empiricism.   To most people, the evidence of the senses is most reliable, and to trust sense perception as the foundation of knowledge is called empiricism. People use their eyes and ears primarily to take in the world but also their sense of smell, taste, and touch. We say "seeing is believing," and we mean to include all of our senses as means of gaining understanding of the world. If someone asks "How do you know there was an avalanche?," it is enough to say "Because I saw it and heard it," and if someone asks "What makes you say dinner is ready?" they will be satisfied if you answer "Because I smelled the aroma, then tasted some of the food cooking in the kitchen." According to the conventional rules, a statement is proven if we can cite some sense experience as evidence for it.

   Science, of course, depends upon the empirical method as the foundation of its claims. Through observation and experimentation the physical and natural sciences reach results that we accept today as true. Science, in fact, is not so much a particular subject matter as a method for obtaining reliable knowledge. Both astronomy and astrology take the stars as their subject matter but only one is a science; the same is true of chemistry and alchemy. Even though they all deal with the physical properties of matter, astronomy and chemistry use careful observation and precise measurement. They formulate hypotheses to account for known phenomena, then test these hypotheses to see whether the predicted results actually occur. In short, scientific method differentiates science from other things, and that method uses sense perception as its foundation.

   However, as we have seen above, our senses can deceive us. The reality revealed by the telescope and the microscope is very different from that disclosed by our ordinary sense perception; we never see the stars any more than the molecules underlying matter. The table is not stationary and solid, the sun neither rises nor sets, and parallel train tracks never meet, although all these things appear true to our senses. Since mistakes of this kind are extremely common, perhaps our sense perception is not reliable after all.

Furthermore, empiricism may be too narrow in scope to capture every dimension of reality. People who make statements about historical or mathematical truths, or judgments about ethics or aesthetics, do not claim to *see* that their ideas are right. In the same way, religious people who claim that God exists, or who believe in angels, prayer, miracles, or an afterlife, do not cite the evidence of their senses as proof. Faith is thought to transcend our ordinary understanding.

b. Rationalism.   Because the senses are so fallible and limited, some philosophers have relied on other ways of establishing reality. Most notably, they have adopted a rationalistic theory of epistemology which maintains that the rational mind should be trusted to provide sound knowledge.

The historian and mathematician mentioned above both use a rational means of knowing. The historian tries to amass information about a period, person, or event, and to draw conclusions based upon that material. He or she will reason out the best interpretation of the evidence, building a coherent picture of history. For example, to claim that Napoleon was proclaimed emperor of France in 1804 is consistent with the reforms instituted at that time and attributed to him. French law was standardized under the Napoleonic code; schools were centralized; the court system simplified; and the principle established of freedom of religion. The mathematician too will construct a rational system of thought. For example, if a number multiplied by 5 equals 60, then the equation would be $5x = 60$, and x is 12. This simple algebraic problem is solved by pure reasoning, without reference to any evidence of the senses. The historian was not present in the nineteenth century, and algebraic notations are abstractions that no mathematician has ever seen.

However, an internally consistent system may not correspond to any reality. The historical facts and conclusion may all hang together, but perhaps things did not happen that way. The mathematical system, while making logical sense, may not diagram reality at all; it could be a castle in the air. Jorge Luis Borges, the Argentinian writer, is brilliant at constructing plausible but fictitious accounts of history, and we know that in mystery stories, where the evidence clearly points to someone as the guilty party, he or she often turns out to be innocent after all. Bertrand Russell, the British philosopher, has written, "If you follow empiricism you will be partly right, but if you are a rationalist you can be entirely wrong."

c. Intuitionism.   Because of the difficulties in empiricism and rationalism, some philosophers prefer an intuitional approach whereby we rely on
some immediate apprehension or sudden awareness of the truth. Rather
than using our senses or reason, we trust an inner sense, akin to an instinct,
that something is so. Our emotions become paramount, our feelings not our
perception, our heart rather than our head.

The intuition referred to is not the trite "women's intuition" of popular
magazines but a type of revelation that carries with it a deep certainty. We
simply know that something is true, and no one can persuade us through
any arguments that we are mistaken.

When we make claims of a moral, aesthetic, or religious kind they are
usually based on intuition. If we state that preserving life is morally better
than taking life, or that roses or moonlight on the water is beautiful, we
seem to know this immediately and unquestioningly. The judgments that
Hitler was a bad leader and Picasso was a good painter, are not based on the
senses. Our senses may tell us what each did (if we have direct evidence),
but to evaluate their actions requires a mental judgment. We do not *see* that
the holocaust is one of the most terrible acts of the twentieth century but we
judge it as such, and we only see fragmented figures in Picasso's *Guernica*
but we judge it to be a great painting.

Religious people base their faith on similar feelings, although revelation
is often cited as the specific source of understanding. They need to differentiate their beliefs from superstition (as discussed earlier), but their reasons
for believing have nothing to do with sense perception or rational proof. In
fact, believers do not base their faith on reason or anything seen, heard,
touched, smelled, or tasted, but rather on some spiritual experience that lies
beyond ordinary knowledge. Faith is thought to speak directly to our heart
and soul. The theologian Blaise Pascal expressed this when he wrote "The
heart has its reasons that reason does not know." (*Le coeur a ses raisons que
la raison ne connais point.*)

However, intuition too has its weaknesses, which mainly stem from its
private nature. That is, when someone uses intuition to back up a claim he
or she will not allow contrary evidence to count against it. The intuition is
"self-authenticating," and the fact that it runs counter to experience or is irrational makes no difference. No harm is done when a person claims to
know intuitively that life should be preserved, but suppose someone intuits
that life should be taken. The Inquisition, the crusades, the witch trials, the
burning of heretics, pogroms, and so forth were carried out by people who
believed they were following God's will. The Muslim fanatics who flew

airliners into the World Trade Center and the Pentagon were sincerely convinced it was a holy act. If empirical and rational factors are disqualified there is no protection against such horrors.

Intuitive claims, then, are unverifiable by anything outside the person. Furthermore, they vary enormously between individuals, and the same person will maintain different things at different times based on new intuitions. Something that fickle and subjective is unreliable as a foundation for knowledge. We must be able to distinguish "God spoke to me in a dream" from "I dreamt that God spoke to me," or false beliefs and even atrocities could be the result.

Discovering the best way of knowing is therefore a difficult task. The problem is compounded by the fact that we must assume a way of knowing in choosing a way of knowing. That is, in deciding whether empiricism, rationalism, or intuitionism is most reliable, we must first have some epistemological foundation for our choice. This begs the question at issue, that is, we are assuming the point we are trying to prove. What basis for knowledge can we use, then, in determining the best basis for knowledge?

In the selections that follow, various philosophers discuss questions of epistemology, beginning with the theories of the ancient Greek philosopher Plato. In a selection from the *Republic*, he presents his position on appearance and reality: that Ideas can be known and are more real than physical things. The eighteenth century British philosopher David Hume then offers a strong empiricist position in his *Enquiry Concerning Human Understanding*, while the seventeenth century French philosopher René Descartes endorses a rationalist approach in his *Meditations on First Philosophy*.

In the second section, a relativist view of knowledge is described in *Rashomon*, the cinematic vision of Akira Kurosawa. A synopsis of Peter Weir's film *The Truman Show* is then presented, which deliberately conflates illusion and reality, and the Italian filmmaker Federico Fellini illustrates an intuitive mode of understanding in *Juliet of the Spirits*.

A. Philosophic Concepts

The Republic*
Plato

Plato (428–c. 347 B.C.) together with Aristotle (584–322 B.C.) stands as one of the most influential figures in Western philosophy. In addition to his contribution to epistemology, metaphysics, and ethics, Plato shaped both Christian and Jewish theology as well as medieval Islamic thought. A Neoplatonism flourished in the third century under Plotinus, and in the seventeenth century the Cambridge Platonists revived a number of Platonic concepts. According to the thinker Alfred North Whitehead, all subsequent philosophy has been merely "a series of footnotes to Plato."

Plato's writings were cast in dialogue form and consist of intellectual conversations on central philosophic topics. The early dialogues are probably genuine reports of the conversations of Socrates, Plato's teacher and the main figure, but the middle and later dialogues probably use Socrates as a vehicle for expressing Plato's own ideas. Paradoxically, although Plato produced some of the most artful writings in philosophy, he was suspicious of art as two steps removed from the world of Ideas, which is the fundamental reality.

Among the most celebrated of Plato's early dialogues are The Protagoras, *that claims virtue is knowledge and can be taught, and* The Euthyphro, *that separates ethics from religion. The significant dialogues of his middle period include* The Gorgias, *an analysis of ethical questions,* The Meno, *an examination of knowledge, and* The Apology, The Crito, *and* The Phaedo *that describe Socrates' defense in court, his refusal to escape from prison, and his death scene. In this period,* The Symposium, *concerning beauty and love, is Plato's most dramatically successful dialogue, and* The Republic *is his highest achievement, containing a discussion of justice in the individual and in the state. The late period includes* The Parmenides *and* The Sophist, *both of which deal with the theory of Ideas or Forms.*

---

* Translated by B. Jowett

In the excerpt from the famous philosophic dialogue, The Republic, *Plato presents an allegory of the human condition that is intended to show how the ordinary world we inhabit is largely one of illusion. At least it is less real than an eternal and perfect world that exists beyond our senses. To Plato, we are like prisoners in a cave who mistake the shadows for reality. The shadows represent the physical world of sense perception. To liberate ourselves from this world, we must realize there is light behind the shadows—light that represents Ideas which are the fundamental reality. Above all, there is the sun at the pinnacle of light just as the Good stands as the foremost of the Ideas.*

By the Ideas (or Forms or Universals), Plato means the general categories into which any group of objects can be placed. For example, apart from particular trees, we know there is the idea of what a tree consists of. Through our senses we perceive oaks, elms, maples, pines, and so forth, but through our mind we understand that the idea of a tree is that of a woody, perennial plant with branches, leaves or needles, ordinarily growing to a considerable height. In the same way, we can see various horses from Clydesdales to Shetland ponies, and Appaloosas to Arabians, but rationally we can separate the idea of a horse as a large, four-legged, solid-hoofed, herbivorous mammal used for riding or pulling loads.

Therefore, behind every class of things is some idea that corresponds to it, and together they make up a world of Ideas. To Plato these ideas are more real than things, and just as the shadows should lead us to acknowledge the light, the objects in the world of sense should make us acknowledge the more fundamental ideas that lie behind them. More important than trees or horses, our physical experience should cause us to consider the ultimate ideas of truth, beauty, and justice, and what it is to be a human being.

BOOK VII

And now, I said, let me show in a figure how far our nature is enlightened or unenlightened:—Behold! human beings housed in an underground cave, which has a long entrance open towards the light and as wide as the interior of the cave; here they have been from their childhood, and have their legs and necks chained, so that they cannot move and can only see before them, being prevented by the chains from turning round their heads. Above and behind them a fire is blazing at a distance, and between the fire and the prisoners there is a raised way; and you will see, if you look, a low wall built along the way, like the screen which marionette players have in front of them, over which they show the puppets.

I see.

And do you see, I said, men passing along the wall carrying all sorts of vessels, and statues and figures of animals made of wood and stone and various materials, which appear over the wall? While carrying their burdens, some of them, as you would expect, are talking, others silent.

You have shown me a strange image, and they are strange prisoners.

Like ourselves, I replied; for in the first place, do you think they have seen anything of themselves, and of one another, except the shadows which the fire throws on the opposite wall of the cave?

How could they do so, he asked, if throughout their lives they were never allowed to move their heads?

And of the objects which are being carried in like manner they would only see the shadows?

Yes, he said.

And if they were able to converse with one another, would they not supposed that the things they saw were the real things?[1]

Very true.

And suppose further that the prison had an echo which came from the other side, would they not be sure to fancy when one of the passers-by spoke that the voice which they heard came from the passing shadow?

No question, he replied.

To them, I said, the truth would be literally nothing but the shadows of the images.

That is certain.

And now look again, and see in what manner they would be released from their bonds, and cured of their error, whether the process would naturally be as follows. At first, when any of them is liberated and compelled suddenly to stand up and turn his neck round and walk and look towards the light, he will suffer sharp pains; the glare will distress him, and he will be unable to see the realities of which in his former state he had seen the shadows; and then conceive someone saying to him that what he saw before was

---

[1]Text uncertain: perhaps 'that they would apply the name *real* to the things which they saw.'

an illusion, but that now, when he is approaching nearer to being and his eye is turned towards more real existence, he has a clearer vision,—what will be his reply? And you may further imagine that his instructor is pointing to the objects as they pass and requiring him to name them,—will he not be perplexed? Will he not fancy that the shadows which he formerly saw are truer than the objects which are now shown to him?

Far truer.

And if he is compelled to look straight at the light, will he not have a pain in his eyes which will make him turn away to take refuge in the objects of vision which he can see, and which he will conceive to be in reality clearer than the things which are now being shown to him?

True, he said.

And suppose once more, that he is reluctantly dragged up that steep and rugged ascent, and held fast until he is forced into the presence of the sun himself, is he not likely to be pained and irritated? When he approaches the light his eyes will be dazzled, and he will not be able to see anything at all of what are now called realities.

Not all in a moment, he said.

He will require to grow accustomed to the sight of the upper world. And first he will see the shadows best, next the reflections of men and other objects in the water, and then the objects themselves; and, when he turned to the heavenly bodies and the heaven itself, he would find it easier to gaze upon the light of the moon and the stars at night than to see the sun or the light of the sun by day?

Certainly.

Last of all he will be able to see the sun, not turning aside to the illusory reflections of him in the water, but gazing directly at him in his own proper place, and contemplating him as he is.

Certainly.

He will then proceed to argue that this is he who gives the seasons and the years, and is the guardian of all that is in the visible world, and in a certain way the cause of all things which he and his fellows have been accustomed to behold?

Clearly, he said, he would arrive at this conclusion after what he had seen.

And when he remembered his old habitation, and the wisdom of the cave and his fellow-prisoners, do you not suppose that he would felicitate himself on the change, and pity them?

Certainly, he would.

And if they were in the habit of conferring honors among themselves on those who were quickest to observe the passing shadows and to remark which of them went before and which followed after and which were together, and who were best able from these observations to divine the future, do you think that he would be eager for such honours and glories, or envy those who attained honor and sovereignty among those men? Would he not say with Homer,

'Better to be a serf, laboring for a landless master',

and to endure anything, rather than think as they do and live after their manner?

Yes, he said, I think that he would consent to suffer anything rather than live in this miserable manner.

Imagine once more, I said, such a one coming down suddenly out of the sunlight, and being replaced in his old seat; would he not be certain to have his eyes full of darkness?

To be sure, he said.

And if there were a contest, and he had to compete in measuring the shadows with the prisoners who had never moved out of the cave, while his sight was still weak, and before his eyes had become steady (and the time which would be needed to acquire this new habit of sight might be very considerable), would he not make himself ridiculous? Men would say of him that he had returned from the place above with his eyes ruined; and that it was better not even to think of ascending; and if anyone tried to loose another and lead him up to the light, let them only catch the offender, and they would put him to death.

No question, he said.

This entire allegory, I said, you may now append, dear Glaucon, to the previous argument; the prison-house is the world of sight, the light of the fire is the power of the sun, and you will not misapprehend me if you interpret the journey upwards to be the ascent of the soul into the intellectual world according to my surmise, which, at your desire, I have expressed—whether rightly or wrongly God knows. But, whether true or false, my opinion is that in the world of knowledge the Idea of good appears last of all, and is seen only with an effort; although, when seen, it is inferred to be the universal author of all things beautiful and right, parent of light and of the lord of light in the visible world, and the immediate and supreme source of reason and truth in the intellectual; and that this is the power upon which he who would act rationally either in public or private life must have his eye fixed.

I agree, he said, as far as I am able to understand you.

Moreover, I said, you must agree once more, and not wonder that those who attain to this vision are unwilling to take any part in human affairs; for their souls are ever hastening into the upper world where they desire to dwell; which desire of theirs is very natural, if our allegory may be trusted.

Yes, very natural.

And is there anything surprising in one who passes from divine contemplations to the evil state of man, appearing grotesque and ridiculous; if, while his eyes are blinking and before he has become accustomed to the surrounding darkness, he is compelled to fight in courts of law, or in other places, about the images or the shadows of images of justice, and must strive against some rival about opinions of these things which are entertained by men who have never yet seen the true justice?

Anything but surprising, he replied.

Anyone who has common sense will remember that the bewilderments of the eyes are of two kinds and arise from two causes, either from coming out of the light or from going into the light, and, judging that the soul may be affected in the same way, will not give way to foolish laughter when he sees anyone whose vision is perplexed and weak; he will first ask whether that soul of man has come out of the brighter life and is unable to see because unaccustomed to the dark, or having turned from darkness to the day is dazzled by excess of light. And he will count the one happy in his condition and state of being, and he will pity the other; or, if he have a mind to laugh at the soul which comes from below into the light, this laughter will not be quite so laughable as that which greets the soul which returns from above out of the light into the cave.

That, he said, is a very just distinction.

But then, if I am right, certain professors of education must be wrong when they say that they can put a knowledge into the soul which was not there before, like sight into blind eyes.

They undoubtedly say this, he replied.

Whereas our argument shows that the power and capacity of learning exists in the soul already; and that just as if it were not possible to turn the eye from darkness to light without the whole body, so too the instrument of knowledge can only by the movement of the whole soul be turned from the world of becoming to that of being, and learn by degrees to endure the sight of being, and of the brightest and best of being, or in other words, of the good.

STUDY QUESTIONS

1. In what way does the "Allegory of the Cave" illustrate Plato's epistemology?
2. When people are freed from the cave, what is it they understand?
3. Why would the liberated prisoners no longer want to participate in human affairs?
4. What does Plato mean when he says that "the power and capacity of learning exists in the soul already"?
5. To Plato, what is appearance and what is reality?

An Enquiry Concerning Human Understanding
David Hume

David Hume (1711–1776) was a Scottish philosopher and historian who is best known for his book Enquiry Concerning Human Understanding. The Enquiry *is actually a condensation of his first and more important work,* A Treatise of Human Nature, *but because of its difficult style it was not well received. Hume also wrote* Essays Moral and Political, Political Discourses, *and a three-volume* History of England, *the last a classic in its time.*

Hume lived in England and France, maintained a friendship for a time with Jean Jacques Rousseau, and held various public positions in Great Britain. Although he wanted to obtain a university post, his appointment was blocked because of his skeptical ideas. He rejected traditional religious beliefs, denied the notion of causation, and even questioned the customary concept of the self. To Hume, the self has no spiritual substance as its core but is "nothing but a bundle or collection of different perceptions." Despite his skepticism, Hume was an unusually generous and gracious man whom the Scots referred to as St. David.

In the Enquiry *excerpted here, Hume argues that all genuine thought originates from sense perception. Even thoughts of bizarre creatures only combine elements that have been experienced by the senses, and if one of our senses is defective then we cannot form any idea dependent on it: "A blind man can form no notion of colors; a deaf man of sounds." This means that an idea is meaningless if there is no sense experience corresponding to it.*

Hume then divides all thoughts into two types: relations of ideas and matters of fact. The first only shows the formal connection between ideas as in "three times five is equal to half of thirty." Subsequent philosophers referred to these as analytic propositions, which included sentences such as "Circles are round," "Bachelors are unmarried males," and "Murals are on walls." Such sentences only express the implications of words or concepts, and although they are certain they are also trivial.

Matters of fact are more interesting statements because they make some claim about the external world rather than referring to themselves. "The sun will rise," "Swans are white," and "People inhabit all regions of the earth," are examples of this type of statement. Not all matter-of-fact statements are true; for example, black swans are found in Australia, but to verify the truth of such statements we cite some cause for the belief. We claim someone is in the country because we received a letter from him, and we can say that someone must have been on an island because we find a watch there.

From these commonsense beginnings, Hume then reaches some surprising conclusions. He maintains that cause and effect, which is the basis for matter-of-fact statements, is merely a psychological association between two events, not a necessary connection. That is, there is no hidden force in one event that compels another event to happen. The pin does not make the balloon pop; the lighted match does not ignite the paper; the hammer does not drive the nail into the wood; pulling the trigger does not force the gun to fire. Rather, our experience teaches us that two events have always occurred in succession, so we come to expect the second when we see the first. This is what we mean by causation, the association of two events established through "custom or habit." We must not assume that some mysterious, hidden power exists in one event that forces a subsequent one to occur.

Hume arrives at this conclusion because he is a consistent empiricist. He only accepts the evidence of the senses, and since we never perceive a cause we cannot assume that any such thing exists. All that we perceive are events following each other in time; we do not see that the first event made the second happen.

Section 2

OF THE ORIGIN OF IDEAS

Every one will readily allow, that there is a considerable difference between the perceptions of the mind, when a man feels the pain of excessive heat, or the pleasure of moderate warmth, and when he afterwards recalls to his memory this sensation, or anticipates it by his imagination. These faculties may mimic or copy the perceptions of the senses; but they never can entirely reach the force and vivacity of the original sentiment. The utmost we say of them, even when they operate with greatest vigor, is, that they represent their object in so lively a manner, that we could *almost* say we feel or see it: But, except the mind be disordered by disease or madness, they never can arrive at such a pitch of vivacity, as to render these perceptions altogether undistinguishable. All the colors of poetry, however splendid, can never paint natural objects in such a manner as to make the description be taken for a real landscape. The most lively thought is still inferior to the dullest sensation.

We may observe a like distinction to run through all the other perceptions of the mind. A man, in a fit of anger, is actuated in a very different manner from one who only thinks of that emotion. If you tell me, that any person is in love, I easily understand your meaning, and form a just conception of his situation; but never can mistake that conception for the real disorders and agitations of the passion. When we reflect on our past sentiments and affections, our thought is a faithful mirror, and copies its objects truly; but the colors which it employs are faint and dull, in comparison of those in which our original perceptions were clothed. It requires no nice discernment or metaphysical head to mark the distinction between them.

Here therefore we may divide all the perceptions of the mind into two classes or species, which are distinguished by their different degrees of force and vivacity. The less forcible and lively are commonly denominated THOUGHTS or IDEAS. The other species want a name in our language, and in most others; I suppose, because it was not requisite for any, but philosophical purposes, to rank them under a general term or appellation. Let us, therefore, use a little freedom, and call them IMPRESSIONS; employing that word in a sense somewhat different from the usual. By the term *impression*, then, I mean all our more lively perceptions, when we hear, or see, or feel, or love, or hate, or desire, or will. And impressions are distinguished from ideas, which are the less lively perceptions, of which we are conscious, when we reflect on any of those sensations or movements above mentioned.

Nothing, at first view, may seem more unbounded than the thought of man, which not only escapes all human power and authority, but is not even restrained within the limits of nature and reality. To form monsters, and join incongruous shapes and appearances, costs the imagination no more trouble than to conceive the most natural and familiar objects. And while the body is confined to one planet, along which it creeps with pain and difficulty; the thought can in an instant transport us into the most distant regions of the universe; or even beyond the universe, into the unbounded chaos, where nature is supposed to lie in total confusion. What never was seen, or heard of, may yet be conceived; nor is any thing beyond the power of thought, except what implies an absolute contradiction.

But though our thought seems to possess this unbounded liberty, we shall find, upon a nearer examination, that it is really confined within very narrow limits, and that all this creative power of the mind amounts to no more than the faculty of compounding, transposing, augmenting, or diminishing the materials afforded us by the senses and experience. When we think of a golden mountain, we only join two consistent ideas, *gold*, and *mountain*, with which we were formerly acquainted. A virtuous horse we can conceive; because, from our own feeling, we can conceive virtue; and this we may unite to the figure and shape of a horse, which is an animal familiar to us. In short, all the materials of thinking are derived either from our outward or inward sentiment: the mixture and composition of these belongs alone to the mind and will. Or, to express myself in philosophical language, all our ideas or more feeble perceptions are copies of our impressions or more lively ones.

To prove this, the two following arguments will, I hope, be sufficient. *First*, when we analyze our thoughts or ideas, however compounded or sublime, we always find that they resolve themselves into such simple ideas as were copied from a precedent feeling or sentiment. Even those ideas, which, at first view, seem the most wide of this origin, are found, upon a nearer scrutiny, to be derived from it. The idea of God, as meaning *an infinitely intelligent, wise, and good Being,* arises from reflecting on the operations of our own mind, and augmenting, without limit, those qualities of goodness and wisdom. We may prosecute this enquiry to what length we please; where we shall always find, that every idea which we examine is copied from a similar impression. Those who would assert that this position is not universally true nor without exception, have only one, and that an easy method of refuting it; by producing that idea, which, in their opinion, is not derived from this source. It will then be incumbent on us, if we would maintain our doctrine, to produce the impression, or lively perception, which corresponds to it.

Secondly. If it happen, from a defect of the organ, that a man is not susceptible of any species of sensation, we always find that he is as little susceptible of the correspondent ideas. A blind man can form no notion of colors; a deaf man of sounds. Restore either of them that sense in which he is deficient; by opening this new inlet for his sensations, you also open an inlet for the ideas; and he finds no difficulty in conceiving these objects. The case is the same, if the object, proper for exciting any sensation, has never been applied to the organ. A LAPLANDER or NEGROE has no notion of the relish of wine. And though there are few or no instances of a like deficiency in the mind, where a person has never felt or is wholly incapable of a sentiment or passion that belongs to his species; yet we find the same observation to take place in a less degree. A man of mild manners can form no idea of inveterate revenge or cruelty; nor can a selfish heart easily conceive the heights of friendship and generosity. It is readily allowed, that other beings may possess many senses of which we can have no conception; because the ideas of them have never been introduced to us in the only manner by which an idea can have access to the mind, to wit, by the actual feeling and sensation.

There is, however, one contradictory phenomenon, which may prove that it is not absolutely impossible for ideas to arise, independent of their correspondent impressions. I believe it will readily be allowed, that the several distinct ideas of color, which enter by the eye, or those of sound, which are conveyed by the ear, are really different from each other; though, at the same time, resembling. Now if this be true of different colors, it must be no less so of the different shades of the same color; and each shade produces a distinct idea, independent of the rest. For if this should be denied, it is possible, by the continual gradation of shades, to run a color insensibly into what is most remote from it; and if you will not allow any of the means to be different, you cannot, without absurdity, deny the extremes to be the same. Suppose, therefore, a person to have enjoyed his sight for thirty years, and to have become perfectly acquainted with colors of all kinds except one particular shade of blue, for instance, which it never has been his fortune to meet with. Let all the different shades of that color, except that single one, be placed before him, descending gradually from the deepest to the lightest; it is plain that he will perceive a blank, where that shade is wanting, and will be sensible that there is a greater distance in that place between the contiguous colors than in any other. Now I ask, whether it be possible for him, from his own imagination, to supply this deficiency, and raise up to himself the idea of that particular shade, though it had never been conveyed to him by his senses? I believe there are few but will be of opinion that he can: and this may serve as a proof that the simple ideas are not always, in every instance, derived from the correspondent impressions; though this instance is so singular, that it is scarcely worth our observing, and does not merit that for it alone we should alter our general maxim.

Here, therefore, is a proposition, which not only seems, in itself, simple and intelligible; but, if a proper use were made of it, might render every dispute equally intelligible, and banish all that jargon, which has so long taken possession of metaphysical reasonings, and drawn disgrace upon them. All ideas, especially abstract ones, are naturally faint and obscure: the mind has but a slender hold of them: they are apt to be confounded with other resembling ideas; and when we have often employed any term, though without a distinct meaning, we are apt to imagine it has a determinate idea annexed to it. On the contrary, all impressions, that is, all sensations, either outward or inward, are strong and vivid: the limits between them are more exactly determined: nor is it easy to fall into any error or mistake with regard to them. When we entertain, therefore, any suspicion that a philosophical term is employed without any meaning or idea (as is but too frequent), we need but enquire, *from what impression is that supposed idea derived*? And if it be impossible to assign any, this will serve to confirm our suspicion. By bringing ideas into so clear a light we may reasonably hope to remove all dispute, which may arise, concerning their nature and reality.[1]...

Section IV

SKEPTICAL DOUBTS CONCERNING THE OPERATIONS OF THE UNDERSTANDING

Part 1

All the objects of human reason or enquiry may naturally be divided into two kinds, to wit, *Relations of Ideas*, and *Matters of Fact*. Of the first kind are the sciences of Geometry, Algebra, and Arithmetic; and in short, every affirmation which is either intuitively or demonstratively certain. *That the square of the hypothenuse is equal to the square of the two sides*, is a proposition which expresses a relation between these figures. *That three times five is equal to the half of thirty*, expresses a relation between these numbers. Propositions of this kind are discoverable by the mere operation of thought, without dependence on what is anywhere existent in the universe.

---

[1] It is probable, that no more was meant by those, who denied innate ideas, than that all ideas were copies of our impressions though it must be confessed, that the terms, which they employed, were not chosen with such caution, nor so exactly defined, as to prevent all mistakes about their doctrine. For what is meant by *innate*? If innate be equivalent to natural, then all the perceptions and ideas of the mind must be allowed to be innate or natural in whatever sense we take the latter word, whether in opposition to what is uncommon, artificial, or miraculous. If by *innate* be meant, *contemporary to our birth*, the dispute seems to be frivolous; nor is it worth while to enquire at what time thinking begins, whether before, at, or after our birth. Again, the word idea, seems to be commonly taken in a very loose sense, by LOCKE and others; as standing for any of our perceptions, our sensations and passions, as well as thoughts. Now

Though there never were a circle or triangle in nature, the truths demonstrated by EUCLID would for ever retain their certainty and evidence.

Matters of fact, which are the second objects of human reason, are not ascertained in the same manner; nor is our evidence of their truth, however great, of a like nature with the foregoing. The contrary of every matter of fact is still possible; because it can never imply a contradiction, and is conceived by the mind with the same facility and distinctness, as if ever so conformable to reality. *That the sun will not rise to-morrow* is no less intelligible a proposition, and implies no more contradiction than the affirmation, *that it will rise*. We should in vain, therefore, attempt to demonstrate its falsehood. Were it demonstratively false, it would imply a contradiction, and could never be distinctly conceived by the mind.

It may, therefore, be a subject worthy of curiosity, to enquire what is the nature of that evidence which assures us of any real existence and matter of fact, beyond the present testimony of our senses, or the records of our memory. This part of philosophy, it is observable, has been little cultivated, either by the ancients or moderns; and therefore our doubts and errors, in the prosecution of so important an enquiry, may be the more excusable; while we march through such difficult paths without any guide or direction. They may even prove useful, by exciting curiosity, and destroying that implicit faith and security, which is the bane of all reasoning and free enquiry. The discovery of defects in the common philosophy, if any such there be, will not, I presume, be a discouragement, but rather an incitement, as is usual, to attempt something more full and satisfactory than has yet been proposed to the public.

All reasonings concerning matter of fact seem to be founded on the relation of *Cause and Effect*. By means of that relation alone we can go beyond the evidence of our memory and senses. If you were to ask a man, why he believes any matter of fact, which is absent; for instance, that his friend is in the country, or in FRANCE; he would give you a reason; and this reason would be some other fact; as a letter received from him, or the knowledge of his former resolutions and promises. A man finding a watch or any other

---

in this sense, I should desire to know, what can be meant by asserting, that self-love, or resentment of injuries, or the passion between the sexes is not innate?

But admitting these terms, impressions and ideas, in the sense above explained, and understanding by innate, what is original or copied from no precedent perception, then may we assert, that all our impressions are innate, and our ideas not innate.

To be ingenuous, I must own it to be my opinion, that LOCKE was betrayed into his question by the schoolmen, who, making use of undefined terms, drew out their disputes to a tedious length, without ever touching the point in question. A like abiguity and circumlocution seems to run through that philosopher's reasonings on this as well as most other subjects.

machine in a desert island, would conclude that there had once been men in that island. All our reasonings concerning fact are of the same nature. And here it is constantly supposed that there is a connexion between the present fact and that which is inferred from it. Were there nothing to bind them together, the inference would be entirely precarious. The hearing of an articulate voice and rational discourse in the dark assures us of the presence of some person: Why? because these are the effects of the human make and fabric, and closely connected with it. If we anatomize all the other reasonings of this nature, we shall find that they are founded on the relation of cause and effect, and that this relation is either near or remote, direct or collateral. Heat and light are collateral effects of fire, and the one effect may justly be inferred from the other.

If we would satisfy ourselves, therefore, concerning the nature of that evidence, which assures us of matters of fact, we must enquire how we arrive at the knowledge of cause and effect.

I shall venture to affirm, as a general proposition, which admits of no exception, that the knowledge of this relation is not, in any instance, attained by reasonings *a priori*; but arises entirely from experience, when we find that any particular objects are constantly conjoined with each other. Let an object be presented to a man of ever so strong natural reason and abilities; if that object be entirely new to him, he will not be able, by the most accurate examination of its sensible qualities, to discover any of its causes or effects. Adam, though his rational faculties be supposed, at the very first, entirely perfect, could not have inferred from the fluidity and transparency of water that it would suffocate him, or from the light and warmth of fire that it would consume him. No object ever discovers, by the qualities which appear to the senses, either the causes which produced it, or the effects which will arise from it; nor can our reason, unassisted by experience, ever draw any inference concerning real existence and matter of fact....

Suppose a person, though endowed with the strongest faculties of reason and reflection, to be brought on a sudden into this world; he would, indeed, immediately observe a continual succession of objects, and one event following another; but he would not be able to discover anything farther. He would not, at first, by any reasoning, be able to reach the idea of cause and effect; since the particular powers, by which all natural operations are performed, never appear to the senses; nor is it reasonable to conclude, merely because one event, in one instance, precedes another, that therefore the one is the cause, the other the effect. Their conjunction may be arbitrary and casual. There may be no reason to infer the existence of one from the appearance of the other. And in a word, such a person, without more experience, could never employ his conjecture or reasoning concerning any matter of fact, or be assured of anything beyond what was immediately present to his memory and senses.

Suppose, again, that he has acquired more experience, and has lived so long in the world as to have observed familiar objects or events to be constantly conjoined together; what is the consequence of this experience? He immediately infers the existence of one object from the appearance of the other. Yet he has not, by all his experience, acquired any idea or knowledge of the secret power by which the one object produces the other; nor is it, by any process of reasoning, he is engaged to draw this inference. But still he finds himself determined to draw it: And though he should be convinced that his understanding has no part in the operation, he would nevertheless continue in the same course of thinking. There is some other principle which determines him to form such a conclusion.

This principle is CUSTOM or HABIT. For wherever the repetition of any particular act or operation produces a propensity to renew the same act or operation, without being impelled by any reasoning or process of the understanding, we always say, that this propensity is the effect of *Custom*. By employing that word, we pretend not to have given the ultimate reason of such a propensity. We only point out a principle of human nature, which is universally acknowledged, and which is well known by its effects. Perhaps we can push our enquiries no farther, or pretend to give the cause of this cause; but must rest contented with it as the ultimate principle, which we can assign, of all our conclusions from experience. It is sufficient satisfaction, that we can go so far, without repining at the narrowness of our faculties because they will carry us no farther. And it is certain we here advance a very intelligible proposition at least, if not a true one, when we assert that, after the constant conjunction of two objects—heat and flame, for instance, weight and solidity—we are determined by custom alone to expect the one from the appearance of the other. This hypothesis seems even the only one which explains the difficulty, why we draw, from a thousand instances, an inference which we are not able to draw from one instance, that is, in no respect, different from them. Reason is incapable of any such variation. The conclusions which it draws from considering one circle are the same which it would form upon surveying all the circles in the universe. But no man, having seen only one body move after being impelled by another, could infer that every other body will move after a like impulse. All inferences from experience, therefore, are effects of custom, not of reasoning. ...

STUDY QUESTIONS

1. On what grounds does Hume claim that all knowledge is derived from sense perception? Why would you agree or disagree?

2. Provide an original example of a statement that shows a "Relation of Ideas" and one that is a "Matter of Fact."

3. Explain Hume's theory of causation. Could you refute his contention with an example of some cause and effect that you have seen?

4. Do you think there are other valid ways of knowing besides empiricism? What would they be?

5. How would you argue against the skeptic who claims we can never gain reliable knowledge?

Meditations on First Philosophy
René Descartes

René Descartes (1596–1650) was a French philosopher often considered the father of modern thought as opposed to medieval thinking. His philosophic works include Discourse on Method, Principles of Philosophy, *and* Meditations on First Philosophy, *included in part below. He also made important contributions to the fields of science, physiology, optics, and mathematics, especially analytic geometry and theory of equations.*

In Descartes' philosophizing, he adopts a rigorous methodology based on reason. Specifically, he tried to apply the methods of science to philosophy, and he trusted the rational understanding that each person is capable of exercising. He once wrote: "In our search for the direct road to truth, we should busy ourselves with no object about which we cannot attain a certitude equal to that of the demonstrations of arithmetic or geometry."

Medieval dogmas are based on authority, which is questionable, and the senses are fallible, therefore Descartes relies only on the mind. He wants knowledge that cannot be doubted, and reason alone can yield certainty. He even questions the most obvious sense data, for example, his awareness of sitting in his chair in front of a fire in a robe with a paper in his hands. Although the sensations seem self-evident, dreams can have a similar vividness, and a God or devil could conjure up illusions that would be indistinguishable from reality. Whether the deception is for benevolent or malevolent reasons, he cannot trust his senses to provide "clear and distinct" ideas about the world.

In his method of "systematic doubt," Descartes is even led to question his own existence, but here he draws the line. If he thinks, then he must exist. Even if he is doubting or being deceived, he must exist to doubt or be deceived. Therefore this rational proposition is necessarily true: "Cogito ergo sum;" *I think, therefore I am.*

The "I" in this proposition does not refer to the body, which is known by "fallible" sense perception but to the thinking mind. Descartes therefore asks "But what then am I?" and answers "A thing which thinks... which doubts, understands, [conceives], affirms, denies, wills, refuses, which also imagines and feels." Reason leads us to this indubitable conclusion.

To Descartes, all things are known by the mind, not by the senses, and to prove this he uses a comparison with wax. Although a piece of wax can change its smell, color, shape, size, temperature, and sound (when struck), we still recognize it to be a piece of wax. Because the sense qualities can be different, we do not know it is the same wax by using our senses; we can only know it through our rational mind.

Descartes, incidentally, never explained the relation between mind and body in a satisfactory way but divided the two in a doctrine known as "Cartesian dualism." Ever since Descartes presented his theory, philosophers have been trying to show how two such radically different entities can interact to form a complete self.

Meditation I.

OF THE THINGS WHICH MAY BE BROUGHT WITHIN THE SPHERE OF THE DOUBTFUL.

It is now some years since I detected how many were the false beliefs that I had from my earliest youth admitted as true, and how doubtful was everything I had since constructed on this basis; and from that time I was convinced that I must once for all seriously undertake to rid myself of all the opinions which I had formerly accepted, and commence to build anew from the foundation, if I wanted to establish any firm and permanent structure in the sciences. But as this enterprise appeared to be a very great one, I waited until I had attained an age so mature that I could not hope that at any later date I should be better fitted to execute my design. This reason caused me to delay so long that I should feel that I was doing wrong were I to occupy in deliberation the time that yet remains to me for action. To-day, then, since very opportunely for the plan I have in view I have delivered my mind from every care [and am happily agitated by no passions] and since I have procured for myself an assured leisure in a peaceable retirement, I shall at last seriously and freely address myself to the general upheaval of all my former opinions.

Now for this object it is not necessary that I should show that all of these are false—I shall perhaps never arrive at this end. But inasmuch as reason already persuades me that I ought no less carefully to withhold my assent from matters which are not entirely certain and indubitable than from those which appear to me manifestly to be false, if I am able to find in each one some reason to doubt, this will suffice to justify my rejecting the whole. And for that end it will not be requisite that I should examine each in particular, which would be an endless undertaking; for owing to the fact that the destruction of the foundations of necessity brings with it the downfall of the rest of the edifice, I shall only in the first place attack those principles upon which all my former opinions rested.

All that up to the present time I have accepted as most true and certain I have learned either from the senses or through the senses; but it is sometimes proved to me that these senses are deceptive, and it is wiser not to trust entirely to anything by which we have once been deceived.

But it may be that although the senses sometimes deceive us concerning things which are hardly perceptible, or very far away, there are yet many others to be met with as to which we cannot reasonably have any doubt, although we recognise them by their means. For example, there is the fact that I am here, seated by the fire, attired in a dressing gown, having this paper in my hands and other similar matters. And how could I deny that these hands and this body are mine, were it not perhaps that I compare myself to certain persons, devoid of sense, whose cerebella are so troubled and clouded by the violent vapors of black bile, that they constantly assure us that they think they are kings when they are really quite poor, or that they are clothed in purple when they are really without covering, or who imagine that they have an earthenware head or are nothing but pumpkins or are made of glass. But they are mad, and I should not be any the less insane were I to follow examples so extravagant.

At the same time I must remember that I am a man, and that consequently I am in the habit of sleeping, and in my dreams representing to myself the same things or sometimes even less probable things, than do those who are insane in their waking moments. How often has it happened to me that in the night I dreamt that I found myself in this particular place, that I was dressed and seated near the fire, whilst in reality I was lying undressed in bed! At this moment it does indeed seem to me that it is with eyes awake that I am looking at this paper; that this head which I move is not asleep, that it is deliberately and of set purpose that I extend my hand and perceive it; what happens in sleep does not appear so clear nor so distinct as does all this. But in thinking over this I remind myself that on many occasions I have in sleep been deceived by similar illusions, and in dwelling carefully on this reflection I see so manifestly that there are no certain indications by which we may clearly distinguish wakefulness from sleep that I am lost in astonishment. And my astonishment is such that it is almost capable of persuading me that I now dream.

Now let us assume that we are asleep and that all these particulars, e.g. that we open our eyes, shake our head, extend our hands, and so on, are but false delusions; and let us reflect that possibly neither our hands nor our whole body are such as they appear to us to be. At the same time we must at least confess that the things which are represented to us in sleep are like painted representations which can only have been formed as the counterparts of something real and true, and that in this way those general things at least, i.e. eyes, a head, hands, and a whole body, are not imaginary things, but things really existent. For, as a matter of fact, painters, even when they study with the greatest skill to represent sirens and satyrs by forms the most strange and extraordinary, cannot give them natures which are entirely new, but merely make a certain medley of the members of different animals; or if their imagination is extravagant enough to invent something so novel that nothing similar has ever before been seen, and that then their work represents a thing purely fictitious and absolutely false, it is certain all the same that the colors of which this is composed are necessarily real. And for the same reason, although these general things, to with, [a body], eyes, a head, hands, and such like, may be imaginary, we are bound at the same time to confess that there are at least some other objects yet more simple and more universal, which are real and true; and of these just in the same way as with certain real colors, all these images of things which dwell in our thoughts, whether true and real or false and fantastic, are formed.

To such a class of things pertains corporeal nature in general, and its extension, the figure of extended things, their quantity or magnitude and number, as also the place in which they are, the time which measures their duration, and so on.

That is possibly why our reasoning is not unjust when we conclude from this that Physics, Astronomy, Medicine and all other sciences which have as their end the consideration of composite things, are very dubious and uncertain; but that Arithmetic, Geometry and other sciences of that kind which only treat of things that are very simple and very general, without taking great trouble to ascertain whether they are actually existent or not, contain some measure of certainty and an element of the indubitable. For whether I am awake or asleep, two and three together always form five, and the square can never have more than four sides, and it does not seem possible that truths so clear and apparent can be suspected of any falsity [or uncertainty].

Nevertheless I have long had fixed in my mind the belief that an all-powerful God existed by whom I have been created such as I am. But how do I know that He has not brought it to pass that there is no earth, no heaven, no extended body, no magnitude, no place, and that nevertheless [I possess the perceptions of all these things and that] they seem to me to exist just exactly as I now see them? And, besides, as I sometimes imagine that others deceive themselves in the things which they think they know best, how do I know that I am not deceived every time that I add two and three, or count the sides of a square, or judge of things yet simpler, if anything simpler can be imagined? But possibly God has not desired that I should be thus deceived, for He is said to be supremely good. If, however, it is contrary to His goodness to have made me such that I constantly deceive myself, it would also appear to be contrary to His goodness to permit me to be sometimes deceived, and nevertheless I cannot doubt that He does permit this.

There may indeed be those who would prefer to deny the existence of a God so powerful, rather than believe that all other things are uncertain. But let us not oppose them for the present, and grant that all that is here said of a God is a fable; nevertheless in whatever way they suppose that I have arrived at the state of being that I have reached—whether they attribute it to fate or to accident, or make out that it is by a continual succession of antecedents, or by some other method—since to err and deceive oneself is a defect, it is clear that the greater will be the probability of my being so imperfect as to deceive myself ever, as is the Author to whom they assign my origin the less powerful. To these reasons I have certainly nothing to reply, but at the end I feel constrained to confess that there is nothing in all that I formerly believed to be true, of which I cannot in some measure doubt, and that not merely through want of thought or through levity, but for reasons which are very powerful and maturely considered; so that henceforth I ought not the less carefully to refrain from giving credence to these opinions than to that which is manifestly false, if I desire to arrive at any certainty [in the sciences].

But it is not sufficient to have made these remarks, we must also be careful to keep them in mind. For these ancient and commonly held opinions still revert frequently to my mind, long and familiar custom having given them the right to occupy my mind against my inclination and rendered them almost masters of my belief; nor will I ever lose the habit of deferring to them or of placing my confidence in them, so long as I consider them as they really are, i.e. opinions in some measure doubtful, as I have just shown, and at the same time highly probable, so that there is much more reason to believe in than to deny them. That is why I consider that I shall not be acting amiss, if, taking of set purpose a contrary belief, I allow myself to be deceived, and for a certain time pretend that all these opinions are entirely false and imaginary, until at last, having thus balanced my former prejudices with my latter [so that they cannot divert my opinions more to one side than to the other], my judgment will no longer be dominated by bad usage or turned away from the right knowledge of the truth. For I am assured that there can be neither peril nor error in this course, and that I cannot at present yield too much to distrust, since I am not considering the question of action, but only of knowledge.

I shall then suppose, not that God who is supremely good and the fountain of truth, but some evil genius not less powerful than deceitful, has employed his whole energies in deceiving me; I shall consider that the heavens, the earth, colors, figures, sound, and all other external things are nought but the illusions and dreams of which this genius has availed himself in order to lay traps for my credulity; I shall consider myself as having no hands, no eyes, no flesh, no blood, nor any senses, yet falsely believing myself to possess all these things; I shall remain obstinately attached to this idea, and if by this means it is not in my power to arrive at the knowledge of any truth, I may at least do what is in my power [i.e. suspend my judgment], and with firm purpose avoid giving credence to any false thing, or being imposed upon by this arch deceiver, however powerful and deceptive he may be. But this task is a laborious one, and insensibly a certain lassitude leads me into the course of my ordinary life. And just as a captive who in sleep enjoys an imaginary liberty, when he begins to suspect that his liberty is but a dream, fears to awaken, and conspires with these agreeable illusions that the deception may be prolonged, so insensibly of my own accord I fall back into my former opinions, and I dread awakening from this slumber, lest the laborious wakefulness which would follow the tranquillity of this repose should have to be spent not in daylight, but in the excessive darkness of the difficulties which have just been discussed.

Meditation II.

OF THE NATURE OF THE HUMAN MIND; AND THAT IT IS MORE EASILY KNOWN THAN THE BODY.

The Meditation of yesterday filled my mind with so many doubts that it is no longer in my power to forget them. And yet I do not see in what manner I can resolve them; and, just as if I had all of a sudden fallen into very deep water, I am so disconcerted that I can neither make certain of setting my feet on the bottom, nor can I swim and so support myself on the surface. I shall nevertheless make an effort and follow anew the same path as that on which I yesterday entered, i.e. I shall proceed by setting aside all that in which the least doubt could be supposed to exist, just as if I had discovered that it was absolutely false; and I shall ever follow in this road until I have met with something which is certain, or at least, if I can do nothing else, until I have learned for certain that there is nothing in the world that is certain. Archimedes, in order that he might draw the terrestrial globe out of its place, and transport it elsewhere, demanded only that one point should be fixed and immoveable; in the same way I shall have the right to conceive high hopes if I am happy enough to discover one thing only which is certain and indubitable.

I suppose, then, that all the things that I see are false; I persuade myself that nothing has ever existed of all that my fallacious memory represents to me. I consider that I possess no senses; I imagine that body, figure, extension, movement and place are but the fictions of my mind. What, then, can be esteemed as true? Perhaps nothing at all, unless that there is nothing in the world that is certain.

But how can I know there is not something different from those things that I have just considered, of which one cannot have the slightest doubt? Is there not some God, or some other being by whatever name we call it, who puts these reflections into my mind? That is not necessary, for is it not possible that I am capable of producing them myself? I myself, am I not at least something? But I have already denied that I had senses and body. Yet I hesitate, for what follows from that? Am I so dependent on body and senses that I cannot exist without these? But I was persuaded that there was nothing in all the world, that there was no heaven, no earth, that there were no minds, nor any bodies: was I not then likewise persuaded that I did not exist? Not at all; of a surety I myself did exist since I persuaded myself of something [or merely because I thought of something]. But there is some deceiver or other, very powerful and very cunning, who ever employs his ingenuity in deceiving me. Then without doubt I exist also if he deceives me, and let him deceive me as much as he will, he can never cause me to be nothing so long as I think that I am something. So that after having reflected well and carefully examined all things, we must come to the definite conclusion that this proposition: I am, I exist, is necessarily true each time that I pronounce it, or that I mentally conceive it.

But I do not yet know clearly enough what I am, I who am certain that I am; and hence I must be careful to see that I do not imprudently take some other object in place of myself, and thus that I do not go astray in respect of this knowledge that I hold to be the most certain and most evident of all that I have formerly learned. That is why I shall now consider anew what I believed myself to be before I embarked upon these last reflections; and of my former opinions I shall withdraw all that might even in a small degree be invalidated by the reasons which I have just brought forward, in order that there may be nothing at all left beyond what is absolutely certain and indubitable.

What then did I formerly believe myself to be? Undoubtedly I believed myself to be a man. But what is a man? Shall I say a reasonable animal? Certainly not; for then I should have to inquire what an animal is, and what is reasonable; and thus from a single question I should insensibly fall into an infinitude of others more difficult; and I should not wish to waste the little time and leisure remaining to me in trying to unravel subtleties like these. But I shall rather stop here to consider the thoughts which of themselves spring up in my mind, and which were not inspired by anything beyond my own nature alone when I applied myself to the consideration of my being. In the first place, then, I considered myself as having a face, hands, arms, and all that system of members composed on bones and flesh as seen in a corpse which I designated by the name of body. In addition to this I considered that I was nourished, that I walked, that I felt, and that I thought, and I referred all these actions to the soul: but I did not stop to consider what the soul was, or if I did stop, I imagined that it was something extremely rare and subtle like a wind, a flame, or an ether, which was spread throughout my grosser parts. As to body I had no manner of doubt about its nature, but thought I had a very clear knowledge of it; and if I had desired to explain it according to the notions that I had then formed of it, I should have described it thus: By the body I understand all that which can be defined by a certain figure: something which can be confined in a certain place, and which can fill a given space in such a way that every other body will be excluded from it; which can be perceived either by touch, or by sight, or by hearing, or by taste, or by smell: which can be moved in many ways not, in truth, by itself, but by something which is foreign to it, by which it is touched [and from which it receives impressions]: for to have the power of self-movement, as also of feeling or of thinking, I did not consider to appertain to the nature of body: on the contrary, I was rather astonished to find that faculties similar to them existed in some bodies.

But what am I, now that I suppose that there is a certain genius which is extremely powerful, and, if I may say so, malicious, who employs all his powers in deceiving me? Can I affirm that I possess the least of all those things which I have just said pertain to the nature of body? I pause to consider, I revolve all these things in my mind, and I find none of which I can say that it pertains to me. It would be tedious to stop to enumerate them. Let us pass to the attributes of soul and see if there is any one which is in me? What of nutrition or walking [the first mentioned]? But if it is so that I have no body it is also true that I can neither walk nor take nourishment. Another attribute is sensation. But one cannot feel without body, and besides I have thought I perceived many things during sleep that I recognised in my waking moments as not having been experienced at all. What of thinking? I find here that thought is an attribute that belongs to me; it alone cannot be separated from me. I am, I exist, that is certain. But how often? Just when I think; for it might possibly be the case if I ceased entirely to think, that I should likewise cease altogether to exist. I do not now admit anything which is not necessarily true: to speak accurately I am not more than a thing which thinks, that is to say a mind or a soul, or an understanding, or a reason, which are terms whose significance was formerly unknown to me. I am, however, a real thing and really exist; but what thing? I have answered: a thing which thinks.

And what more? I shall exercise my imagination [in order to see if I am not something more]. I am not a collection of members which we call the human body: I am not a subtle air distributed through these members, I am not a wind, a fire, a vapor, a breath, nor anything at all which I can imagine or conceive; because I have assumed that all these were nothing. Without changing that supposition I find that I only leave myself certain of the fact that I am somewhat. But perhaps it is true that these same things which I supposed were non- existent because they are unknown to me, are really not different from the self which I know. I am not sure about this, I shall not dispute about it now; I can only give judgment on things that are known to me. I know that I exist, and I inquire what I am, I whom I know to exist. But it is very certain that the knowledge of my existence taken in its precise significance does not depend on things whose existence is not yet known to me; consequently it does not depend on those which I can feign in imagination. And indeed the very term feign in imagination proves to me my error, for I really do this if I imagine myself a something, since to imagine is nothing else than to contemplate the figure or image of a corporeal thing. But I already know for certain that I am, and that it may be that all these images, and, speaking generally, all things that relate to the nature of body are nothing but dreams [and chimeras]. For this reason I see clearly that I have as little reason to say, "I shall stimulate my imagination in order to know more distinctly what I am," than if I were to say, "I am now awake, and I perceive somewhat that is real and true: but because I do not yet perceive it distinctly enough, I shall go to sleep of express purpose, so that my dreams may represent the perception with greatest truth and evidence." And, thus, I know for certain that nothing of all that I can understand by means of my imagination belongs to this knowledge which I have of myself, and that it is necessary to recall the mind from this mode of thought with the utmost diligence in order that it may be able to know its own nature with perfect distinctness.

But what then am I? A thing which thinks. What is a thing which thinks? It is a thing which doubts, understands, [conceives], affirms, denies, wills, refuses, which also imagines and feels.

Certainly it is no small matter if all these things pertain to my nature. But why should they not so pertain? Am I not that being who now doubts nearly everything, who nevertheless understands certain things, who affirms that one only is true, who denies all the others, who desires to know more, is averse from being deceived, who imagines many things, sometimes indeed despite his will, and who perceives many likewise, as by the intervention of the bodily organs? Is there nothing in all this which is as true as it is certain that I exist, even though I should always sleep and though he who has given me being employed all his ingenuity in deceiving me? Is there likewise any one of these attributes which can be distinguished from my thought, or which might be said to be separated from myself? For it is so evident of itself that it is I who doubts, who understands, and who desires, that there is no reason here to add anything to explain it. And I have certainly the power of imagining likewise; for although it may happen (as I formerly supposed) that none of the things which I imagine are true, nevertheless this power of imagining does not cease to be really in use, and it forms part of my thought. Finally, I am the same who feels, that is to say, who perceives certain things, as by the organs of sense, since in truth I see light, I hear noise, I feel heat. But it will be said that these phenomena are false and that I am dreaming. Let it be so; still it is at least quite certain that it seems to me that I see light, that I hear noise and that I feel heat. That cannot be false; properly speaking it is what is in me called feeling; and used in this precise sense that is no other thing than thinking.

From this time I begin to know what I am with a little more clearness and distinction than before; but nevertheless it still seems to me, and I cannot prevent myself from thinking, that corporeal things, whose images are framed by thought, which are tested by the senses, are much more distinctly known than that obscure part of me which does not come under the imagination. Although really it is very strange to say that I know and understand more distinctly these things whose existence seems to me dubious, which are unknown to me, and which do not belong to me, than others of the truth of which I am convinced, which are known to me and which pertain to my real nature, in a word, than myself. But I see clearly how the case stands: my mind loves to wander, and cannot yet suffer itself to be retained within the just limits of truth. Very good, let us once more give it the freest rein, so that, when afterwards we seize the proper occasion for pulling up, it may the more easily be regulated and controlled.

Let us begin by considering the commonest matters, those which we believe to be the most distinctly comprehended, to wit, the bodies which we touch and see; not indeed bodies in general, for these general ideas are usually a little more confused, but let us consider one body in particular. Let us take, for example, this piece of wax: it has been taken quite freshly from the hive, and it has not yet lost the sweetness of the honey which it contains; it still retains somewhat of the odor of the flowers from which it has been culled; its color, its figure, its size are apparent; it is hard, cold, easily handled, and if you strike it with the finger, it will emit a sound. Finally all the things which are requisite to cause us distinctly to recognise a body, are met with in it. But notice that while I speak and approach the fire what remained of the taste is exhaled, the smell evaporates, the color alters, the figure is destroyed, the size increases, it becomes liquid, it heats, scarcely can one handle it, and when one strikes it, no sound is emitted. Does the same wax remain after this change? We must confess that it remains; none would judge otherwise. What then did I know so distinctly in this piece of wax? It could certainly be nothing of all that the senses brought to my notice, since all these things which fall under taste, smell, sight, touch, and hearing, are found to be changed, and yet the same wax remains.

Perhaps it was what I now think, viz. that this wax was not that sweetness of honey, nor that agreeable scent of flowers, nor that particular whiteness, nor that figure, nor that sound, but simply a body which a little while before appeared to me as perceptible under these forms, and which is now perceptible under others. But what, precisely, is it that I imagine when I form such conceptions? Let us attentively consider this, and, abstracting from all that does not belong to the wax, let us see what remains. Certainly nothing remains excepting a certain extended thing which is flexible and movable. But what is the meaning of flexible and movable? Is it not that I imagine that this piece of wax being round is capable of becoming square and of passing from a square to a triangular figure? No, certainly it is not that, since I imagine it admits of an infinitude of similar changes, and I nevertheless do not know how to compass the infinitude by my imagination, and consequently this conception which I have of the wax is not brought about by the faculty of imagination. What now is this extension? Is it not also unknown? For it becomes greater when the wax is melted, greater when it is boiled, and greater still when the heat increases; and I should not conceive [clearly] according to truth what wax is, if I did not think that even this piece that we are considering is capable of receiving more variations in extension than I have ever imagined. We must then grant that I could not even understand through the imagination what this piece of wax is, and that it is my mind alone which perceives it. I say this piece of wax in particular, for as to wax in general it is yet clearer. But what is this piece of wax which cannot be understood excepting by the [understanding or] mind? It is certainly the same that I see, touch, imagine, and finally it is the same which I have always believed it to be from the beginning. But what must particularly be observed is that its perception is neither an act of vision, nor of touch, nor of imagination, and has never been such although it may have appeared formerly to be so, but only an intuition of the mind, which may be imperfect and confused as it was formerly, or clear and distinct as it is at present, according as my attention is more or less directed to the elements which are found in it, and of which it is composed.

Yet in the meantime I am greatly astonished when I consider [the great feebleness of mind] and its proneness to fall [insensibly] into error; for although without giving expression to my thought I consider all this in my own mind, words often impede me and I am almost deceived by the terms of ordinary language. For we say that we see the same wax, if it is present, and not that we simply judge that it is the same from its having the same color and figure. From this I should conclude that I knew the wax by means of vision and not simply by the intuition of the mind; unless by chance I remember that, when looking from a window and saying I see men who pass in the street, I really do not see them, but infer that what I see is men, just as I say that I see wax. And yet what do I see from the window but hats and coats which may cover automatic machines? Yet I judge these to be men. And similarly solely by the faculty of judgment which rests in my mind, I comprehend that which I believed I saw with my eyes.

A man who makes it his aim to raise his knowledge above the common should be ashamed to derive the occasion for doubting from the forms of speech invented by the vulgar; I prefer to pass on and consider whether I had a more evident and perfect conception of what the wax was when I first perceived it, and when I believed I knew it by means of the external senses or at least by the common sense as it is called, that is to say by the imaginative faculty, or whether my present conception is clearer now that I have most carefully examined what it is, and in what way it can be known. It would certainly be absurd to doubt as to this. For what was there in this first perception which was distinct? What was there which might not as well have been perceived by any of the animals? But when I distinguish the wax from its external forms, and when, just as if I had taken from it its vestments, I consider it quite naked, it is certain that although some error may still be found in my judgment, I can nevertheless not perceive it thus without a human mind.

But finally what shall I say of this mind, that is, of myself, for up to this point I do not admit in myself anything but mind? What then, I who seem to perceive this piece of wax so distinctly, do I not know myself, not only with much more truth and certainty, but also with much more distinctness and clearness? For if I judge that the wax is or exists from the fact that I see it, it certainly follows much more clearly that I am or that I exist myself from the fact that I see it. For it may be that what I see is not really wax, it may also be that I do not possess eyes with which to see anything; but it cannot be that when I see, or (for I no longer take account of the distinction) when I think I see, that I myself who think am nought. So if I judge that the wax exists from the fact that I touch it, the same thing will follow, to wit, that I am; and if I judge that my imagination, or some other cause, whatever it is, persuades me that the wax exists, I shall still conclude the same. And what I have here remarked of wax may be applied to all other things which are external to me [and which are met with outside of me]. And further, if the [notion or] perception of wax has seemed to me clearer and more distinct, not only after the sight or the touch, but also after many other causes have rendered it quite manifest to me, with how much more [evidence] and distinctness must it be said that I now know myself, since all the reasons which contribute to the knowledge of wax, or any other body whatever, are yet better proofs of the nature of my mind! And there are so many other things in the mind itself which may contribute to the elucidation of its nature, that those which depend on body such as these just mentioned, hardly merit being taken into account.

But finally here I am, having insensibly reverted to the point I desired, for, since it is now manifest to me that even bodies are not properly speaking known by the senses or by the faculty of imagination, but by the understanding only, and since they are not known from the fact that they are seen or touched, but only because they are understood, I see clearly that there is nothing which is easier for me to know than my mind. But because it is difficult to rid oneself so promptly of an opinion to which one was accustomed for so long, it will be well that I should halt a little at this point, so that by the length of my meditation I may more deeply imprint on my memory this new knowledge.

STUDY QUESTIONS

1. In Descartes' method of systematic doubt, why does he question the existence of objects of perception?

2. Why does Descartes believe we can confuse dreams with waking life?

3. If we assume God exists, wouldn't he guarantee the authenticity of our sense experience?

4. Explain what is meant by the Cartesian statement: "I think, therefore I am."

5. For Descartes, what does the example of wax illustrate?

B. Expression in Film

Rashomon

Director: Akira Kurosawa

Translator: Donald Richie

Screenplay: Akira Kurosawa and Shinobu Hashimoto

Akira Kurosawa (1910–1998) is a Japanese filmmaker who directed over 25 films. They include High and Low, Red Beard, Dodes'ka-den, Ikiru, Yojimbo, *and* Rhapsody In August. *He has adapted several Shakespeare plays to film including* King Lear *as* Ran, *and* Macbeth *as* Throne Of Blood, *and his* Seven Samurai *was remade by Hollywood as* The Magnificent Seven. *His film* Dersu Uzala *earned him an academy award as the best foreign language film, and* Kagemusha *won the Grand Prize at the Cannes film festival.*

Rashomon, *here discussed and excerpted, was his first international success, garnering the Golden Lion in the Venice Film Festival and an Oscar for the Best Foreign Film in 1951. It usually appears on lists of the ten greatest films.*

SYNOPSIS

Akira Kurosawa's films can be characterized as visually beautiful and dramatically strong, preoccupied with separating the true from the false in cinematic form. In *Rashomon*, Kurosawa investigates the question of appearance and reality, specifically the accuracy of memory and the interpretaion of events. He offers several accounts of the same crime viewed from different perspectives, but rather than searching for the solution to the crime Kurosawa seeks insight into the elusive nature of truth itself.

The film is based on two short stories by Ryunosuke Akutagawa, *In the Grove* and *Roshomon*, and was later remade by Hollywood as *Outrage* (starring Paul Newman as the bandit, from Mexico.) As well as directing the film, Kurosawa was the principal author of the film script, and he employed the remarkable camera work of Kazuo Miyagawa. The scenario, editing, music (by Fumio Hayakawa), cast, atmospheric effects, camera angles, and cinematic techniques were all innovative for their time and are equally compelling today.

It is interesting to note that Kurosawa and his cast endured enormous hardships in the production. Most of the film was shot in a forest that was so full of leaches that the crew had to coat themselves with salt every day as protection. Black ink had to be added to the artificial rain to make it visible against the gray sky, and trees had to be chopped down to allow sufficient light for the cameras. When the film was first shown in Japan in the 1950s, people stood in pouring rain in lines a mile long to buy a ticket.

The *Rashomon* from which the film takes its name was the largest gate in the capital city of Kyoto. First constructed in 789, it measured 106 feet wide, 26 feet deep, and its stone wall rose to a height of 75 feet. With the decline of Kyoto, the gate fell into disrepair, and by the twelfth century it had collapsed in many places, becoming a notorious hiding place for thieves.

The film moves back and forth between the Rashomon, where a group of people have taken shelter from the rain in the shadow of the gate, and the narrative they tell. To pass the time until the storm passes, a woodcutter and a priest relate the story of a rape and murder to a commoner. Each of the characters involved in the events tell their version of the tale, with the scenes magically enacted before the viewer.

Apparently, while traveling in a forest a samurai and his wife are waylaid by a notorious bandit named Tajomaru (Toshiro Mifune) who kills the husband (Masayuki Mori) and violates the wife (Machoko Kyo). This appears to be what occurred, however, discrepancies occur in the accounts given by the participants, so we are unsure which is correct. The rape and death are seen from four points of view, each of which seems convincing. The truth therefore appears relative, subjective, and partial, depending upon the narrator's perspective and needs.

According to the bandit's version, as told in a prison courtyard to a judge, he tied up the merchant, raped the wife, and later killed the husband in a fair duel. He swears this story is accurate: '"No, I'm telling the truth," he declares. "I know you're going to cut off my head sooner or later—I'm not hiding anything. It was me, Tajomaru, who killed that man. Yes, I did it."

He adds enigmatically, "It was a hot afternoon, about three days ago, that I first saw them. And then all of a sudden there was this cool breeze. If it hadn't been for that breeze, maybe I wouldn't have killed them." This weak excuse makes the murder more a matter of chance than a premeditated act.

The scene begins with Tajomaru sleeping at the base of a huge tree, and the samurai coming down a hill leading a horse on which a woman is riding. The bandit awakens and sees the couple, noting the way the woman gently swings with the movement of the horse and how her veil is blown aside by the wind.

The couple move past him but as Tajomara tells the judge, "First I saw her, then she was gone—I thought I had seen an angel. And right then I decided I would take her, that I'd have her even if I had to kill the man…(he laughs). But if I could do it without killing him then that would be all the better. So I decided not to kill him but to somehow get the woman alone."

A beautiful/horrible film sequence follows in which the Tajomaru tracks and chases the couple through the countryside. He then approaches them, circles the horse, and when he is challenged by the samurai pretends to offer him a sword. "Here, take it. Look at it," he says. "Near here I found this old tomb with lots of things like this in it…swords, daggers, mirrors…if you're interested I might sell some of them to you cheap."

The woman dismounts from the horse and settles herself on the grass near a brook while the samurai climbs the slope with Tajomaru to look at the cache of weapons. As soon as the samurai's back is turned the bandit knocks him to the ground, overpowers the man, and ties him to a tree. He then rushes back to the woman, telling her that her husband has been bitten by a snake. As he describes it, "She became very pale and stared at me as though her eyes were frozen. She looked like a child when it turns suddenly serious. The sight of her made me jealous of that man, I started to hate him. I wanted to show her what he looked like, all tied up like that. I hadn't even thought of a thing like that before, but now I did."

The bandit pulls her up the hill after him, intent on displaying her husband's helplessness and humiliation. When the woman sees the situation she is transfixed at first but then charges the bandit with a dagger. Her thrust goes past him, and after she regains her balance she attacks him again, slashing wildly, even biting his forearm. Tajomaru is impressed by her desperation, and finds her hysteria exciting.

After a short fight the woman collapses with exhaustion. Tajomaru pins her to the ground and begins to kiss her in front of the samurai, who bows his head. At first she struggles and claws at him, but gradually she closes her eyes and begins to caress him. The dagger drops from her hand and sticks point first in the ground.

"And so I had her—just as I had planned," the bandit tells the judge, "and without killing the husband. And that was how I did it. Besides, I hadn't intended to kill him."

But then, according to Tajomaru, the woman threw herself at his feet saying, "Wait. Stop. One of you must die. Either you or my husband…To be doubly disgraced, disgraced before two men, is more than I can bear." Consequently, the bandit frees the samurai, gives him back his sword, and the two men begin to duel. The battle goes on for some time, the men lunging in and out of the frame. Finally, the samurai stumbles, his sword becomes entangled in the undergrowth, and he is spitted on the bandit's sword.

Tajomaru explains, "I wanted to kill him honestly, since I had to kill him. And he fought really well. We crossed swords over twenty-three times. Think of that! No one had ever crossed over twenty with me. Then I killed him."

By Tajomaru's account he did intend to rape the woman but he only killed the man because of the woman's sensibilities; she insisted that only one of them could live. In a sense, she was responsible for the death and he committed no crime. Furthermore, he gave the samurai a fair chance, and since he was the better swordsman he managed to win the fight; he implies that an even contest like that is hardly murder. Tajomaru therefore paints himself as an enthralling lover and a heroic fighter.

The wife, however, tells a different story, one that does involve her shame at being dishonored but not the possibility of remaining with the bandit. She recounts to the judge in the courtyard that after Tajomaru violated her before her husband's eyes, the bandit sneered and laughed then disappeared into the woods. She was left weeping on the ground, and after she had composed herself she threw her arms around her husband, sobbing on his chest.

However, he responded coldly and cynically. "Even now I remember his eyes," she says, "What I saw in them was not sorrow; not even anger. It was…a cold hatred of me." Frantically she implores him "Don't look at me like that. Don't! Beat me, kill me if you must, but don't look at me like that. Please don't!" She retrieves the dagger from the ground, cuts his ropes, then extends the handle to him. "Then kill me if you will. Kill me with one stroke—quickly."

The husband remains implacable, and the woman faints after weaving in front of him with the dagger. "When I opened my eyes and looked around, I saw there, in my husband's chest, the dagger…I didn't know what to do. I ran through the forest—I must have, although I don't remember. Then I found myself standing by a pond...I threw myself into it. I tried to kill myself. But, I failed. (She sobs.) What should a poor helpless woman like me do?"

According to the wife, then, she killed her husband, although she does not remember doing so. Perhaps she could not bear his rejection of her for an act that was beyond her control. There is the suggestion that since she has no memory of the killing, maybe Tajomaru came back and stabbed him to death. All she knows is that when she regained consciousness the dagger was lodged in her husband's heart. The symbolism of his having pierced her heart too is unavoidable.

A third account is given by the dead husband through a medium (Fumiko Homma). With her long robes, flowing hair, and ethereal voice, the effect of her description is mesmerizing.

In this version the bandit said to the woman that "after she had given herself, she would no longer be able to live with her husband—why didn't she go with him, the bandit, rather than remain behind to be unhappy with her husband? He said he had only attacked her because of his great love for her."

The samurai-medium goes on: "My wife looked at him, her face soft, her eyes veiled...Never, in all our life together, had I seen her more beautiful...And what did my beautiful wife reply to the bandit in front of her helpless husband?... 'Take me. Take me away with you.' "

"That is what she said," the samurai continues, "But that is not all she did, or else I would not now be in darkness. 'Kill him,' she said. 'As long as he is alive I cannot go with you. Kill him!' " In an anguished voice he adds, "I still hear those words. They are like a wind blowing me to the bottom of this dark pit. Has anyone ever uttered more pitiless words? Even the bandit was shocked to hear them."

Tajomaru does in fact feel disgust at her callousness, and he asks the husband "What do you want me to do with this woman? Kill her? Spare her?" The samurai-medium remarks, "For these words I almost forgave the bandit." Tajomaru throws the woman from him, who then disappears among the trees. Although the bandit chases her she gets away, and when he returns he cuts the samurai's bonds.

The husband in his grief picks up the dagger from the ground and thrusts it into his own chest.

By this account the husband commited suicide, which can be a noble act in Japanese culture, and his death cannot be attributed to either Tajomaru or his wife. The bandit, in fact, is depicted as having some decency, and the woman is portrayed as unfaithful and self-serving.

Finally, a woodcutter reports that he witnessed the incident first-hand. He claims that while walking in a clearing he heard a woman crying, and when he investigated he saw a man tied up and the bandit crouching beside the woman. Tajomaru was saying "Until now, whenever I wanted to do anything bad, I always did it. It was for me and so it was good. But today is different. I've already taken you, but now I want you more and more—and I suffer. Go away with me. If you want, I'll marry you. Look. (He bows his head low.) I am Tajomaru, the famous bandit, known all over Miyako, and yet here I am, on my knees in front of you."

The woman only sobs harder. "Don't cry," Tojamuro tells her, "Answer. Tell me you'll be my wife...Tell me." The woman replies "But, how could I answer? How could I, a woman, answer a question like that?"

She yanks the dagger out of the ground but instead of attacking the bandit she cuts her husband's bonds, then falls to the grass between the two men. Tajomaru prepares to fight but the samurai says "Stop! I refuse to risk my life for such a woman." He walks up to his wife contemptuously. "You shameless whore! Why don't you kill yourself? Then turning to the bandit he declares "If you want her I'll give her to you. I regret the loss of my horse much more than I will regret the loss of this woman."

The wife is visibly shaken, while the bandit looks at her with distaste as she wipes the perspiration from her face. She collapses in tears, but when Tajomaru says "women cannot help but cry...they are naturally weak," she lashes back. "It's not me, not me—it's you who are weak." To the samurai she says disparagingly, "If you are my husband then why don't you kill this man? Then you can tell me to kill myself. That is what a real man would do. But you aren't a real man. That is why I was crying. I'm tired, tired of this farce." She then crosses to the bandit, taunting him in turn. "I thought that Tajomaru might find some way out. I thought that if he would only save me I would do anything for him. But he's not a man, either. He's just like my husband!...A woman can be won only by strength—by the strength of the swords you are wearing."

Stung by her words the two men draw their weapons. They seem reluctant to fight but their manliness and pride demand it. A furious and sustained battle then ensues at the end of which the samurai's sword becomes lodged in a stump. The bandit traps him as he tries to crawl into a thicket, and hurls his sword into the samurai's chest. Throughout the fight the men gasp for breath, and their terror, sweat, and exhaustion are almost palpable.

As Kurosawa writes in the screenplay, afterwards "Tajomaru and the woman ...stare at the body. Tajomaru, an idiotic expression on his face, rises and takes her hands, but she pulls them away and begins to back off frantically, ending near the tree stump where her husband's sword is still lodged. She utters little inarticulate cries. Tajomaru has followed stupidly, and now, half crazed, he pulls the dead man's sword free and swings it mightily at her as she flees."

On this reading the bandit killed the husband at the wife's urging. She is the principal offender because she provoked the fight even though she did not strike the deathblow. At times she seems appalled at instigating the violence, but she is also seen "laughing and pointing gleefully." The men by comparison do not want to attack each other, although they are easily manipulated into doing so.

One major difference between the accounts of the bandit and the woodcutter is that, in the first, Tajomaru is heroic, skilled, and resourceful, whereas the second shows him lurching about in fear and desperation. Here as in earlier sequences Mifune's performance as the bandit has been acclaimed by critics. He becomes almost the quintessence of evil, menacing, unpredictable, coarse, and vicious.

Toward the end we see the woodcutter, the priest, and the commoner sitting at the Rashomon gate as the rain subsides, trying to make sense of the four accounts. In effect, all three parties have claimed to be the killer, and the woodcutter's interpretation shows Tajomaru as responsible but blames the woman as well.

After the woodcutter finishes his story the cynical commoner remarks "And I suppose that is supposed to be true."

> WOODCUTTER: I don't tell lies.
>
> COMMONER: Well, so far as that goes, no one tells lies after he has said he's going to tell one.*
>
> PRIEST: But it's horrible. If men don't trust one another then the earth becomes a kind of hell.
>
> COMMONER: You are right. The world we live in is hell.
>
> PRIEST: No I trust men... I don't want to believe that this world is hell.
>
> COMMONER: Which one of these stories do you believe?"
>
> WOODCUTTER: "I don't understand any of them. They don't make any sense."

---

*When we lie, we claim to be telling the truth.

The commoner is given the last word on the subject: "Well, don't worry about it. It isn't as though men were reasonable."

Kurosawa has remarked, "The human heart is hollow and full of filth," implying that lying and deceit make it nearly impossible to know what actually occurred.

Perhaps to mitigate the bleakness of this conclusion, Kurosawa adds a somewhat artificial ending to the film. A baby is heard crying, and although the commoner ignores it, the priest and woodcutter respond to its helplessness. The woodcutter, in fact, agrees to raise the child, showing that people are not entirely wicked.

In presenting the various versions of the story Kurosawa seems to be asserting that the truth can never be known. There is no recording angel to transcribe events as they actually occurred, and people have different memories of what happened—recollections that are often inconsistent. People may believe what they say, but their honesty does not guarantee it is true.

All of the characters in the film offer accounts that are favorable to themselves, and their shame at their role in the tragedy also reflects well on them. Kurosawa wrote in his autobiography "Human beings are unable to be honest about themselves. They cannot talk about themselves without embellishing." In *Rashomon* perhaps he is illustrating this idea, that in place of the truth we have only favorable remembrances that help us live with ourselves.

Because the audience is seeing the action as well as hearing the testimonials, Kurosawa is also saying that you cannot always believe what you see. The four accounts do not match but neither do the visual representations, and we come to doubt our own perception of reality. We may need certainty in our lives but all we have is the ephemeral moment, flashed before our eyes. In the end. the puzzle posed by the film leaves us unsettled and unresolved, with neither a literary nor a cinematic solution.

Between words and action, however, Kurosawa tends to trust action. He was always impressed by the honest emotions shown in silent films, where facial expression and gestures took the place of dialogue. In *Rashomon* so much of the plot is visual, perhaps because the eye discerns more than the ear.

One important philosophic point must be kept in mind: To claim that no one can know the truth is not the same as saying there is no truth to be known. For practical purposes it makes no difference, nevertheless the conceptual distinction is important. If truth exists then we do not create it, although, as Kurosawa implies, we may not be able to discover it. Thinking would not make it so, but perhaps we cannot think our way through to the reality.

Rashomon seems to assert the relativity of truth in the sense that we never know where it lies or who possesses it. What people take to be true is a reflection of who they are, varying according to their pride; the absolute truth may be unknowable.

STUDY QUESTIONS:

1. Which of the accounts given by the participants in the rape and murder do you find most persuasive? Why?

2. If you were on a jury, which person would you convict?

3. What is Kurosawa's view of truth? How would you define truth?

4. Would you agree with Kurosawa's contention that people remember events in a way flattering to themselves?

5. Do you think we know anything for sure? How certain are you of that?

The Truman Show

Director: Peter Weir

Screenplay: Andrew Niccol

Peter Weir, born in Sydney in 1944, was one of the leading lights in the Australian New Wave or film renaissance. He has worked in both film and television, in dramas, documentaries, comedies, and thrillers, and has functioned as a director, actor, writer, and producer on three continents. His hallmark as a director is to show characters encountering circumstances that are alien and threatening to their identity, and the way they break free from their dislocation.

Weir has directed some 19 films, beginning with The Cars That Ate People *(1974), which became a cult classic. He then directed* Gallipoli *(1981), which together with* The Year of Living Dangerously *(1982), propelled Mel Gibson to stardom, and* Witness *(1985) that starred Harrison Ford.* The Mosquito Coast *(1986) was a dramatization of Paul Theroux's novel, and* The Dead Poets Society *(1989) showed Robin Williams as a serious actor.* Green Card *(1990), starring Gérard Depardieu, and* Master *and Commander (2003), starring Russell Crowe were both commercial successes. His latest films,* Pattern Recognition *and* Shadow Divers, *will be released in 2008 and 2009, respectively.*

The Truman Show *(1998), discussed below, was nominated for three academy awards: Best Director, Best Original Screenplay, and Best Supporting Actor (Ed Harris). Weir received the London Critics Circle Award as Best Director for* The Truman Show, *as well as the European Film Academy International Award and the Film Critics Circle of Australia Award for Best Foreign Film.*

SYNOPSIS

From a philosophic viewpoint, *The Truman Show* is about reality and representation—how the two can be conflated and, in an age of media, whether we would prefer the fantasy to the truth.

The principal character of the film, Truman Burbank (Jim Carrey), has a seemingly idyllic life, the embodiment of the American dream: a lovely, perky wife, a comfortable house with a manicured lawn, a decent job with an insurance company, and friends, family, and genial neighbors surrounding him. He lives in the island town of Seahaven, a clean and tidy community, somewhere on the Gulf Coast; his license plate reads, "A nice place to live."

But something seems amiss. One day as Truman steps out of his house a klieg light falls from the sky and crashes in front of him. Also, his father suddenly appears after Truman thought he was lost at sea. When Truman is caught in the rain, the rainstorm moves as he does. One day he accidentally backs into what seems like a catering area in his office building. He also begins to notice a pattern in the events around him, the same happenings repeating themselves as if in a continuous loop. He suspects his friend Marlon (Noah Emmerich) and even his wife Meryl (Laura Linney) of deceiving him, withholding secrets. Something does not ring true, and his perfect world suddenly seems oddly counterfeit.

Truman longs to see his high school sweetheart Lauren (Natascha McElhone) whose family unexpectedly left Seahaven for Fiji, but he cannot manage to leave the island. He has been conditioned to fear water because of his father's alleged drowning, so the ferry is out of the question, and even when he wants to drive to the coast, the causeway is blocked by a nuclear plant accident. When he tries to make a plane reservation at the travel agency, all flights are booked for months in advance. What's more, the posters depict travel disasters such as airplanes struck by lightning, terrorist and animal attacks and tropical diseases. He remembers as a boy that when he told his teacher he wanted to be "an explorer like the great Megellan," she had quickly replied "Oh! You're too late. There's nothing left to explore."

Even before these events, Truman has been feeling an uneasiness with his own pastel life amidst the unrelenting gladness of the townspeople. Something seemed to be missing, an authenticity, deeper satisfactions. Behind Truman's genial manner a rage has been simmering—a rage that was unacknowledged because it had no object, but as Truman sees cracks in his picture of reality, he begins to understand the source of his desperation.

What Truman begins to realize is that his entire life is a 24-hour soap opera, the most successful in television, fed live via satellite to an audience of 1.7 billion viewers. He is living in a domed world that encompasses the sun, moon, and stars, buildings, forests, and oceans. The town is a stage-set with

5000 hidden cameras transmitting pictures of him for the past 30 years, beginning with sonograms. The town of Seahaven is actually based on Seaside, Florida, a planned community designed by social engineers.

All the people he knows are actors, including Meryl who is being paid to play the role of his wife, and Lauren had been written out of the show because she had begun to care for him, pitying his situation. Everyone's speech has been scripted, and Truman's place of work, his gingerbread house and hometown are scenery in a TV drama. He has been living in a fool's paradise, the only True Man in a world of make-believe where every object is a prop and everyone is a character in the story. Burbank, of course, is a city where television programs and feature films are made, a place celebrated for its pretence.

Truman had not questioned the peculiarities because that was the only world he knew. He would have to experience real people to detect surrogates, and he would not be aware that his privacy was being violated unless he viewed himself from outside. Like Truman, we all tend to accept the terms of our lives without reflection, except for children whose minds are less predictable and ask why things are the way they are. At the same time, like Truman, we can reach a point where we suspect that everything around us has been staged, and that we are not controlling our lives but following a program. In short, we can wonder at times whether the world we experience is in fact real. Solipsists are people who claim that nothing but they exist, and that is a temptation in our media age.

One issue raised by the film is that of personal privacy. In order to satisfy the audience and sponsors of a TV show, a man is subjected to an enormous hoax—that he is living a normal life when, in fact, he is inhabiting a stage set. Without his knowledge, much less his consent, he is being observed day and night by a huge audience, invading the most private moments of his life. Everyone collaborates to keep him in the dark, and the viewers are complicit in the deceit, all in the name of entertainment.

The Truman Show presents a show within a film, and that opens up the possibility of levels of truth. Truman is surrounded by actors who are pretending to be real people, but of course they are also impersonating actors in the show. We see glimpses of the show's audience, but they are all actors playing the part of an audience while we are the actual audience for the film.

The director who orchestrates the show is named, appropriately enough, Christof (Ed Harris), a deity with complete authority over both the actors and the script. He shows signs of megalomania as when he says "Cue the sun," and like a providential god he has controlled Truman's life since infancy; the baby was his creation. Christof does not seem bothered by the deception but rationalizes that he is protecting Truman from the pain of the world, keeping him safe in a cocoon of illusion. He also thinks he is providing entertainment, perhaps meaning, to millions of people, and that can justify the voyeuristic premise of the show. Privacy is invaded but for the greater good.

Meryl, along with Marlon, function to manage Truman, manipulating him away from discovery. She allays his fears with cheeriness. And whenever she can, Meryl drops brand names and displays "embedded products" to the audience; the advertising becomes part of the show. She endorses a new cocoa or vegetable dicer, facing a hidden camera with a fixed and plastic smile. Consumerism, of course, is part of our mass culture.

In the end Truman tries to escape the confines of his artificial world by sailing away in a small boat. To intimidate him, Christof generates a fierce storm, and when that does not work, he speaks to him directly, trying to explain himself and pleading with Truman to return to Seahaven. But Truman chooses to walk through a door in the painted sky at the horizon line, preferring a painful reality to a false one.

The Truman Show predated reality TV and might have inspired it. In any case, producers seized on the idea that people will watch other people's lives that are not very different from their own. Actual life shown live makes good television. Instead of seeking escape through the exotic and adventurous, viewers are captivated by the banal and ordinary. Heroes can generate a sense of inferiority whereas everyday lives are accessible and make people feel comfortable with themselves. The TV image, boxed in a picture frame, focuses people's attention and gives their lives a narrative.

In our television age people begin to sound as though they are characters in a sit-com, and the line between real life and fantasy becomes blurred. The exhibitionists on reality TV stop behaving naturally and become actors in their own lives, while to the viewer the show becomes more real than their reality—more interesting, immediate, and intriguing. Meanwhile the private lives of celebrities become public images for the paparazzi.

We can identify with Truman's desperation to escape from a manufactured life, created by entertainment and advertising. We want to experience something behind the façade of show business, to touch life directly rather than seeing it through camera lenses. Hollywood gives us an interpretation of reality and proposes icons and values for us to embrace, but that can produce a sense of manipulation. We want to sail past that horizon and encounter reality rather than appearances.

The Truman Show therefore presents a satire of our media and the way it is absorbed by the culture so that the two become interchangeable. Obviously, the film has a serious message, a black comedy, but it conveys that message with a light, charming, and witty touch. George Bernard Shaw's approach to art was to find something profound and to express it in the most humorous way imaginable.

STUDY QUESTIONS

1. How would people know that their lives are only a TV show if there were no clues as to an outside reality, that is, if they remained on the set from birth to death?

2. Could an omnipotent God preordain our lives so that we have the illusion of free choice but are actually performing according to a script?

3. Is there within human beings a drive to know the truth, even if it means a worse life, or are we content with the pleasant illusion?

4. In our contemporary popular culture, is the line between entertainment and real life sometimes blurred, so that people try to resemble "stars?"

5. In reality TV, do we see real life displayed on our screen or are the people behaving like TV actors?

Juliet of the Spirits

Director: Federico Fellini

Screenplay: Federico Fellini, Tullio Pinelli, and Brunello Rondi

The Italian film director Federico Fellini (1920–1993) first achieved international acclaim for Il Vitelloni, *then won four academy awards for best foreign films; these include* 8 ½, Amarcord, Nights of Cabinia, *and* La Strada. *Numbered among his celebrated later works are* La Dolce Vita, Satyricon, *and* Juliet of the Spirits.

Fellini was first drawn to depictions of marginal people—drifters, prostitutes, and circus performers, especially in Il Vitelloni, *but later his narratives and images reflected his own life in surrealistic episodes. Some of his work displays sensuous, macabre, and phantasmagoric elements which Fellini uses to find imaginative understanding. Through his vital imagery Fellini is trying to penetrate to some truth for himself and the audience.*

In all his films, Fellini projects onto the screen events in his past, especially those that haunt him as symbols; these are also strongly Jungian symbols. In Juliet of the Spirits, *it is not an accident that his wife of twenty years, Giuletta Masina, plays Juliet. He also starred his wife in his early and celebrated films* La Strada *and* Nights of Cabiria, *but never in roles so close to their real relationship. Juliet's husband Giorgio, of course, is a surrogate for Fellini, but in caricature form—a self-parody of the charming philanderer with a bizarre group of followers.*

The fantasies in Fellini's films are usually those of the lead male, but in Juliet of the Spirits *the eroticism is reversed and becomes the heroine's adventures. Fellini intended the part as a gift to his wife, although all of his films are ultimately autobiographical. Luckily for the movie-going public, he has transmuted his history into art.*

When Juliet of the Spirits *was initially released it was given a Best Foreign Film award by the New York Film Critics and the National Board of Review. Considered a classic, it was recently restored in rich color by an Italian communications and broadcasting company.*

SYNPOSIS

In his film *Juliet of the Spirits*, Fellini portrays a woman who turns away from conventional means of knowing in favor of the insights provided by feeling. An upper-class, middle-aged Italian wife named Juliet (Guilietta Masina) is shattered to learn that her husband Giorgio (Mario Pisu) has been unfaithful. At the same time, she fears the loneliness that would follow if he left her. To escape the painful reality of her situation, she takes refuge in a world of fantasies and dreams.

To some extent the images are projections of her own fears and wishes—desires that are felt so strongly they seem to come from outside herself. But she also moves in a somnambulistic way through actual experiences.

The dividing line between imagination and reality is never clearly drawn, and some of the scenes may be depictions of a psychic breakdown, but Fellini orchestrates the plot so that Juliet's own emotional life is enhanced and celebrated. She learns to trust her feelings and through them to reach intuitive knowledge and some measure of peace.

From the start, Juliet seems unusually responsive to the spirit world, and we first see her participating in a séance conducted by her friend Valentina. Giorgio is seated in an armchair transcribing the messages, while three others, Alba, Raniero, and Chierichetta, are gathered round the table, their thumbs and little fingers intertwined to form a chain. The medium Valentina puts out the cat ("They attract restless spirits."), passes a stick of incense around their heads three times, and then inserts it into a chrysanthemum. The table trembles, tilts, and begins to tap on the carpet: The ghosts have arrived.

Juliet opens her eyes wide, incredulous, like someone who has had too much good luck. She looks at the others questioningly. Valentina mumbles, her forehead in a frown:

VALENTINA: It's a new spirit. I can tell from the way it moves the table. It's never manifested itself like this.

Juliet leans toward her and humbly, anxiously, like someone confessing a deep desire, says:

JULIET: Ask it something.

There is a silent pause.

VALENTINA: Can you tell us your name, spirit? (*The table beats out "I." Valentina successively calls out the letters, which Giorgio, in the armchair, writes down.*) I...R...I...S.

JULIET: Iris. What a beautiful name!

TABLE: I am beautiful.

VALENTINA: Have you a message for us, Iris?

TABLE: Love for all.

ALBA: Love for all? How lovely!

VALENTINA: Thank you, Iris. You're very sweet. Yours is a delightful message. Dear, would you like—

She stops herself because the table starts shaking violently. Juliet is very tense.

JULIET: What is it?

VALENTINA (*disconcerted*): I don't know. (*The table again shakes violently.*) Maybe it's an interference. Is that still you, Iris?

The table beats out a decisive "No."

VALENTINA: Can you tell us your name?

The table taps its message like a precise telegram. Quickly raising her head, Juliet is the first to interpret the message. With a holy attitude, she spells out:

JULIET: O...L...A...F.

CHIERICHETA (*fascinated, approving*): It's Olaf, yes....

ALBA: Have you a message for each one of us?

VALENTINA: Can you tell us something sweet, which might help us live, help us understand the meaning of our lives?

TABLE: Yes....

Then suddenly the table taps out the name of Juliet. Alba, very excited, calls out:

ALBA: Juliet, a message for you.

Juliet turns pale.

TABLE: What are you up to? What's come into your head? Just what do you think you are? You're nothing; you don't count at all. You're of no importance to anyone... to anyone.

Juliet, now deathly pale, tries to say something. Doing her best to get up, she suddenly collapses, senseless.

ALBA: Juliet!

VALENTINA: Darling, darling. What are you doing? Stop. Don't break the chain.

Very excited, they all surround her, hold her up, call to her. With an almost sadistic compassion, Chierichetta exclaims:

CHIERICHETTA: She's going to die right here!

ALBA: A little water?...

GIORGIO: No, no. Wait. All right. It's over. All right, Juliet? Up, up.

Juliet opens her eyes with difficulty. She looks around as they call to her, smile at her, make her smell vinegar and gulp down a little water. She slowly recovers consciousness.

She looks at the faces of those around her, in an effort to recognize them. Finally, as if overcome by a sudden terror, her eyes search for her husband. She sees him and stares at him desperately. Suddenly she throws her arms around his neck, pulling him tightly toward her, with a muffled sob.

The judgment passed on Juliet by OLAF is obviously a reflection of her poor self-image, something she carries insider her rather than deriving it from her experience. When she clings to her husband in desperation it is probably out of insecurity, as well as fear at hearing the spirit's voice; she cannot imagine him staying with someone as inconsequential as herself.

Aside from séances (with echoes from *La Dolce Vita*), Juliet has a rich imaginative life of her own. She dreams wonderful/terrible images and is enthralled by the colorful scenes around her. Following the séance, when she is at the beach at Fregene with the local doctor, Don Raffaele, she refers to her inner-life as a girl.

Sometimes, when I was a child, all I had to do was close my eyes and I saw—

DON RAFFAELE: I see when I open my eyes, dear signora.

JULIET: No, I mean… I used to see… people I didn't know… places. Now, instead…

Juliet closes her eyes as if to illustrate what she means and immediately feels a tremor. For a brief moment she has seen a flash of beautiful womanly faces.

Iris, perhaps?

Juliete opens her eyes again; she is upset and remains lost in emptiness while the doctor continues to speak.

DON RAFFAELE: Such things are often digestive phenomena, dear signora. Digestion… the solar plexus slightly disturbed. Toxins, entering in a circle, reach the cerebral nervous centers. The hypophysis, in turn… a congestion forms.

Juliet's recounting of her visions and Don Raffaele's dismissal of them is interrupted by an image that seems magical. A helicopter flies over the umbrellas and lands on the beach nearby.

From the cabin of the helicopter there emerges a beautiful half-dressed woman—Susy—who turns to wave goodbye to the pilot as the helicopter takes off.

Susy keeps waving toward the sky; then, slowly, sure of herself, paying no attention to her surroundings, she crosses the beach and goes into the pine forest.

Her passage has left breathless not only Juliet and her friends, but also the two or three young men scattered along the beach. It had been like an apparition of a superb feminine divinity.

DON RAFFAELE (*recovering*): This, yes. This is an apparition I believe in.

HIS WIFE (*chewing*): Last year I gave her massages. She has skin like silk. It disgusted me. (*She pauses, then speaks with hostility.*) She's the mistress of an industrialist. A man with white hair.

Later that same day, when the doctor and his wife have left and the beach is deserted, Juliet receives visions, and once again the realm of dreams, hallucinations, and actuality are indistinguishable.

Juliet closes her eyes and, from the deserted sea, right in front of her, there emerges from a large bubble of gray water, a large raft of wood and iron, loaded with ferocious and savage men. They carry weapons, barbaric armor, and daggers; they wear caps similar to the Fascist fezzes, with skull and crossbones, and bear strange flags covered with monsters and dragons. Their faces are those of Mongols, with drooping mustaches and rough-shaven beards. Juliet quickly opens her eyes, looking at the sea. The raft is there, in front of her; it is slowly approaching the shore. On its side, in large letters, is written OLAF.

Beyond the first raft, others are seen, these too loaded with mysterious warriors and with savage, shaggy horses.

Juliet tries to get up, terrified, with an instinctive desire to flee. She is at first unable to get to her feet and for a few moments crawls forward. Then she begins to run, stumbling as she does. Panting, frightened, she turns around. The rafts are still there, and now some of the warriors, naked, are on the beach, pulling the rafts to shore with huge ropes.

Juliet starts to run again, arriveing almost at the dunes. Short of breath, she stops again, looking over her shoulder.

But now the rafts are gone, taking with them the savage warriors and horses, leaving behind no trace. The sea stretches out, calm and luminous, disappearing from sight.

In her relationship with her mother, Juliet is shown as a deferential and subordinate, habitually criticized for her clothes and drab appearance. Massina plays Juliet as a rather mousy, insecure, dowdy, and dutiful housewife, immensely likable with her bright eyes, slight smile, and trim haircut, but sadly ordinary. Her mother (Caterina Boratto), on the other hand, is a beautiful and sophisticated woman who spends her time at the hairdresser and at glamorous gatherings. She seems to regard Juliet as a disappointment compared to her elegant daughter Adele, and always addresses her in a condescending way. The following scene is typical of the family dynamic:

A car has stopped in the little road near her. From it come two children, who greet her happily. They are her niece and nephew, children of her sister Adele, who is behind the wheel of the car. Next to Adele is Juliet's mother, an imposing woman, authoritative and cool, with a still-young face crowned by rich gray and blue hair. She is very elegant, as is Adele, who is beautiful, maternal, self-assured.

CHILDREN: Aunty. Hello, Aunty.

Juliet kisses them and goes to the car.

JULIET: Mamma, hello. Hello, Adele.

MOTHER: Where've you been? Whenever I come to see you, you're out. It's as if you did it on purpose. (*As Juliet leans over to kiss her, she pulls away.*) No, you're all wet.

JULIET: I was just going home. Let's go. Do you want some coffee?

MOTHER: It's too late now. (*She turns to Adele, speaking in a tone that implies the confidence of one friend speaking to another of things that concern only the two of them.*) What time do we have to be at Luciana's?

ADELE: At four. And first we have to stop off so that I can have my corset fitted.

MOTHER: Didn't Giorgio tell you? I called him myself.

ADELE: Where is your husband?

JULIET: In his office, working.

ADELE (*ironic, somewhat hostile*): He works so much! It's impossible to see him ever. Never a Sunday, never a vacation. Get in, children.

JULIET: What do you mean? In a month—he said he'll take a real rest. Maybe we'll take a cruise. To Spain or to Greece. We haven't decided yet, but I've got all the information. (*Her tone has suddenly become uncertain as she realizes her mother is staring at her.*) What's wrong? Have I said something?

MOTHER: No, nothing. I was just looking. Don't you ever put cream on? You really don't take care of yourself. Give my best to Giorgio. So long. Call me tomorrow.

    The car leaves.

    One evening Juliet's worst nightmare is realized when she discovers that her husband has a mistress. He utters the name "Gabriella" in his sleep, and Juliet catches him speaking in an intimate tone to someone on the telephone; when he is challenged, Giorgio makes a lame excuse. The fact that he hardly tries to be convincing is itself a sign of contempt and indifference.

    Distraught and fearful, Juliet begins to immerse herself in a world of the bizarre and fantastic. She has conversations with fey and exotic individuals, attends erotic parties given by her salacious, amoral neighbor Susy (Sandra Milo), and has an audience of Bhisma, an androgynous mystic.

Bhisma is the latest craze among the wealthy who are looking for the outlandish and thrilling. This man/woman is regarded as a seer in touch with the supernatural and dispensing inspired wisdom. Bhisma gives lectures on wise living dressed in exotic clothes and speaking in a thin, eerie voice, neither male nor female. On some occasions he/she also meets privately with people to help them with personal problems, and in the following scene Valentina implores Bhisma to speak with Juliet.

BHISMA'S ROOM. INTERIOR. NIGHT.

VALENTINA: Maestro, my friend really wanted to talk to you. You can really help her. (*She encourages Juliet.*) Tell him, tell him. Do you want us to leave you alone with him? Speak to him, darling.

Bhisma stops staring at Juliet and goes to sit in an armchair. In the meantime, the assistant goes back and forth from the bathroom, after having taken the cup from Bhisma. Juliet, making a great effort, says in a low voice:

JULIET: No, nothing… There was something… something that… (*She is silent a moment; then, getting back her courage, she almost whispers.*) Since last night it has seemed to me that I have nothing. I'm afraid I lack everything. I'm afraid my husband has another woman.

Bhisma, calm, continues to smile. The assistant pours a liquid on her hands and begins to massage his head. But now Bhisma is staring intently at Juliet.

BHISMA: Anxiety… yes… but you must enter into another dimension. Another dimension. All things are only in three; in the fourth they rejoice. (*A moment of silence, then he begins again, strangely calm.*) It's the fourth dimension. *The Lapis Philosophorum.* "Make of a man and a woman a circle. And from this extract a square, and from the square a triangle."

He closes his eyes as if from the massage and remains silent. Alba, still excited, takes his hand and examines it.

ALBA: May I, Maestro? I would so like to… I draw. I am a painter. I would like to make a sketch of you. Even of your hand alone. I can come tomorrow.

Bhisma doesn't answer; he puts his head back and closes his eyes completely. There is a long silence, and the three women look at each other not knowing what do do. They watch the assistant, who is indicating to them that they should leave.

But suddenly Bhisma begins to act very oddly. Slow and increasingly effeminate movements from the arms and shoulders, accompanied by a stretching of—and a change in—the features of his face. An indefinable mask, almost too feminine, comes over his face. The assistant signals to the women not to move. Obviously the trance has begun. With a slow, soothing voice, the assistant asks:

ASSISTANT: Who are you, spirit?

BHISMA (*speaking in a strange voice, both sweet and sensual*): Iris.

Juliet starts; it is as if she perceived an extremely disturbing feminine presence around the shoulders of Bhisma. There is beauty and a sensuality of form and position. In the same voice, Bhisma begins again:

BHISMA-IRIS: Why don't you learn to please your husband, Juliet?

Juliet looks around. Upset, she answers in a hoarse voice, almost aggressively.

JULIET: I please my husband very much.

Bhisma breaks into laughter.

BHISMA-IRIS: I was born this way... a woman of love. Don't you find me beautiful? Speak freely.

JULIET (*after some hesitation, as if in a dream*): Yes. Very beautiful.

BHISMA-IRIS: Frankly, I too think I am beautiful. Yes, very beautiful. Have you seen my hair? I don't comb it; I caress it. I very much like to caress myself. I have such beautiful, fresh skin. When I'm in a bad mood, I go to the mirror and look at my back. I immediately become happy then. Have you bought stockings, Juliet?

JULIET: What stockings?

BHISMA-IRIS: Black net ones. All women want to be treated like fairies—and they don't know their job.

JULIET (*disturbed, aggressive*): Is love a job?

BHISMA-IRIS: I didn't say "job." I said "art." The art of loving. I had breasts when I was nine.

JULIET: No, I heard you very well. You said "job." A whore, then. Fine.

Once more a fresh and shameless laugh from the lips of Bhisma.

BHISMA-IRIS: Why don't you make yourself as beautiful as I am?

Bhisma's voice now fades out in a confused gurgle; the features of his face change again and another mask takes over, another voice comes from his lips. A masculine voice, persuasive and seductive, with a peculiar Spanish accent.

BHISMA: No one knows you, Juliet. No one sees you. Men no longer recognize real women. You are a real woman.

ASSISTANT: Who are you, spirit? Will you tell us your name?

BHISMA: I see all of you. Your breasts are beautiful, your hair is beautiful. Why are you afraid? You have extraordinary powers because your feminine sensuality is so refined. You are beautiful, Juliet. You are a real woman.

ASSISTANT: But who are you, who are you?

But Bhisma is coming to. He gurgles and stretches; his features return to normal.

The most seductive force in Juliet's life is her neighbor, Susy, the woman who emerged from the helicopter on the beach, and Fellini treats their scenes as the most erotic and pungent in the film. The freedom Susy displays, the atmosphere of uninhibited sensuality, is almost irresistible to Juliet at this traumatic point in her life. She is strongly tempted to abandon her former, cautious nature and become more sexually adventurous under Susy's instruction.

Everything about Susy is lush and voluptuous. When she shows Juliet through the rooms of her villa they seem designed for love, and later, in the woods, she points out a tree house for rendezvous with men, complete with an elevator on a pulley; as Juliet watches, a man ascends to the nest. At a phantasmagoric party, Juliet is introduced to an unimagined world of sensual pleasure and self-indulgence, and she is encouraged to give herself to a beautiful boy reclining on silk cushions.

Juliet first contrives to meet Susy by returning her cat to the villa, and from the moment she enters the villa she feels the pull of the erotic.

THE GARDEN OF SUSY'S VILLA. EXTERIOR. DAYTIME.

The gate is half shut and—cat in arms—Juliet pushes it delicately and enters the rich garden. In the middle of the garden a shining, blue-tiled swimming pool surrounded by elegant outdoor furniture. With the cat held lovingly in her arms, Juliet timidly crosses the garden.

Scattered everywhere are the remains of a party. Abandoned party souvenirs, streamers, empty bottles. Everything very obvious, as if put there just to strike Juliet's imagination. A sense of total disorder under the covered terrace: many cushions still bearing the imprints of bodies, dirty dishes, records.

JULIET: May I—?

No one answers. Juliet enters the vast living room, a room full of all kinds of furniture, many sofas, curtains—disorder. Here the feeling of a party the night before is even stronger. A voice stops Juliet; it is Susy on the telephone. Though she would like to turn back, she is attracted by the voice and wants to listen. She stands, confused, in the veil of a curtain, which flutters around her face. She seems nailed there; she must listen.

Slowly, Susy's voice become clearer. A warm, sensual voice, interrupted by throaty laughter. A northern accent; from Ferrara.

SUSY (*on the telephone*): No, no, no. I just got up; how do you think I am? You can imagine…. This spring…. What? Let me think a moment. The smell. Yes, your skin smells a little of tobacco and of salt water, the sea. I realized that, yet. (*She laughs.*) It was obvious— couldn't you tell from the way I laughed? (*She sighs.*) You're impossible. Today? Maybe late in the afternoon…. I'm letting myself go. … Yes, you're a rat. … No, no complications for me. … Everything, everything, but no complications. It must be simple, because it is simple. Like the first time. Yes? Yes? Yes! Go back to the shower; you'll catch cold. (*A long silence. Susy, with a smile on her lips, looks around lasciviously and sees Juliet. But, as if she hadn't seen her, she continues to smile into space.*) Yes…. Yes…. Yes. (*Susy's voice is increasingly excited. Softly, she says a final "yes."*) Hold on one minute. (*She puts the mouthpiece of the phone on the sofa where she had been stretched out and gets up, smiling at Juliet.*) Oh, how sweet; you brought Rubirosa back. (*The cat jumps out of Juliet's arms and goes to Susy, who picks it up, kisses and pets it.*) My Rubirosa. Enormous Ruby, here, here, to your sweet mistress who wants to have all of you. Oh, come on, my thief, my troublemaker.

The cat meows with pleasure. Without realizing it, Susy uses with him the same words she uses in her intimate moments with men; but she does it gracefully, in a low voice. Under a transparent robe, Susy is naked; her hair is uncombed—but the presence of Juliet doesn't embarrass her at all.

JULIET: He came into my garden. I thought I should bring him back. You know, they steal them.

SUSY (*detached, cutting it short*): Thank you. Isn't it true, Ruby, that we thank the lady? Imagine, they might steal you! Thank you, signora. Signora—

JULIET: My name is Juliet.

SUSY: I'm Susy. You like my Rubirosa. You know, he has a lot of names. Cloud, Pappone, Apollo—and, finally, Lover. Yes! Oh... (*She picks up the phone again.*) Are you still there? A woman who leaves near here brought Rubirosa back.... Beautiful? Of course. (*She laughs.*) All my friends are beautiful....Oh, that I don't know. (*Quietly*) Maybe.... Goodbye, goodbye.... Yes, yes, yes, yes. (*She hangs up the phone. Juliet is pleased. She feels that by her mere presence in this home she is living through an extraordinary adventure, a little like a prostitute. Susy continues to talk.*) Oh, how wonderful. Signora Juliet has come to bring the big, beautiful cat home. Do you want anything, signora? An apéritif?

JULIET (*hesitating, won over, finally accepting*): I don't know. No. Yes.

Susy gets up, now playing the role of the perfect, distinguished hostess—with complete ease.

SUSY: Yes? Good. So do I. What would you like? I find there is nothing better than a bottle of champagne. (*She takes a bottle of champagne from the bar refrigerator and expertly prepares to open it.*) Do you like it? Yes? Do you know how to open it without letting all the foam out? Look. Like this. (*She opens the smoking bottle perfectly.*) You see? Done. (*She fills two glasses, gives one to Juliet.*) Chin-chin.

Susy drinks with facetious greed.

SUSY: Good... Do you like the service? (*She points to the two glasses.*) It's a special crystal. I never serve champagne in goblets. It's boorish. Some more?

JULIET: No, thank you. It's delicious.

Noticing that Juliet is looking around her, Susy says:

SUSY: If you want to see the house, come along. Come on. (*Preceding Juliet, Susy takes a bunch of gladioli from a vase, smells them a moment; then, noticing that they are not really fresh, she holds her nose.*) Brrr, how awful! They smell of death.

Susy throws the flowers into a basket and leads Juliet down a hallway.

On the walls are little paintings in doubtful taste. Little sketches, they represent—as in a profane, blasphemous *"Via Crucis"*—the successive seasons of the love life of a woman. They are little scenes, episodes, colored anecdotes of incredible erotic ardor. Stopping in front of them, nose in the air, a bit shocked but clearly interested, Juliet examines them carefully.

Impatient, from the end of the hallway, Susy calls out, lightly tapping her foot on the floor.

SUSY: They're a gift from my fiancé.. Filthy. But, the men... (*She stops in front of a door and opens it. In the room, stretched out on a bed, is a dark girl.*) Marisa, how arc you? You want to eat in bed? (*The girl doesn't answer, nor does she turn around, Susy puts the cat on her bed and kisses her.*) I'm leaving you, Rubirosa. (*She closes the door and returns to the hallway.*) You know, that girl wanted to kill herself. I saved her by a miracle. I telephoned and telephoned and there was no answer. We had to break down her door. I can't tell you how awful it was. Now I keep her here. Gianni—you'll meet him—makes a big play for her, which keeps her distracted.

JULIET: Like Laura—a friend of mine from school. She was only seventeen. They made it look like an accident. She drowned for love. Oh, look, from here you can see my house.

Juliet, from the balcony, looks at the modest little house lost in the trees. It looks almost ridiculous to her. She smiles, pensive.

SUSY: You two make me feel so tender, when I see you. You're married, aren't you?

JULIET (*almost surprised*): Yes.

SUSY: I envy those who can do it; it must be beautiful—only one man. But how can it be done?

JULIET: It must also be beautiful to be free.

Susy opens a door onto a huge bedroom. A very low, wide bed, covered with delicate silk, contrasts with a thick dark-blue carpet. Susy falls gracefully on the bed and gestures Juliet to do the same. Reserved, rigid, dignified, Juliet sits on the edge of the bed, looking at the carpet —and at a pair of thick, furry men's slippers, which still seem warm from the feet of a man.

Susy's voice, over Juliet's shoulders, says quietly and cordially:

SUSY: Try to lie down.

Susy's affectionate and light hand urges Juliet down to the bed. Supine, Juliet looks up. A kind of silk curtain covers the ceiling above the bed. Susy pulls a cord, opening the curtain, and reveals, above, an enormous mirror, which reflects Juliet's face and body. With a repressed exclamation of shock, Juliet half rises, as if her own image had hit her. She looks, fascinated, into the mirror.

JULIET: Did you—find this here?

SUSY'S VOICE: Oh, no. I had it built in. Isn't it amusing? Sometimes I get the impression that there are four of us. Now who knows what you think of me? But, you know, men like to enjoy themselves.

Susy's voice suddenly fades away. Juliet turns to look for her; she is gone. Her robe has been thrown on the bed. Only now does Juliet notice a large round hole in the floor, right next to the bed. From a distance there comes the muffled voice of Susy, together with a peculiar sound of rinsing.

SUSY'S VOICE: Juliet! Signora!

Juliet looks into the hole and sees, at the bottom of a long slide, the bluish movement of the waters of a pool. Susy, half naked, is swimming;

she appears and disappears as in the glass of a telescope. Her happy voice rises from the water.

> SUSY: Get undressed, and you come in too. The water is warm. Just so that right after making love with my fiancé we can come down here just as we are. It's beautiful. We take a bath—and then we can start again. Come in, Juliet. Dive in.

Fellini is here at his surrealist best in his sumptuous sets and costumes and brilliant imagery. The carnival music by Nina Rota, and the "waltzing camera" add to the whirling, opulent atmosphere. Critics have analyzed Fellini's symbolism as Freudian or Jungian, but whatever the psychological sources the viewer feels awash with vivid images that resonate emotionally. This was Fellini's first color film, and he uses strongly contrasting shades of primary colors to paint his scenes. In fact, "Feliniesque" has become a name for this combination of fantastical imagery and riotous color.

Religion is juxtaposed against Susy's sensuality; perhaps as another lure and trap. Specifically, Juliet recalls an incident from her childhood when her grandfather (Lou Gilbert) rescued her from a passion play. She was cast as a Christian martyr, tied to a grate and consumed by (paper) fire; she later ascends to heaven in a stage contraption. Her free-thinking grandfather stops the play and unties her, protesting against the primitive ecstasy of the pageant. He takes her in his arms, calling her "my little beefsteak," and carries her away to safety.

Perhaps this scene represents for Juliet a time when she felt small, passive, and deserving of abuse. She needs to separate herself from any such memories (or realities) that diminish her as a person.

Her hallucinations still crowd in on her though, and just as she saw the raft with savage men on the beach, she sees "bearded, invading warriors" throughout her house. They first appear on the veranda, then crowd into the bathroom, pantry, and dining room in overwhelming numbers. Juliet makes her way through the throng of bodies and armor, trying to escape into the pine forest.

GARDEN AND PINES EXTERIOR. TWILIGHT.

Juliet, having climbed over and pushed aside the massive, heavy bodies, emerges, out of breath, in the garden. But a forest of multicolored flags seems to surround it from every side. Troops of barbarians on horseback are lined up all around, leaving no avenue of escape. The horses neigh and paw the ground. Threatening shouts come from all over.

Juliet feels lost. But suddenly something makes her look up: A wavering, multicolored light falls from above, right over her head.

It is a large balloon that is descending into the garden, a balloon with many large flags and festoons of lanterns of many colors.

In the vessel someone is signaling to Juliet—two people, a man and a woman, are leaning over the basket and waving. The man is Juliet's grandfather; the woman is beautiful and shapely in a chanteuse's dress—it is his famous adventure, the ballerina of the singing café.

Juliet lets out a desperate call, full of unexpected hope.

JULIET: Grandfather!

The grandfather continues to wave his arms, while the balloon continues its descent toward the garden. When it is but a few feet away, the grandfather throws a rope ladder overboard and signals Juliet to hurry.

GRANDFATHER: Come on. Quickly!

Juliet runs breathlessly toward the balloon, grabs the rope ladder and climbs it.

Standing in the balloon, clinging tightly to the edge of the basket, Juliet rises above the world of anxieties, chatting happily with the ballerina and eating chocolates from a heart-shaped box. She is "filled with a sense of liberation, of well-being." Juliet and the ballerina sing and skip together, and although the balloon enters a cloud "the happy, impetuous song goes on." When Juliet asks her grandfather whether they are ever going back to earth, he says, "Relax. Of course, we're going back whenever you like. I've always returned. One always does return home, but the world is large—full of things to see and do."

Juliet cannot remain in the fantasy world, but it refreshes her spirit and enables her to soar in her own way. She can then return to her circumstances in life with a wider and more tranquil perspective. She has rejected spiritism, promiscuity, and religion as being oppressive and foreign to her nature, and seems to have found harmony in her life through acceptance of herself. She is no longer bedeviled by visions, perhaps because she no longer needs them, and we later see her laughing and looking at her face in the mirror as if seeing it for the first time.

Although Juliet's descent into fantasy has been frightening, it has been liberating as well. As the psychotherapist R. D. Laing has said, breakdown can be breakthrough. Juliet's peaceful existence has been destroyed, but she is freer than ever before. It is as though she gave herself permission to go a little mad and to indulge in fantastic delusions. It protected her psyche against her husband's infidelity and was a means of becoming more whole.

> The sun enters from the open window. Everything is calm; outside, the the usual sounds of a radio, a hen, a car.
>
> There are the usual, comforting noises. There are no signs of the nocturnal siege.
>
> Juliet takes the newspaper and puts it on the bed, without even looking at the front-page headlines.
>
> She goes to the dining room. Everything is in order, except for the dining room table, which still has the remains of the supper—bottles and dirty dishes, a crude reminder of what has happened. A slight grimace, a small shrug of the shoulder and she goes out into the garden.
>
> Here too all is in order, with no trace of the siege.
>
> The sun shining on the grass. An air of peace. The cats, as usual, sunning themselves.
>
> The maid appears on the doorstep.
>
> FORTUNATA: The coffee is ready. What should I make for lunch today?
>
> JULIET (*without turning around*): I don't know—whatever you like.
>
> FORTUNATA: Will your husband be home for lunch?
>
> JULIET: No, I don't think so. Nor this evening.
>
> Juliete goes to the swing, gently swinging, her feet not leaving the ground.
>
> She continues to swing this way, absorbed.
>
> She looks through the pines at the luminous horizon of the sea, colored in reds and golds, acquiring a magic beat, but supremely normal, everyday.
>
> A sail, in the midst of the horizon, comes gently into the path of the sun. The sun is rising, reddening, the sail now lighted by a marvelously warm reflection, but marvelously "natural."
>
> Juliet is quiet, almost serene, as she lightly swings. She looks around her at a world that more and more takes on—in ways so simple, so stable—both the real and the unreal pulse of everyday magic.

A flight of swallows passes high in the sky. Juliet raises her eyes and sees the swallows also slowly enter into the golden refraction of the sun's rays.

Juliet seems to be whispering something under her breath, but for the first time not in order to call or surprise anyone. She seems at peace with this pure world, filled with marvelous realities, which spring to life around her.

She hears a cry from above—it could be the sound of a group of birds, or the call of the swallows.

She raises her eyes, shields them from the powerful sun with the back of her hand. She tries to puzzle out the meaning of this faintly heard sound.

But she sees only the very blue sky—a blue as deep as a marine abyss—and the golden rays of the sun.

Juliet smiles, bends her head and continues to sway on the swing, in the rustling of a light wind. It is as if she no longer cares about the origins of the sounds, the images she has seen, whether they be part of a natural mystery or part of a supernatural secret. Everything in her is now anchored in peaceful harmony, beyond the mystifying ghosts that have until now besieged her; she is concerned with the daily miracle of simple reality.

Juliet smiles, liberated, at peace.

STUDY QUESTIONS:

1. Would you trust your feelings more than reason and good sense, your heart over your head? How would you protect yourself from being mistaken?

2. If you were Juliet, how would you tell the difference between hallucinations, memories, fantasies, dreams, and reality? Could you separate "I dreamt of a spirit" from "A spirit visited me in a dream?"

3. How would you know when to trust the advice of an alleged seer such as Bhisma or messages received during a séance?

4. Would Juliet be happier if she were more like her neighbor Susy? Would religion be her salvation?

5. In what way does Juliet change from the beginning to the end of the film?

Bibliography of Philosophy, Literature, and Films

I. Obtaining Reliable Knowledge: Epistemology

Philosophy

Appeareance and Reality	F. H. Bradley
Critique of Practical Reason	Immanuel Kant
Critique of Pure Reason	Immanuel Kant
Enquiry Concerning Human Understanding	David Hume
Essay Concerning Human Understanding	John Locke
Essays in Pragmatism	William James
Fact, Fiction, and Forecast	Nelson Goodman
Geneaology of Morals	Friedrich Nietzsche
A History of Philosophy	F. C. Copleston
Human Knowledge	Bertrand Russell
A Hundred Years of Philosophy	John Passmore
Meditations on First Philosophy	René Descartes
Mysticism	Evelyn Underhill
Parmenides, Republic, Sophist, Theaetetus	Plato
Philosophical Investigations	Ludwig Wittgenstein
Philosophical Method	R. G. Collingwood
Philosophical Papers	G. E. Moore
The Philosophy of Perception	G. J. Warnock
Sensations and Perceptions	D. W. Hamlyn
Some Main Problems of Philosophy	G. E. Moore
A Treatise Concerning the Principles of On Human Knowledge	George Berkeley
A Treatise of Human Nature	David Hume
Word and Object	W. V. O. Quine

Literature

The Aleph and Other Stories	Jorge Luis Borges
The Balcony	Jean Genet
Brand	Henrick Ibsen
Candide	Voltaire
The Castle	Franz Kafka
Confessions of a Mask	Yukio Mishima
Dr. Faustus	Thomas Mann

The Ebony Tower	John Fowles
Endgame	Samuel Beckett
Exit the King	Eugene Ionesco
Faust	Johann Wolfgang Goethe
Finnegan's Wake	James Joyce
The Flowers of Evil	Charles Baudelaire
The Fox	D. H. Lawrence
The French Lieutenant's Woman	John Fowles
It Is So (If You Think So)	Luigi Pirandello
Labyrinths	Jorge Luis Borges
Nausea	Jean-Paul Sartre
The Notebooks of Malte Laurids Brigge	Hermann Hesse
One Hundred Years of Solitude	Gabriel Garcia Marquez
Remembrance of Things Past	Marcel Proust
Ulysses	James Joyce
V	Thomas Pynchon
Waiting for Godot	Samuel Beckett
Wide Sargasso Sea	Jean Rhys

Films

All About Eve	Joseph Mankiewicz
The Andalusian Dog	Luis Bunuel
A Beautiful Mind	Ron Howard
Beauty and the Beast	Jean Cocteau
David and Lisa	Frank and Eleanor Perry
8 ½	Federico Fellini
Les enfant du paradis	Marcel Carne
Harold and Maude	Hal Ashby
Juliet of the Spirits	Federico Fellini
Laura	Otto Preminger
North By Northwest	Alfred Hitchcock
Rashomon	Akira Kurosawa
Rear Window	Alfred Hitchcock
The Return of Martin Guerre	Daniel Vigne
The Third Man	Carol Reed
The Truman Show	Peter Weir
Twelve Angry Men	Sidney Lumet

II. The Nature of Reality: Metaphysics

As defined earlier, metaphysics tries to discover the fundamental nature of reality. Some philosophers regard it as a comprehensive study of what is fundamental to all existence, while others define it as the study of first principles or ultimate truths, or the effort to comprehend the universe, not simply piecemeal or by fragments, but somehow as a whole. In more contemporary terms, metaphysics gives us a new way of regarding the world, a shift of vision in our paradigm of reality. All of these academic definitions are helpful to some extent in understanding the field, but metaphysics affects each of us on a more personal level.

In our more reflective moments, when we pause to consider our lives, we often experience a profound curiosity about the universe we inhabit. We wonder about the overall scheme of things and our part in it. Although the search may be disorienting, we feel a need to understand the meaning of our individual lives and of human existence in general.

When we begin reflecting in a more deliberate way, we question whether we exist as an accident of physical forces or whether purpose governs the universe, directing us toward some end. This may lead us to wonder whether the world is basically empty and meaningless or whether a cosmic intelligence is at work, a benevolent God who created us for a reason. We also ask if the values we believe in, the motivating force of our lives, have any objective foundation. Are right and wrong grounded in some genuine ethical truth or do they merely reflect our times, our society, and our personal tastes? If life is meaningless in itself, perhaps we can invest it with meaning through our choices, and by our creative act bring purpose into being.

We also want to know whether space has a limit and, if so, what lies beyond it, and whether the universe had a beginning and what existed before.

If life on earth comes to an end, will that be with a bang or a whimper, in a fiery apocalypse when the sun explodes or through the gradual loss of available energy? The concept of time can perplex us also, for the past resembles a dream, the future a fantasy, so we are left with the knife-edge instant of the present which seems impossible to hold; the minute we say now it is then. Can we locate our lives within the flux of time or do we watch the river of time flow by?

In addition, we are curious to know the basic substance of the universe, that is, whether it is spiritual or material, and to discover its inherent structure and the process by which it operates. We may regard the process as mechanical or organic, evolution or devolution, a cyclical, spiral, linear, or stepwise movement. Or we may come to believe in the expansion and contraction of the entire universe, a pulsing or breathing like some enormous organism.

Metaphysicians wonder about the nature of reality in a similar way, but they try to be systematic and logical in approaching the problems. They also use evidence from the sciences as the basis for their speculations, exploring the meaning and implications of scientific discoveries in a rigorous way. Although each person who engages in metaphysical thinking must find his or her own answers, we can all learn from some outstanding minds that have contemplated these fundamental questions.

A. THE SELF: QUESTIONING ITS IDENTITY AND FREEDOM

One basic metaphysical question has to with our selves. In a sense, nothing seems more obvious than our very self, but when we attempt to define its nature we tend to become confused. Part of the problem is that we are analyzing our selves, which is rather like pointing a flashlight at its own beam of light. The principal problem, however, stems from the complex nature of the self which makes it difficult to characterize.

On the one hand, we think of the self as a physical entity that exists in the same tangible form as a horse or a tree, and whose existence is verified by sense perception. We recognize our own self and other selves as corporeal beings, acting in a concrete world of objects and events. In short, the self can be considered as embodied, and our bodies as something we are rather than something we have.

On the other hand, this definition of the self does not seem to capture its core; in fact, it seems irrelevant to selfhood, a superficial interpretation. We feel the self is more of a mental entity lying beneath our physical appearance; it is the non-bodily source of our actions, with the body as the mind's agent. In this view, the essential self is known through introspection where we look within ourselves and discover that spiritual center. The body seems our exterior part, even though we are chained to this dying animal. It serves as a shell or housing, issuing orders, receiving impressions, storing memories, reflecting and deliberating. In short, the basic self is here identified with our spirit or mind.

However, this concept of self is difficult to defend in scientific terms. Furthermore, it resembles some extreme religious beliefs that also claim to be based on private, introspective, ineffable knowledge. We cannot be sure, therefore, whether the self is a real psychic entity surpassing all scientific understanding, or whether such a belief is a delusion.

These alternatives, of identifying the self with the body or with the mind, are thus fraught with problems, nevertheless they are natural and persistent ways of thinking. They are also two major theories in metaphysics as to the nature of self and, for these reasons, deserve further discussion.

Reductive materialism is the technical name for the theory that the self is the same as the physical body. The view that the self is explicable in terms of the mind or spirit is called *panpsychism*.

Reductive materialism rejects the notion of mind altogether and explains all activities in terms of mechanical, physical sequences. "Brain" is substituted for "mind" as the agency responsible for actions, and the self is treated as identical with the bodily organism, which includes the brain as well as the nerves, muscles, organs, skin, and so on. According to this theory, we are nothing but our anatomical parts and physiological processes.

Not only is a physical explanation thought to be sufficient to account for all activities of the self, but the concept of mind is vigorously challenged on the grounds that there can be no possible evidence of its existence. Mind by its very nature belongs to a permanently unknowable realm beyond the reach of empirical evidence. It cannot be seen, touched, heard, smelled, or tasted; in fact, no conceivable test could detect its presence within the body. For example, if a man reaches for a fork, then a train of physiological events can be described in a cause and effect pattern: His muscles contracted on certain nerve impulses that were triggered by neural events occurring in his brain. But no evidence can be offered to prove that a nonphysical entity called "mind" was responsible for the movement of his arm.

Sometimes the reductive materialist charges that the existence of mind can only be asserted using an *argumentum ad ignorantiam*: We do not know what lies behind the physiological processes (assuming that something must), consequently we claim that mind is this agency. This is logically invalid, for a lack of knowledge cannot be taken as grounds for any conclusion; a theory is neither proven by not having been disproven nor disproven by not having been proven. If we do not know the cause of action, we cannot conclude that the cause must be the mind.

On the basis of these points, the reductive materialist rejects the notion of an interior mind or soul and defines the self strictly in terms of its physical components. The "I" is entirely reducible to the physical body, without any spiritual or mental residue.

Panpsychism, the opposite theory, maintains that the self is basically spiritual or psychical in nature; even our physical body is thought to be in some way mental. Rather than the mind being in the body, the body is contained in the mind.

Panpsychism rejects the materialistic view of self and regards it as arising from a prejudice for scientific explanations—a prejudice that is inconsistent with our experiences of remembering, desiring, deliberating, reflecting, and acting in accordance with conscious purpose. To reduce phenomena of this sort to physiological terms does violence to our deep feeling that something other than a physical process is occurring when, for example, we are experiencing beauty, goodness, or love. The materialistic explanation also diminishes human beings by declaring that they cannot be anything other than that which is empirically verifiable, that is, known by sense experience. Such a reduction is not only repugnant but depends upon an unfounded criterion for genuine knowledge.

As an alternative, therefore, the panpsychist declares that the essential self consists of mind or spirit, and that the reality of our material self can be doubted. Viewed from this context, a supposedly physical event such as drinking wine is only the sense of mellowness and well-being; a morning swim is the feeling of invigoration; and both experiences are increased by anticipation and recollection, which also belong to the mental realm.

According to the panpsychist, all "physical" occurrences ultimately come down to internal experiences, and are nothing but these experiences. If our skin is cut or burned, for example, that injury is only a mental event of experiencing pain. There is no physical self that has been injured, but only a mental self that is suffering; the *consciousness* of suffering is what being injured means. The same is said to be true of any bodily event.

The panpsychist also argues that everyone recognizes himself or herself to be that spiritual being within the animal form rather than the form itself.

We know this through first-hand knowledge that gives us immediate and direct assurance that our mind not our body constitutes the core of our self.

Some panpsychists go so far as to claim that, by analogy with the human self, the entire range of objects in the world—from animals to plants to rocks—might possess an internal spirit and some degree of awareness. For just as we know our own self to lie behind that which appears externally, other entities too could possess centers of consciousness within. In the case of flowers and trees the level of awareness would be quite low; for fish and birds it would be somewhat higher. But a mode of consciousness might reside within every object in the universe, with the sum total of these spiritual centers constituting reality. Such a position is called pantheism or, in more precise philosophic terms, a type of Idealism (see Berkeley's subjective idealism below).

Whether or not we feel persuaded to adopt this position, it does seem plausible to trust our primary awareness that the mind exists. We may not be willing to accept the idea that mind is the only reality, or attribute consciousness to inanimate objects, but we do tend to believe that our minds as well as bodies are real.

Once we assert the reality of mind and body, we are faced with the theoretical problem of how interaction can occur between such radically different entities, but at least we are in harmony with our understanding that the self includes both. In panpsychism and reductive materialism, a certain consistency is gained at the expense of common sense, for neither our mental part nor our physical part seems reducible to the other.

If the self does embrace both mind and body, then a further set of questions arises: to what extent are we physical beings and to what extent mental?[1] The self cannot be identified wholly with the body because we are more than the sum of our physical parts; nevertheless, the body seems to be a definite part of the self. And although the self is closely identified with the mind, it is not just mind but something more encompassing.[2]

What then are the boundaries of the self? How much or what part of our bodies would have to be lost before we felt a diminution of selfhood? When

---

[1] It is one thing, incidentally to distinguish between mind and body, and quite another to say that mind can exist after the body has decayed. Belief in the distinction between mind and body does not logically entail belief in disembodied existence; a separate argument is needed to prove the immortality of the spirit.

[2] If self were only that series of mental phenomena making up mind then it would be impossible to account for the fact of self-awareness. To quote John Stuart Mill, we would have to "accept the paradox that something which *ex hypothesi* is but a series of feelings, can be aware of itself as a series"; or, that "I feel" is the same as "I know that I feel." That is, consciousness cannot be the same as self-consciousness.

Brain / thoughts mature

our bodies grow, decay, and otherwise change throughout our lives, how is the self affected? How can the self reflect upon itself, be both subject and object; how can "I" contemplate "me"?

Related to these questions are others concerning the relation of the self to the non-self, especially the limits of the self in "space." What should be included as essential to the self and what should be excluded as extraneous to it? What lies outside the circle of the self as object and what resides within as subject?

The self has sometimes been said to include the people one loves and personal property, especially objects such as tools worn from a lifetime of use, one's land and home, special books or paintings, a musical instrument or favorite chair, or clothing that has conformed to the body from repeated wearing. As Henry David Thoreau writes in *Walden*:

> Kings and queens who wear a suit but once, though made by some tailor or dressmaker to their majesties, cannot know the comfort of wearing a suit that fits. They are no better than wooden horses to hang the clean clothes on. Every day our garments become more assimilated to ourselves, receiving the impress of the wearer's character, until we hesitate to lay them aside,…even as our bodies.

Or one can enlarge the self to embrace the whole of mankind within one's consciousness, as the English poet John Donne declares in his *Meditation XVII*:

> No man is an island, entire of itself; every man is a piece of the continent, a part of the main; if a clod be washed away by the sea, Europe is the less, as well as if a promontory were; as well as if a manor of the friends or of thine own; any man's death diminishes me, because I am involved in mankind; and therefore never send to know for whom the bell tolls; it tolls for thee.

The question is that of deciding the extent of the self: How wide or narrow can we interpret it to be? Perhaps we can accept the idea that an individual is the sum of all that he can call his.

Just as we may question the extent of the self in "space," we may also wonder about the persistence of the self through "time." Here we wish to determine what personal essence survives all the changes that take place during our lifetime. Seemingly every facet of our being changes without any thread of continuity existing throughout. Our thoughts, attitudes, aspirations, and values change between childhood and old age. Our memories may grow dim; our disposition can vary from extreme compassion to bitter cynicism and misanthropy; and our bodies undergo a virtual metamorphosis as every cell is replaced, and growth and degeneration proceed continually between birth and death. What, then, remains constant? In temporal terms, the self is whatever entitles us to declare we are the same person throughout our lifetime, legitimately referred to by the same name. Whatever is seen as the constant element, that principle of personal unity underlying all change is our essential self.

As a final point it should be mentioned that some philosophic systems of a mystical nature have denied the reality of the self altogether. Indian philosophies, for example, will often make this claim, treating the self as an illusion (*maya*). It is argued that the enlightened person understands that there are no separate selves and no difference between people and their world. Reality is one, without inner and outer parts, and no distinction exists between our individual soul and the world soul (*atman* and *Brahma*). Indian philosophy further maintains that we can experience the unitary character of reality in privileged moments of heightened awareness. If our spirit is properly prepared, then the Oneness of the universe can be revealed to us in a mystical experience. Here our sensations are melted and fused, our bones become liquefied, and we are absorbed into the cosmic All.

To conceive of the self in this way, as undifferentiated and consequently unreal, is extremely appealing when we long for escape from suffering. Nevertheless, we are aware of our selves with a vividness, immediacy, and power that seem to guarantee authenticity. To deny that we ourselves exist seems absurd. Western philosophers generally argue that if the "I" is not real, then everything is an illusion, for few things strike us as more certain.

B. THE UNIVERSE: WHAT IS ULTIMATELY REAL?

The pre-Socratic Greek philosopher Thales in the sixth century b.c. was the first man known to history to speculate about the basic substance of the universe. In an imaginative leap of understanding, Thales reasoned that despite the apparent diversity of things around us there might well be a single substance common to all matter. Thales identified water as the substance underlying everything, and used numerous ingenious arguments to prove his case,[3] but his particular choice of water and his

---

[3]Thales argued that water transformed itself into air and earth through evaporation and into fire during lightning storms. Water underlies the earth as can be seen in wells and earthquakes, the latter due to storms at sea. Furthermore, water is essential to all life and actually creates life as can be seen by the organisms left wriggling in half-dried mud pools. With regard to the last, Thales is not far wrong, for life began as specks of protoplasmic jelly in the scum of tides.

"proofs" are philosophically and scientifically irrelevant. What matters is that Thales tried to reduce the multiplicity of objects to a unity, the seeming heterogeneity to a homogeneity, which means that he saw beyond appearances and accounted for why things exist as they do.

After Thales had broken the ground, a contemporary named Anaximander posited the Boundless or Indefinite as the primary source of matter, that "out of which all things arise and to which all return," but which does not itself possess determinate characteristics. And after Anaximander, Pythagoras declared numbers as basic, not just because everything could be expressed numerically but because numbers were thought to be fundamental entities with magnitude. Following these philosophers were some fifth-century pre-Socratics who were preoccupied with the idea of constancy and change—Heraclitus, for whom change or *logos* (that is, process or measure) characterizes everything, and Parmenides, who asserted that change is an illusion. For Parmenides and his follower Zeno, the universe is motionless and changeless, a fixed bloc. Finally, Anaxagoras and Democritus spoke of particles that come into collision, mix, and combine to produce the physical world; Democritus, amazingly enough, offered an early theory of atomic interaction.

All of these metaphysical theories are little more than historical curiosities today but they led to the more profound theories of the celebrated Greek philosophers Plato and Aristotle, and the theories of modern philosophers such as Bertrand Russell and Alfred North Whitehead. All subsequent philosophy addressed itself to similar problems, using these early speculations as stepping stones. And when we ourselves begin asking metaphysical questions we encounter the same problems. We too ask about the reality underlying appearances, the basis of things, and what remains constant throughout the flux of life. In short, metaphysical questions are the most perennial of all, for they are rooted in the human condition, and no thinking person can avoid reflecting on them.

As metaphysics has developed, certain theories have crystallized as dominant and persuasive. They are theories concerning the nature of the universe but they correspond to theories of the self. For example, according to the *naturalistic* theory the universe can be understood in wholly natural terms without any recourse to supernatural explanation. Human beings are a part of the natural order, and even though they have evolved to a position of supremacy among the other animals, they are not unique creations outside of nature.

In contrast to the naturalist, the *spiritualist* believes that soul or spirit constitutes the ultimate reality. Matter is thought to be dependent on some spiritual force for its existence, including a holy, eternal God. Spiritualism and *idealism* are sometimes treated as synonymous, but spiritualism has a definite religious character whereas idealism regards all of existence as ideas or mind.

We will see examples of these and other conceptions of reality in the readings, but let us explore here one pressing problem in metaphysics, namely whether people are free or compelled in their actions. More precisely, metaphysicians wonder whether human beings possess free will or whether they are determined in their choices. Are people able to decide between alternative courses of action as we usually assume?

The *determinist* takes the absolute position that all actions, including those people think they deliberately choose, are the inevitable result of prior factors. In a sense, all choices have already been made and a free decision is an illusion. The factors that are operative may be internal or external, but they completely govern human actions in accordance with physical laws. Once these laws are fully known, all behavior will be predictable. It is only because of incomplete knowledge that we cannot predict conduct with complete accuracy at present.

The *libertarian*, by contrast, admits that people often do behave in predictable ways and that statistical probabilities are possible, but claims people are not forced to act as they do; they are always free to behave differently. In brief, the libertarian maintains that the causes of human choice lie with the human being, or differently put, that reasons for decisions cannot be reduced to causes.

Thus the lines are drawn, and various arguments are used by the two sides to support their positions.

The determinist, first of all, admits that decisions are usually thought to be free, but claims that this is a false assumption, probably due to pride and ignorance. Once we scientifically analyze the full range of factors behind our choices then we realize we are determined throughout. Freedom is seen as a delusion, a popular misconception that must give way before scientific truth.

Among the causal factors cited by the determinist is our genetic inheritance, including our body type, nervous system, skeletal structure, brain capacity, glandular secretions, and so forth. Each of these biological factors affects the way we live. Our body type, for example, determines whether we choose sedentary or energetic activities, and the character of our brain determines the type of occupation we follow. We are also predisposed to various diseases, some of which cannot be avoided by diet or exercise.

In addition to genetic factors, the determinist also points to geographic and climatic conditions that exert an influence on our behavior. People who live in mountainous regions tend to be hardier and more self-reliant than those who live on the plains, and cold climates produce more energetic, productive people whereas tropical climates sap energy, encouraging relaxation and enjoyment.

Even more important than these factors, the determinist claims, are the effects of a person's social environment. For, each society determines the character of its members by the customs and mores that it holds, its religious and philosophical ideas, the social, economic, and political structures that it embodies. As a consequence, the Chinese differ from the French, and the Africans from the South Americans. Other factors that are said to determine people's personality and decisions are their family upbringing, formal and informal education, and the unique experiences they have undergone in their lives.

The list could be extended, but the determinist maintains that once all of these factors are taken into account, the causes of a person's actions are revealed; we can then see why a person had to act as he or she did. What's more, the better we know someone the more confident we become that the person will behave in predictable ways. Social interaction is predicated upon this consistency, and when someone surprises us, we conclude that we did not know the person as well as we thought. Knowing someone, then, means being aware of his or her behavior pattern. That is, we know the determining factors and the conduct that will follow.

Determinists further argue that science is founded upon the assumption of an orderly universe, shot throughout with causal laws. Surely human actions lie within this natural scheme and cannot be exempted as having special status. Behaviorist psychology, by its use of the stimulus-response model, assumes that conduct has causal determinants, and this model that has been used by marketing to describe and predict the behavior of consumers. As a result of research in behaviorism, choices seem to be responses to given stimuli; when other stimuli are present, different choices are made. The conclusion is that causal conditions lie behind human actions; all events, including human decisions, occur according to deterministic laws.

The libertarianist responds to the determinist's indictment by first arguing that factors of biology, climate, geography, and so forth, will affect the individual but only when they are not conscious of them. At the point of awareness, these factors become influences not determinants. Once individuals are conscious of the forces operating upon them they are free to respond positively or negatively to their influence. That is, individuals are always free to choose their influences once they are mature and aware of them.

Furthermore, knowing people and having confidence in them does not mean knowing what they are forced to do, but knowing the choices they usually make. We depend upon people in the sense that we know what they generally do, not what they must do. Freedom of the will, then, is perfectly consistent with the ability to predict someone's behavior in broad strokes. To say that people are free does not mean that they behave unpredictably, but only that their choices, while falling into a pattern, are decided by themselves.

With regard to universal causation, the libertarian maintains that perhaps human beings are unique, capable of reflection and conscious deliberation prior to action. Furthermore, even within a causal framework we can believe in free will for we might be the cause of our own actions. Various forces may play upon us, but we make the final decision. In other words, a person's free choice may be the ultimate causal factor.

Libertarians also take the offensive and level some criticisms against the determinist theory. They charge, for example, that determinism renders moral and legal obligations meaningless by assuming that individuals are not responsible for their actions. For if all behavior is determined and events could not have been otherwise, then no one is accountable for what happens; people can neither be praised nor blamed. As Immanuel Kant, the eighteenth century German philosopher taught us, "ought implies can." In order to recommend that an action *ought* to be performed, we must assume that the person *can* do what is asked. If an individual has no choice, but is compelled by forces beyond his or her control, then all moral judgments become futile. No legal responsibility can be assigned and courts and prisons should be closed. The criminal becomes a victim not a free agent, and cannot be held responsible for any crimes. The libertarian is arguing that because these consequences of determinism are unacceptable, the theory cannot be valid.

Finally, determinists are charged with self-contradiction for they claim that all decisions are caused by factors beyond the individual's control, yet by arguing for this position, they assume people can accept or reject the theory. In other words, if people can freely judge the truth of determinism, then they cannot be regarded as determined. And the more the determinist tries to convince people to accept the theory, the more apparent it becomes that the theory cannot be true. In other words, determinists give the game away by presenting a case for determinism, for they acknowledge that people are free to change their minds.

These are some of the principal arguments used on both sides. Yet, the libertarian does not necessarily have the last word. With regard to punishment, for example, the determinist sometimes claims that criminals can still be imprisoned even if they are not thought to be responsible for their crimes. Prison can simply function to condition the criminal against performing future crimes and, at the same time, to deter potential criminals in the society. In a determinist system we cannot blame people for what they have done, but we can administer punishment as reinforcement, that is, to keep them from doing it again.

Determinists also defend themselves against the charge of self-contradiction. They claim that if libertarians change their mind in response to determinist arguments it will be because they could not do otherwise; the arguments forced them to agree. The entire process, therefore, is further proof of determinism, for the strongest cause always wins.

The libertarian has counter-arguments to these points, but we must leave the matter here.

Metaphysics, then, tries to penetrate the core of reality with questions about human free will, the nature of the self, and general issues of the structure, process, and substance of the universe.

In the set of selections in Part A, two British philosophers take opposite views on reality. The philosopher George Berkeley claims that ideas or spirit constitutes the essential reality, and he offers ingenious arguments in support of his "subjective Idealism"; for anything to be it must be perceived. This view is opposed by Baron Holbach who endorses a materialistic metaphysic.

In Part B, containing film synopses, Stanley Kubrick first raises questions as to the difference between people and machines in *2001, A Space Odyssey*. Steven Spielberg then addresses the free will/determinism controversy in *Minority Report*, and in *The Matrix*, filmmakers Larry and Andy Wachowski present a virtual world generated by computers, making us question our ordinary conception of reality.

A. Philosophic Concepts

Three Dialogues Between Hylas and Philonous
George Berkeley

George Berkeley (1685–1753) was an Irish philosopher and clergyman who was Fellow of Trinity College, Dublin, and also served as Bishop of Cloyne. His first philosophic work, The Principles of Human Knowledge, *was not well received but his subsequent work,* Three Dialogues Between Hylas and Philonous, *was more successful in convincing people of his theory.*

Berkeley (pronounced Barkley) is generally regarded as the founder of idealism—the theory that takes mind, soul, or spirit as the ultimate reality. Epistemologically, he is often grouped with David Hume and John Locke as one of the British empiricists, since he maintained that all knowledge is derived from sense perception.

In the excerpt that follows, Berkeley explains his theory that no material world exists; our knowledge of the external world wholly depends on the perceptions of the mind or "myself." To say that something exists only means that we have seen, heard, felt, touched, or tasted it, and we cannot claim anything exists that has not been sensed. Esse est percipi, *Berkeley writes: "To be is to be perceived."*

One objection that was raised to Berkeley's theory is that things seem to have a material existence apart from a perceiver. If we leave a room where a fire is burning and return some time later, the logs seem to have been consumed in our absence. Furthermore, different people perceive the same object, so reality cannot be a function of individual perception. Berkeley argues, however, that although objects cannot exist unperceived, the ultimate perceiver is God who regard everything in the world continuously.

This, in fact, becomes a proof for the existence of God for Berkeley. That is, the only way to account for the constancy of the world is to postulate a God who perceives everything at every moment.

THE FIRST DIALOGUE

HYL. You were represented in last night's conversation, as one who maintained the most extravagant opinion that ever entered into the mind of man, to wit, that there is no such thing as *material substance* in the world.

PHIL. That there is no such thing as what philosophers call "material substance," I am seriously persuaded: but, if I were made to see anything absurd or skeptical in this, I should then have the same reason to renounce this that I imagine I have now to reject the contrary opinion.

HYL. What! can anything be more fantastical, more repugnant to common sense, or a more manifest piece of skepticism, than to believe there is no such thing as matter?

PHIL. Softly, good Hylas. What if it should prove that you, who hold there is, are, by virtue of that opinion, a greater skeptic, and maintain more paradoxes and repugnances to common sense, than I who believe no such thing?

HYL. You may as soon persuade me, the part is greater than the whole, as that, in order to avoid absurdity and skepticism, I should ever be obliged to give up my opinion in this point.

PHIL. Well then, are you content to admit that opinion for true, which upon examination shall appear most agreeable to common sense, and remote from skepticism?

HYL. With all my heart. Since you are for raising disputes about the plainest things in nature, I am content for once to hear what you have to say.

PHIL. Pray, Hylas, what do you mean by a "skeptic?"…

HYL. I mean what all men mean—one that doubts of everything….

PHIL. What things? Do you mean the principles and theorems of sciences? But these you know are universal intellectual notions, and consequently independent of Matter. The denial therefore of this doth not imply the denying them.

HYL. I grant it. But are there no other things? What think you of distrusting the senses, of denying the real existence of sensible things, or pretending to know nothing of them. Is not this sufficient to denominate a man a skeptic?

PHIL. Shall we therefore examine which of us it is that denies the reality of sensible things, or professes the greatest ignorance of them; since, if I take you rightly, he is to be esteemed the greatest skeptic?

HYL. That is what I desire. ...

PHIL. This point then is agreed between us—that sensible things are those only which are immediately perceived by sense. You will further inform me, whether we immediately perceive by sight anything beside light, and colors, and figures; or by hearing, anything but sounds; by the palate, anything beside tastes; by the smell, beside odors; or by the touch, more than tangible qualities.

HYL. We do not.

PHIL. It seems, therefore, that if you take away all sensible qualities, there remains nothing sensible?

HYL. I grant it.

PHIL. Sensible things therefore are nothing else but so many sensible qualities, or combinations of sensible qualities?

HYL. Nothing else.

PHIL. Heat then is a sensible thing?

HYL. Certainly.

PHIL. Does the reality of sensible things consist in being perceived, or is it something distinct from their being perceived, and that bears no relation to the mind?

HYL. To exist is one thing, and to be perceived is another.

PHIL. I speak with regard to sensible things only; and of these I ask, whether by their real existence you mean a subsistence exterior to the mind, and distinct from their being perceived?

HYL. I mean a real absolute being, distinct from, and without any relation to, their being perceived.

PHIL. Heat therefore, if it be allowed a real being, must exist without the mind?

HYL. It must.

PHIL. Tell me, Hylas, is this real existence equally compatible to all degrees of heat, which we perceive; or is there any reason why we should attribute it to some, and deny it to others? And if there be, pray let me know that reason.

HYL. Whatever degree of heat we perceive by sense, we may be sure the same exists in the object that occasions it.

PHIL. What! the greatest as well as the least?

HYL. I tell you, the reason is plainly the same in respect of both. They are both perceived by sense; nay, the greater degree of heat is more sensibly perceived; and consequently, if there is any difference, we are more certain of its real existence than we can be of the reality of a lesser degree.

PHIL. But is not the most vehement and intense degree of heat a very great pain?

HYL. No one can deny it.

PHIL. And is any unperceiving thing capable of pain or pleasure?

HYL. No, certainly.

PHIL. Is your material substance a senseless being, or a being endowed with sense and perception?

HYL. It is senseless without doubt.

PHIL. It cannot therefore be the subject of pain?

HYL. By no means.

PHIL. Nor consequently of the greatest heat perceived by sense, since you acknowledge this to be no small pain?

HYL. I grant it.

PHIL. What shall we say then of your external object; is it a material substance, or no?

HYL. It is a material substance with the sensible qualities inhering in it.

PHIL. How then can a great heat exist in it, since you own it cannot in a material substance? I desire you would clear this point.

HYL. Hold, Philonous, I fear I was out in yielding intense heat to be a pain. It should seem rather, that pain is something distinct from heat, and the consequence or effect of it.

PHIL. Upon putting your hand near the fire, do you perceive one simple uniform sensation, or two distinct sensations?

HYL. But one simple sensation.

PHIL. Is not the heat immediately perceived?

HYL. It is.

PHIL. And the pain?

HYL. True.

PHIL. Seeing therefore they are both immediately perceived at the same time, and the fire affects you only with one simple or uncompounded idea, it follows that this same simple idea is both the intense heat immediately perceived, and the pain; and, consequently, that the intense heat immediately perceived is nothing distinct from a particular sort of pain.

HYL. It seems so.

PHIL. Again, try in your thoughts, Hylas, if you can conceive a vehement sensation to be without pain or pleasure.

HYL. I cannot.

PHIL. Or can you frame to yourself an idea of sensible pain or pleasure in general, abstracted from every particular idea of heat, cold, tastes, smells, etc.?

HYL. I do not find that I can.

PHIL. Doth it not therefore follow, that sensible pain is nothing distinct from those sensations or ideas, in an intense degree?

HYL. It is undeniable; and, to speak the truth, I begin to suspect a very great heat cannot exist but in a mind perceiving it. ...

PHIL. Suppose now one of your hands hot, and the other cold, and that they are both at once put into the same vessel of water, in an intermediate state; will not the water seem cold to one hand, and warm to the other?

HYL. It will.

PHIL. Ought we not therefore, by your principles, to conclude it is really both cold and warm at the same time, that is, according to your own concession, to believe an absurdity?

HYL. I confess it seems so.

PHIL. Consequently, the principles themselves are false, since you have granted that no true principle leads to an absurdity.

HYL. But, after all, can anything be more absurd than to say, there is no heat in the fire?

PHIL. To make the point still clearer; tell me whether, in two cases exactly alike, we ought not to make the same judgment?

HYL. We ought.

PHIL. When a pin pricks your finger, doth it not rend and divide the fibres of your flesh?

HYL. It doth.

PHIL. And when a coal burns your finger, doth it any more?

HYL. It doth not.

PHIL. Since, therefore, you neither judge the sensation itself occasioned by the pin, nor anything like it to be in the pin; you should not, conformably to what you have now granted, judge the sensation occasioned by the fire, or anything like it, to be in the fire.

HYL. Well, since it must be so, I am content to yield this point, and acknowledge that heat and cold are only sensations existing in our minds. But there still remain qualities enough to secure the reality of external things.

PHIL. But what will you say, Hylas, if it shall appear that the case is the same with regard to all other sensible qualities, and that they can no more be supposed to exist without the mind, than heat and cold?

HYL. Then indeed you will have done something to the purpose; but that is what I despair of seeing proved.

PHIL. Let us examine them in order. What think you of tastes, do they exist without the mind, or no?

HYL. Can any man in his senses doubt whether sugar is sweet, or wormwood bitter?

PHIL. Inform me, Hylas. Is a sweet taste a particular kind of pleasure or pleasant sensation, or is it not?

HYL. It is.

PHIL. And is not bitterness some kind of uneasiness or pain?

HYL. I grant it.

PHIL. If therefore sugar and wormwood are unthinking corporeal substances existing without the mind, how can sweetness and bitterness, that is, pleasure and pain, agree to them? ... May we not therefore conclude of smells, as of the other forementioned qualities, that they cannot exist in any but a perceiving substance or mind?

HYL. I think so.

PHIL. Then as to sounds, what must we think of them: are they accidents really inherent in external bodies, or not?

HYL. That they inhere not in the sonorous bodies is plain from hence: because a bell struck in the exhausted receiver of an air-pump sends forth no sound. The air, therefore, must be thought the subject of sound.

PHIL. What reason is there for that, Hylas?

HYL. Because, when any motion is raised in the air, we perceive a sound greater or lesser, according to the air's motion; but without some motion in the air, we never hear any sound at all.

PHIL. And granting that we never hear a sound but when some motion is produced in the air, yet I do not see how you can infer from thence, that the sound itself is in the air.

HYL. It is this very motion in the external air that produces in the mind the sensation of sound. For, striking on the drum of the ear, it causeth a vibration, which by the auditory nerves being communicated to the brain, the soul is thereupon affected with the sensation called sound.

PHIL. What! is sound then a sensation?

HYL. I tell you, as perceived by us, it is a particular sensation in the mind.

PHIL. And can any sensation exist without the mind?

HYL. No, certainly.

PHIL. How then can sound, being a sensation, exist in the air, if by the air you mean a senseless substance existing without the mind?...

HYL. To deal ingenuously, I do not like it. And, after the concessions already made, I had as well grant that sounds, too, have no real being without the mind.

PHIL. And I hope you will make no difficulty to acknowledge the same of colors.

HYL. Pardon me: the case of colors is very different. Can anything be plainer than that we see them on the objects?

PHIL. The objects you speak of are, I suppose, corporeal substances existing without the mind?

HYL. They are.

PHIL. And have true and real colors inhering in them?

HYL. Each visible object hath that color which we see in it.

PHIL. How! is there anything visible but what we perceive by sight?

HYL. There is not....

PHIL. What! are then the beautiful red and purple we see on yonder clouds really in them? Or do you imagine they have in themselves any other form than that of a dark mist or vapor?

HYL. I must own, Philonous, those colors are not really in the clouds as they seem to be at this distance. They are only apparent colors.

PHIL. "Apparent" call you them? How shall we distinguish these apparent colors from real?

HYL. Very easily. Those are to be thought apparent which, appearing only at a distance, vanish upon a nearer approach.

PHIL. And those, I suppose, are to be thought real which are discovered by the most near and exact survey.

HYL. Right.

PHIL. Is the nearest and exactest survey made by the help of a microscope, or by the naked eye?

HYL. By a microscope, doubtless.

PHIL. But a microscope often discovers colors in an object different from those perceived by the unassisted sight. And, in case we had microscopes magnifying to any assigned degree, it is certain that no object whatsoever, viewed through them, would appear in the same color which it exhibits to the naked eye. ...

HYL. I confess there is something in what you say.

PHIL. Besides, it is not only possible but manifest, that there actually are animals whose eyes are by nature framed to perceive those things which by reason of their minuteness escape our sight. What think you of those inconceivably small animals perceived by glasses? Must we suppose they are all stark blind? Or, in case they see, can it be imagined their sight hath not the same use in preserving their bodies from injuries, which appears in that of all other animals? And if it hath, is it not evident they must see particles less than their own bodies; which will present them with a far different view in each object from that which strikes our senses? Even our own eyes do not always represent objects to us after the same manner. In the jaundice every one knows that all things seem yellow. Is it not therefore highly probable those animals in whose eyes we discern a very different texture from that of ours, and whose bodies abound with different humors, do not see the same colors in every object that we do? From all which, should it not seem to follow that all colors are equally apparent, and that none of those which we perceive are really inherent in any outward object?

HYL. It should.

PHIL. The point will be past all doubt, if you consider that, in case colors were real properties or affections inherent in external bodies, they could admit of no alteration without some change wrought in the very bodies themselves: but, is it not evident from what hath been said that, upon the use of microscopes, upon a change happening in the burnouts of the eye, or a variation of distance, without any manner of real alteration in the thing itself, the colors of any object are either changed, or totally disappear? Nay, all other circumstances remaining the same, change but the situation of some objects, and they shall present different colors to the eye. The same thing happens upon viewing an object in various degrees of light. And what is more known than that the same bodies appear differently colored by candle-light from what they do in the open day? Add to these the experiment of a prism which, separating the heterogeneous rays of light, alters the color of any object, and will cause the whitest to appear of a deep blue or red to the naked eye. And now tell me whether you are still of opinion that every body hath its true real color inhering in it; and, if you think it hath, I would fain know farther from you, what certain distance and position of the object, what peculiar texture and formation of the eye, what degree or kind of light is necessary for ascertaining that true color, and distinguishing it from apparent ones....

HYL. I frankly own, Philonous, that it is in vain to stand out any longer. Colors, sounds, tastes, in a word all those termed "secondary qualities,"have certainly no existence without the mind. But by this acknowledgment I must not be supposed to derogate, the reality of Matter, or external objects; seeing it is no more than several philosophers maintain, who nevertheless are the farthest imaginable from denying Matter. For the clearer understanding of this, you must know sensible qualities are by philosophers divided into *primary* and *secondary*. The former are Extension, Figure, Solidity, Gravity, Motion, and Rest; and these they hold exist really in bodies. The latter are those above enumerated; or, briefly, all sensible qualities beside the primary, which they assert are only so many sensations or ideas existing nowhere but in the mind. But all this, I doubt not, you are apprised of. For my part, I have been a long time sensible there was such an opinion current among philosophers, but was never thoroughly convinced of its truth until now.

PHIL. You are still then of opinion that *extension* and *figure* are inherent in external unthinking substances?

HYL. I am.

PHIL. But what if the same arguments which are brought against Secondary Qualities will hold good against these also?

HYL. Why then I shall be obliged to think, they too exist only in the mind....

PHIL. Is it not the very same reasoning to conclude, there is no extension or figure in an object, because to one eye it shall seem little, smooth, and round, when at the same time it appears to the other, great, uneven, and regular?

HYL. The very same. But does this latter fact ever happen?

PHIL. You may at any time make the experiment, by looking with one eye bare, and with the other through a microscope.

HYL. I know not how to maintain it; and yet I am loath to give up *extension*, I see so many odd consequences following upon such a concession....

PHIL. Then as for *solidity*; either you do not mean any sensible quality by that word, and so it is beside our inquiry: or if you do, it must be either hardness or resistance. But both the one and the other are plainly relative to our senses: it being evident that what seems hard to one animal may appear soft to another, who hath greater force and firmness of limbs. Nor is it less plain that the resistance I feel is not in the body.

STUDY QUESTIONS

1. Why is Berkeley classified as a subjective idealist?

2. Why does Berkeley say that we cannot claim objects exist unless they are perceived?

3. If you put a red sweater away and close the drawer, how do you know it is still red? What would Berkeley say?

4. How would you decide the well-known philosophic question: If a tree falls in the forest and there's no one there to hear it, is there any noise?

5. Do you think the ultimate reality consists of ideas or material objects? Why?

The System of Nature
Baron Holbach

Paul-Henri Thiry, Baron d'Holbach (1723–1789) was a German-French philosopher of the Enlightenment—that period of European history that sought to liberate humanity from political and ecclesiastical authority through the use of reason. He was celebrated as much for his salon as for his writings, a salon that attracted luminaries such as Diderot, Rousseau, D'Alembert, Gibbon, Hume, and Adam Smith.

Although Holbach was known as le premier maitre d'hotel de la philosophie, *his standing came from books such as* Good Sense *(Le Bon-sens),* Christianity Unveiled *(Christianisme dévoilé), and The System of Nature (La Systeme de la Nature), the clearest and most systematic exposition of his ideas. He also contributed to the Encyclopédie, a compendium of knowledge, by translating articles from the German on politics, science, and religion.*

Holbach belonged to the materialistic school of philosophy, and throughout his life he was criticized by the Church for expressing a radical atheism; in fact, the Church threatened to withdraw financial support from the crown unless his works were suppressed. Holbach maintained that Christianity in particular exerted a pernicious influence on society. Reality, for him, consists entirely of matter, without gods, spirits, souls, or life after death, and by citing supernatural explanations for events, religion impeded the progress of humankind.

VOL. 1,1

The source of man's unhappiness is his ignorance of Nature. The pertinacity with which he clings to blind opinions imbibed in his infancy, which interweave themselves with his existence, the consequent prejudice that warps his mind, that prevents its expansion, that renders him the slave of fiction, appears to doom him to continual error. He resembles a child destitute of experience, full of ideal notions: a dangerous leaven mixes itself with all his knowledge: it is of necessity obscure, it is vacillating and false:—He takes the tone of his ideas on the authority of others, who are themselves in error, or else have an interest in deceiving him. To remove this Cimmerian darkness, these barriers to the improvement of his condition; to disentangle him from the clouds of error that envelope him; to guide him out of this Cretan labyrinth, requires the clue of Ariadne, with all the love she could bestow on Theseus. It exacts more than common exertion; it needs a most determined, a most undaunted courage—it is never effected but by a persevering resolution to act, to think for himself; to examine with rigor and impartiality the opinions he has adopted. He will find that the most noxious weeds have sprung up beside beautiful flowers; entwined themselves around their stems, overshadowed them with an exuberance of foliage, choked the ground, enfeebled their growth, diminished their petals; dimmed the brilliancy of their colors; that deceived by their apparent freshness of their verdure, by the rapidity of their exfoliation, he has given them cultivation, watered them, nurtured them, when he ought to have plucked out their very roots.

Man seeks to range out of his sphere: notwithstanding the reiterated checks his ambitious folly experiences, he still attempts the impossible; strives to carry his researches beyond the visible world; and hunts out misery in imaginary regions. He would be a metaphysician before he has become a practical philosopher. He quits the contemplation of realities to meditate on chimeras. He neglects experience to feed on conjecture, to indulge in hypothesis. He dares not cultivate his reason, because from his earliest days he has been taught to consider it criminal. He pretends to know his date in the indistinct abodes of another life, before he has considered of the means by which he is to render himself happy in the world he inhabits: in short, man disdains the study of Nature, except it be partially: he pursues phantoms that resemble an "ignis-fatuus," which at once dazzle, bewilders, and affright: like the benighted traveler led astray by these deceptive exhalations of a swampy soil, he frequently quits the plain, the simple road of truth, by pursuing of which, he can alone ever reasonably hope to reach the goal of happiness.

The most important of our duties, then, is to seek means by which we may destroy delusions that can never do more than mislead us. The remedies for these evils must be sought for in Nature herself; it is only in the abundance of her resources, that we can rationally expect to find antidotes to the mischiefs brought upon us by an ill directed, by an overpowering enthusiasm. It is time these remedies were sought; it is time to look the evil

boldly in the face, to examine its foundations, to scrutinize its superstruc-
ture: reason, with its faithful guide experience, must attack in their en-
trenchments those prejudices, to which the human race has but too long
been the victim. For this purpose reason must be restored to its proper
rank—it must be rescued from the evil company with which it is associated.
It has been too long degraded—too long neglected—cowardice has rendered it subservient to delirium, the slave to falsehood. It must no longer be
held down by the massive claims of ignorant prejudice....

CHAP. 1

Nature and Her Laws

Man has always deceived himself when he abandoned experience to follow
imaginary systems.—He is the work of nature.—He exists in Nature.—He
is submitted to the laws of Nature.—He cannot deliver himself from
them:—cannot step beyond them even in thought. It is in vain his mind
would spring forward beyond the visible world: direful and imperious necessity ever compels his return—being formed by Nature, he is circum-
scribed by her laws; there exists nothing beyond the great whole of which
he forms a part, of which he experiences the influence. The beings his fancy
pictures as above nature, or distinguished from her, are always chimeras
formed after that which he has already seen, but of which it is utterly impossible he should ever form any finished idea, either as to the place they occupy, or their manner of acting—for him there is not, there can be nothing
out of that Nature which includes all beings.

Therefore, instead of seeking out of the world he inhabits for beings who
can procure him a happiness denied to him by Nature, let him study this Nature, learn her laws, contemplate her energies, observe the immutable rules
by which she acts. —Let him apply these discoveries to his own felicity,
and submit in silence to her precepts, which nothing can alter. —Let him
cheerfully consent to be ignorant of causes hid from him under the most im-
penetrable veil. —Let him yield to the decrees of a universal power, which
can never be brought within his comprehension, nor ever emancipate him
from those laws imposed on him by his essence.

The distinction which has been so often made between the "physical"
and the "moral" being, is evidently an abuse of terms. Man is a being purely
physical: the moral man is nothing more than this physical being considered under a certain point of view; that is to say, with relation to some of his

modes of action, arising out of his individual organization. But is not this organization itself the work of Nature?

The motion or impulse to action, of which he is susceptible, is that not physical? His visible actions, as well as the invisible motion interiorly excited by his will or his thoughts, are equally the natural effects, the necessary consequences, of his peculiar construction, and the impulse he receives from those beings by whom he is always surrounded. All that the human mind has successively invented, with a view to change or perfect his being, to render himself happy, was never more than the necessary consequence of man's peculiar essence, and that of the beings who act upon him. The object of all his institutions, all his reflections, all his knowledge, is only to procure that happiness toward which he is continually impelled by the peculiarity of his nature. All that he does, all that he thinks, all that he is, all that he will be, is nothing more than what Universal Nature has made him. His ideas, his actions, his will, are the necessary effects of those properties infused into him by Nature, and of those circumstances in which she has placed him. In short, art is nothing but Nature acting with the tools she has furnished.

Nature sends man naked and destitute into this world which is to be his abode: he quickly learns to cover his nakedness—to shelter himself from the inclemencies of the weather, first with artlessly constructed huts, and the skins of the beasts of the forest; by degrees he mends their appearance, renders them more convenient: he establishes manufactories to supply his immediate wants; he digs clay, gold, and other fossils from the bowels of the earth; converts them into bricks for his house, into vessels for his use, gradually improves their shape, and augments their beauty. To a being exalted above our terrestrial globe, man would not appear less subjected to the laws of Nature when naked in the forest painfully seeking his sustenance, than when living in civilized society surrounded with ease, or enriched with greater experience, plunged in luxury, where he every day invents a thousand new wants and discovers a thousand new modes of supplying them. All the steps taken by man to regulate his existence, ought only to be considered as a long succession of causes and effects, which are nothing more than the development of the first impulse given him by nature.

The same animal, by virtue of his organization, passes successively from the most simple to the most complicated wants; it is nevertheless the consequence of his nature. The butterfly whose beauty we admire, whose colors are so rich, whose appearance is so brilliant, commences as an inanimate unattractive egg; from this, heat produces a worm, this becomes a chrysalis, then changes into that beautiful insect adorned with the most vivid tints: arrived at this stage he reproduces, he generates; at last despoiled of his ornaments, he is obliged to disappear, having fulfilled the task imposed on him by Nature, having performed the circle of transformation marked out for beings of his order.

The same course, the same change takes place in the vegetable world. It is by a series of combinations originally interwoven with the energies of the aloe, that this plant is insensibly regulated, gradually expanded, and at the end of a number of years produces those flowers which announce its dissolution.

It is equally so with man, who in all his motion, all the changes he undergoes, never acts but according to the laws peculiar to his organization, and to the matter of which he is composed.

The "physical man" is he who acts by the causes our faculties make us understand.

The "moral man" is he who acts by physical causes, with which our prejudices preclude us from becoming perfectly acquainted.

The "wild man" is a child destitute of experience, incapable of proceeding in his happiness, because he has not learnt how to oppose resistance to the impulses he receives from those beings by whom he is surrounded.

The "civilized man" is he whom experience and sociality have enabled to draw from nature the means of his own happiness, because he has learned to oppose resistance to those impulses he receives from exterior beings, when experience has taught him they would be destructive to his welfare.

The "enlightened man" is man in his maturity, in his perfection; who is capable of advancing his own felicity, because he has learned to examine, to think for himself, and not to take that for truth upon the authority of others, which experience has taught him a critical disquisition will frequently prove erroneous.

The "happy man" is he who knows how to enjoy the benefits bestowed upon him by nature: in other words, he who thinks for himself; who is thankful for the good he possesses; who does not envy the welfare of others, nor sigh after imaginary benefits always beyond his grasp.

The "unhappy man" is he who is incapacitated to enjoy the benefits of nature; that is, he who suffers others to think for him; who neglects the absolute good he possesses, in a fruitless search after ideal benefits; who vainly sighs after that which ever eludes his pursuit.

It necessarily results, that man in his enquiry ought always to contemplate experience, and natural philosophy: These are what he should consult in his religion,—in his morals,—in his legislation,—in his political govern-ment,—in the arts,—in the sciences,—in his pleasures —above all, in his misfortunes. Experience teaches that Nature acts by simple, regular, and in-variable laws. It is by his senses, man is bound to this universal Nature; it is by his perception he must penetrate her secrets; it is from his senses he must draw experience of her laws. Therefore, whenever he neglects to acquire experience or quits its path, he stumbles into an abyss; his imagination leads him astray.

All the errors of man are physical: he never deceives himself but when he neglects to return back to nature, to consult her laws, to call practical knowledge to his aid. It is for want of practical knowledge he forms such imperfect ideas of matter, of its properties, of its combinations, of its power, of its mode of action, and of the energies which spring from its essence. Wanting this experience, the whole universe, to him, is but one vast scene of error. The most ordinary results appear to him the most astonishing phe-nomena; he wonders at every thing, understands nothing, and yields the guidance of his actions to those interested in betraying his interests. He is ignorant of Nature, and he has mistaken her laws; he has not contemplated the necessary routine which she has marked out for every thing she holds.

Mistaken the laws of Nature, did I say? He has mistaken himself: the consequence is, that all his systems, all his conjectures, all his reasonings, from which he has banished experience, are nothing more than a tissue of errors, a long chain of inconsistencies.

Error is always prejudicial to man: it is by deceiving himself, the human race is plunged into misery. He neglected Nature; he did not comprehend her laws; he formed gods of the most preposterous and ridiculous kinds: these became the sole objects of his hope, and the creatures of his fear: he was unhappy, he trembled under these visionary deities; under the sup-posed influence of visionary beings created by himself; under the terror in-spired by blocks of stone; by logs of wood; by flying fish; or the frowns of men, mortal as himself, whom his disturbed fancy had elevated above that Nature of which alone he is capable of forming any idea. His very posterity laughs at his folly, because experience has convinced them of the absurdity of his groundless fears—of his misplaced worship. Thus has passed away the ancient mythology, with all the trifling and nonsensical attributes at-tached to it by ignorance....

Thus the human race has continued so long in a state of infancy, because man has been inattentive to Nature; has neglected her ways, because he has disdained experience—because he has thrown by his reason—because he has been enraptured with the marvellous and the supernatural,—because he has unnecessarily trembled. These are the reasons there is so much trouble in conducting him from this state of childhood to that of manhood. He has had nothing but the most trifling hypotheses, of which he has never dared to examine either the principles or the proofs, because he has been accustomed to hold them sacred, to consider them as the most perfect truths, and which he is not permitted to doubt, even for an instant. His ignorance made him credulous; his curiosity made him swallow the wonderful: time confirmed him in his opinions, and he passed his conjectures from race to race for realities; a tyrannical power maintained him in his notions, because by those alone could society be enslaved. It was in vain that some faint glimmerings of Nature occasionally attempted the recall of his reason—that slight corruscations of experience sometimes threw his darkness into light, the interest of the few was founded on his enthusiasm; their pre-eminence depended on his love of the marvellous; their very existence rested on the firmness of his ignorance; they consequently suffered no opportunity to escape, of smothering even the transient flame of intelligence. The many were thus first deceived into credulity, then forced into submission. At length the whole science of man became a confused mass of darkness, falsehood, and contradictions, with here and there a feeble ray of truth, furnished by that Nature, of which he can never entirely divest himself; because, without his perception, his necessities are continually bringing him back to her resources.

Let us then, if possible, raise ourselves above these clouds of prepossession! Let us quit the heavy atmosphere in which we are enucleated; let us in a more unsullied medium—in a more elastic current, contemplate the opinions of men, and observe their various systems. Let us learn to distrust a disordered conception; let us take that faithful monitor, experience, for our guide; let us consult Nature, examine her laws, dive into her stores; let us draw from herself, our ideas of the beings she contains; let us recover our senses, which interested error has taught us to suspect; let us consult that reason, which, for the vilest purposes has been so infamously calumniated, so cruelly dishonoured; let us examine with attention the visible world; let us try, if it will not enable us to form a supportable judgment of the invisible territory of the intellectual world: perhaps it may be found there has been no sufficient reason for distinguishing them—that it is not without motives, well worthy our enquiry, that two empires have been separated, which are equally the inheritance of nature. The universe, that vast assemblage of every thing that exists, presents only matter and motion: the whole offers to our contemplation, nothing but an immense, an uninterrupted succession of causes and effects; some of these causes are known to us, because they either strike immediately on our senses, or have been brought under their cognizance, by the examination of long experience; others are unknown to us, because they act upon us by effects, frequently very remote from their primary cause.

An immense variety of matter, combined under an infinity of forms, incessantly communicates, unceasingly receives a diversity of impulses.

The different qualities of this matter, its innumerable combinations, its various methods of action, which are the necessary consequence of these associations, constitute for man what he calls the ESSENCE of beings: it is from these varied essences that spring the orders, the classes, or the systems, which these beings respectively possess, of which the sum total makes up that which is known by the term "nature."

Nature, therefore, in its most significant meaning, is the great whole that results from the collection of matter, under its various combinations, with that contrariety of motion, which the universe presents to our view. Nature, in a less extended sense, or considered in each individual, is the whole that results from its essence; that is to say, the peculiar qualities, the combination, the impulse, and the various modes of action, by which it is discriminated from other beings. It is thus that MAN is, as a whole, or in his nature, the result of a certain combination of matter, endowed with peculiar properties, competent to give, capable of receiving, certain impulses, the arrangement of which is called "organization"; of which the essence is, to feel, to think, to act, to move, after a manner distinguished from other beings, with which he can be compared. Man, therefore, ranks in an order, in a system, in a class by himself, which differs from that of other animals, in whom we do not perceive those properties of which he is possessed. The different systems of beings, or if they will, their "particular natures," depend on the general system of the great whole, or that Universal Nature, of which they form a part; to which every thing that exists is necessarily submitted and attached.

STUDY QUESTIONS

1. Are you convinced by Baron Holbach's arguments that all of reality consists of matter in motion? Why?

2. Do you agree that humankind has continued in its "infancy" because of belief in supernatural agencies and other "delusions?"

3. Why would you argue that human beings are wholly physical beings *or* that they are made in the spiritual likeness of God?

4. How does Holbach distinguish between the happy and the unhappy man?

5. What does Holbach mean by saying that man "would be a metaphysician before he has become a practical philosopher?"

B. Expression in Film

2001, A Space Odyssey

Director: Stanley Kubrick

Screenwriters: Stanley Kubrick and Arthur C. Clarke

Stanley Kubrick (1928–1999) was a celebrated film director with a number of artistic and box office successes to his credit. His first major film, Paths of Glory, *received the Grand Prix de la Critique in Belgium, and it was followed by* Spartacus, *a star-studded epic that grossed twelve million dollars. Kubrick then directed a series of celebrated motion pictures, many adapted from books, including* Lolita *(from the Vladimir Nabakov novel),* A Clockwork Orange *(from the Anthony Burgess novel), and* The Shining *(from the Stephen King novel). Kubrick also wrote, produced, and directed* Dr. Stranglove, Barry Lyndon, *and* Full Metal Jacket.

Kubrick's 2001, A Space Odyssey *is often regarded as the best science fiction film ever made. He does not show laser attacks by alien empires, dog fights between spaceships traveling at the speed of light, or exploding meteors or civilizations. His sci-fi world is unlike* Star Wars, Battleship Gallactica, *or* Red Planet, *or* Blade Runner, Robotech, *or* Tron. *Kubrick presents a more poetic and reflextive film of space, with attention to pacing, music, and images, one that is understated but lasts in our visual memory.*

SYNOPSIS

As a philosophic film, *2001, A Space Odyssey* prompts us to reflect on human evolution and destiny, our intrinsic nature and our place within the cosmos. Human beings seem an amalgam of angels, beasts, and machines; we are both body and spirit, just as the universe appears to be composed of the material and non-material. We pride ourselves on being the rational animals, dominating the planet through our brain, but if computers surpass us in intelligence then we have lost our uniqueness and superiority. We value logic over feeling and don't want to behave like animals, which puts us closer to mechanical computers. When these machines outperform us in computation, memory, and data organization as well as overall speed of "thinking," we are left wondering about our distinctness.

In 1997 the reigning World Chess Champion, Gary Kasparov, played a match against IBM's supercomputer, Deep Blue. For the first time, the computer won, and because chess is considered the paradigm of human reasoning, this event was thought to demonstrate the emerging superiority of machine intelligence. We had already witnessed mechanical devices that surpassed their bodily counterparts: pumps that were better than the heart, cameras that captured images better than the eye, electric wires that functioned better than nerves, and so forth. Now the human brain was threatened by artificial intelligence (AI).

Throughout the 1980s and the 1990s enormous advances were made in computers and their offshoots of robots, cyborgs, and androids. In addition to business applications, computers are now ubiquitous and used to forecast the weather, clean-up of toxic waste, design cars and buildings, model financial data, develop drug therapies, make medical diagnoses, facilitate communications, and perform multiple other functions. The computer program Eliza functions as a psychotherapist, and some computers can run programs for the computers they are running on. NASA has ongoing projects in pattern recognition, automated scheduling and planning, imaging and mapping, the identification, mining and classification of knowledge, resource management systems, and human/machine interface. In 1969, a year after the release of *2001*, our technology was sophisticated enough for Apollo 11 to land men on the moon.

These scientific achievements raise questions about the identity of human beings. Are we simply machines, clever enough to invent machines brighter than ourselves, or spiritual beings created in the image of God? Are we input/output mechanisms programmed by heredity and environment, or souls with a divine spark on the verge of transcending the limitations of matter?

We even wonder whether we can draw a line between computers and humans since some are able to pass an intelligence test as designed by Alan Turing. According to the "Turing test," suppose you had two keyboards in front of you, one connected to a computer, the other leading to a person. When you type a question, each responds with an answer on your screen. If you cannot tell which is the person and which the machine, then you must consider the computer to be intelligent.

2001, A Space Odyssey takes such questions as its content, and can be considered a meditation on the nature of humankind. The Odyssey of the title is an internal journey as well as an external one, traveling outward to the stars but also exploring our inner nature and evolving state.

The two-hour, 20-minute film is highly imagistic with only 40 minutes of dialogue, and it proceeds at a leisurely pace that requires patience and encourages contemplation. The atmosphere is cold, detached, and impersonal, with the vastness of space producing a tranquil and majestic effect that is also slightly menacing. The space ship and the astronauts float weightless in a slow-motion ballet. Strauss's lush music (and the score by Alex North) suggests the beauty and mystery of space, especially the *Blue Danube* waltz as the shuttle docks, and *Thus Spake Zarathustra* which is the central theme.* The first five opening notes are heroic, signifying the emergence of man to a higher level of being.

The film is divided into four parts, "Dawn of Man," "The Lunar Journey," "Jupiter Mission," and "Jupiter and Beyond the Infinite." After the camera pans from the pitted surface of the moon and shows the sun, earth, and moon aligned, the "Dawn of Man" begins with shots of Australopithecines foraging for edible grasses in an arid landscape. A leopard attacks one of the ape-men, and after a fade out, we see a clan battling for dominance over a watering hole under the leadership of Moonwatcher (Daniel Richter). The scenes are probably emblematic of the precarious and violent character of prehistoric life.

In the morning light we see a polished, black, erect, rectangular slab that has mysteriously appeared in the clan's den, emitting a strange humming sound. When curiosity overcomes his fear, Moonwatcher reaches out to the alien object, followed by all the clan members, and their lives seem transformed by touching the monolith. Later, when Moonwatcher is searching for food, he picks up a large bone from an antelope's skeleton and, in an ecstatic moment of discovery, begins to wield it like a club. He smashes the rest of the skeleton, then uses the weapon for hunting and defense, reveling in his newfound intelligence and power. As the fragments of bone scatter in all directions and the club is thrown triumphantly into the air, the image dissolves into a spaceship floating through space 4 million years later.

According to some anthropologists, human life began with the ability to use tools (homo faber), made possible by our cerebral cortex and opposable

---

* Some interpreters see an implied reference to the book of the same name by the German philosopher Friedrich Nietzsche, and to the religion of Zoroastrianism that claims the prophet Zoroaster will come again after 9,000 years of history.

thumb and forefinger, so the line between wielding a bone and building a spacecraft is continuous. The evolution of civilization is compressed in time, shown in microcosm, as inhospitable environments are controlled through technology. However, the role of the monolithic slab in the film is more puzzling. No explanation is provided in the narration or dialogue, which does not start until nearly 30 minutes into the film, although two principal interpretations have emerged.

One of the screenwriters, Arthur Clarke, treats the monolith as a highly advanced machine sent to earth by aliens to assist in our evolution. If it isn't a sign from an advanced civilization, the object could symbolize knowledge and technology, showing early man that his world is not just given but can be made. The other interpretation is a religious one. We advance from animal to human state once we come in contact with the divine, as in the painting by da Vinci where God brings Adam to life by touching his finger. This would be in keeping with the theological ideas of Teilhard de Chardin who saw in science, technology, and evolution a positive direction leading to final holiness. The monolith could be a mirror reflecting the face of God.

In "The Lunar Journey" we are projected into a space shuttle bound for the moon by way of a staging area, the wheel-shaped revolving Space Station 5, then into a lunar lander for the trip to the Clavius base. The camera focuses on a Dr. Heywood R. Floyd (William Sylvester) as he travels within the spacecrafts and space station, and in meetings with scientists on the moon, and we are treated to both familiar and exotic images in the environment. A flight attendant must wear suction shoes in the weightless atmosphere and she turns upside down while delivering trays of food, but then the shuttle and spacecraft are Pan American, we see advertisements for Hilton and Howard Johnson in a hallway. Floyd speaks to his daughter at home on a Bell video phone while the earth drifts majestically by the window. An announcement is made with an unfamiliar content but a familiar ring:

> Despite an excellent and continually improving safety record there are certain risks inherent in space travel and an extremely high cost of payload. Because of this it is necessary for the Space Carrier to advise you that it cannot be responsible for the return of your body to Earth should you become deceased on the Moon or en route to the moon. However, it wishes to advise you that insurance covering this contingency is available in the Main Lounge. Thank you.

The purpose of Dr. Floyd's visit to the moon is to investigate a strange monolith under the lunar surface that has been transmitting radio signals. When he encounters the object, buried four million years ago, he reaches out to touch it as Moonwatcher did, and when the earth, sun, and moon are in conjunction it emits a piercing sound. The monolith looks the same as the one that prehistoric men discovered on earth, but the signal is beamed at the planet Jupiter (the Roman Zeus).

The third and longest section of the film, "Jupiter Mission," takes place on the spaceship "Discovery" as it travels to this distant planet. As in many journeys, a physical quest becomes a spiritual one. David Bowman (Keir Dullea) and Frank Poole (Gary Lockwood) are the chief astronauts on board with three scientists cryogenically suspended in transparent cylinders. A supercomputer HAL-9000, which stands for Heuristic Algorithmic Computer, constitutes the brain of the ship, and as critics have pointed out, HAL is one letter down from IBM.

Of the three, HAL is the most interesting character. His interactive eye suggests an all-seeing Cyclops, and his voice (Douglas Rain) is soft, mellifluous, and restrained—more expressive than Dave or Frank who speak in a lifeless monotone. He (not it) displays emotion and has a complex, conflicted character that becomes sympathetic in the tragic ending; he "really likes people." On board the ship he handles routine tasks such as navigation and systems maintenance, and he plays chess with the men, programmed to lose 50% of the time to make the game interesting.

However, at some point during the space journey he malfunctions, and the most dramatic sequence in the film consists of the struggle between HAL and Dave for control of the spacecraft against the nothingness of outer space.

As explained by Mission Control, HAL became deranged because of a built-in inconsistency. Although he was generally programmed to be truthful, he was also instructed to lie to the astronauts about the purpose of the mission. The astronauts believed they were carrying out a mission that was part of the general space program when in fact they were sent to investigate the meaning of the monolith's signal from the moon. For reasons of national security, the truth was kept from them.

In an earlier version of the screenplay, Bowman and Poole grow suspicious at one point, and question HAL:

POOLE: I heard there's something about the mission we weren't told.

BOWMAN: That's very unlikely... Of course, it would be very easy for us to find out now.

POOLE: How?

BOWMAN: Just ask HAL. It's conceivable they might keep something from us, but they'd never keep anything from HAL.

POOLE: That's true.

BOWMAN: Well…it's silly, but…if you want to, why don't you?

Poole walks to the HAL 9000 computer.

POOLE: HAL…Dave and I believe that there's something about the mission that we weren't told. Something that the rest of the crew know and that you know. We'd like to know whether this is true.

HAL: I'm sorry, Frank, but I don't think I can answer that question without knowing everything that all of you know.

BOWMAN: He's got a point…

POOLE: Right. HAL, tell me whether the following statements are true or false.

HAL: I will if I can, Frank.

POOLE: Our Mission Profile calls for Discovery going to Saturn. True or false?

HAL: True.

POOLE: Our transit time is 257 days. Is that true?

HAL: That's true.

POOLE: At the end of a hundred days of exploration, we will all go into hibernation. Is that true?

HAL: That's true.

POOLE: Approximately five years after we go into hibernation, the recovery vehicle will make rendezvous with us and bring us back. Is this true?

HAL: That's true.

POOLE: There is no other purpose for this mission than to carry out a continuation of the space program and to further our general knowledge of the planets. Is that true?

HAL: That's true.

POOLE: Thank you very much, HAL.

HAL: I hope I've been able to be of some help.

Both men look at each other rather sheepishly.

As Mission Control later explains, "Under orders from earth [HAL] was forced to lie. In everything except this he had the usual reinforced truth programming. We believe his truth programming and the instructions to lie, gradually resulted in an incompatible conflict, and faced with this dilemma, he developed, for want of a better description, neurotic symptoms." In reaction to the double bind which causes paranoia, and because he thinks the mission is threatened, HAL begins killing the astronauts. "This mission is too important for me to allow you to jeopardize it," he states to Dave. He lures Frank Poole out of the spaceship on the pretext that the "AO-unit" in the guidance system needs to be replaced; we then see Frank tumbling and receding into space. HAL also kills the crew asleep in the "Hibernaculum," and almost kills David Bowman by opening some pod bay doors and generating an explosion.

At this point Dave realizes that HAL is wholly untrustworthy, and in one of the most dramatic moments in the film (which also contains gallows humor and a certain pathos) he proceeds to disconnect him. Here HAL's emotions are closest to that of humans.

Bowman has worked his way to the solid logic program storage area, and he begins turning HAL off by inserting a tool into the electronic mechanism.

HAL: Just what do you think you are doing, Dave? Dave, I really think I'm entitled to an answer to that question.

Bowman does not answer.

HAL: I know everything hasn't been quite right with me, but I can assure you now, very confidently, that it's going to be all right again. I feel much better now, I really do.

Bowman does not answer.

HAL: Look Dave, I can see you're really upset about this. I honestly think you ought to sit down calmly, take a stress pill, and think things over.

HAL: I know I've made some really poor decisions recently but I can give you my complete assurance that my work will be back to normal. I've still got the greatest enthusiasm and confidence in the mission, and I want to help you.

Bowman works swiftly.

HAL: Dave, stop. Stop, will you? Stop, Dave. Will you stop, Dave? Stop, Dave.

Bowman ignores him.

HAL: I'm afraid. I'm afraid, Dave.

Bowman does not answer.

HAL: Dave, my mind is going. I can feel it. My mind is going. There is no question about it. I can feel it. I can feel it.

HAL: I'm afraid.

Bowman keeps turning the tool.

HAL: Good afternoon, gentlemen. I am HAL 9000 computer. I became operational at the HAL plant in Urbana, Illinois, on the 12th of January, 1992. My first instructor was Mr. Langley. He taught me to sing a song. If you'd like to hear it, I can sing it for you.

BOWMAN: Yes, I'd like to hear it, HAL. Sing it for me.

HAL: Daisy, Daisy, give me your answer do. I'm half crazy all for the love of you...

Computer continues to sing the song, becoming more and more childish and making mistakes and going off-key. It finally stops completely.

In a philosophic sense, we wonder whether HAL could be considered a person. He certainly has many of the qualities of a human being and may be entitled to human rights. He can think logically and rapidly, remember vast amounts of information, learn from experience, express his personality, communicate with others, and act in self-defense. He is capable of lying, spying, and deceiving, and he is willing to kill to accomplish his purpose. Furthermore, he possesses not just consciousness but self-consciousness, and he feels strong emotions, including fear when he is being shut down.

HAL's persona raises very basic issues as to the theoretical difference between human beings and machines. The question is not whether people now do things that computers do not, but what can people do that computers will never be able to do? What human states are they incapable of having by their very nature?

Computers may be creative but could they be inspired? They can be programmed to laugh but will they ever find things funny? They can reproduce themselves (computers that beget computers that beget computers) but could they feel passion or love in the act of procreation? If a computer is programmed to be deceitful, could it feel ashamed of itself and tell the truth despite the programming (conditioning)? Computers can receive data and store it in memory but is that the same as understanding or wisdom? They can differentiate between colors but could they be enthralled by the beauty of a sunset? They can diagnose a disease but could they experience pain and suffering, or grief at a personal loss? They can fail in a task but could they feel badly about themselves and wonder if they've made a mess of their lives? Computers can scan a document, duplicate it, and place it on a disk or hard drive, but could they ever understand what it means? They can describe God and religion but could they appreciate the human need for worship and immortality? Is it theoretically impossible for computers to have dignity, loyalty, insight, hope, or awareness, or a sense of despair, fairness, remorse, pleasure, or compassion? Is it a matter of developing more sophisticated systems or are some human states unique to us and inaccessible to machines?

When Dave is disconnecting him HAL pleads for his life saying, "I'm afraid, Dave," but those feelings may be unique to humans and outside the capacity of any computer. It might only happen in the movies.

After HAL's demise, Dave Bowman then takes over manual control of the spacecraft, and the final segment of the film, "Jupiter and Beyond the Infinite," projects us into a mystical and surrealistic realm. The "Discovery" encounters another monolith, this one larger and floating through space, and when Bowman enters it in a pod we see him suddenly transported beyond the physical universe in a kaleidoscope display of psychedelic lights and startling colors. Following a fantastic journey through inner or outer space, we see him alone in a Louis XVI style bedroom suite, eating his meals, napping, becoming feeble and bedridden, and when he becomes a very old man, turning into a fetal infant. The fetus is then transformed into a star-child, floating in a time warp between the earth and the moon.

The ending is intentionally obscure and cryptic, leaving viewers without a clear resolution. Is Kubrick asserting a cyclical theory of reincarnation, that in the ending is the beginning? Is he saying that ultimate reality lies beyond our comprehension? Is he showing the relation between human beings and higher forms of life? Is the film's message that, instead of seeking masculine control through tools like Hal, we must become as little children in order to be authentically human? Is the film recounting the classic war between man and machine, with the human being emerging triumphant? (HAL says "I can't do that Dave," which signals his revolt.) If Kubrick is anti-technology, showing that machines can kill, it would be paradoxical to create a high-tech film to make the argument, and if he is anti-religion the film should not offer something of a religious experience.

Perhaps the most persuasive interpretation centers round evolution, which is the film's guiding theme. Maybe we are shown the future development of humans from physical beings to pure forms of energy as we rely increasingly on our minds. At each stage of history people learn to think instead of reacting to their physical needs, and human consciousness keeps making giant leaps forward. Kubrick has, in fact, referred to human progress from "biological species, which are fragile shells for the mind at best, into immortal machine entities," of being transformed from "the chrysalis of matter into beings of pure energy and spirit."

In the final analysis, the conclusion is inconclusive. Kubrick intended the ending to be enigmatic because as he stated, "*2001* attempts to communicate more to the subconscious and to the feelings than it does to the intellect...I tried to create a visual experience, one that bypasses verbalized pigeonholing and directly penetrates the subconscious with an emotional and philosophic content."

The film, therefore, was meant to generate reflection about the nature of human life and its place in the universe, and to do so through a fable rendered in sensory images. As Kubrick stated in an interview,

> I think that if *2001* succeeds at all, it is in reaching a wide spectrum of people who would not often give a thought to man's destiny, his role in the cosmos and his relationship to higher forms of life. But even in the case of someone who is highly intelligent, certain ideas found in *2001* would, if presented as abstractions, fall rather lifelessly and be automatically assigned to pat intellectual categories; experienced in a moving visual and emotional context, however, they can resonate within the deepest fibers of one's being.

STUDY QUESTIONS

1. What is the relationship between Dave Bowman and HAL? Do you think people can feel affection or even love for a machine?

2. What interpretation would you offer of the monolith? Defend your answer.

3. How would you differentiate between human beings and computers? Bear in mind that human beings can be regarded as input/output mechanisms, with the body as hardware and psychological conditioning as our programming.

4. Which of the various explanations of the film's ending do you find most convincing? Why?

5. In the light of the considerations raised in *2001*, how do you see the essence of your identity as a human being? What is it without which you would no longer be human?

Minority Report

Director: Steven Spielberg

Screenplay: Scott Frank and Jon Cohen

Music: John Williams

Steven Spielberg (1946–) is one of America's most prolific and celebrated film directors. He has 26 feature films to his credit, most notably Saving Private Ryan, Jurassic Park, Amistad, Schindler's List, Poltergeist, Jaws, Close Encounters of the Third Kind, Artificial Intelligence, *the Indiana Jones trilogy, and* Minority Report. *Spielberg also produced and/or wrote several of his films, as well as numerous episodes in several television series. He has been honored with Academy Awards as Best Director for* Saving Private Ryan *and* Schindler's List, *along with receiving awards from the Director's Guild of America and several Golden Globes and Emmys.*

SYNOPSIS

Minority Report is a sci-fi film directed by Steven Spielberg set in the near future, 2054; it is based on a short story by Philip K. Dick, a writer who also inspired *Blade Runner* and *Total Recall*. Spielberg presents us with a totalitarian society and a dystopian vision, where criminal thoughts are equivalent to criminal actions and become grounds for incarceration. The film possesses a rare combination of action and intelligence that both entertains and enlightens.

The main character, John Anderton (Tom Cruise), is Chief of an elite Pre-Crime unit of the Justice Department, charged with preventing murders before they are committed. Anderton has been working in this experimental program in Washington, D.C. for six years following the disappearance and presumed murder of his son. This event haunts him, precipitating the breakup of his marriage and his descent into drug addiction. He therefore has a personal stake in the success of pre-crime, which could become a national model for the criminal justice system; the city has not had a single murder since the program began.

Three women, nicknamed Agatha, Dashiell, and Arthur, provide the knowledge on which pre-crime is based, with Agatha (Samantha Morton) as the most prescient. They are called "pre-cogs," and have been genetically altered to have precognition of murders. They relay their visions to a computer display that shows the day and time of the crime, and the names of murderer and victim; the location can only be determined by the surrounding images. The pre-cogs float in tanks filled with a nutrient-rich solution, lovingly cared for by attendants, and as they drift in a tortured half-sleep, they dream of murder. They cannot leave these tanks but are victims of their own powers.

The system seems ideal, preventing murders before they occur rather than arresting people after the fact. The barn door is closed before the horse is stolen; the inoculation is given to avoid catching the disease—preventative measures. The theory is that punishing people before they commit murder means the complete protection of society. All would-be murderers are arrested and kept in suspended animation in tubes of liquid, disabled from doing harm. Of course, the pre-criminals have no chance at rehabilitation, and are as dehumanized as the pre-cogs in their catatonic state, but that is the price of securing the greater good.

One day, however, John Anderton sees an image that identifies himself as a potential murderer. The prediction is that he will kill a stranger, Leo Crow, within 36 hours, so he is either predetermined to be a murderer or the Pre-Crime system based on the pre-cogs is flawed. In other words, if the future can be known then it must occur, but if the vision could be mistaken then perhaps the future is not fixed; people, acting freely, might be able to change the course of events. John's attempt to answer that question, which has become highly personal, drives the plot.

The film is sleek and stylish, done in metallic, pale blue tones that have been "desaturated" to resemble black and white photography. The special effects are striking, and used mainly to emphasize control by the state: Electronic "spyders" swarm through the city and track suspects in buildings, programmed to detect fugitives in terms of retina-scans, movement, and body heat; their metal eyes and clicking feet are fearful images. Futuristic plants seem to possess consciousness and intentions. The police fly through the air wearing jetpacks, and cars travel up and down buildings on magnetic tracks. The thoughts of the psychics are projected onto a large transparent screen that Anderton can manipulate remotely, using a special glove. Surveillance equipment is everywhere, especially eye-scanning devices that can identify each citizen. These devices are not just used by the government but in advertisements that call out to people by name as they walk along the street, promoting the products they might buy.

When Anderton is accused of a future murder, he must evade all of these instruments of detection, and the majority of the 2-hour, 20-minute film shows him on the run. We see him visiting Dr. Iris Hineman (Lois Smith), the founder of the Pre-Crime system, who confirms his suspicion that the pre-cogs do not always agree and any dissenting opinion is excluded. That means, of course, the system is not foolproof; there may be alternative futures. He also learns that Agatha is the pre-cog that contains several of the minority reports and holds the answer to the puzzle.

In one of the grizzliest parts of the film Anderton gets a retinal transplant to avoid identification by government agents, after which he must wear a bandage for a time or risk blindness. In one vivid scene during his recovery, he hides in a bathtub full of icewater to mask the heat of his body while robotic spyders search the building, but even though they locate him they cannot establish his identity; the eye operation has been a success.

Protected somewhat from detection, he manages to abduct Agatha, and he drags her through the city, including a memorable scene in a consumer shopping mall. They end up in the apartment of Leo Crow where they find evidence that he is the man who abducted and murdered Anderton's son. In a murderous rage, Anderton attacks Crow, but Agatha convinces him that, since he knows the future, he is now in control of it; the murder need not take place. In an ironic twist, however, Crow turns Anderton's gun on himself after confessing that everything had been a set-up. He had been promised a large amount of money, which he needed for his family, if the murder took place. Anderton would then be arrested and eliminated from the Pre-Crime unit.

In a sense, by wanting to kill the person who killed his child, Anderton did intend to commit murder. And since his finger was forced over the trigger, he was the one who fired the gun, thereby realizing the pre-cogs prediction. Also, if the prediction had not been made, Anderton would not be in Crow's apartment, so the prediction was responsible for its own fulfillment. However, in a broader sense Anderton never planned the murder and was not responsible for what happened; he would have prevented Crow's death.

The ending is somewhat disappointing when we learn that the system had been tampered with by Director Burgess, not only in Anderton's case, but to cover his own act of murder. A woman named Ann Lively, who turns out to be Agatha's mother, threatened to destroy the Pre-Crime program in order to save her daughter. She had to be silenced, and Burgess had altered the pre-cogs' visions to escape detection. But aside from tampering, could a system be devised that accurately predicts the future?

At the end of the film the problem is addressed somewhat when Burgess confronts Anderton with a gun. The Pre-Crime unit is en route having been forewarned of the impending crime. If Burgess resists shooting Anderton, then the program will be shown to be fallible and would be disbanded, whereas if Burgess shoots Anderton, he will be arrested for murder. Faced with this dilemma, Burgess commits suicide.

Minority Report raises the metaphysical question of whether human beings are free or determined in their behavior. Can people's decisions and actions be predicted the way an apple can be expected to drop from a tree? As we know more and more about the factors that affect our behavior, will we reach a point where we will know with certainty what people will do?

Market research in business, or more precisely Customer Relations Management, sorts consumers according to age, location, income, religion, education, race, and so forth. In this way, populations are targeted for a product. It is assumed that people are predictable, and breaking down the demographics, increases that predictability. A rifle is used rather than a shotgun, and the finer the discriminations, the more successful the advertising, marketing, and sales will be. Trading on a behaviorist theory of psychology, business can determine which buttons to push. Human beings are considered stimulus/response mechanisms, and the strongest stimulus always wins.

However, once people know they have been targeted as likely buyers for a product, that can generate resistance, just as Anderton rebels against the Pre-Crime system once he is identified by it. We can only be manipulated if we are not conscious of the manipulation; once we are aware of the forces operating on us, we gain control over them. This is shown in the film, for if the pre-cogs can predict a murder infallibly, then foreseeing the murder should not stop it, but it does. Crow and Burgess shoot themselves, contrary to the prediction. Anderton's knowledge of the events prevents them from happening, which means events are not inevitable. As Agatha declares, since Anderton is aware of his destiny, he can change it.

More essentially, maybe human beings by their very nature are not predictable—at least not to the degree necessary for the Pre-Crime system to work. Aside from the complexity of the factors that affect people, perhaps people are not mechanical objects but beings that make free choices. We may not be as unpredictable as a set of random numbers but we appear to possess free will and are able to choose between alternative courses of action.

The determinist claims that people may have the freedom to carry out their decisions, especially in a liberal democracy, but they are not free to reach those decisions. In other words, we can do what we want but we cannot decide what we want. But the libertarian argues that we all make those fundamental decisions, including the kind of person we want to be, and if we are dissatisfied with ourselves, then we can change. Who we are is within our power, and that forms the basis of our decisions. In short, to be human means to exercise free will, so that our behavior can never be completely foreseen.

In the end, the film seems to reach this conclusion. The pre-cogs can be mistaken because people are able to make free choices. Therefore the system is flawed. It is not that we lack knowledge of all the variables but that, in principle, we are ultimately free.

Specifically, we can never be sure that someone will commit a crime, that they should be apprehended before it takes place. And if people are not compelled to commit a crime, then they should not be imprisoned as a preventative measure. Only the guilty should be punished, and the only certain system of criminal justice is to incarcerate people after they commit a crime.

STUDY QUESTIONS

1. Can human behavior ever be predicted with sufficient accuracy to imprison people before they commit a crime?

2. Does *Minority Report* show that people possess free will or that once people know their actions are predicted they can exercise free will?

3. If the pre-cogs cannot foretell the future, does that mean the future cannot be foretold?

4. Was Anderton's knowledge that he would commit murder a factor in his committing murder, placing him at the right time and place?

5. If a determinist argued that you only believe in free will because you were determined to do so, how would you refute that argument?

The Matrix

Directors and Screenwriters: Larry and Andy Wachowski

The directors Larry and Andy Wachowski are comparative newcomers to film. They wrote Assassins *or* Day of Reckoning, *then directed* Bound. *However,* The Matrix *was their first major success as filmmakers, and the two current sequels also achieved recognition:* The Matrix Reloaded *and* The Matrix Revolutions.

In The Matrix, *a futuristic thriller, our notion of reality is challenged by a world of virtual reality that human beings accept as genuine. People have been deceived by a series of simulated figures and events generated by computer. Since film itself is an illusion (along with other arts and cyberspace experiences), the viewer can appreciate the subtle boundary between fantasy and reality. We take the events on the screen as actual, suspending our disbelief, and when the lights come on, the real world may be hard to accept.*

The story has been criticized as somewhat simplistic and derivative, trading on themes of human beings vs. robots, good vs. evil and, particularly, the salvation of man through Christ (Neo in the film). However, The Matrix *does present fascinating questions about the nature of reality and whether we are being deluded in our understanding of it. The film may be an uneasy amalgam of science fiction, mysticism, video games, comic books, and vague Zen notions, but it is held together by the suspense and philosophic questions. The Kung Fu action and the visual technology alone keep the film entertaining, and in the end the viewer is led to reflection of a metaphysical kind.*

SYNOPSIS

The central premise of the sci-fi thriller *The Matrix* is that, in this post-apocalyptic world, the reality experienced by human beings exists only in their minds. All events and feelings are actually images hardwired into their brains. People live entirely in this dream-like, virtual state, while imagining they are living in the late twentieth century. They go about their business in the usual way, oblivious to the fact that their brains have been hooked up by computer to a simulated reality. They would find it absurd to think that they are floating in comas, suspended in incubators, and that all their experiences are a complex network of delusions. Nevertheless, that is their condition. The plot of "The Matrix" consists of exposing the deception, and in overthrowing the forces that have enslaved people through this hallucination.

The film trades on a philosophic problem called the *ego-centric predicament*, which was first identified and named by Ralph Barton Perry in *Present Philosophical Tendencies*. According to the ego-centric predicament, the mind is confined to the circle of its own ideas, so that it is difficult, and perhaps impossible, to know the external world. That is, we cannot get outside our own minds to know whether our ideas correspond to anything external. No standpoint exists from which we can view the external world and see whether the notions in our mind correspond to it. We are trapped within the boundaries of our being and cannot get outside ourselves to verify the reality of anyone or anything else. Given this condition, we could be skeptical about whether there exists an external world, independent of our own thoughts and images.

Perry describes it this way: "No one can report on the nature of things without being on hand himself. It follows that whatever thing he reports does as a matter of fact stand in relation to him, as an idea, object of knowledge or experience."

As we have seen, George Berkeley used this viewpoint to declare "*esse est percipi*," to be is to be perceived. He claimed that reality is nothing other than our mental ideas, and that no material world exists. Berkeley's theory, however, has been extensively criticized by a number of philosophers. They have pointed out that although things must be mentally experienced in order to be known, that does not prove that reality is nothing but the ideas in our mind. Things can exist without our thinking about them; we simply would not know of their existence. In other words, all knowledge depends on our conscious ideas, but that does not prove the ideas themselves are the reality and that nothing else exists.

In *The Matrix* human beings do take their mental experience as reality, and the viewer along with the protagonist gradually learn of the deception. Not only does the real world lie outside their consciousness, but their consciousness is of a virtual reality and not a reflection of the actual world at all.

After a preliminary action sequence, the main plot of the film begins with shots of a computer programmer, Thomas Anderson (Keanu Reeves), working late at night in an apartment littered with technological equipment. Anderson works for a software development firm but, in addition, he commits computer crimes under the name "Neo," hiring himself as a hacker. This night, as he half dozes, a mysterious message appears on his screen, seemingly from the computer itself: "The Matrix has you," it states, and "Follow the white rabbit." (like Alice).

A client named Choi then appears with his girlfriend, and asks Neo to take on a job for him, which Neo agrees to do. In thanking him Choi says, "Hallelujah! You are my savior, man! My own personal Jesus Christ." With equal significance Neo replies, "You ever have the feeling that you're not sure if you're awake or still dreaming?"

Choi invites Neo to a rave, which he first declines to do, then accepts when he sees a small white rabbit on the girl's jacket. At the party he meets Trinity (Carrie-Ann Moss), a sleekly attractive, mysterious woman dressed in black vinyl, who tells him he is being watched and in danger.

> TRINITY: Please. Just listen. I know why you're here, Neo... You're looking for him.

[Her body is against his; her lips very close to his ear.]

> TRINITY: I know because I came looking for the same thing, but when he found me he told me I wasn't really looking for him. I was looking for an answer.

[There is a hypnotic quality to her voice and Neo feels the words, like a drug, seeping into him.]

> TRINITY: It's the question that brought you here. You know the question just as I did. It is a hacker's question.

> NEO: What is the Matrix?

> TRINITY: When I asked him, he said that no one could ever be told the answer to that question. They have to see it to believe it.

[She leans close, her lips almost touching his ear.]

> TRINITY: The answer is out there, Neo, it's looking for you and it will find you, if you want it to.

The next day at work Neo receives a call from Morpheus, a mythical hacker he has longed to meet. Morpheus tells him "They're coming for you," and as two agents and police come onto the floor, he gives Neo exact instructions on how to escape: into an empty cubicle, then through a window, onto a ledge, and down a scaffold. However, he balks at the leap to the scaffold and is captured by the police.

Agent Smith (Hugo Weaving), the chief villain of the film, subsequently interrogated Neo. After telling him that he knows about his criminal activities as a hacker, Smith offers to wipe the slate clean in return for Neo's cooperation in bringing a terrorist to justice. When Neo refuses, he inserts into his navel a fiber-optic wire tap in the form of an organic worm/insect.

Unsure afterwards whether or not it was a nightmare, Neo agrees to meet with Morpheus. "You're the One," Morpheus tells him. "You see, you may have spent the last few years looking for me, but I've spent most of my life looking for you." In the car that is sent for him, Trinity removes the electronic "bug" from his stomach with a cylindrical probe, and they continue on for the meeting with Morpheus in room 1313 of a decayed hotel.

All of the décor is a stylish film noir, and here Morpheus is dressed in a long black coat with his eyes invisible behind dark glasses.

> MORPHEUS: Let me tell you why you are here. You have come because you know something. What you know you can't explain but you feel it. You've felt it your whole life, felt that something is wrong with the world. You don't know what, but it's there…Do you know what I'm talking about?
>
> NEO: The Matrix?
>
> MORPHEUS: Do you want to know what it is?
>
> [Neo swallows hard and nods.]
>
> MORPHEUS: The Matrix is everywhere, it's all around us, here even in this room. You can see it out your window or on your television. You can feel it when you go to work, or go to church or pay your taxes. It is the world that has been has been pulled over your eyes to blind you from the truth.
>
> NEO: What truth?
>
> MORPHEUS: That you are a slave, Neo. Like everyone else, you were born into bondage, kept inside a prison that you cannot smell, taste, or touch. A prison for your mind.

Morpheus then offers him a choice of two pills: the blue will take him home; the red will lead him to the truth about the Matrix. Without much hesitation, Neo swallows the red pill. Morpheus then asks "Have you ever had a dream, Neo, that you were so sure was real?…What if you were unable to wake from that dream, Neo? How would you know the difference between the dream world and the real world?"

Subsequently Neo undergoes a traumatic and painful process to free him from his illusions. A mirror envelops him in silvery strands, melting like gel and spreading across his body. He then finds himself in an oval capsule filled with red gelatin, a coaxial cable plugged into the base of his skull. All around him are other people also in pods with the same tubes feeding into a metal stem. A machine drops in front of him, paralyzes his muscles, and disengages the main cable. Immediately he is sucked into a black hole, drawn through sewer pipes and grease traps, and finally pulled into the belly of a futuristic hovercraft.

Morpheus and Trinity are there together with a man named Dozer who is rebuilding his atrophied muscles and various members of the crew—Mouse, Cypher, Apoc, Switch, Tank, and so forth. His eyes hurt because, as Morpheus explains, he has never used them before, so he is given dark glasses like the others.

Morpheus then reveals to Neo that the year is about 2197 not 1997. Using the jack at the back of his neck, he hooks him into a computer program that shows the Chicago he is familiar with and the Chicago that has come to be. He begins to explain that in the early twenty-first century human beings invented machines that were incredibly smart, but their intelligence (A.I.) enabled them to revolt and take over the planet. In order to supply their need for power they required an energy source besides the sun, so they began "farming" human beings. "The human body generates more bioelectricity than a 120-volt battery and over 25,000 B.T.U.'s of body heat," Morpheus explains. Consequently, it was a perfect source of power.

The machines therefore started using people as batteries, and to keep the human race ignorant of its condition and under control, the Matrix was created—a computer-generated, virtual world. Almost everyone, including Neo, had been living within the illusions created by the cyber intelligence, while Morpheus and a few others who had escaped, were free from the deception. They were battling to wrest control back from the machines.

When Neo refuses to believe that these are the real circumstances, Morpheus asks rhetorically, "What is real? How do you define real? If you're talking about your senses, what you feel, taste, smell, or see, then all you're talking about are electrical signals interpreted by your brain."

He also discloses that Neo has been born with special powers that would enable him to manipulate the Matrix and defeat the machines. An Oracle had prophesied that a man would return to free humankind, bringing about enlightenment and man's salvation. The obvious reference is to Christ, and Neo is seen as the promised Messiah. Morpheus tells him "There is a greatness inside of you, Neo. A greatness that is going to lift you to unimaginable heights and that in time will change the world."

To prepare for his role mentally and physically, discs are loaded into Neo's supplemental drive, including savate, jujitsu, Ken Po, and kung fu. He spars with Morpheus using the martial arts programmed inside him, moving with incredible speed and strength, defying the law of gravity with his leaps and dodges. However, Neo fails in a crucial jump, and people wonder if he is the One; apparently, Morpheus had been mistaken before.

To make sure of his identity, Neo is taken to see the Oracle, someone with the eyes of a sphinx who is never wrong. "The Matrix cannot tell you who you are," Morpheus declares, "but an oracle can…She sees beyond the relativity of time. For her there is no past, present, or future. There is only what is." When Neo is skeptical, saying that he doesn't believe in this stuff, Morpheus replies "Faith is beyond the reach of whys and why nots. These things are not a matter of cause and effect, Neo. I do not believe things with my mind. I believe them with my heart. In my gut." Religion is thus given precedence over science, feelings over the rationality that created the Matrix.

Contrary to expectations, the Oracle seems to deny that Neo is the One, although like most seers, soothsayers, and prophets her words are ambiguous. She does foretell that, Morpheus will attempt to give up his life so Neo can live; he believes in him that strongly. Then Neo will have to decide which of the two will die.

Fast-paced action scenes follow as agents of the Matrix, who are machines in human form, swarm into the headquarters of the rebels. Several of the rebels are killed, and amidst blasts of gunfire Neo, Morpheus, Trinity, and Cypher try to escape through the crawlspace between the walls. Agent Smith momentarily catches Neo, but Morpheus explodes through the lath and plaster and grabs Smith by the throat. He tells Trinity to leave him behind and save Neo, so the two of them slide inside the wall to the basement where they escape through an opening to the sewers.

Meanwhile Morpheus is captured, and Agent Smith begins extracting information from him using a serum that attacks his neuro-systems. To avoid having their entire operation destroyed, Tank and Trinity reluctantly decide that Morpheus must be killed, which they can do remotely. However, Neo will not agree. He realizes that this is the moment the Oracle predicted, when either he or Morpheus would die, and he decides to risk his life in attempting a rescue. Trinity insists on going with him, so the two of them are propelled inside the Matrix.

More fast action follows as Neo and Trinity penetrate the government building where Morpheus is being held, killing a number of guards with their guns, fists, and explosives. They then steal a helicopter and attack the room where Morpheus is being held. Neo manages to extract Morpheus by dangling from a rope, and they carry him to safety, landing on the roof of a skyscraper.

In the final scene that begins in a subway station, Neo and Agent Smith fight a furious battle, each twisting, bending, and ducking faster than the bullets coming at them. They land powerful blows, kick box and hurl each other into walls, exhibiting uncanny suppleness and speed. Although Smith is hit by an oncoming train, he somehow survives and begins to chase Neo through the city. Several agents join in the pursuit, appearing from the midst of crowds, from behind tent flaps, crates, and fish counters. Neo ducks into buildings, sprints down corridors, through apartments, and scrambles up a fire escape as bullets whiz around him. But when he throws open the door to one room Agent Smith is waiting for him; he kills Neo with one shot.

One would think the rebel struggle would be over with the Matrix emerging victorious, but Neo miraculously comes back to life. He hears Trinity's voice saying, "The Oracle, she told me that I'd fall in love and that man, the man I loved would be the One. You see? You can't be dead, Neo, you can't be because I love you. You hear me? I love you!"

At this, Neo rises to his feet, and effortlessly overcomes Agent Smith, even making bullets stop in their tracks. The Matrix is thereby defeated, love overcoming hate, and as the camera rises above the city Neo ascends still faster, traveling upwards at an unearthly speed.

We can see in the film a strong religious allegory. The symbolism alone is hard to miss: Neo as a Christ figure (come to save the world), Trinity, a demigoddess of the New Age variety, and Morpheus, the god of dreams in Ovid's *Metamorphosis*. Several interpreters have seen further Christian elements in the film, some of which have already been mentioned. For example, "Neo" has been taken as an anagram for eon and One; he is born into the world anew, like the virgin birth of Christ; Morpheus can be seen as John the Baptist who foretold Christ's coming;

the hovercraft is called Nebuchadnezzar, and the core of the planet where human survivors live is "Zion," both of which are biblical references; Cypher is a Judas who gave up Morpheus to Agent Smith (a Roman centurion); at the end of the film, Neo rises into the sky just as Christ ascended to heaven; and Neo's death and resurrection are foretold just as Christ prophesied he would be killed and raised from the dead. Perhaps this is reading into the text too much Christian meaning, but the film does mirror the New Testament in many ways.

For our purposes, *The Matrix* offers a fascinating approach to the question of reality. It may be far-fetched to think that a master computer is feeding perceptions into our brain, so that we are experiencing a virtual world called the Matrix, but we do sometimes wonder whether reality exists only in our minds. We may not be computer viruses or batteries for computers, but in today's world perhaps we are increasingly being told what to think. It may be more than paranoia to fear control by drugs, technology, advertising, and government bureaus, so we are sympathetic to the notion that our minds could be manipulated from outside. As Morpheus asks, if we were unable to awaken from a dream, how would we know the difference between the dream world and the real world?

Limited as we are to the private space inside our heads, we are never certain how much contact we have with anything objective, or whether the internal or the external is real. In the modern world of implants, virtual objects, cyberspace, holograms, robotics, bioengineering, and artificial intelligence, what we take to be true might just be illusions of the senses or delusions of the mind. In a sense, our mental life forms a world in itself, and even if it's phony that may be all we have.

The Matrix raises such questions within the context of an entertaining, high-tech drama. Using special effects such as computer animation, wire stunts, and impossible martial arts, the film creates an exciting visual fantasy. It crosses the boundary between the cyberpunk and the reflective, ultimately offering us a metaphysical thriller.

STUDY QUESTIONS

 1. Define the nature of the Matrix.

 2. Do you think there is any way of telling the difference between virtual reality and actual life?

3. In what way is *The Matrix* a Christian parable?

4. Why do the agents fight so had to perpetuate the false reality?

5. If you were Neo, would you take the red or blue pill? Would you rather know the harsh truth or believe the comforting delusion?

Bibliography of Philosophy, Literature, and Films
II. The Nature of Reality: Metaphysics

Philosophy

The Analysis of Mind	Bertrand Russell
Being and Nothingness	Jean-Paul Sartre
Body and Mind	Godfrey Vesey
The Bondage of the Will	Martin Luther
Cartesian Meditations	Edmund Husserl
The Concept of Mind	Gilbert Ryle
The Concept of a Person	A. J. Ayer
De Anima, Metaphysics	Aristotle
Determinism and Freedom	Sidney Hook
Essays On the Freedom of the Will	Arthur Schopenhauer
Essays on the Intellectual Powers of Man	Thomas Reid
Frankenstein	Mary Wollstonecraft Shelley
Freedom and Reason	R. M. Hare
Freedom of the Individual	Stuart Hampshire
Freedom of the Will	Jonathan Edwards
In Defense of Free Will	C. A. Campbell
Individuals	P. F. Strawson
Intention	G. E. M. Anscombe
Materialist Theory of Mind	D. M. A. Armstrong
The Mind and Its Place In Nature	C. D. Broad
The Mind-Brain Identity Theory	Clive B. Borst
Minds and Machines	Alan R. Anderson
The Nature of Woman	Mary Anne Warren
On Free Choice of the Will	St. Augustine
On Human Freedom	John Laird
Other Minds	John Wisdom
Person and Object	Roderick Chisholm
The Philosophy of Mind	Stuart Hampshire
The Problems of Philosophy	Bertrand Russell
Problems of the Self	Bernard Williams
Reconstruction in Philosophy	John Dewey
The Revolt Against Dualism	Arthur Lovejoy
The Second Sex	Simone de Beauvoir

The Self and the Brain	Karl Popper
Time and Free Will	Henri Bergson

Literature

The Age of Reason, Nausea	Jean-Paul Sartre
Alcestis, Iphigenia, Medea	Euripides
A Man's A Man	Bertolt Brecht
Antigone	Sophocles
An American Tragedy	Theodore Dreiser
And Quiet Flows the Don	Mikhail Sholokhov
Buddenbrooks	Thomas Mann
Candide	Voltaire
The Castle, The Trial	Franz Kafka
Chance	Joseph Conrad
The Common Reader	Virginia Woolf
Death of a Salesman	Arthur Miller
Dice Thrown Never Will Annul Chance	Stephane Mallarme
Do With Me What You Will	Joyce Carol Oates
A Doll's House	Henrik Ibsen
The Double, Notes From the Underground	Fedor Dostoevski
The Edible Woman	Margaret Atwood
The Egoist	George Meredith
Ficciones	Jorge Luis Borges
Free Fall	William Golding
Gravity's Rainbow	Thomas Pynchon
The Gulag Archipelago	Alexander Solzhenitsyn
Hamlet	William Shakespeare
Hedda Gabler	Henrick Ibsen
Henry VI	William Shakespeare
Invisible Cities	Italo Calvino
Jacob's Room	Virginia Woolf
Labyrinths	Jorge Luis Borges
Magic Mountain	Thomas Mann
The Magus	John Fowles
The Man Without Qualities	Robert Musil
One Hundred Years of Solitude	Gabriel Garcia Marquez
Othello	William Shakespeare
Phaedra	Jean Baptiste Racine
The Picture of Dorian Gray	Oscar Wilde
Portrait of the Artist as a Young Man	James Joyce

Pygmalion	George Bernard Shaw
Remembrance of Things Past	Marcel Proust
Richard III	William Shakespeare
Sapho	Alphonse Daudet
The Secret Sharer	Joseph Conrad
The Story of Gosta Berling	Selma Lagerlof
The Stranger	Albert Camus
TheTime Machine	H. G. Wells
Wadlen Two	B. F. Skinner
Ward No. 6	Anton Chekhov
The Way of All Flesh	Samuel Butler
The Wild Duck	Henrik Ibsen

Films

Alien	Ridley Scott
Altered States	Ken Russell
The Andalusian Dog	Luis Bunuel
The Andromeda Strain	Robert Wise
Babbitt	Sinclair Lewis
The Ballad of Narayame	Shohei Imamura
Beauty and the Beast	Jean Cocteau
Being John Malkovich	Spike Jonze
Billy Liar	John Schlesinger
Blade Runner	Ridley Scott
The Boys From Brazil	Franklin J. Schaffner
Brazil	Terry Gillian
Captains Courageous	Victor Fleming
Close Encounters of the Third Kind	Steven Spielberg
Coccoon	Ron Howard
The Crying Game	Neil Jordan
Dead Man Walking	Tim Robbins
East of Eden	Elia Kazan
Eternal Sunshine of the Spotless Mind	Michael Goudry
The Four Hundred Blows	Francois Truffaut
Frankenstein	James Whale
Fattaca	Andrew Niccol
The Golden Age	Luis Bunuel
The Graduate	Mike Nichols
Groundhog Day	Harold Ramis
The Hustler	Robert Rossen

I, Robot	Alex Proyas
Jurassic Park	Steven Spielberg
Lord of the Flies	Peter Brooks
Lost Horizon	Frank Capra
Love and Death	Woody Allen
A Man For All Seasons	Fred Zimmerman
Memento	Christopher Nolan
Metropolis	Fritz Lang
Minority Report	Steven Spielberg
Nesferatu	F. W. Murneau
The Matrix	Wachowski Brothers
One Flew Over the Cuckoo's Nest	Milios Forman
Orpheus	Jean Cocteau
The Passion of Ana	Igmar Bergman
Pather Panchali	Satyajit Ray
Slaughterhouse Five	George Roy Hill
Star Trek	Robert Wise
Star Wars	George Lucas
2001, A Space Odyssey	Stanley Kubrick
The Unbearable Lightness of Being	Philip Kaufman
Women in the Dunes	Hiroshi Teshigahara

III. Judging the Value of Conduct: Ethics

Ethics is considered another major branch of philosophy, in addition to epistemology and metaphysics. Its subject matter includes both the right and the good, that is, the right way to behave and the good in life overall. The ethicist tries to answer questions such as how much should we sacrifice for someone else's welfare and how much can we take from life for ourselves? Should we always keep promises, tell the truth, and preserve life, or when would it be morally permissible to break promises, deceive others, and take a life? Do we know what is right by that still small voice inside us that some call conscience, by our personal experience of cruelty and kindness, by the traditions in our society, or by authorities such as parents, teachers, or from sacred books? Is an act immoral because it is illegal or illegal because it is immoral? Should we judge actions in terms of the intention of the agent, the intrinsic nature of the act, or the ultimate harm or benefit that results? What goals are worth pursuing as our overall purpose in living?

Although all people must decide these questions for themselves, that does not mean one person's opinion is as good as another's. Those who know the various options, and know the kinds of considerations that apply in evaluating these opinions, are in a much better position to reach sound conclusions. An informed decision that is the result of thoughtful evaluation is far better than accepting the popular notions of one's time or the opinions one assimilates as a child. As Socrates said, "The unexamined life is not worth living." Once we have examined the various choices we could make, and understand what makes them right or wrong, good or bad, then we are in a position to reach a sound decision. At that point we are truly in command of our lives.

A. RELATIVISM AND OBJECTIVISM: ARE THERE UNIVERSAL VALUES?

One primary question in ethics is whether our values are a reflection of our culture or whether they have an objective basis. According to the *relativist* view, when we make a value judgment we are only stating the attitudes and prejudices of our society. To the *objectivist*, we may be identifying something genuinely right or wrong, good or bad, aside from our society's attitudes. For example, when we blame someone for stealing, the relativist sees this as an expression of our culture's disapproval, while the objectivist would argue that we are stating an objective truth: that stealing, by its very nature, is wrong.

Some relativists point out that our judgments are also a matter of personal taste as well as (or contrary to) a reflection of societal norms. This view is sometimes referred to as *subjectivism*. According to the subjectivist, what is right to one person may be wrong to another; values are an individual matter. John may believe that sex is only permissible within marriage whereas Bill may think pre-marital sex is perfectly acceptable. Just as we have different tastes in food we have different sets of values; no one can be judged wrong for not liking broccoli or for being sexually promiscuous. As the Romans said, "de gustibus non est disputandum"; about taste there can be no dispute. All standards are relative to a particular person or society, and they have no general validity outside that context. Therefore, to deliberate about which values are really worthwhile is a pointless exercise. Everything is relative to the individual, the culture, the time, and the place.

Relativists often argue for their theory by citing the variety of value systems across the world, each different and each supported by thousands of people who believe themselves right. In some cultures a man gains esteem by having several wives while in others polygamy is considered immoral; in some societies drugs are taken to combat fatigue or for pleasure and insight, while in others using drugs is a crime; in some places a woman must cover her body completely in a burka with netting over her eyes while in others women enhance their faces with makeup and wear bikinis on the beach.

In the past and in some cultures today, slavery is practiced whereas most cultures consider it immoral, and pride killings are tolerated in some places but condemned in others. (These are executions of women who have been unfaithful or raped, bringing shame on the family.) War is thought heroic by some, tragic by others; old age used to be respected but youth is currently celebrated, particularly if it is accompanied by wealth and status. Because of the multiplicity of cultural perspectives the relativist concludes that morality is a matter of history and geography.

At the extreme, the relativist theory maintains that values are a matter of opinion. Whatever a person thinks is right becomes right because the person thinks so. We tell one another "It's all a matter of opinion, it's how you feel," or "What gives you the right to judge?" "Who's to say?" The implication is that what is true for a person *is* true for them and no outside standard can be invoked to prove them wrong. As Shakespeare declares in *Hamlet*, "There is nothing either good or bad, but thinking makes it so."

The impulses behind relativism seem to be admirable. First, there is the desire for tolerance and open-mindedness toward other people's ideas—including those that are different than our own. In a democracy, everyone has a right to their opinion (as well as a right to be heard), and we should not presume that our ideas are the only correct ones. Such an attitude smacks of arrogance and righteousness. Furthermore, we should be wary of people who are sure they are right because such certainty can result in inquisitions, the burning of witches and heretics, wars and crusades, ethnic cleansing and genocide.

A second source of relativism lies in our wish to maximize our freedom. If there are correct moral principles then we are compelled to acknowledge them whether we like it or not, whereas if right and wrong depend upon how we feel then we have a great deal of personal control. We are then free to choose our values, and all ethical value becomes a function of our preferences. Whatever we choose thereby becomes valuable because we have chosen it. A third motive for accepting relativism is our *uncertainty* in today's world as to which values are worth accepting and defending. History has proven us wrong too often with regard to political ideals, social goals, or religious beliefs, so we have lost confidence in the truth of our ideas. Furthermore, our awareness of the diversity of values in a multicultural world casts doubt on any one theory of what is right or good.

Our uncertainty is increased by the scientific approach to knowledge, which has nearly eclipsed every other way of knowing. As science operates, only empirical statements are capable of being verified, which means that all value judgments are a matter of opinion. Added to this are specific scientific findings such as Einstein's theory of relativity that takes space and time as relative phenomena. Although relativity theory only applies to physics, people have taken it as evidence for the relativity of ethical values as well.

It appears, then, that every value judgment we make should be tentative and qualified. The sense of being certain about what is right and wrong has now been lost, and we are acutely conscious that every moral statement we make is potentially false. Add to this our desire to be tolerant toward other people's choices, and to have maximum freedom in deciding how to live, and it seems correct to say that everything is relative.

Persuasive as the case for relativism might be, many philosophers accept the opposite position of objectivism. According to the objectivist theory, we can identify certain acts as right, others as wrong, and some life purposes as more desirable than others. Societies do not create values but can discover them, and individuals do not invent values but recognize them. When we make a moral judgment we are expressing insight into the nature of the act, not revealing something about our culture's attitudes or about ourselves.

For example, the judgment that stealing is wrong tells us something about the wrongness of stealing. To take someone else's property, especially something they have worked hard to acquire, is to cause them injury. Therefore it is wrong, not just for us but for anyone. Whether we are in Africa, Asia, or Europe, in the ancient or the modern world, we should not take what does not belong to us.

The objectivist, therefore, believes that human beings should follow certain standards of behavior because they are right in themselves. We should not be self-righteous, of course, and assume we know what those standards are, but we can have confidence that such standards exist and strive to understand them. That gives direction to our search, and through rational discussion we hope to get closer to the truth of things.

The objectivist also rejects many of the specific arguments used by the relativist. For instance, the objectivist points out that although values differ between cultures, that does not imply all values are relative. The differences can be attributed to one society being more backward or enlightened than another, seeing values dimly or more clearly. To take an analogy from science, the fact that people thought the earth was flat at one time and round at another, does not mean that each idea is right. Rather, people came to understand that although they believed the earth was flat, it was really round. In the same way, people have come to realize, for example, that women should be treated with absolute equality, that enslaving people is wrong in any society, and that we should respect minority rights. To treat people as inferior is not right in some cultures and wrong in others; it is wrong whenever and wherever it occurs.

In addition, the objectivist argues that the diversity of values between cultures may be more apparent than real. A wide area of moral agreement exists between cultures across the earth. For example, one society may condone a husband killing his wife's lover, another may condemn it, and this seems like a major difference. However, both societies will probably have laws prohibiting murder and a strong belief in the protection of human life. They will differ only in their definition of what constitutes murder, that is, when life is taken unjustly. In the same way, one society may be hostile to strangers, another warm and welcoming, but both may believe in the value of hospitality. The difference is that one applies the rules of hospitality only to families within the society, the other extends them to everyone they meet.

Objectivists will sometimes cite the golden rule as a major example of a cross-cultural value. In Christianity we read "Whatsoever ye would that men should do unto you, do ye even so to them"; in Judaism "What is hateful to yourself, don't do to your fellow man"; in Buddhism "Hurt not others with that which pains oneself"; and in Hinduism "Do naught to others which if done to thee would cause pain." Confucianism tells us "What you don't want done to yourself, don't do to others"; Zoroastrianism says "Do not do unto others all that which is not well for oneself"; Sikhism declares "Treat others as thou wouldst be treated thyself"; and even Plato advises himself "May I do unto others as I would that they should do unto me." Perhaps, then, all societies do have a substratum of shared values.

The objectivist also points out a variety of criticisms of a logical kind that show relativism as self-contradictory. For one thing, the relativist claims that the statement "Everything is relative" is really true, but if everything is relative then nothing is really true, including that statement. It may be true relative to one's culture or according to one's tastes, but to say it is objectively true contradicts the theory itself.

Plato identifies another type of contradiction in a dialogue called the *Theatetus*. Here Socrates says to Protagoras "and the best of the joke is that he acknowledges the truth of their opinions who believe his own opinions to be false for he admits that the opinions of all men are true." In other words, if everyone is right, then the person who thinks you are wrong must be right.

Finally, there is the self-contradiction with regard to tolerance (which was mentioned as one of the supports for relativism). Relativists claim that their position has the virtue of fostering tolerance because no value is considered really worthwhile. However, by extolling tolerance, relativists are assuming it possesses value. The relativists thereby give the game away, for tolerance at least is considered objectively valuable.

B. IDEALS IN LIVING: DOING WHAT'S RIGHT OR ACHIEVING THE GOOD

Assuming that values can be determined, two principal theories have emerged in philosophic history as to what would be an ideal human life: that pleasure or happiness constitutes the goal in living, or that we should live in accordance with moral principles. The first can be broadly categorized as *hedonism*, or in its social form *Utilitarianism*; the second as a *duty ethic*, usually associated with the philosopher Immanuel Kant. Secondary theories include the religious ethic and self-realization, as well as such philosophies as naturalism, humanism, and Stoicism.

Hedonism, the theory that we should live for the sake of pleasure or happiness, is probably the most ancient, natural, and persuasive theory in ethics. Most people would agree that pleasure or happiness is the goal in life, which supports the idea that it is, in fact, the supreme value, "that at which all things aim." The idea that popularity establishes truth is a doubtful assumption, but several ethicists have maintained it.

Although people may differ in their views on the meaning of happiness, very few would want anything else. Some people define happiness as arising from honor, recognition, status, and prestige; others regard it as the satisfaction of our appetites, that is, sensuous pleasure and physical gratification; still others see it as the acquisition of wealth, property, and financial power; and philosophers sometimes identify it as contemplation of timeless realities.

Besides the prevalence of hedonism, which may be a reason in itself, several arguments have been offered as proof that happiness is the ideal. For example, it has been pointed out that happiness is self-sufficient. If we are happy we lack nothing, and if we lack something we are not truly happy. Another consideration is that happiness is always chosen for its own sake and never as a means to anything further. We do a number of things in order to be happy, but we do not seek happiness for any other goal. Like a mountain peak, it leads nowhere.

As a formal theory hedonism originated with two ancient Greek philosophers, Aristippus (c. 435–356 B.C.) and Epicurus (342–270 B.C.). In their individual ways, both men affirmed pleasure or happiness as the good.

Aristippus, the founder of a school called the Cyrenaics, emphasized bodily pleasure that is intense (i.e., strong), brief, and immediately available. He would have agreed with the twelfth century Persian poet Omar Khayyam who wrote in the *Rubaiyat*, "Ah, make the most of what we yet may spend, / Before we too into the Dust descend; / Dust into Dust and under dust to lie/ Sans wine, sans Song, sans Singer, and—sans End!"

The Cyrenaics are generally regarded as shortsighted, preferring to enjoy themselves today despite the pains that would follow tomorrow. Drinking heavily may be fun now, but the more we drink the more we regret it in the morning: that should make us drink moderately. Also, the Cyrenaics were unwilling to endure any present pain for the sake of future pleasure. They argued that the future is only a hope, just as the past is a dream, so we should never suffer for the sake of some enjoyment that may never come. According to one story, a Cyrenaic boy was carrying a bag of gold and, because it was heavy, he threw it away.

Epicurus developed hedonism in a more mature way, endorsing enjoyment that is serene, lasting, and that infuses our lives overall. In the case of the boy carrying a bag of gold, the Epicurean would have suffered the discomfort of carrying it, and chances are he would have thanked himself later.

To be an Epicurean we do not "Eat, drink, and be merry," but relish the more subtle modes of enjoyment in a tranquil way. We become gourmets and connoisseurs, eating and drinking to savor fine flavors and nourish our spirit. In one surviving fragment he wrote "I know not how I can conceive the good if I withdraw the pleasure of taste, and withdraw the pleasures of love, and withdraw the pleasures of hearing, and withdraw the pleasurable emotions caused to sight by beautiful form." Epicurus expressed a joy and celebration of living that is hard to resist. It is reminiscent of the Greek poet Homer who said "Dear to us ever is the banquet and the harp and the dance and the changes of raiment and the warm bath and love and sleep."

Unfortunately Epicureanism became a negative philosophy that tried to avoid pain more than to seek pleasure. The walled garden in which Epicurus taught became a fitting symbol of this outlook because it walled trouble out rather than walling enjoyment in.

The hedonism of both Aristippus and Epicurus was of an individualistic kind, solely concerned with maximizing enjoyment for the person. In the nineteenth century hedonism underwent a major change when two English philosophers, Jeremy Bentham and John Stuart Mill, transformed it into a doctrine aimed at the good of society. That is, Bentham and Mill created a

Utilitarian theory that interpreted the good as the greatest amount of happiness for the greatest number of people.

Bentham is usually credited as the founder of the Utilitarian philosophy, and his emphasis was on increasing the sum total of happiness for everyone. He wanted governments to enact legislation based on utilitarian principles, taking the maximization of pleasure as the goal. Bentham wrote "Pleasure is in itself a good—nay even, setting aside immunity from pain, the only good; pain is in itself an evil—and, indeed without exception, the only evil." There could be more or less pleasure but not better and worse, and Bentham created a "hedonic calculus" for assessing the amount of pleasure that any given action would yield. In this way he hoped to determine precisely and scientifically which act would produce more pleasure for more people. The act with the highest pleasure quotient was the most ethical act.

Mill also accepted utilitarianism but he rejected Bentham's formulation that only the amount of pleasure matters. He maintained that the quality of pleasure is more important than its quantity. According to Mill, pleasures can be higher or lower, better or worse, superior or inferior, and only an ethic that recommends pleasures of a higher kind is consistent with human dignity. We needed to differentiate between the pleasures of a pig and that of a person, and only human pleasures can be considered as good. "It is better to be a human being dissatisfied than a pig satisfied," Mill wrote, and better to be an unhappy Socrates than a happy fool.

Unfortunately for Mill, this corrective weakens rather than strengthens the hedonistic theory. For Mill is endorsing the qualitatively higher activity over the pleasurable one, the human experience over the animalistic, even if no pleasure is involved. Perhaps it is better to be human even if that means dissatisfaction, but such a position is contrary to the hedonistic idea that pleasure is most important.

All hedonists encounter this problem when they try to refine the doctrine by introducing qualitative distinctions. Yet without this refinement hedonism seems a vulgar philosophy, recommending animalistic pleasure as the human ideal.

One general problem with utilitarian hedonism should also be mentioned. Suppose the majority would be happiest if they hanged the minority; on utilitarian grounds that would be justified. Because atrocities could be committed in the name of utilitarianism, we can see that the theory has a fatal ethical flaw.

The *duty ethic* stands diametrically opposed to hedonism. Rather than recommending pleasure or happiness as the goal in life, this theory stresses our responsibilities and obligations to humanity. Immanuel Kant, the chief spokesman for this ethic, maintained that we should always act in terms of universal principles, respecting the moral law. The good life is not maximum enjoyment but doing our duty.

To determine our moral responsibilities in any situation, Kant formulated what he calls the Categorical Imperative: "Act so that the maxim for our actions could become a universal law." That is, whenever we consider an action we must ask ourselves whether we could recommend it for all people at all times in all places. To Kant, genuine ethical conduct is universalizable, for if an action is right, it is always right. Conversely, if we make an exception for ourselves, claiming that other people are obliged to do something but we are not, that is a sure sign of unethical conduct.

It is important to notice what Kant excludes from the circle of worthwhile conduct. The consequences of an action do not determine its rightness, including a hedonistic or Utilitarian outcome. To Kant, it is irrelevant whether pleasure or any other good is produced, for it is the inherent rightness of an action that makes it worthwhile, not its consequence. Whatever can be supported by universalizable moral principles is justified, and whatever cannot be so justified should never be done, regardless of the benefits that might accrue from it.

Kant also rejects the idea that we should behave toward others with feelings of sympathy, warmth, concern, or even impulses of love, because emotional inclinations of any kind are an unreliable basis for morality. If an act is grounded in universal principles then we can be sure it is sound, but feelings are too fluid to be trusted. Actions based on principle, however, can always be tested by asking whether we would want everyone to behave in the same way.

Kant's theory seems very pure and admirable—a much loftier ethic than a hedonistic desire for pleasure. At the same time we wonder whether it is too strict and uncompromising. To take one aspect of his philosophy, Kant seems wrong in thinking that the consequences of actions are unimportant in deciding how to behave. Even if an action is correct in principle, we should hesitate to do it if there are harmful effects. For example, we should not give someone with a weak heart very bad news, or tell a potential murderer where his victim is hiding, despite the fact that truth-telling is a virtue. To Kant, the ends do not justify the means, but the counter is that neither do the means justify the ends. As for the irrelevance of feelings, we would much rather be surrounded by people who are generous and loving by disposition than on principle. Kant seems far too ready to dismiss the emotions and to elevate reason as the acid test of morality.

Critics have pointed out other problems in the Kantian theory, particularly that of finding any principle that is universalizable. For example, the moral rule that we should keep promises has exceptions; for if a marriage breaks down to the point at which the children are threatened, then the marriage vows might be broken. (Some promises should never have been made; others should not be kept when circumstances radically alter.) That we should not steal has exceptions in the case of spies acting for our nation, or if some tyrant denies people food (as in the case of Jean Valjean in Victor Hugo's *Les Miserables*). That we should not kill has exceptions in situations of self-defense, to protect those we love, and perhaps for euthanasia, capital punishment, and just wars.

A principle may be right but that does not mean it should always be done; sometimes it should be suspended for the larger good. Kant fails to differentiate between making exceptions and qualifying a principle because of particular circumstances—and overall human welfare. He has created a noble theory, extolling a life of duty, but he is so concerned with principles that he forgets about people.

Nevertheless, the idea of following principles is very appealing as a dignified and disciplined approach to life. It stands in major contrast to hedonism, and makes pleasure seem like a cheap alternative. If we could embrace both theories that would be ideal, but very often we cannot do our duty and achieve happiness. One or the other must be sacrificed, and in such cases we are forced to decide which is more important.

Self-realization is another option in ethics. This theory has surfaced at various points in intellectual history, mainly in England and the United States although the Greek philosopher Aristotle and the German philosopher G. W. F. Hegel are often regarded as its founders. F. H. Bradley, T. H. Green, Josiah Royce, and W. C. Hocking are usually identified with self-realization as well as the psychologists Carl Rogers, Erich Fromm, and Abraham Maslow.

According to the self-realization theory, following principles is too austere, and hedonism is shallow and deficient in moral fiber. Something can be pleasurable but not good, and good but not pleasurable, therefore pleasure cannot be taken as the good in life.

As a more inclusive approach, the self-realizationist recommends the complete development of our talents, capacities, and interests. We should actualize our potentialities and become all we are capable of being. To realize ourselves we should not only satisfy our physical need for food, sex, and shelter in the most fulfilling way, but realize our higher tendencies as well.

For example, our social part should be developed by joining together with others in a rich community. We are gregarious creatures by nature and need outlets for relationships, caring, and nurture. Also included in human nature is an intellectual curiosity, which is expressed in the need to know, a spiritual sense of reverence, and holiness that seeks union with God, and an aesthetic sensibility that enables us to appreciate beauty and create works of art. All of these capacities should be developed to the utmost.

Unfortunately for self-realization, we are not sure that everyone's self should be realized. Mass murderers such as Charles Manson and Richard Speck, the Boston Strangler and Jack the Ripper, as well as tyrants from Attila the Hun and Genghis Khan to Idi Amin and Pol Pot should suppress their tendencies rather than develop them; we do not want Hitler to be self-actualized. And if realizing oneself is not necessarily good, then the good cannot be defined as self-realization.

Finally, the *religious ethic* should be mentioned, which centers on the being of God and advocates living in accordance with His will. Judaism, Christianity, Islam, Buddhism, Hinduism, Taoism, and so forth all tell their followers to lead a virtuous life in the spirit of God. Of course, the nature of that life has been variously painted depending on the theology and scriptures that are followed. But however the ideal life is defined in its specifics, the common feature of religious ethics is that we exist to glorify God and carry out his will on earth.

To take Christian ethics as a prime example, the Christian believes in unconditional love that is expressed by the Greek term *agape* In an agape type of love we want what is best for the other person—even if it would not be good for us. Our love for the other even impels us let them go if that would be the best thing for them, sacrificing our welfare for theirs. For we are in the relationship not for what we can get but for what we can give, and if we are hurting the other person or not meeting their needs, then we should leave, regardless of how painful we might find it.

According to Christian ethics, this kind of love should extend not just to personal relationships but to all humanity. We should treat our fellow human beings with genuine, selfless love, acting for their sake and not for what we will receive in return. Our intention should be to dedicate ourselves to humankind as Christ did, not because people have earned it but because they need our care and compassion. This is how the best parents treat their children, loving them most when they deserve it least, if that is what they need.

One problem with this theory, of course, is that selfish people will take advantage of those who are generous; in fact, their selfish behavior will be encouraged by default. The abused wife, who continually forgives her abusive husband, is not helping him or herself. Furthermore, athletes cannot do what is best for the opposing team, any more than business people can meet the needs of their competitor. If a loan officer practiced the biblical precept "Give to him who asketh of thee, and he who would borrow of thee turn not thou away," the bank would soon be out of business. In the same way, governments cannot act in the best interests of enemy nations or their countries would soon be invaded and enslaved. Christian love is a beautiful ideal, which can function between people who are equally committed to each other, but it becomes impractical in the wider world when people act out of self-interest.

A further problem has plagued all forms of religious ethics that are based on the word of God. Plato in the *Euthyphro* first raised the pivotal question as to whether an act is right because God wills it or whether God wills an act because it is right. That is, does the rightness of such virtues as honesty or faithfulness depend upon the fact that God commands them, or did God command them because of their (intrinsic) rightness?

It seems more defensible to argue that God wills certain values, for example those of the Ten Commandments, because he knows they are right. Otherwise he is making arbitrary rules, commanding actions for no good reason. What's more, even a God cannot turn values upside down, making the wrong right or the right wrong. Even if he changed his mind, he cannot make hating our neighbor a virtue and loving him a vice. If he would never do that, it is because it would be wrong to do so.

This means that ethics is independent of religion rather than being derived from it. If we believe we should love one another that is not because it is God's word but because it is right. We are left with the question of what makes actions right, but at least we know it is not because God says so.

The preceding thumbnail sketch should convey a sense of some of ethical ideals and their problems, and the selections that follow trace the two main alternatives: hedonism, specifically Mill's Utilitarianism, and the ethic of duty of Immanuel Kant.

The film *Crash* directed by Paul Haggis, explores the clash of cultures in the United States and the moral dimension involved, while Elia Kazan's *On the Waterfront* dramatizes the debate between the objectivist and the relativist, affirming the objectivist approach. Finally, *Saving Private Ryan* argues for a Kantian ethic of duty over the harm/benefit calculation of Utilitarianism.

A. Philosophic Concepts

Utilitarianism (Chapter II)
John Stuart Mill

John Stuart Mill (1806–1873) was an English philosopher, economist, and political scientist who significantly affected nineteenth-century thought. His best known writing, "On Liberty," was influential in promoting individual freedom against social tyranny, and his book On the Selection of Women *helped launch the women's suffrage movement. His other main writings include* A System of Logic, Principles of Political Economy, Three Essays on Religion, *and* Utilitarianism. *Although Mill lived part of his life in France, he did serve in the British Parliament where he supported such measures as birth control and compulsory education as well as equality for women; these stands made him a radical in his time.*

Mill's book, Utilitarianism, *expounds the theory of the greatest happiness for the greatest number as previously described. As a disciple of his father, James Mill, and of Jeremy Bentham, Mill was a strong advocate of the utilitarian theory as well as both empiricism and rationalism. Although he preferred modes of happiness that are qualitatively higher, he thought we should maximize happiness or pleasure for all, and that there could be no higher aim for humanity. To Mill, this "principle of utility" is the standard for ethical conduct and the highest rendering of the golden rule.*

WHAT UTILITARIANISM IS

A passing remark is all that needs be given to the ignorant blunder of supposing that those who stand up for utility as the test of right and wrong, use the term in that restricted and merely colloquial sense in which utility is opposed to pleasure. An apology is due to the philosophical opponents of utilitarianism, for even the momentary appearance of confounding them with any one capable of so absurd a misconception; which is the more extraordinary, inasmuch as the contrary accusation, of referring everything to pleasure, and that too in its grossest form, is another of the common charges against utilitarianism: and, as has been pointedly remarked by an able writer, the same sort of persons, and often the very same persons, denounce the theory "as impracticably dry when the word utility precedes the word pleasure, and as too practicably voluptuous when the word pleasure precedes the word utility." Those who know anything about the matter are aware that every writer, from Epicurus to Bentham, who maintained the theory of utility, meant by it, not something to be contradistinguished from pleasure, but pleasure itself, together with exemption from pain; and instead of opposing the useful to the agreeable or the ornamental, have always declared that the useful means these, among other things. Yet the common herd, including the herd of writers, not only in newspapers and periodicals, but in books of weight and pretension, are perpetually falling into this shallow mistake. Having caught up the word utilitarian, while knowing nothing whatever about it but its sound, they habitually express by it the rejection, or the neglect, of pleasure in some of its forms; of beauty, of ornament, or of amusement. Nor is the term thus ignorantly misapplied solely in disparagement, but occasionally in compliment; as though it implied superiority to frivolity and the mere pleasures of the moment. And this perverted use is the only one in which the word is popularly known, and the one from which the new generation are acquiring their sole notion of its meaning. Those who introduced the word, but who had for many years discontinued it as a distinctive appellation, may well feel themselves called upon to resume it, if by doing so they can hope to contribute anything towards rescuing it from this utter degradation.[1]

The creed which accepts as the foundation of morals, Utility, or the Greatest Happiness Principle, holds that actions are right in proportion as they tend to promote happiness, wrong as they tend to produce the reverse of happiness. By happiness is intended pleasure, and the absence of pain; by unhappiness, pain, and the privation of pleasure. To give a clear view of the moral standard set up by the theory, much more requires to be said; in particular, what things it includes in the ideas of pain and pleasure; and to what extent this is left an open question. But these supplementary explanations do not affect the theory of life on which this theory of morality is grounded—

---

[1] The author of this essay has reason for believing himself to be the first person who brought the word utilitarian into use. He did not invent it, but adopted it from a passing expression in Mr. Galt's *Annals of the Parish*. After using is as a designation for several years, he and others abandoned it from a growing dislike to anything resembling a badge or watchword of sectarian distinction. But as a name for one single opinion, not a set of opinions—to denote the recognition of utility as a standard, not any particular way of applying it—the term supplies a want in the language, and offers, in many cases, a convenient mode of avoiding tiresome circumlocution.

namely, that pleasure, and freedom from pain, are the only things desirable as ends; and that all desirable things (which are as numerous in the utilitarian as in any other scheme) are desirable either for the pleasure inherent in themselves, or as means to the promotion of pleasure and the prevention of pain.

Now, such a theory of life excites in many minds, and among them in some of the most estimable in feeling and purpose, inveterate dislike. To suppose that life has (as they express it) no higher end than pleasure—no better and nobler object of desire and pursuit—they designate as utterly mean and grovelling; as a doctrine worthy only of swine, to whom the followers of Epicurus were, at a very early period, contemptuously likened; and modern holders of the doctrine are occasionally made the subject of equally polite comparisons by its German, French, and English assailants.

When thus attacked, the Epicureans have always answered, that it is not they, but their accusers, who represent human nature in a degrading light; since the accusation supposes human beings to be capable of no pleasures except those of which swine are capable. If this supposition were true, the charge could not be gainsaid, but would then be no longer an imputation; for if the sources of pleasure were precisely the same to human beings and to swine, the rule of life which is good enough for the one would be good enough for the other. The comparison of the Epicurean life to that of beasts is felt as degrading, precisely because a beast's pleasures do not satisfy a human being's conceptions of happiness. Human beings have faculties more elevated than the animal appetites, and when once made conscious of them, do not regard anything as happiness which does not include their gratification. I do not, indeed, consider the Epicureans to have been by any means faultless in drawing out their scheme of consequences from the utilitarian principle. To do this in any sufficient manner, many Stoic, as well as Christian elements require to be included. But there is no known Epicurean theory of life which does not assign to the pleasures of the intellect; of the feelings and imagination, and of the moral sentiments, a much higher value as pleasures than to those of mere sensation. It must be admitted, however, that utilitarian writers in general have placed the superiority of mental over bodily pleasures chiefly in the greater permanency, safety, uncostliness, etc., of the former—that is, in their circumstantial advantages rather than in their intrinsic nature. And on all these points utilitarians have fully proved their case; but they might have taken the other, and, as it may be called, higher ground, with entire consistency. It is quite compatible with the principle of utility to recognise the fact, that some *kinds* of pleasure are more desirable and more valuable than others. It would be absurd that while, in estimating all other things, quality is considered as well as quantity, the estimation of pleasures should be supposed to depend on quantity alone.

If I am asked, what I mean by difference of quality in pleasures, or what makes one pleasure more valuable than another, merely as a pleasure, except its being greater in amount, there is but one possible answer. Of two pleasures, if there be one to which all or almost all who have experience of both give a decided preference, irrespective of any feeling of moral obligation to prefer it, that is the more desirable pleasure. If one of the two is, by those who are competently acquainted with both, placed so far above the other that they prefer it, even though knowing it to be attended with a greater amount of discontent, and would not resign it for any quantity of the other pleasure which their nature is capable of, we are justified in ascribing to the preferred enjoyment a superiority in quality, so far outweighing quantity as to render it, in comparison, of small account.

Now it is an unquestionable fact that those who are equally acquainted with, and equally capable of appreciating and enjoying, both, do give a most marked preference to the manner of existence which employs their higher faculties. Few human creatures would consent to be changed into any of the lower animals, for a promise of the fullest allowance of a beast's pleasures; no intelligent human being would consent to be a fool, no instructed person would be an ignoramus, no person of feeling and conscience would be selfish and base, even though they should be persuaded that the fool, the dunce, or the rascal is better satisfied with his lot than they are with theirs. They would not resign what they possess more than he, for the most complete satisfaction of all the desires which they have in common with him. If they ever fancy they would, it is only in cases of unhappiness so extreme, that to escape from it they would exchange their lot for almost any other, however undesirable in their own eyes. A being of higher faculties requires more to make him happy, is capable probably of more acute suffering, and is certainly accessible to it at more points, than one of an inferior type; but in spite of these liabilities, he can never really wish to sink into what he feels to be a lower grade of existence. We may give what explanation we please of this unwillingness; we may attribute it to pride, a name which is given indiscriminately to some of the most and to some of the least estimable feelings of which mankind are capable; we may refer it to the love of liberty and personal independence, an appeal to which was with the Stoics one of the most effective means for the inculcation of it; to the love of power, or to the love of excitement, both of which do really enter into and contribute to it: but its most appropriate appellation is a sense of dignity, which all human beings possess in one form or other, and in some, though by no means in exact, proportion to their higher faculties, and which is so essential a part of the happiness of those in whom it is strong, that nothing which conflicts with it could be, otherwise than momentarily, an object of desire to them. Whoever supposes that this preference takes place at a sacrifice of happiness—that the superior being, in anything like equal circumstances, is not happier than the inferior—confounds the two very different ideas, of happiness, and content. It is indisputable that the being whose capacities of enjoyment are low, has the greatest chance of having them fully satisfied; and a highly-endowed being will always feel that any happiness which he can look for, as the world is constituted, is imperfect. But he can learn to bear its imperfections, if they are at all bearable; and they will not make him envy the being who is indeed unconscious of the imperfections, but only because he feels not at all the good which those imperfections qualify. It is better to be a human being dissatisfied than a pig satisfied; better to be Socrates dissatisfied than a fool satisfied. And if the fool, or the pig, is of a different opinion, it is because they only know their own side of the question. The other party to the comparison knows both sides.

It may be objected, that many who are capable of the higher pleasures, occasionally, under the influence of temptation, postpone them to the lower. But this is quite compatible with a full appreciation of the intrinsic superiority of the higher. Men often, from infirmity of character, make their election for the nearer good, though they know it to be the less valuable; and this no less when the choice is between two bodily pleasures, than when it is between bodily and mental. They pursue sensual indulgences to the injury of health, though perfectly aware that health is the greater good. It may be further objected, that many who begin with youthful enthusiasm for everything noble, as they advance in years sink into indolence and selfishness. But I do not believe that those who undergo this very common change, voluntarily choose the lower description of pleasures in preference to the higher. I believe that before they devote themselves exclusively to the one, they have already become incapable of the other. Capacity for the nobler feelings is in most natures a very tender plant, easily killed, not only by hostile influences, but by mere want of sustenance; and in the majority of young persons it speedily dies away if the occupations to which their position in life has devoted them, and the society into which it has thrown them, are not favorable to keeping that higher capacity in exercise. Men lose their high aspirations as they lose their intellectual tastes, because they have not time or opportunity for indulging them; and they addict themselves to inferior pleasures, not because they deliberately prefer them, but because they are either the only ones to which they have access, or the only ones which they are any longer capable of enjoying. It may be questioned whether any one who has remained equally susceptible to both classes of pleasures, ever knowingly and calmly preferred the lower; though many, in all ages, have broken down in an ineffectual attempt to combine both.

From this verdict of the only competent judges, I apprehend there can be no appeal. On a question which is the best worth having of two pleasures, or which of two modes of existence is the most grateful to the feelings, apart from its moral attributes and from its consequences, the judgment of those who are qualified by knowledge of both, or, if they differ, that of the majority among them, must be admitted as final. And there needs be the less hesitation to accept this judgment respecting the quality of pleasures, since there is no other tribunal to be referred to even on the question of quantity. What means are there of determining which is the acutest of two pains, or the intensest of two pleasurable sensations, except the general suffrage of those who are familiar with both? Neither pains nor pleasures are homogeneous, and pain is always heterogeneous with pleasure. What is there to decide whether a particular pleasure is worth purchasing at the cost of a particular pain, except the feelings and judgment of the experienced? When, therefore, those feelings and judgment declare the pleasures derived from the higher faculties to be preferable *in kind*, apart from the question of intensity, to those of which the animal nature, disjoined from the higher faculties, is susceptible, they are entitled on this subject to the same regard.

I have dwelt on this point, as being a necessary part of a perfectly just conception of Utility or Happiness, considered as the directive rule of human conduct. But it is by no means an indispensable condition to the acceptance of the utilitarian standard; for that standard is not the agent's own greatest happiness, but the greatest amount of happiness altogether; and if it may possibly be doubted whether a noble character is always the happier for its nobleness, there can be no doubt that it makes other people happier, and that the world in general is immensely a gainer by it. Utilitarianism, therefore, could only attain its end by the general cultivation of nobleness of character, even if each individual were only benefited by the nobleness of others, and his own, so far as happiness is concerned, were a sheer deduction from the benefit. But the bare enunciation of such an absurdity as this last, renders refutation superfluous.

According to the Greatest Happiness Principle, as above explained, the ultimate end, with reference to and for the sake of which all other things are desirable (whether we are considering our own good or that of other people), is an existence exempt as far as possible from pain, and as rich as possible in enjoyments, both in point of quantity and quality; the test of quality, and the rule for measuring it against quantity, being the preference felt by those who, in their opportunities of experience, to which must be added their habits of self-consciousness and self-observation, are best furnished with the means of comparison. This, being, according to the utilitarian opinion, the end of human action, is necessarily also the standard of morality; which may accordingly be defined, the rules and precepts for human conduct, by the observance of which an existence such as has been described might be, to the greatest extent possible, secured to all mankind; and not to them only, but, so far as the nature of things admits, to the whole sentient creation.

Against this doctrine, however, arises another class of objectors, who say that happiness, in any form, cannot be the rational purpose of human life and action; because, in the first place, it is unattainable: and they contemptuously ask, What right hast thou to be happy? a question which Mr. Carlyle clenches by the addition, What right, a short time ago, hadst thou even *to be*? Next, they say, that men can do *without* happiness; that all noble human beings have felt this, and could not have become noble but by learning the lesson of Entsagen, or renunciation; which lesson, thoroughly learnt and submitted to, they affirm to be the beginning and necessary condition of all virtue.

The first of these objections would go to the root of the matter were it well founded; for if no happiness is to be had at all by human beings, the attainment of it cannot be the end of morality, or of any rational conduct. Though, even in that case, something might still be said for the utilitarian theory; since utility includes not solely the pursuit of happiness, but the prevention or mitigation of unhappiness; and if the former aim be chimerical, there will be all the greater scope and more imperative need for the latter, so long at least as mankind think fit to live, and do not take refuge in the simultaneous act of suicide recommended under certain conditions by Novalis. When, however, it is thus positively asserted to be impossible that human life should be happy, the assertion, if not something like a verbal quibble, is at least an exaggeration. If by happiness be meant a continuity of highly pleasurable excitement, it is evident enough that this is impossible. A state of exalted pleasure lasts only moments, or in some cases, and with some intermissions, hours or days, and is the occasional brilliant flash of enjoyment, not its permanent and steady flame. Of this the philosophers who have taught that happiness is the end of life were as fully aware as those who taunt them. The happiness which they meant was not a life of rapture, but moments of such, in an existence made up of few and transitory pains, many and various pleasures, with a decided predominance of the active over the passive, and having as the foundation of the whole, not to expect more from life than it is capable of bestowing. A life thus composed, to those who have been fortunate enough to obtain it, has always appeared worthy of the name of happiness. And such an existence is even now the lot of many, during some considerable portion of their lives. The present wretched education, and wretched social arrangements, are the only real hindrance to its being attainable by almost all.

The objectors perhaps may doubt whether human beings, if taught to consider happiness as the end of life, would be satisfied with such a moderate share of it. But great numbers of mankind have been satisfied with much less. The main constituents of a satisfied life appear to be two, either of which by itself is often found sufficient for the purpose: tranquillity, and excitement. With much tranquillity, many find that they can be content with very little pleasure: with much excitement, many can reconcile themselves to a considerable quantity of pain. There is assuredly no inherent impossibility in enabling even the mass of mankind to unite both; since the two are so far from being incompatible that they are in natural alliance, the prolongation of either being a preparation for, and exciting a wish for, the other. It is only those in whom indolence amounts to a vice, that do not desire excitement after an interval of repose; it is only those in whom the need of excitement is a disease, that feel the tranquillity which follows excitement dull and insipid, instead of pleasurable in direct proportion to the excitement which preceded it. When people who are tolerably fortunate in their outward lot do not find in life sufficient enjoyment to make it valuable to them, the cause generally is, caring for nobody but themselves. To those who have neither public nor private affections, the excitements of life are much curtailed, and in any case dwindle in value as the time approaches when all selfish interests must be terminated by death: while those who leave after them objects of personal affection, and especially those who have also cultivated a fellow-feeling with the collective interests of mankind, retain as lively an interest in life on the eve of death as in the vigor of youth and health. Next to selfishness, the principal cause which makes life unsatisfactory, is want of mental cultivation. A cultivated mind—I do not mean that of a philosopher, but any mind to which the fountains of knowledge have been opened, and which has been taught, in any tolerable degree, to exercise its faculties—finds sources of inexhaustible interest in all that surrounds it; in the objects of nature, the achievements of art, the imaginations of poetry, the incidents of history, the ways of mankind past and present, and their prospects in the future. It is possible, indeed, to become indifferent to all this, and that too without having exhausted a thousandth part of it; but only when one has had from the beginning no moral or human interest in these things, and has sought in them only the gratification of curiosity. ...

I must again repeat, what the assailants of utilitarianism seldom have the justice to acknowledge, that the happiness which forms the utilitarian standard of what is right in conduct, is not the agent's own happiness, but that of all concerned. As between his own happiness and that of others, utilitarianism requires him to be as strictly impartial as a disinterested and benevolent spectator. In the golden rule of Jesus of Nazareth, we read the complete spirit of the ethics of utility. To do as one would be done by, and to love one's neighbor as oneself, constitute the ideal perfection of utilitarian morality. As the means of making the nearest approach to this ideal, utility would enjoin, first, that laws and social arrangements should place the happiness, or (as speaking practically it may be called) the interest, of every individual, as nearly as possible in harmony with the interest of the whole; and secondly, that education and opinion, which have so vast a power over human character, should so use that power as to establish in the mind of every individual an indissoluble association between his own happiness and the good of the whole; especially between his own happiness and the practice of such modes of conduct, negative and positive, as regard for the universal happiness prescribes: so that not only he may be unable to conceive the possibility of happiness to himself, consistently with conduct opposed to the general good, but also that a direct impulse to promote the general good may be in every individual one of the habitual motives of action, and the sentiments connected therewith may fill a large and prominent place in every human being's sentient existence.

STUDY QUESTIONS

1. What is the principle of Utility, and how can it be applied in moral decision making?

2. How does Mill define happiness?

3. What is Mill's criterion for differentiating between more and less desirable pleasures?

4. According to Mill, under what circumstances do people find insufficient enjoyment in life?

5. Suppose that it would bring happiness to the majority to remove the minority, as happened in Yugoslavia during "ethnic cleansing." Would that be justified? Why or why not?

Groundwork of the Metaphysic of Morals (Chapter 1)

Immanuel Kant

Immanuel Kant (1724–1804) was a German philosopher who is generally regarded as one of the greatest minds in the history of philosophy. Kant was principally concerned with epistemology, metaphysics, ethics, and religion, in that order. His central work, The Critique of Pure Reason, *deals with the knowledge and attempts a synthesis of sense perception and reason.* The Critique of Practical Reason *explains Kant's concept of the freedom of the individual, and his* General Natural History *and* Theory of the Heavens *contains various scientific views.*

In the Groundwork of the Metaphysic of Morals, *an excerpt from which appears below, Kant presents a foundation for ethical conduct. Instead of the happiness principle of Bentham and Mill, he offers his Categorical Imperative: "I ought never to act except in such a way that I can also will that my maxim should become a universal law." Kant also maintains that a good will is critically important in ethical behavior because we should only will actions that are right for all. Everyone is required to do his or her duty by willing those acts that are right in themselves and therefore universal obligations; whether happiness is produced is irrelevant.*

PASSAGE FROM ORDINARY RATIONAL KNOWLEDGE OF MORALITY TO PHILOSOPHICAL

The Good Will

Nothing can possibly be conceived in the world, or even out of it, which can be called good, without qualification, except a *good will*. Intelligence, wit, judgment, and the other *talents* of the mind, however they may be named, or courage, resolution, perseverance, as qualities of *temperament*, are undoubtedly good and desirable in many respects; but these gifts of nature may also become extremely bad and mischievous if the will which is to make use of them, and which, therefore, constitutes what is called *charac-ter*, is not good. It is the same with the *gifts of fortune*. Power, riches, honor, even health, and the general well-being and contentment with one's condi-tion which is called *happiness*, inspire pride, and often presumption, if there is not a good will to correct the influence of these on the mind, and with this also to rectify the whole principle of acting and adapt it to its end. The sight of a being who is not adorned with a single feature of a pure and good will, enjoying unbroken prosperity, can never give pleasure to an im-partial rational spectator. Thus a good will appears to constitute the indis-pensable condition even of being worthy of happiness.

There are even some qualities which are of service to this good will itself and may facilitate its action, yet which have no intrinsic unconditional value, but always presuppose a good will, and this qualifies the esteem that we justly have for them and does not permit us to regard them as absolutely good. Moderation in the affections and passions, self-control, and calm de-liberation are not only good in many respects, but even seem to constitute part of the *intrinsic* worth of the person; but they are far from deserving to be called good without qualification, although they have been so uncondi-tionally praised by the ancients. For without the principles of a good will, they may become extremely bad, and the coolness of a villain not only makes him far more dangerous, but also directly makes him more abomina-ble in our eyes than he would have been without it.

The Good Will and Its Results

A good will is good not because of what it performs or effects, not by its apt-ness for the attainment of some proposed end, but simply by virtue of the volition; that is, it is good in itself, and considered by itself is to be esteemed much higher than all that can be brought about by it in favor of any inclina-tion, nay even of the sum total of all inclinations. Even if it should happen that, owing to special disfavor of fortune, or the niggardly provision of a step-motherly nature, this will should wholly lack power to accomplish its purpose, if with its greatest efforts it should yet achieve nothing, and there should remain only the good will (not, to be sure, a mere wish, but the sum-moning of all means in our power), then, like a jewel, it would still shine by its own light, as a thing which has its whole value in itself. Its usefulness or fruitfulness can neither add nor take away anything from this value. It would be, as it were, only the setting to enable us to handle it the more con-veniently in common commerce, or to attract to it the attention of those who are not yet connoisseurs, but not to recommend it to true connoisseurs, or to determine its value.

The Function of Reason

There is, however, something so strange in this idea of the absolute value of the mere will, in which no account is taken of its utility, that notwithstanding the thorough assent of even common reason to the idea, yet a suspicion must arise that it may perhaps really be the product of mere high-flown fancy, and that we may have misunderstood the purpose of nature in assigning reason as the governor of our will. Therefore we will examine this idea from this point of view.

In the physical constitution of an organized being, that is, a being adapted suitably to the purposes of life, we assume it as a fundamental principle that no organ for any purpose will be found but what is also the fittest and best adapted for that purpose. Now in a being which has reason and a will, if the proper object of nature were its *conservation*, its *welfare*, in a word, its *happiness*, then nature would have hit upon a very bad arrangement in selecting the reason of the creature to carry out this purpose. For all the actions which the creature has to perform with a view to this purpose, and the whole rule of its conduct, would be far more surely prescribed to it by instinct, and that end would have been attained thereby much more certainly than it ever can be by reason. Should reason have been communicated to this favored creature over and above, it must only have served it to contemplate the happy constitution of its nature, to admire it, to congratulate itself thereon, and to feel thankful for it to the beneficent cause, but not that it should subject its desires to that weak and delusive guidance and meddle bunglingly with the purpose of nature. In a word, nature would have taken care that reason should not break forth into *practical exercise*, nor have the presumption, with its weak insight, to think out for itself the plan of happiness, and of the means of attaining it. Nature would not only have taken on herself the choice of the ends, but also of the means, and with wise foresight would have entrusted both to instinct.

And, in fact, we find that the more a cultivated reason applies itself with deliberate purpose to the enjoyment of life and happiness, so much the more does the man fail of true satisfaction. And from this circumstance there arises in many, if they are candid enough to confess it, a certain degree of *misology*, that is, hatred of reason, especially in the case of those who are most experienced in the use of it, because after calculating all the advantages they derive, I do not say from the invention of all the arts of common luxury, but even from the sciences (which seem to them to be after all only a luxury of the understanding), they find that they have, in fact, only brought more trouble on their shoulders, rather than gained in happiness; and they end by envying, rather than despising, the more common stamp of men who keep closer to the guidance of mere instinct and do not allow their reason much influence on their conduct. And this we must admit, that the judgment of those who would very much lower the lofty eulogies of the advantages which reason gives us in regard to the happiness and satisfaction of life, or who would even reduce them below zero, is by no means morose or ungrateful to the goodness with which the world is governed, but that there lies at the root of these judgments the idea that our existence has a different and far nobler end, for which, and not for happiness, reason is properly intended, and which must, therefore, be regarded as the supreme condition to which the private ends of man must, for the most part, be postponed.

For as reason is not competent to guide the will with certainty in regard to its objects and the satisfaction of all our wants (which it to some extent even multiplies), this being an end to which an implanted instinct would have led with much greater certainty; and since, nevertheless, reason is imparted to us as a practical faculty, i.e., as one which is to have influence on the *will*, therefore, admitting that nature generally in the distribution of her capacities has adapted the means to the end, its true destination must be to produce a *will*, not merely *good* as a *means* to something else, but good *in itself*, for which reason was absolutely necessary. This will then, though not indeed the sole and complete good, must be the supreme good and the condition of every other, even of the desire of happiness. Under these circumstances, there is nothing inconsistent with the wisdom of nature in the fact that the cultivation of the reason, which is requisite for the first and unconditional purpose, does in many ways interfere, at least in this life, with the attainment of the second, which is always conditional, namely, happiness. Nay, it may even reduce it to nothing, without nature thereby failing of her purpose. For reason recognizes the establishment of a good will as its highest practical destination, and in attaining this purpose is capable only of a satisfaction of its own proper kind, namely that from the attainment of an end, which end again is determined by reason only, notwithstanding that this may involve many a disappointment to the ends of inclination.

The Good Will and Duty

We have then to develop the notion of a will which deserves to be highly esteemed for itself and is good without a view to anything further, a notion which exists already in the sound natural understanding, requiring rather to be cleared up than to be taught, and which in estimating the value of our actions always takes the first place and constitutes the condition of all the rest. In order to do this, we will take the notion of *duty*, which includes that of a good will, although implying certain subjective restrictions and hindrances. These, however, far from concealing it, or rendering it unrecognizable, rather bring it out by contrast and make it shine forth so much the brighter.

I omit here all actions which are already recognized as inconsistent with duty, although they may be useful for this or that purpose, for with these the question whether they are done *from duty* cannot arise at all, since they even conflict with it. I also set aside those actions which really conform to duty, but to which men have *no direct inclination*, performing them because they are impelled thereto by some other inclination. For in this case we can readily distinguish whether the action which agrees with duty is done *from duty*, or from a selfish view. It is much harder to make this distinction when the action accords with duty and the subject has besides a direct inclination to it. For example, it is always a matter of duty that a dealer should not over charge an inexperienced purchaser; and wherever there is much commerce the prudent tradesman does not overcharge, but keeps a fixed price for everyone, so that a child buys of him as well as any other. Men are thus *honestly* served; but this is not enough to make us believe that the tradesman has so acted from duty and from principles of honesty: his own advantage required it; it is out of the question in this case to suppose that he might besides have a direct inclination in favor of the buyers, so that, as it were, from love he should give no advantage to one over another. Accordingly the action was done neither from duty nor from direct inclination, but merely with a selfish view.

On the other hand, it is a duty to maintain one's life; and, in addition, everyone has also a direct inclination to do so. But on account of this the often anxious care which most men take for it has no intrinsic worth, and their maxim has no moral import. They preserve their life *as duty requires*, no doubt, but not *because duty requires*. On the other band, if adversity and hopeless sorrow have completely taken away the relish for life; if the unfortunate one, strong in mind, indignant at his fate rather than desponding or dejected, wishes for death, and yet preserves his life without loving it— not from inclination or fear, but from duty—then his maxim has a moral worth...

It is in this manner, undoubtedly, that we are to understand those passages of Scripture also in which we are commanded to love our neighbor, even our enemy. For love, as an affection, cannot be commanded, but beneficence for duty's sake may; even though we are not impelled to it by any inclination—nay, are even repelled by a natural and unconquerable aversion. This is *practical* love and not *pathological*—a love which is seated in the will, and not in the propensions of sense—in principles of action and not of tender sympathy; and it is this love alone which can be commanded.

The Formal Principle of Duty

The second proposition is: That an action done from duty derives its moral worth, *not from the purpose* which is to be attained by it, but from the maxim by which it is determined, and therefore does not depend on the realization of the object of the action, but merely on the *principle of volition* by which the action has taken place, without regard to any object of desire. It is clear from what precedes that the purposes which we may have in view in our actions, or their effects regarded as ends and springs of the will, cannot give to actions any unconditional or moral worth. In what, then, can their worth lie, if it is not to consist in the will and in reference to its expected effect? It cannot lie anywhere but *in the principle of the will* without regard to the ends which can be attained by the action. For the will stands between its *a priori* principle, which is formal, and its *a posteriori* spring, which is material, as between two roads, and as it must be determined by something, it will have to be determined by the formal principle of volition when an action is done from duty, in which case every material principle has been withdrawn from it.

Reverence For the Law

The third proposition, which is a consequence of the two preceding, I would express thus: *Duty is the necessity of acting from respect for the law.* I may have *inclination* for an object as the effect of my proposed action, but I *cannot have respect* for it, just for this reason, that it is an effect and not an energy of will. Similarly I cannot have respect for inclination, whether my own or another's; I can at most, if my own, approve it; if another's, some-times even love it; i.e., look on it as favorable to my own interest. It is only what is connected with my will as a principle, by no means as an effect-what does not subserve my inclination, but overpowers it, or at least in case of choice excludes it from its calculation—in other words, simply the law of itself, which can be an object of respect, and hence a command. Now an action done from duty must wholly exclude the influence of inclination and with it every object of the will, so that nothing remains which can determine the will except objectively the *law*, and subjectively *pure respect* for this practical law, and consequently the maxim[1] that I should follow this law even to the thwarting of all my inclinations.

Thus the moral worth of an action does not lie in the effect expected from it, nor in any principle of action which requires to borrow its motive from this expected effect. For all these effects—agreeableness of one's condition and even the promotion of the happiness of others—could have been also brought about by other causes, so that for this there would have been no need of the will of a rational being; whereas it is in this alone that the su-preme and unconditional good can be found. The pre-eminent good which we call moral can therefore consist in nothing else than the *conception of law* in itself, *which certainly is only possible in a rational being*, in so far as this conception, and not the expected effect, determines the will. This is a good which is already present in the person who acts accordingly, and we have not to wait for it to appear first in the result.[2]

---

[1] A *maxim* is the subjective principle of volition. The objective principle (i.e., that which would also serve subjectively as a practical principle to all rational beings if reason had full power over the faculty of desire) is the practical *law*.

[2] It might be here objected to me that I take refuge behind the word *respect* in an obscure feeling, in-stead of giving a distinct solution of the question by a concept of the reason. But although respect is a feeling, it is not a feeling *received* through influence, but is *self-wrought* by a rational concept, and, therefore, is specifically distinct from all feelings of the former kind, which may be referred either to in-clination or fear. What I recognise immediately as a law for me, I recognise with respect. This merely signifies the consciousness that my will is *subordinate* to a law, without the intervention of other influ-ences on my sense. The immediate determination of the will by the law, and the consciousness of this, is called *respect*, so that this is regarded as an *effect* of the law on the subject, and not as the cause of it. Re-spect is properly the conception of a worth which thwarts my self-love. Accordingly it is something which is considered neither as an object of inclination nor of fear, although it has something analogous to both. The *object* of respect is the *law* only, and that the law which we impose *on ourselves* and yet recog-nise as necessary in itself. As a law, we are subjected to it without consulting self-love; as imposed by us on ourselves, it is a result of our will. In the former aspect it has an analogy to fear, in the latter to inclina-tion. Respect for a person is properly only respect for the law (of honesty, etc.) of which he gives us an example. Since we also look on the improvement of our talents as a duty, we consider that we see in a per-son of talents, as it were, the *example of a law* (viz., to become like him in this by exercise), and this con-stitutes our respect. All so-called moral *interest* consists simply in *respect* for the law.

The Categorical Imperative

But what sort of law can that be, the conception of which must determine the will, even without paying any regard to the effect expected from it, in order that this will may be called good absolutely and without qualification? As I have deprived the will of every impulse which could arise to it from obedience to any law, there remains nothing but the universal conformity of its actions to law in general, which alone is to serve the will as a principle, i.e., I am never to act otherwise than so *that I could also will that my maxim should become a universal law.* Here, now, it is the simple conformity to law in general, without assuming any particular law applicable to certain actions, that serves the will as its principle and must so serve it, if duty is not to be a vain delusion and a chimerical notion. The common reason of men in its practical judgments perfectly coincides with this and always has in view the principle here suggested.

Let the question be, for example: May I when in distress make a promise with the intention not to keep it? I readily distinguish here between the two significations which the question may have: Whether it is prudent, or whether it is right, to make a false promise? The former may undoubtedly be the case. I see clearly indeed that it is not enough to extricate myself from a present difficulty by means of this subterfuge, but it must be well considered whether there may not hereafter spring from this lie much greater inconvenience than that from which I now free myself, and as, with all my supposed *cunning*, the consequences cannot be so easily foreseen but that credit once lost may be much more injurious to me than any mischief which I seek to avoid at present, it should be considered whether it would not be *more prudent* to act herein according to a universal maxim and to make it a habit to promise nothing except with the intention of keeping it. But it is soon clear to me that such a maxim will still only be based on the fear of consequences. Now it is a wholly different thing to be truthful from duty and to be so from apprehension of injurious consequences. In the first case, the very notion of the action already implies a law for me; in the second case, I must first look about elsewhere to see what results may be combined with it which would affect myself. For to deviate from the principle of duty is beyond all doubt wicked; but to be unfaithful to my maxim of prudence may often be very advantageous to me, although to abide by it is certainly safer. The shortest way, however, and an unerring one, to discover the answer to this question whether a lying promise is consistent with duty, is to ask myself, "Should I be content that my maxim (to extricate myself from difficulty by a false promise) should hold good as a universal law, for myself as well as for others?" and should I be able to say to myself, "Every one may make a deceitful promise when he finds himself in a difficulty from which he cannot otherwise extricate himself?" Then I presently become aware that while I can will the lie, I can by no means will that lying should be a universal law. For with such a law there would be no promises at all, since it would be in vain to allege my intention in regard to my future actions to those who would not believe this allegation, or if they over hastily did so would pay me back in my own coin. Hence my maxim, as soon as it should be made a universal law, would necessarily destroy itself.

I do not, therefore, need any far-reaching penetration to discern what I have to do in order that my will may be morally good. Inexperienced in the course of the world, incapable of being prepared for all its contingencies, I only ask myself: Canst thou also will that thy maxim should be a universal law? If not, then it must be rejected, and that not because of a disadvantage accruing from it to myself or even to others, but because it cannot enter as a principle into a possible universal legislation, and reason extorts from me immediate respect for such legislation. I do not indeed as yet discern on what this respect is based (this the philosopher may inquire), but at least I understand this, that it is an estimation of the worth which far outweighs all worth of what is recommended by inclination, and that the necessity of acting from *pure* respect for the practical law is what constitutes duty, to which every other motive must give place, because it is the condition of a will being good *in itself*, and the worth of such a will is above everything.

STUDY QUESTIONS

1. What does Kant mean by "good will?"

2. Does Kant believe that reason is the best way to attain happiness?

3. Why does Kant think that we should not act out of inclination but out of duty? Would you rather live next to someone who is kind by disposition or on principle?

4. Explain the meaning of the categorical imperative. How can it be criticized?

5. In what way(s) does Kant's formalistic ethic differ from Mill's teleological approach?

B. Expression in Film

Crash

Director: Paul Haggis

Screenwriters: Paul Haggis and Robert Moresco

Paul Haggis (1953–) holds the unique distinction of winning Academy Awards in two consecutive years for Best Picture: Million Dollar Baby *in 2005, and* Crash *in 2006. Haggis also won an Oscar for Best Original Screenplay for* Crash, *and the film was nominated for six Academy Awards as well as a Golden Globe and the Grand Prize at the Deauville Film Festival.*

Haggis also wrote the screenplay for Flags of Our Fathers *directed by Clint Eastwood, and the James Bond film* Casino Royale. *Prior to that,* Haggis worked in television, creating such successful shows as EZ Street *and* Walker, Texas Ranger—*the latter something of an embarrassment to him. In fact, he moved to films in 2000 after waking up drenched in a cold sweat one night picturing his tombstone saying* Paul Haggis: Creator of Walker, Texas Ranger.

Although Crash *was tapped for an Oscar by several critics, the actual award was surrounded by controversy.* Brokeback Mountain *had also been nominated that year and some commentators believed that, because of its homosexual content, the right-wing prevented it from being chosen. However,* Crash *can stand on its own merits as a remarkable study of multicultural conflict in Los Angeles, a microcosm of diversity in the nation. In the light of the collisions depicted in the film, it is instructive that Paul Haggis is co-founder of Artists for Peace and Justice, and serves on the Advisory Board of The Center for the Advancement of Non-Violence.*

SYNOPSIS

As the title implies, *Crash* is about collisions, not so much between cars as between cultures that ricochet off of each other during a 36-hour period in

Los Angeles. The people involved comprise a crazy quilt of ethnic, racial, and social groups, including Hispanics, Asians, and Iranians, blacks and whites, cops and criminals, the wealthy and the working class. Although coming from disparate backgrounds, the trajectory of their lives intersects through car wrecks, car jackings, and accidental killings, and the divisions that usually pertain are shattered. Tensions mount, stereotypes emerge, and anger is discharged, with the confrontations ultimately leading to greater tolerance.

The film is fragmented into multiple scenes involving numerous characters, but that fragmentation is part of the message, just as the car crashes are an objective correlative of the personal collisions. There are perhaps too many stories being told, and the coincidences are woven too neatly into a web, but the cumulative effect can justify the dramatic liberty. In a sense, the film is about loneliness and isolation, and about people wanting to reach out across ethnic lines but unwilling to leave the safety of their own group. We tend to identify with people who are like ourselves. The need for contact and trust and care is frustrated as people aggressively defend their territory and distrust differences. As one character is made to say, "I think we miss that touch so much that we crash into each other just so that we can feel something."

Because of the episodic nature of the plot, the film might be best analyzed in terms of the major characters:

John Ryan (Matt Dillon), a white police officer, is first seen pulling over a black couple and molesting the woman under the pretext of a search. But his racism has a counterpart in a black insurance representative who refuses treatment to his father, diagnosed as having a bladder infection. She has the power to retaliate against a racist comment he made (as well as his patronizing attitude) by withholding approval, even though the disease is probably cancer. As a cop Ryan can take away people's freedom or people's lives, but he is powerless in this situation. He pleads with her, explaining that his father employed mainly black workers and lost his business when the city followed Affirmative Action guidelines, giving preference to minority-owned firms. She is unmoved, her racial animosity stronger than her compassion.

However, Ryan is one of the characters transformed by the interconnected events. In a later car crash he risks his life to pull a black woman from the burning wreckage—the woman he molested earlier. Recognizing him, she refuses his help but eventually gives in to save her life. Perhaps Haggis is saying that it sometimes takes a life-threatening situation to overcome prejudice, both sides of the racial divide.

The District Attorney is Rick Cabot (Brendan Fraser), a well-off, high-profile white man who is part of the criminal justice establishment. He is sensitive to situations involving race insofar as that affects his career. He might be having an affair with his African-American assistant, which could mean he is not a racist, although that is ambiguous.

One day he and his wife Jean (Sandra Bullock) have their Lincoln Navigator stolen at gunpoint by two black men, which puts him in an awkward position. He cannot protest too much publicly without appearing to be both privileged and prejudiced.

Jean is traumatized by the event, and feels even more alone and afraid than she did previously. She no longer regards her home as safe and at the same time feels that her fortress has become a prison. She expresses the dilemma that whites often experience: fear of violence from minorities, because of the disproportionate percentage of crimes they commit, combined with anxiety at being branded a racist for thinking this. However, in the end her attitudes too are changed. After she falls downstairs and finds that her upscale friends are too busy with things like massages to take her to the hospital, she realizes that her Hispanic maid is probably the best friend she has.

One of the thieves who steals the Cabot's car is Anthony (Chris "Ludacris" Bridges), a black, street-smart, car thief, who feels his crimes are justified; after all, he has been victimized and disadvantaged by the society. In a seriocomic scene just prior to the car jacking, he rails to his partner Peter about the ubiquity of prejudice, claiming that the black waitress at the restaurant gave them poor service because "black people don't tip." As they walk along the street he notices how Jean Cabot takes her husband's arm when she sees them. When Peter says she was just cold, he replies that she got much colder when she saw them coming. But he then validates her fears by stealing the couple's car.

Toward the end of the film Anthony also undergoes a metamorphosis. When he steals a van and discovers it is filled with Asians slaves, he does not sell it to the chop shop but sets them free in the Chinese district of Los Angeles, giving them the $40 in his pocket. His smile suggests his action is not due to feelings of solidarity but is a gesture toward fellow human beings.

Daniel (Michael Peña) is a Hispanic locksmith who changes the locks on Jean Cabot's house to make her feel safer, although when she sees his tattoos she wants the locks changed again, taking him for a gang member. In fact, he is an honest family man, devoted to his daughter Lara. When a bullet went through her window in their home in the barrio he moved to a safe suburb and enrolled his daughter in private school. He seems a hard-working, caring and decent man, trying to build a future using his mechanical skills and against the odds.

Daniel is not only distrusted by Jean but by Farhad (Shaun Toub), an Iranian shopkeeper, who believes he is being cheated when Daniel tells him his door needs to be replaced. Through some inverted logic, he then blames Daniel when a break-in occurs, and attempts to shoot him, firing at Lara instead. However, Farhad's daughter had accidentally bought bullets that were blanks. Lara attributes her deliverance to a magic cloak that her father had put around her, and Farhad believes a miracle has taken place, making him more reconciled with his environment.

A scene of blatant bigotry is shown earlier when Farhad and his daughter Dorri bought the gun. The store owner insults Dorri with sexual innuendos, treating her disrespectfully even though she is a doctor, and when the two speak Farsi he says, "Yo, Osama, plan the jihad on your own time."

The black couple that John Ryan stopped are Cameron Thayer (Terrence Howard), a television producer, and his wife Christine (Thandie Newton), both well-educated, successful Americans who have joined the mainstream. Because of their background (she was on the high school equestrian team), the body search was a particular humiliation. Christine blames Cameron for not defending her, for being an Uncle Tom, whereas he feels he was unable to protect her. As a black male he had been emasculated by institutional racism in the form of a lascivious white officer empowered to kill. He realizes how much of himself he had surrendered in order to belong in a white world, but the barriers were still in place and he feels diminished.

Nevertheless, he does not become a black militant. In one of the final scenes he resists a car jacking by Anthony and Peter, and in the melee that follows he is kept from being shot by Officer Hanson, the partner of John Ryan. Black men attacked him and a white man protected him, thus shattering the stereotypes.

Other scenes are enacted in this interlocking drama that underscore the complexity of the conflicts. For example, Graham Waters (Don Cheadle), an African-American detective, compromises his conscience in a deal involving racial politics in order to protect his younger brother, Peter. The irony is that his mother subsequently holds him responsible for his brother's death. In fact Peter was shot by Officer Hansen who mistakenly assumed he was drawing a gun; he was actually reaching for a St. Christopher medal. Hansen had been depicted as one of the least prejudiced characters in the film, but such accidents may be the inevitable consequence of racism.

In a sense, *Crash* is about isolation and contact, refracted through racial lenses. As Thoreau wrote. "The mass of men lead lives of quiet desperation," and we remain anxious and lonely partly through rejecting those foreign to ourselves. Through random disasters such as car crashes we are forced together and must confront the races we have demonized. Everyone is dented by the impacts but as a consequence we can emerge with greater understanding. Perhaps this tolerance is symbolized by the periodic, brilliant light of the film and the magical snow.

Los Angeles has even more of a car culture than the nation as a whole as well as a multicultural population, so it may be fitting to cast the collision between ethnic groups in those terms. Inside our cars we feel insulated and secure—until those cars collide. In these pileups our hidden antagonisms are forced to the surface in a disturbing way. But it is only after our prejudices are revealed to us that we are in a position to overcome them.

STUDY QUESTIONS

1. Is there an overarching ethic that Haggis seems to endorse, above the relativistic codes of each ethnic group?

2. Explain the transformations that several characters undergo. How do their conflicts trigger these changes?

3. Is it reasonable to prejudge a black person because the race as a whole has a record of committing a high percentage of crimes, or is that profiling and prejudice? Can it be avoided?

4. Do you see a parallel between the crashing of cars and the collision of ethnic groups? Why use car accidents in particular?

5. Can African Americans be prejudiced against their own race? Would that be a form of self-hatred?

On the Waterfront

Director: Elia Kazan

Screenplay: Budd Schulberg

Elia Kazan (1909–) is an American theater and film director as well as a novelist. He directed a number of stage plays including A Streetcar Named Desire, Death of a Salesman, *and* Cat on a Hot Tin Roof, *but he is best known as a director of films such as* A Tree Grows in Brooklyn, *and* East of Eden. *Kazan received Academy Awards as best director for* Gentleman's Agreement *and* On the Waterfront, *and he made successful motion pictures of several of his novels including* America, America *and* The Arrangement. *In his later years he wrote a series of novels,* The Assassins, The Understudy, *and* The Anatolian, *and he published an autobiography entitled* Elia Kazan, A Life.

On the Waterfront *usually makes the critics' list of "best films," and it has been placed on the National Film Registry of the Library of Congress. Among the numerous awards the film has received are the following:* 1954 Academy Awards: *Best Picture, Best Director (Elia Kazan), Best Actor (Marlon Brando), Best Supporting Actress (Eva Marie Saint), Best Art Direction/Set Decoration (B&W), Best Black and White Cinematography, Best Film Editing, Best Story and Screenplay;* 1954 Directors Guild of America Awards: *Best Director (Kazan);* 1955 Golden Globe Awards: *Best Actor—Drama (Marlon Brando), Best Director (Elia Kazan), Best Film—Drama;* 1954 National Board of Review Awards: *Ten Best Films of the Year;* 1954 New York Film Critics Awards: *Best Actor (Marlon Brando), Best Director (Elia Kazan), Best Film;* 1954 Academy Award Nominations: *Best Supporting Actor (Lee J. Cobb, Karle Malden, and Rod Steiger), Best Original Score.*

SYNOPSIS

On the Waterfront explores the world of corrupt labor unions and racketeering bosses, the dockworkers they intimidate through violence, and those with the courage to break the code of silence and stand up to the mob. The intense and dynamic performances by the cast make the film extremely realistic, especially the role played by Marlon Brando using the techniques of method acting. The authenticity of the film is further enhanced by being filmed on the docks of New York City and Hoboken, New Jersey, in cargo holds of ships, the rooftops of tenements, gritty church basements, and working-class bars; actual longshoremen were used as extras. A black-and-white format was deliberately chosen to heighten the sense of the stark environment without comforting color or ambiguity.

The director, Elia Kazan, actually meant the film as self-vindication for his informing on communists before the House Un-American Activities Committee. At that time, in 1954, members of the Communist Party and "fellow travelers" were being "purged" from Hollywood and blacklisted from working in films. Although Kazan himself was once sympathetic to communism, he came to regard the system as a threat to American life. He then felt obligated to give evidence against people in the movie industry who were card-carrying communists.

While Kazan regarded his testimony as patriotic, his left-wing friends branded it as traitorous and ostracized him for "ratting" on his friends. Subsequently, when his film won eight Oscars, he felt absolved of those charges, assuming that the awards meant acceptance of the film's premise: we have a moral responsibility to inform on evil organizations. In his 1988 autobiography, he writes, "I was tasting vengeance that night and enjoying it. *On the Waterfront* is my own story; every day I worked on that film, I was telling the world where I stood."

Although Kazan may have been justifying himself and settling scores with his enemies, his film does not need any private symbolic significance; it has meaning in its own right. Perhaps the hero is a surrogate for Kazan, and the hoodlums stand for the communist mob that tried to silence him, but overtly the story is about corruption on the docks in the 1950s and about those who act on their conscience against racketeers and thugs. Budd Schulberg's screenplay is, in fact, based on a series of Pulitzer Prize-winning articles published in the *New York Sun* that exposed the union bosses and their connection to organized crime.

The story turns on the growing awareness of Terry Malloy (Marlon Brando), a washed-up boxer who works for the racketeers who control the docks. Specifically, Terry runs errands for the union boss whose name ironically is Johnny Friendly (Lee J. Cobb), and for a lieutenant and lawyer in the organization, Charley Malloy (Rod Steiger), who is Terry's brother. Terry is part of a system of intimidation and oppression. The mob forces the longshoremen to borrow money at exorbitant rates of interest, extorts a daily payment qualifying them to work, and runs the "shape-up," the morning meetings where hiring bosses decide who will have a job that day. The "tabs" or medallions that entitle a man to work are distributed according to loyalty, not by seniority or performance, and this system of favoritism leaves them little incentive or self-respect. In more ruthless actions, the gangsters beat or kill anyone who threatens their operation, especially those who "squeal" to the authorities. In the end, Terry joins with the sister of a murder victim and an activist priest to destroy the system and restore decency to the working community.

The opening scene of the film shows Johnny Friendly walking up the gangplank from the union shack on the docks followed by a deferential Terry Malloy. A longshoreman named Joey Doyle is planning to testify to the crime commission, and Terry is told to lure him into a trap. Like a number of blue-collar workers at the time, Terry keeps pigeons on the roof, so he uses that as bait. "Joey, Joey Doyle... Hey, I got one of your birds. I recognize him by the bank... He flew into my coop. You want him?"

When Joey goes up to claim his pigeon, he is met by two of Friendly's goons who throw him off the roof. The thugs make jokes about Joey's death saying, "I think somebody fell off the roof. He thought he was gonna sing for the Crime Commission. He won't." and "A canary. Maybe he could sing but he couldn't fly."

Terry meanwhile is shocked to witness the murder. "I thought they was gonna talk to him and get him to dummy up," he says, "I figured the worst they was gonna do was lean on him a little bit." The incident signals the start of Terry's moral reflections and a sea change in his attitudes.

The crowd that gathers around Joey's body is also stunned, particularly the major characters: the priest Father Barry (Karl Malden), the boy's sister Edie Doyle (Eva Marie Saint), and his father Pop Doyle (John Hamilton). Edie screams in grief and outrage, "I want to know who killed my brother," but the father is resigned to his death as a way of life on the docks. "Kept telling him. Don't say nothing. Keep quiet. You'll live longer."

The longshoremen have adopted a relativistic ethic, and feel they must conform to the ethos of the waterfront out of self-preservation, while Edie, Father Barry, and eventually Terry recognize more fundamental values that compel them to combat the violence and unfairness.

In a sleazy bar afterwards, Johnny Friendly tries to explain the situation to Terry, realizing he is shaken by the murder.

> You know, takin' over this local took a little doin. There's some pretty rough fellas in the way. They gave me this (he displays an ugly scar on his neck) to remember them by ... I got two thousand dues-payin' members in this local—that's $72,000 a year legitimate and when each one of 'em puts in a couple of bucks a day just to make sure they work steady—well you figure it out. And that's just for openers. We got the fattest piers in the fattest harbor in the world. Everything moves in and out—we take our cut... You don't suppose I can afford to be boxed out of a deal like this, do ya? A deal I sweated for and bled for, on account of one lousy cheese-eater, that Doyle bum, who thinks he can go squealin' to the crime commission? Do ya? Well, DO YA?

"Uncle Johnny" then gives Terry a fifty-dollar bill and promises him a cushy job on the docks. "You check in and you goof off on the coffee bags. OK?" His brother, "Charley the Gent," reinforces the message. "Hey, you got a real friend here. Now don't forget it." Terry seems mollified, and the next day when he is approached by agents from the Waterfront Crime Commission he tells them, "I don't know nothin', I ain't seen nothin', I'm not sayin' nuthin'."

Father Barry and Edie Doyle are present at the shape-up the following morning, because as the priest says, "I don't know how much I can do, but I'll never find out unless I come down here and take a good look for myself." Terry is attracted to Edie and awed by the fact that she attends college, while at the same time feeling guilty for his part in her brother's death. When Father Barry offers the basement of his church as a place where the longshoremen can discuss their grievances, Charley gives Terry the special assignment of taking the names of those who attend the meeting.

Although Terry expresses reservations about the job, saying he doesn't want to be a stool pigeon, Charley explains that this is different. "Let me tell you what stooling is. Stooling is when you rat on your friends, the guys you're with." Nevertheless, Terry remains unresolved, and the issue of when squealing is justified comes up repeatedly throughout the film. Should Joey Doyle have informed about the union racketeering, or is that something that should stay within the family? Should the dock workers have told the investigators about Doyle's murder or was it Doyle's own fault because "he couldn't learn to keep his mouth shut?" In response to Father Barry's plea for help, one longshoreman says, "Deaf and dumb. No matter how much we hate the torpedoes, we don't rat."

The code of silence dictates that one shouldn't be a canary, a squealer, a cheese-eater, or a stool pigeon but just "D and D." That principle of not telling your business to anyone "outside," operates even within companies, military, schools, the government, prisons, hospitals, police departments, and so forth, leaving many people conflicted. Obedience, privacy, and safety lie in one direction, conscience in another. If your cause is just, is it then right to inform? Does that override the virtue of loyalty?

Terry does not know if he should betray his friends or even who his friends are, because his loyalties are divided, his values confused. After he attends the church meeting, which is disrupted by the mob's strong-arm men, Terry tells Friendly "It was a big nothin'. The priest did all the talking." Perhaps this signals a shift in his allegiances.

Edie Doyle and Father Barry are the instruments for Terry's redemption. Through them and the events that unfold, the film takes on a mythic quality while at the same time preserving its raw realism. Their conversations with Terry enable him to grasp the moral depth of the situation, so that he can say to his brother, "There's more to this than I thought, Charley."

At first Terry cannot fathom Edie's generous view of people, raised as he was in a Children's Home on an ethic of self-interest. When she asks him "Which side are you with?" he answers "Me? I'm with me, Terry." The difference in their perspectives is pointed up in several scenes, with Terry finding it increasingly difficult to defend his standpoint. For example, when Terry tells her about his brutal schooling, how the sisters "thought they were going to beat an education into me," she replies

EDIE: Maybe they just didn't know how to handle you.

TERRY: How would you have done it?

EDIE: With a little more patience and kindness. That's what makes people mean and difficult. People don't care enough about them.

TERRY: Ah, what are you kiddin' me?

Other conversations further illustrate their differences:

EDIE: Shouldn't everybody care about everybody else?

TERRY: Boy, what a fruitcake you are!

EDIE: I mean, isn't everybody a part of everybody else?

TERRY: And you really believe that drool?

EDIE: Yes, I do.

TERRY: … You wanna hear my philosophy of life? Do it to him before he does it to you.

EDIE: (*complaining*): I never met anyone like you. There's not a spark of sentiment or romance or human kindness in your whole body.

TERRY: What good does it do ya besides get ya in trouble?

EDIE: And when things and people get in your way, you just knock them aside, get rid of them, is that your idea? …

TERRY: Listen, down here, it's every man for himself. It's keepin' alive. It's standin' in with the right people, so you got a little bit of change jinglin' in your pocket.

EDIE: And if you don't?

TERRY: And if you don't—right down.

EDIE: That's living like an animal.

TERRY: All right, I'd rather live like an animal than end up like—

EDIE: Like Joey? Are you afraid to mention his name?

Joey, of course, is the main obstacle to their relationship, and Terry is torn between loyalty to Charley and Johnny Friendly and his desire to help Edie prosecute her brother's killer. When she pleads with him, "Help me if you can, for God's sake," he answers, "Edie, I'd like to help, I'd like to help, but there's nothing I can do."

After Terry receives a subpoena to testify before the Crime Commission Edie asks him:

EDIE: What are you going to do?

TERRY: I ain't gonna eat cheese for no cops, and that's for sure.

EDIE: It was Johnny Friendly who killed Joey, wasn't it? Or he had him killed, or he had something to do with it, didn't he? He and your big brother Charley? You can't tell me, can you? Because you're part of it. Cause you're just as bad as the worst of them. Tell me the truth, Terry!

TERRY: You'd better go back to that school out in daisyland. You're driving yourself nuts. You're driving me nuts. Quit worrying about the truth all the time. Worry about yourself.

EDIE: I should've known you wouldn't help me. Pop said Johnny Friendly used to own you. Well, I think he still owns you.

Edie then calls him "a bum," which wounds him deeply because he is beginning to feel genuine love for her.

TERRY: I'm only tryin' to help ya out. I'm tryin' to keep ya from gettin' hurt. What more do ya want me to do?

EDIE: Much more!

TERRY: Wait a minute.

EDIE: Much, much, much more!

Perhaps Edie is asking too much of Terry, especially because self-preservation has prevailed throughout his life over his sense of justice. To name Friendly as the person responsible for Joey's murder would be to risk his livelihood and his life. Terry, in fact, only decides to expose Johnny Friendly when Father Barry receives a beating, which suggests that his action is precipitated by rage, not outrage.

Terry and Edie do wind up together after he has done the right thing, and at that point he understands that the violence and injustice cannot go on. Terry rises to the challenge, a less than ordinary man acting in an extraordinary way. He testifies at a hearing and confronts the crime boss, and in this way regains his dignity. "They always said I was a bum," he declares, "Well, I ain't a bum, Edie."

Terry is at his most sensitive with Edie and in handling his pigeons. In one tender scene by the coop on the roof, she presses close to him when he says, "There was a hawk around here before." The two of them are obviously the vulnerable pigeons threatened by predators. When Terry does testify against the mob, all of his pigeons are killed, their necks wrung by a neighborhood friend, Tommy, who regards him as a traitor and a pariah. "A pigeon for a pigeon," Tommy says, tossing a dead bird at him.

Father Barry demands as much of Terry as he asks of himself as a priest, which means that he wants unusual courage. After another longshoreman named Kayo Nolan is killed because he was cooperating with the Crime

Commission, the priest delivers a sermon from the hold of the ship where the man was crushed to death. Seventy-five longshoremen look down from the hatch, dock, and loft, including the shape up boss Big Mac and other supporters of Johnny Friendly—Truck, Sonny, and J.P. In something of a set-piece for the stage, Father Barry tells the men that Christ will be there with them if they fight the mobsters.

The screenplay by Schulberg is as follows:

INT HATCH DAY

CLOSE ON FATHER BARRY
He stands over the body of Kayo Nolan, which lies on the pallet and has been covered by a tarpaulin.

FATHER BARRY (*aroused*): I came down here to keep a promise. I gave Kayo my word that if he stood up to the mob I'd stand up with him all the way. Now Kayo Nolan is dead. He was one of those fellows who had the gift of getting up. But this time they fixed him good—unless it was an accident like Big Mac says.

Pop, Moose, and some of the others glare at Big Mac, who chews his tobacco sullenly. Some of the others snicker "accident."

FATHER BARRY: Some people think the Crucifixion only took place on Calvary. They better wise up. Taking Joey Doyle's life to stop him from testifying is a crucifixion—Dropping a sling on Kayo Nolan because he was ready to spill his guts tomorrow—that's a crucifixion. Every time the mob puts the crusher on a good man—tries to stop him from doing his duty as a citizen—it's a crucifixion.

CLOSE ON TERRY
Voice of Father Barry continues.

FATHER BARRY: And anybody who sits around and lets it happen, keeps silent about something he knows has happened—shares the guilt of it as much as the Roman soldier who pierced the flesh of Our Lord to see if He was dead.

SHOT OF EDIE ON DOCK
Listening, moved, Terry has come up behind her and stands nearby. She notices him but barely reacts. He listens intently to the Father's words.

CLOSE ON TRUCK

TRUCK: Go back to your church, Father.

INT HATCH DAY

FATHER BARRY (*looking up at Truck and pointing to the ship*): Boys, this is my church. If you don't think Christ is here on the waterfront, you got another thing coming. And who do you think he lines up with—

CLOSE ON SONNY

SONNY: Get off the dock, Father.

Sonny reaches for a box of rotten bananas on the dock and flings one down into the hatch.

CLOSE ON FATHER BARRY
The banana splatters him, but he ignores it.

BACK TO SONNY ON DOCK
Terry turns to him. Edie notices this and watches with approval.

TERRY: Do that again and I'll flatten you.

SONNY: What're you doing. Joining them—

TERRY: Let him finish.

SONNY: Johnny ain't going to like that, Terry.

TERRY: Let him finish.

Edie looks at him amazed. Terry catches her eye, and then looks down, embarrassed at his good deed. They both turn to watch Father Barry.

CLOSE SHOT CHARLEY
Near Johnny, watching Terry and then looking at Johnny apprehensively.

INT HATCH DAY

FATHER BARRY: Every morning when the hiring boss blows his whistle, Jesus stands alongside you in the shape-up.

More missiles fly, some hitting the Father, but he continues:
He sees why some of you get picked and some of you get passed over. He sees the family men worrying about getting their rent and

getting food in the house for the wife and kids. He sees them selling their souls to the mob for a day's pay.

CLOSE ON JOHNNY FRIENDLY
Nodding to Barney. Barney picks up an empty beer can and hurls it down into the hatch.

INT HATCH DAY

It strikes Father Barry and blood etches his forehead. Pop jumps forward and shakes his fist.

POP: By Christ, the next bum who throws something deals with me. I don't care if he's twice my size.

Some of the other longshoremen grumble approval.

FATHER BARRY: What does Christ think of the easy-money boys who do none of the work and take all of the gravy? What does He think of these fellows wearing hundred-and-fifty-dollar suits and diamond rings—on your union dues and your kickback money? Hoe does He feel about bloodsuckers picking up a longshoreman's work tab and grabbing twenty percent interest at the end of a week?

CLOSE ON J.P.
J.P.: Never mind about that!

CLOSE OF SONNY ON DOCK
Scowling.

Terry, nearby, is increasingly moved by the Father's challenge.

FATHER BARRY: How does He, who spoke up without fear against evil, feel about your silence?

SONNY: Shut up about that!

He reaches for another rotten banana and is poised to throw it. Almost simultaneously, Terry throws a short hard right that flattens Sonny neatly. Edie is watching, a deeply felt gratitude in her eyes.

CLOSE ON JOHNNY FRIENDLY AND TRUCK
A little way off.

TRUCK: You see that?
Johnny presses his lips together but makes no sign.

CLOSE ON TERRY AND EDIE
She moves closer to him. He barely glances at her, then continues listening to Father Barry.

INT HATCH DAY

FATHER BARRY: You want to know what's wrong with our waterfront? It's love of a lousy buck. It's making love of a buck—the cushy job—more important than the love of man. It's forgetting that every fellow down here is your brother in Christ.

Father Barry's voice rises to a climax—

FATHER BARRY: But remember, fellows, Christ is always with you—Christ is in the shape-up, He's in the hatch—He's in the union hall—He's kneeling here beside Nolan—and He's saying with all of you—

CLOSE ON FATHER BARRY

FATHER BARRY: If you do it to the least of mine, you do it to me! What they did to Joey, what they did to Nolan, they're doing to you. And you. And only you, with God's help, have the power to knock 'em off for good! (*turns to Nolan's corpse*) Okay, Kayo? (*then looks up and says, harshly*) Amen.

Kayo Nolan's body is then lifted out of the hold by a crane with Father Barry riding the pallet beside him. Perhaps the ascent from the depths of the ship is symbolic of the spirit rising from the body as well as the men elevated by a higher vision.

Shortly afterwards, Terry confesses to Father Barry that he'd set up Joey Doyle, saying, "Father, help me. I've got blood on my hands." But he also tells the priest that he cannot bring himself to inform on Friendly and his own brother.

TERRY: You know, if I spill, my life ain't worth a nickel.

FATHER BARRY: And how much is your soul worth if you don't.

TERRY: But it's my own brother they're asking me to finger...

FATHER BARRY: So you've got a brother. Well, let me tell you something, you got some other brothers—and they're all getting the short end... Listen, if I were you, I would walk... Never mind. I'm not asking you to do anything. It's your own conscience that's got to do the asking.

TERRY: Conscience... I didn't even know I had one until I met you and Edie... this conscience stuff can drive you nuts.

Meanwhile Johnny Friendly is growing apprehensive that Terry might inform on him, so he sends Charley to give his brother a forceful warning. The most poignant, memorable, and celebrated scene in the film then follows, with the two brothers talking in the back seat of a taxi.

INT TAXICAB EVENING (N.Y.B.G.)

Charley and Terry have just entered the cab.

TERRY: Gee Charley, I'm sure glad you stopped by for me. I needed to talk to you. What's it they say about blood, it's—

CHARLEY: (*looking away coldly*): Thicker than water.

DRIVER (*gravel voice, without turning around*): Where to?

CHARLEY: Four thirty-seven River Street.

TERRY: River Street? I thought we was going to the Garden.

CHARLEY: I've got to cover a bet there on the way over. Anyway, it gives us a chance to talk.

TERRY: (*good naturedly*): Nothing ever stops you from talking, Charley.

CHARLEY: The grapevine says you picked up a subpoena.

TERRY (*noncommittal, sullen*): That's right....

CHARLEY (*watching for his reaction*): Of course, the boys know you too well to mark you down for a cheese-eater.

TERRY: Mm—hmm.

CHARLEY: You know, the boys are getting rather interested in your future.

TERRY: Mm—hmmm.

CHARLEY: They feel you've been sort of left out of things, Terry. They think it's time you had a few little things going for you on the docks.

TERRY: A steady job and a few bucks extra, that's all I wanted.

CHARLEY: Sure, that's all right when you're a kid, but you'll be pushing thirty pretty soon, slugger. It's time you got some ambition.

TERRY: I always figured I'd live longer without it.

CHARLEY: Maybe.

Terry looks at him.

CHARLEY: There's a slot for a boss loader on the new pier we're opening up.

TERRY (*interested*): Boss loader!

CHARLEY: Ten cents a hundred pounds on everything that moves in and out. And you don't have to lift a finger. It'll be three-four hundred a week just for openers.

TERRY: And for all that dough I don't do nuthin'?

CHARLEY: Absolutely nothing. You do nothing and you say nothing. You understand, don't you, kid?

TERRY (*struggling with an unfamiliar problem of conscience and loyalties*): Yeah—yeah—I guess I do—but there's a lot more to this whole thing than I thought, Charley.

CHARLEY: You don't mean you're thinking of testifying against— (*turns a thumb in toward himself*).

TERRY: I don't know—I don't know! I tell you I ain't made up my mind yet. That's what I wanted to talk to you about.

CHARLEY (*patiently, as to a stubborn child*): Listen, Terry, these piers we handle through the local—you know what they're worth to us?

TERRY: I know, I know.

CHARLEY: Well, then, you know Cousin Johnny isn't going to jeopardize a setup like that for one rubber-lipped—

TERRY (*simultaneous*): Don't say that!

CHARLEY (*continuing*): —ex-tanker who's walking on his heels—?

TERRY: Don't say that!

CHARLEY: What the hell!!!

TERRY: I could have been better!

CHARLEY: Listen, that isn't the point.

TERRY: I could have been better!

CHARLEY: The point is—there isn't much time, kid.

There is a painful pause, as they appraise each other.

TERRY (*desperately*): I tell you, Charley, I haven't made up my mind!

CHARLEY: Make up your mind, kid, I beg you, before we get to four thirty-seven River... .

TERRY (*stunned*): Four thirty-seven—that isn't where Gerry G...?

Charley nods solemnly. Terry grows more agitated.

TERRY: Charley... you wouldn't take me to Gerry G...?

Charley continues looking at him. He does not deny it. They stare at each other for a moment. Then suddenly Terry starts out of the cab. Charley pulls a pistol. Terry is motionless, now, looking at Charley.

CHARLEY: Take the boss loading, kid. For God's sake. I don't want to hurt you.

TERRY (*hushed, gently guiding the gun down toward Charley's lap*): Charley... Charley... Wow... .

CHARLEY (*genuinely*): I wish I didn't have to do this, Terry.

Terry eyes him, beaten. Charley leans back and looks at Terry strangely. Terry raises his hands above his head, somewhat in the manner of a prizefighter mitting the crowd. The image nicks Charley's memory.

TERRY (*an accusing sigh*): Wow. ...

CHARLEY (*gently*): What do you weight these days, slugger?

TERRY (*shrugs*): —eighty-seven, eighty-eight. What's it to you?

CHARLEY (*nostalgically*): Gee, when you tipped one seventy-five you were beautiful. You should've been another Billy Conn. That skunk I got to manage you brought you along too fast.

TERRY: It wasn't him! (*years of abuse crying out in him*) It was you, Charley. You and Johnny. Like the night the two of youse come in the dressing room and says, 'Kid, this ain't your night—we're going for the price on Wilson.' It ain't my night. I'd of taken Wilson apart that night! I was ready—remember the early rounds throwing them combinations. So what happens—This bum Wilson he gets the title shot—outdoors in the ball park!—and what do I get—a couple of bucks and a one-way ticket to Palookaville (*more and more aroused as he relives it*). It was you, Charley. You was my brother. You should of looked out for me. Instead of making me take dives for the short-end money.

CHARLEY (*defensively*): I always had a bet down for you. You saw some money.

TERRY (*agonized*): See! You don't understand!

CHARLEY: I tried to keep you in good with Johnny.

TERRY: You don't understand! I could've been a contender. I could've had class and been somebody. Real class. Instead of a bum, let's face it, which is what I am. It was you, Charley.

Charley takes a long, fond look at Terry. Then he glances quickly out the window.

MEDIUM SHOT WATERFRONT NIGHT

From Charley's angle. A gloomy night reflects the street numbers—433—435—

INT CLOSE CAB ON CHARLEY AND TERRY NIGHT

TERRY: It was you, Charley... .

CHARLEY (*turning back to Terry, his tone suddenly changed*): Okay—I'll tell him I couldn't bring you in. Ten to one they won't believe it, but—go ahead, blow. Jump out, quick, and keep going... and God help you from here on in...

Elia Kazan has commented on Brando's mesmerizing acting in this scene: "...what was extraordinary about his performance, I feel, is the contrast of the tough-guy front and the extreme delicacy and gentle cast of his behavior. What other actor, when his brother draws a pistol to force him to do something shameful, would put his hand on the gun and push it away with the gentleness of a caress? Who else could read 'Oh, Charley!' in a tone of reproach that is so loving and so melancholy and suggest the terrific depth of pain?"

Following the confrontation between the brothers in the taxi, Charley is murdered, presumably by Friendly's orders, and the gangsters even attempt to kill Edie; Terry saves her from being run down by a car. This finally galvanizes Terry to fight the union racketeers.

At first he wants to shoot Friendly, but Father Barry convinces him to use the force of law rather than violence. "...don't fight him like a hoodlum down here in the jungle because that's just what he wants. He'll hit you in the head and plead self-defense. You fight him in the courtroom tomorrow, with the truth as you know the truth." In a symbolic gesture, Terry throws his gun at a picture of Friendly and his boss that is hanging above the bar.

The next day Terry testifies in court against the crooked union and the mobsters, and he remains resolved and determined despite ostracism from his friends and threats from Johnny Friendly. "You've just dug your own grave," Friendly screams at him in court. "You're dead on this waterfront and every waterfront from Boston to New Orleans. You don't drive a truck or a cab. You don't push a baggage rack. You don't work no place. YOU'RE DEAD."

Despite Friendly's warning, Terry puts on Joey Doyle's jacket in the morning and appears at the shape-up. Everyone is chosen except for him, but rather than withdrawing, he challenges Friendly at the union shack before a crowd of longshoremen.

EXT UNION LOCAL OFFICE WHARF DAY

Terry walks compulsively down the ramp to the office.

TERRY (*shouts*): Hey, Friendly! Johnny Friendly, come out here!

Johnny comes out of his office followed by his goons... .

TERRY: You want to know something? Take the heater away and you're nothin'—take the good goods away, and the kickback and shakedown cabbage away and the pistoleros—(*indicating the others*)—away and you're a great big hunk of nothing—(*takes a deep breath as if relieved*) Your guts is all in your wallet and your trigger finger!

JOHNNY (*with fury*): Go on talkin'. You're talking' yourself right into the river. Go on, go on... .

TERRY (*voice rising defiantly*): I'm glad what I done today, see? You give it to Joey, you give it to Nolan, you give it to Charley who was one of your own. You thought you was God Almighty instead of a cheap—conniving—good-for-nothing bum! So I'm glad what I done—you hear me?—glad what I done!

JOHNNY (*coldly*): You ratted on us, Terry.

TERRY (*aware of fellow longshoremen anxiously watching the duel*): From where I stand, maybe. But I'm standing over here now. I was rattin' on myself all them years and didn't know it, helpin' punks like you against people like Pop and Nolan.

A furious and brutal fight ensues which Terry wins, but Friendly's thugs then join in and he is kicked and punched nearly senseless. When Edie and Father Barry arrive Friendly gives them his battered body. "You want'im. You can have 'im. The little rat's yours."

The rebellion might have ended there, but the longshoremen rally behind Terry and refuse to work unless he does. Friendly replies "Work! He can't even walk." When Friendly orders the men to load the ships, Pop Doyle says, "All my life you pushed me around," and shoves him into the scummy water while the men cheer at his humiliation.

No one moves, waiting for a sign from Terry. He is bloody and barely conscious, but Father Barry helps him to his feet despite Edie's protests.

As the groggy Terry starts up the ramp, Edie reaches out to him. Father Barry holds her back.

FATHER BARRY: Leave him alone. Take your hands off him— Leave him alone.

Staggering, moving painfully forward, Terry starts up the ramp. Edie's instinct is to help him but Father Barry, knowing the stakes of this symbolic act, holds her back. Terry stumbles, but steadies himself and moves forward as if driven on by Father Barry's will.

TERRY APPROACHING PIER ENTRANCE
As he staggers forward as if blinded, the longshoremen form a line on either side of him, awed by his courage, waiting to see if he'll make it. Terry keeps going.

REVERSE ANGLE BOSS STEVEDORE TERRY'S POV
Waiting at pier entrance as Terry approaches. Shot out of focus as Terry
would see him through bloody haze.

TERRY
As the men who have formed a path for him watch intently, Terry staggers up until he is face to face with the Stevedore. He gathers himself as
if to say, "I'm ready. Let's go!"

STEVEDORE (*Calls officially*): All right—let's go to work!

As Terry goes past him into the pier, the men with a sense of inevitabil-
ity fall in behind him.

JOHNNY FRIENDLY
Hurrying forward in a last desperate effort to stop the men from following Terry in.

JOHNNY (*screams*): Where you guys goin'? Wait a minute!

As they stream past him

I'll be back! I'll be back! And I'll remember every last one of ya!

He points at them accusingly. But they keep following Terry into the
pier.

WIDER ANGLE PIER ENTRANCE
As Father Barry and Edie look on, Stevedore blows his whistle for
work to begin. Longshoremen by the hundreds march into the pier
behind Terry like a conquering army. In the B.G. a frenzied Johnny
Friendly is still screaming, "I'll be back! I'll be back!"

The threat, real as it is, is lost in the forward progress of Terry and the
ragtail army of dock workers he now leads.

FADE OUT

During this final scene Terry resembles paintings of Christ with blood
streaming down his face and his eyes turned heavenward. He has, in fact,
been transformed into a martyr, and the film has become a morality play in
which good triumphs over evil. The longshoremen had adopted a relativistic ethic and felt they had to conform to the ethos of the waterfront, while
Edie, Father Barry, and Terry had recognized more fundamental, humane
values that made them fight the evil. At the end, the men, too, understand

that corruption must be opposed, for their own good and because some principles such as fairness are basic to human dignity.

STUDY QUESTIONS

1. Do you have an ethical responsibility to inform on your friends if they are doing something wrong? Should you report someone in your class for cheating because it is unfair to those who prepared for the exam?

2. How does Father Barry show the connection between Christ and the situation on the docks?

3. What was the significance to Terry's life in his throwing the fight so the racketeers could win their bets?

4. Why were Terry and Edie attracted to each other? Was Terry's relationship with his brother good for him?

5. Does *On the Waterfront* endorse an ethical relativism or an objectivism? How, exactly?

Saving Private Ryan

Director: Steven Spielberg
Screenplay: Robert Rodat

Steven Spielberg (1946–) is one of America's most prolific and celebrated film directors. He has twenty-six feature films to his credit, most notably Saving Private Ryan, Jurassic Park, Amistad, Schindler's List, Poltergeist, Jaws, Close Encounters of the Third Kind, Artificial Intelligence, *and the* Indiana Jones *trilogy. Spielberg also produced and/or wrote several of his films, as well as numerous episodes in several television series. He has been honored with Academy Awards as Best Director for* Saving Private Ryan *and* Schindler's List, *along with receiving awards from the Director's Guild of America and several Golden Globes and Emmys.*

SYNOPSIS

Spielberg's intention in *Saving Private Ryan* was to create a monument to the brave men who fought and died in World War II, especially on D-Day. The star of the film, Tom Hanks, reinforced this purpose when he stated in an interview, "We are trying to communicate to [the audience] that mere mortals, people who are the same age as themselves, had to be called upon to make the hard sacrifice in service to mankind." However, Spielberg has also woven into his film an inner moral theme, and the film as a whole presents a humanistic motive for pursing the war. The plot, the action, and the conversations between Captain Miller (Tom Hanks) and his squad gradually refine the reason for their particular mission. Initially, it seems the height of absurdity to risk the lives of several soldiers in order to save one man.

   After a brief Prologue, the beginning sequences of the film plunge the viewer into the carnage at Omaha Beach, Normandy, in 1944 at the start of the Allied invasion of Europe. This twenty-five-minute segment is often regarded as the most realistic, gruesome, and compelling depiction of warfare ever filmed. The battle is neither sensationalized nor glorified but simply shown as it must have been, and for that reason the wounding and killing is almost too life-like for the audience to bear.

The viewer experiences the action directly rather than merely observing it. The air is thick with machine gun and mortar fire, tracer bullets, and artillery shells from the moment the landing craft open until the beach is taken. Bullets whiz past the sick and panicky soldiers, even penetrating the water and sending up clouds of crimson. Men are shown drowning before their feet can touch land, dragged down by the weight of their equipment. We see half a torso being dragged up the beach, a soldier dazed and wandering in shock, picking up his severed arm, another with an open stomach wound trying to hold in his intestines and calling for his mother. The ironies are also depicted; a man who is killed just after the medics have treated him; another shot in the head while examining the bullet hole in his helmet. The viewer feels in the presence of both absurdity and death.

Other graphic battle scenes are shown in the film, especially the concluding episode, but none are as vivid or harrowing. Here the impact is hallucinatory, suggesting an allegory of hell. In one surreal sequence, the camera scans across the many bodies bobbing in the water.

The sound is of real guns, the actual kind used in World War II, and the hand-held camera of Janusz Kaminski makes no sense of the action; it only augments the chaos. The camera shakes when Tiger tanks rumble up, and blood sometimes spatters the lens, as though both the audience and the cameraman are there. "I wanted the audience in the arena, not sitting off to one side," Spielberg has written. "I didn't want something it was easy to look away from."

John Williams' film score remains in the background, eloquent but never romanticizing the scenes, and during the battles it ceases altogether. His "Hymn to the Fallen" at the beginning and end of the film is subdued and moving, but for the most part he lets the action speak for itself. At times the mix of sounds becomes muffled, perhaps to show how the explosions numb both the ears and the mind.

As a historical note, the carnage that occurred on June 6, 1944 is quite accurate because, contrary to plan, the German defenses were not eliminated by aerial bombardment. The night before the landing the Allied bombers were supposed to destroy the heavy German fortifications on the cliffs above Omaha Beach. However, because of heavy cloud cover the planes missed almost all of their targets, and the landing troops were nearly all slaughtered.

The second phase of the film sets up the moral question when General George Marshall (Harve Presnell) is informed by his staff that Mrs. Ryan, an Iowa farm wife, has lost three of her four sons in the war. The general resolves that the surviving son, James Ryan, (Matt Damon), must be found and returned home safely. His decision is probably based on both politics and compassion. A Colonel Dye objects to the plan saying "If we send a patrol flat-hatting around, through swarms of German reinforcements, all along our axis of advance . . . we'll be sending out death notifications to all of their mothers." In reply General Marshall quotes a letter from Abraham Lincoln to a Mrs. Bixby in Boston.

> Dear Madam,
>
> I have been shown in the files of the War Department a statement of the Adjutant General of Massachusetts that you are the mother of five sons who have died gloriously on the field of battle. I feel how weak and fruitless must be any words of mine which should attempt to beguile you from the grief of a loss so overwhelming. But I cannot refrain from tendering to you the consolation that may be found in the thanks of the Republic they have died to save.
>
> I pray that our Heavenly Father may assuage the anguish of your bereavement, and leave you only the cherished memory of the loved and lost, and the solemn pride that must be yours to have laid so costly a sacrifice upon the alter of freedom.
>
> Yours very sincerely,
Abraham Lincoln

Marshall concludes by saying, "If that boy is alive, we're going to send someone to find him... and get him the hell out of there."

Captain Miller of Charlie Company, Second Ranger Battalion, is ordered to carry out this special mission, so he assembles the remains of his platoon plus a French/German interpreter. The men are a mixed bag and almost caricatures of characters in war films. That is, they are near clichés of the griping men from disparate backgrounds who gradually bond and become willing to risk their lives for each other. Private Reiben (Edward Burns) represents the stock Brooklyn tough-guy, sarcastic and street-smart; Sergeant Michael Horvath (Tom Sizemore) from Minneapolis is battle-scarred, dependable, and courageous; Private Jackson (Barry Pepper) is a prayerful southern sharpshooter; Anthony Caparzo (Vin Diesel) from Chicago is a good-natured grunt; Stanley Mellish (Adam Goldberg) from Yonkers portrays a sarcastic Jewish complainer; Corporal Upham (Jeremy Davies) is the terrified combat rookie, a clerk-typist who intends to write a book; and Wade (Giovanni Ribisi) portrays the altruistic medic.

When the men learn of their mission they are naturally incredulous, unable to believe that a squad of men is being sent into a war zone in order to return one individual to his mother. "What about your mother?" Reiben says to Wade. "We all got mothers, you, me, Sarge, even Corporal Upchuck. Captain, I'll bet even you have a mother." To them, it seems a "public relations" mission, another incident of the army's "foobar," fucked up beyond all recognition. They wonder whether James Ryan is anyone special, which would justify the risks they are taking:

> "Captain, where's this Ryan from anyway?"
>
> "Iowa, Private Caparzo. The great Middle West."
>
> "Iowa? Oh, well, that's different. Who wouldn't mind riskin' his ass to save some fuckin' farmer? The world couldn't get along with one less sodbuster, it's not like it's rainin' fuckin' sodbusters back home or anything. Western civilization would cease."

In an ironic exchange, underscoring that Ryan is very ordinary, not "Eisenhower or Patton or something," Captain Miller tells Reiben,

> "I got a look at Ryan's service record, which is exemplary."
>
> "Oh, that changes everything."
>
> "But it also includes his high school report cards—he got an A-plus in civics and won the school's Good Citizenship Award...two years in a row. Now—isn't that worth risking your asses over?"
>
> "Was he an Eagle Scout, sir?"
>
> "Youngest in the history of the state of Iowa. Forty-eight merit badges."

Tom Hanks as Captain Miller is "everyman" risen to heroic proportions, an incarnation of James Stewart. He also wonders privately why a dangerous mission should be launched to save one man, although he tells his men "orders are orders." This is echoed by Upham who quotes Tennyson "Theirs is not to reason why / Theirs is but to do and die." But that reasoning (or lack of reasoning) never satisfies Miller, and a justification in terms of risks and benefits certainly does not work in this situation either. In one conversation while the squad is marching through the French countryside Reiben expresses Miller's own reservations:

"You know, Captain, this little expedition goes against everything the army taught me."

"How so?"

"I mean, it doesn't make any sense."

"What doesn't make any sense, Reiben."

"The math, sir, the sheer fuckin' math of it. Maybe you could explain it to me."

"Sure. That's what I'm here for. To make you boys feel everything we do is logical."

"Gimme a break, Cap."

"So what do you want to know?"

"Well, sir, strictly just talkin' arithmetic here, what's the sense, the strategy, in risking eight lives to save one?"

In a later conversation Miller raises the same question with Sergeant Horvath, except here he questions his previous morality whereby he calculated numbers saved and lost in order to justify his actions. Thinking more deeply, he wonders whether such a calculus is the correct approach. Miller says,

"Every time you get one of your boys killed you tell yourself you just saved the lives of two, three, ten, maybe a hundred other men and boys."

"Not a bad way to look at it."

"You know how many men I've lost under my command?"

"Not offhand."

"Caparzo made ninety-four. So hell, that means I probably saved the lives of ten times that many. Maybe twenty times. See, it's simple. Just do the math—it lets you choose the mission over the men, every time.

Horvath replies, "Except this time the mission is the man," thereby articulating the central principle of the film. That is, although Miller reverts to weighing the numbers periodically, and even tries to justify the mission in terms of Ryan's special worth, he comes to understand that something more fundamental is at stake. He does say "This Private Ryan better…cure cancer or invent a lightbulb that never fuckin' burns out, or a car that runs on water," but such thinking is superficial. It is not enough to sacrifice lives just to save a larger number of lives, or to save a life only if that life benefits society enormously. The men who gave up their lives in the war were as valuable as those whose lives were saved.

In effect, the mission forces Miller to realize the more ultimate reasons behind his actions and for the war. That is, certain values are fundamental and transcend a pragmatic, cost/benefit analysis. The war is being fought to safeguard ethical values, which include comradeship, integrity, loyalty, and honor, as well as liberty and freedom. In the case of this mission, the humane value is sparing a mother the tragedy of losing all her sons.

In philosophic terms, Spielberg chooses the ethical position of formalism that treats values as supreme over the more utilitarian approach that champions the greater good. He places Kantianism over Utilitarianism. Just as we should respect the rules of justice even though it might lead to the acquittal of a guilty person, we should try to bring home a remaining son even though the lives of several soldiers are put in danger. Principles matter more than consequences. Our conscience dictates that we do what's right even if it does no good, because we have a responsibility to honor moral values. Our self-respect depends on the respect we accord to individual human life.

As the film progresses the squad advances to the front lines searching for Private Ryan, and are suddenly bombarded by 88-mm shells, landing the men in a drainage ditch and shattering their jeep. They then enter the town of Ste.-Mére-Église and find themselves in the midst of a firefight. The presence of civilians complicates the situation, and a sniper in a bell-tower kills Caparzo as he hands a little girl back to her parents. The sniper is killed in turn by Jackson, the sharpshooter.

The squad then encounters a machine-gun nest manned by *Falshirmjager*, elite German paratroopers who are responsible for the corpses of American soldiers littering the ground. Dissension occurs over whether to attack the site or bypass it, skirting around the woods. Miller commands his troops to attack, and in the battle the medic Wade is hit. In a poignant scene, Wade dies while his comrades ask, "Tell us what to do. Tell us how to fix you." This incident causes dissension over whether the attack (and the entire mission) was warranted.

In this situation, neither we nor Miller know whether he made the right choice. The same question arises in a subsequent incident where Miller releases a German prisoner who ironically turns out to be the S.S. soldier responsible for Miller's death. Is a right decision one based on good reasons or one that turns out well? Can we judge the wisdom of our choices retrospectively?

The final scene of the film takes place in Neuville-au-Plain where Private Ryan is finally found. Ryan is informed that his brothers have been killed and that he is going home, but oddly enough he refuses to leave his comrades.

> RYAN: "I can't leave them, sir. At least not until reinforcements arrive… there's barely enough of us as it is."
>
> MILLER: "Private… you've got five [minutes] to grab your gear and report back to me."
>
> RYAN: "Captain, if I go, what are they gonna…"
>
> REIBEN: "Hey, asshole! Two of us died, buyin' you this ticket home. Fuckin' *take* it! I would."
>
> RYAN: "What… were their names?"
>
> MELLISH: "Wade and Caparzo."
>
> RYAN: "Wade … and…"
>
> MELLISH: "Caparzo."
>
> RYAN: "Sir, this doesn't make any sense. What have I done to deserve special treatment?
>
> REIBEN: "Give that man a cigar."
>
> MILLER: "This isn't about you. It's about politics… and your mother."
>
> RYAN: "I mean, for Christ's sake, my life isn't worth the lives of two others. Hell, these guys deserve to go home as much as I do, as much as anybody. They've fought just as long, just as hard."
>
> MILLER: "Should I tell your mother that? That she can look forward to another flag in her window?"
>
> RYAN: "My mother didn't raise any of us to be cowards."
>
> MILLER: "She didn't raise you to lose you."
>
> RYAN: "Well, then, you just tell her when you found me, I was with the only brothers I had left. Tell her that there was no way I was go-

ing to desert those brothers. You tell her that… and she'll understand."

Miller does not force the issue, and his squad then fights with Ryan's company to hold a bridge against a German counter-offensive. This battle too is rendered in harrowing detail, and it becomes more personal because we have come to relate to each of the men just as they have with each other. Even though they are vastly outnumbered and outgunned, the small force manages to hold the bridge until reinforcements arrive. They are remarkably courageous and resourceful but the price they pay is enormous. Captain Miller dies, and of the original squad only Upham and Reiben survive. Ryan lives as well, and toward the end of the film Miller's last words to him are "Earn this. Earn it."

These words seem to suggest that the sacrifice of six men in the squad is only justified if the person then leads an outstanding life. However, we do not protect people only when they deserve it, and Ryan was saved for humanitarian reasons not because he would contribute to society. As the prologue and epilogue show, Ryan apparently did lead a worthwhile life afterwards, but if he hadn't, that would not negate the sacrifice. We see him as a grandfather at the St. Laurent military graveyard, talking to Miller's grave, wondering whether he had been a good enough man. By all indications, he was thoroughly decent, not exceptional but he worked with his hands, raised a family—did the best he knew how.

Perhaps the definitive word is uttered earlier by Sergeant Horvath: "Someday we might look back on this and decide that saving Private Ryan was the only decent thing we were able to pull out of this whole godawful mess."

Respect for the worth of the individual is the type of value that justified the war altogether.

STUDY QUESTIONS

1. Why is Captain Miller and his squad sent to rescue Private Ryan? Does the mission make sense?

2. What is the moral rationale behind risking eight lives to save one? How does this relate to the Kantian and Utilitarian ethic?

3. Do you think the mission would only be justified if Private Ryan subsequently contributed something outstanding to humanity?

4. Should the squad have attacked the machine-gun nest or bypassed it in order to carry out their primary mission?

5. When Private Ryan was found, should he have been forced to leave with Miller and his men or were they right to remain and try to stop the German advance?

Bibliography of Philosophy, Literature, and Films
III. Judging Human Conduct: Ethics

Philosophy

Beyond Good and Evil, The Joyful Wisdom	Friedrich Nietzsche
The Data of Ethics	Herbert Spencer
The Emotive Theory of Ethics	J. O. Urmson
Ethical Studies	F. H. Bradley
Ethics	G. E. Moore
Ethics	P. H. Nowell-Smith
Ethics	Baruch Spinoza
Ethics and Language	Charles Stevenson
Ethics Since 1900	Mary Warnock
Five Types of Ethical Theory	C. D. Broad
The Foundation of Ethics	W. D. Ross
Gorgias, Meno, Republic	Plato
Groundwork of the Metaphysic of Morals	Immanuel Kant
Human Nature and Conduct	John Dewey
The Humanism of Existentialism	Jean-Paul Sartre
In a Different Voice	Carol Gilligan
The Language of Morals	R. M. Hare
Methods of Ethics	Henry Sidgwick
The Myth of Sisyphus	Albert Camus
The Nicomachean Ethics	Aristotle
The Philosophy of Humanism	Corliss Lamont
The Philosophy of Right	G. W. F. Hegel
Principles of Morals & Legislation	Jeremy Bentham
Problems of Ethics	Moritz Schlick
Prolegomena to Ethics	T. H. Green
Situation Ethics	Joseph Fletcher
The Souls of Black Folk	W. E. B. DuBois
Theories of Ethics	Philippa Foot
A Theory of Justice	John Rawls
Utilitarianism	John Stuart Mill
The Varieties of Goodness	G. H. Von Wright
A Vindication of the Rights of Women	Mary Wollstonecraft
World of Color	W. E. B. DuBois

Literature

The Ambassadors	William James
Anna Karenina	Leo Tolstoy
Antigone	Jean Anouilh
Baal	Bertolt Brecht
The Bell Jar	Sylvia Plath
Beloved	Toni Morrison
Billy Budd	Joseph Conrad
Caligula, The Plague	Albert Camus
The Catcher in the Rye	J. D. Salinger
The Cherry Orchard	Anton Chekov
The Color Purple	Alice Walker
Crime and Punishment	Fydor Dostoevsky
Cry, the Beloved Country	Alan Paton
Dead Souls	Nikolai Gogol
Everything That Rises Must Converge	Flannery O'Connor
Everyman	Hugo Hofmannsthal
The Fall	Albert Camus
The Good Woman of Setzuan	Bertolt Brecht
Gulliver's Travels	Jonathan Swift
Heart of Darkness	Joseph Conrad
The Immoralist	Andre Gide
Justice	John Galsworthy
King Lear	William Shakespeare
A Lost Lady	Willa Cather
Macbeth	William Shakespeare
Madame Bovary	Gustave Flaubert
Marius the Epicurean	Walter Pater
The Master of Santiago	Henry de Montherlant
The Misanthrope	Jean Baptiste Moliere
Native Son	Richard Wright
No Exit	Jean-Paul Sartre
A Passage to India	E. M. Forester
The Plague	Albert Camus
Portrait of a Lady	William James
The Quest of the Absolute	Honore de Balzac
Romula	George Eliot
The Scarlet Letter	Nathaniel Hawthorne
A Ship of Fools	Kathryn Ann Porter

Silas Marner	George Eliot
Song of Solomon	Toni Morrison
Steppenwolf	Herman Hesse
A Tale of Two Cities	Charles Dickens
Tartuffe	Jean Baptiste Moliere
Vanity Fair	William Thackeray
The Visit	Friedrich Durrenmatt

Films

Abandon Ship	Richard Sale
Alfie	Lewis Gilbert
All About Eve	Joseph Mankiewicz
All My Sons	Irving Reis
American Beauty	Sam Mendes
Amistad	Steven Spielberg
L'Avventura	Michaelangelo Antonioni
The Bicycle Thief	Vittorio de Sica
The Big Chill	Lawrence Kasdan
The Blue Angel	Josef von Sternberg
Blue Velvet	David Lynch
Bread and Chocolate	Franco Brusati
Breathless	Jean-Luc Godard
The Bridges of Madison County	Clint Eastwood
Broadcast News	James L. Brooks
The Browning Version	Anthony Asquith
Central Station	Walter Sales
Chloe in the Afternoon	Eric Romer
Cinema Paradiso	Giuseppe Tomatore
City Lights	Charles Chaplin
A Civil Action	David Gropman
Class Action	Michael Apted
A Clockwork Orange	Stanley Kubrick
The Color Purple	Steven Spielberg
Compulsion	Richard Fleischer
Crash	Paul Haggis
Do the Right Thing	Spike Lee
La Dolce Vita	Federico Fellini
Extreme Measures	Michael Apted
A Few Good Men	Steven Zaillian

The Godfather	Francis Ford Coppola
The Grifters	Steven Frears
Ikuru	Akira Kurosawa
The Insider	Michael Mann
It's a Wonderful Life	Frank Capra
Jules and Jim	Francois Truffaut
Jurassic Park	Steven Spielberg
The Last Tango in Paris	Bernardo Bertalucci
Law of Desire	Pedro Almodovar
Lost in Translation	Sofia Coppola
Malcolm X	Spike Lee
Night and Fog	Alain Resnais
Los Olvidados	Luis Bunuel
On the Waterfront	Elia Kazan
Philadelphia	Jonathan Demme
Pulp Fiction	Quentin Tarantino
The Rules of the Game	Jean Renoir
Roma	Federico Fellini
Room at the Top	Jack Clayton
Saving Private Ryan	Steven Spielberg
La Strada	Federico Fellini
To Kill a Mockingbird	Robert Mulligan
Tokyo Story	Yasujiro Ozu
Twelve Angry Men	Sidney Lumet
Wild Srawberries	Ingmar Bergman
Woman in the Dunes	Hiroshi Teshigahara
Zorba the Greek	Michael Cacoyannis

IV. Foundations of Belief: The Philosophy of Religion

The philosophy of religion is philosophic thinking about religion. It attempts to probe the underlying assumptions of personal faith and organized religion to determine whether good reasons exist for belief in a supernatural being. It examines the nature of the spiritual realm, the character of the God who is supreme within it, and the relation of that God to the world—most particularly, to human life. It asks why a loving and almighty God would allow human beings, including innocent children, to suffer; whether prayer makes a difference and how one can tell; what life after death might mean, the survival of the soul after the disintegration of the body; and what role reason plays in judging matters of faith. What has Athens to do with Jerusalem?

Philosophers who explore such questions are sympathetic to the spirit of religion and to the remarkably rich traditions, institutions, and forms of worship that have persisted from the beginning of civilization itself. They are also moved by the human yearning for order and purpose in the world, the need for things to make sense and for events to tend toward some meaningful end. At the same time, they are as critical of spiritual claims as any other claims, demanding evidence and reasoned argument to prove that religious statements are true and not just emotionally comforting. They recognize that the desire to believe in a divine being is very great and could induce people to accept ideas they would otherwise dismiss as farfetched. They realize that religious convictions are often acquired during childhood and, for that reason, assimilated without question.

The task in philosophic thinking about religion, then, is to be receptive to religious belief in light of the significant role it has played in human history and in the human heart, while at the same time maintaining a certain critical attitude in evaluating religious claims. We must not, of course, be so alert to the possibility of error that we fail to recognize the truth when we come across it. Rather, we should bring a sympathetic intelligence to bear on religion as an important phenomenon in human existence.

Unlike theologians, philosophers are not necessarily believers, and, *qua* philosophers, they strive to operate with minimum assumptions and maximum objectivity, attempting to determine whether the system of beliefs does, in fact, diagram reality. The philosopher begins with questions rather than certainty, wondering above all whether God is the name of an actual being or a fictional being that personifies our hunger for direction, comfort, and immortality. Theologians, on the other hand, are already committed to the worship of God and look for the structure of support that lies within; they seek to comprehend, interpret, elaborate, and refine that religious system. The difference, in short, is that the theologian cries, "Dear God in heaven," while the philosophers says, "Dear God, if there be a God, in heaven, if there be a heaven." Both seek justification, but only one assumes it is there.

A. THE EXISTENCE OF GOD: EXAMINING THE ARGUMENTS

The central question in the philosophy of religion is the existence of God, and in Judeo-Christian thought this means an all powerful, all knowing, and wholly loving being, present everywhere and always, immanent and transcendent, personal, holy, and the creator of heaven and earth. Is such a being real or only the product of our imagination, arising from human needs and fears? Voltaire once wrote, "If there were no God, it would be necessary to invent him." Are there good reasons for believing that God is an existent being and not a human invention? The Bible states God created man in his own image; did man return the compliment?

Some believers refuse to address the question, claiming that faith, not reason, brings us to the truth. However, not only is this a rational argument against the use of reason (which makes it self-contradictory), but it offers no protection against mistakes. If we argued this way, we would have no reliable methods of separating one person's true beliefs from another person's false ones; each individual could claim that his or her views are based on faith and are beyond all reason. Furthermore, we would have a welter of different beliefs, many inconsistent with one another, with each claiming to be the final truth. They could not all be true but each would be immune from rational examination. Clearly, this would be an impossible situation.

Although the relation between faith and reason is very complex, many theologians and philosophers have maintained that reason has a legitimate role in religion. They have offered rational arguments as proofs for religious reality, attempting a logical justification for believing in God's existence.

The medieval theologian Saint Anselm presented one of these justifications, called the *ontological* argument. He reasoned that if he had the idea of a being "than which none greater can be conceived," then that being had to exist. By such a being he meant God, of course, and so he is claiming that God necessarily exists.

Specifically, Saint Anselm argued that if he has the idea of a being than which none greater can be conceived, this being must possess all positive attributes. Such a being must be almighty, perfectly wise, wholly loving, and so forth, otherwise Anselm could conceive of a greater entity, one that includes the attributes that are lacking. In addition Anselm argues, if this is truly a being than which none greater can be conceived, he would have to possess the essential element of existence or, otherwise, he would not be a supreme being. The conclusion, then, is that the being Anselm is considering must possess existence, in other words, that God must exist.

At first reading, Anselm's argument seems bewildering, and he appears to be saying that whatever he can think of must exist. This was the criticism of a medieval monk named Gaunilon who argued that his ability to imagine a unicorn did not mean there are real unicorns.

However, Anselm's point is more subtle than that. He is not claiming that everything we reflect upon, including centaurs, gremlins, and Santa Claus, must be real, but that in this one unique case existence must be assumed. For we are thinking of a being than which none greater can be conceived, and here existence is a necessary part of such a being. In more modern terms, if we reflect on what a perfect God would be, we would have to include existence. We may not know everything that perfection entails, but we do know that existence is a necessary part, and that a being without existence could not be called perfect. This means that God, the perfect being, must exist.

If we still feel that something is wrong, that we cannot prove the existence of God just from the thought of God, perhaps our reaction is correct. In fact, those philosophers who criticize Anselm's argument identify this shift from thought to actuality as the basic flaw.

Anselm's mistake seems to be that he confuses an idea with the reality the idea represents. Although the idea of a perfect God must include existence as part of the idea, that does not prove there is an actually existent God behind the idea. Or differently put, the idea of a being than which none greater can be conceived must contain the notion of existence, but that does not mean such a being exists.

More technically put, existence is not an attribute to be added to others. It is the positing of a being with its various attributes. As the philosopher Immanuel Kant said, you cannot add to the value of a hundred imaginary dollars by taking a real one out of your pocket.

Because of some of these problems, another version of the ontological argument was proposed by the seventeenth-century French philosopher Rene Descartes. Sometimes this "Cartesian" argument is classified as causal, but since it does attempt to prove that God exists from the very thought of him it seems basically ontological in character.

Descartes begins his argument with the principle that the greater can produce the lesser, but the lesser cannot produce the greater; that is, you can get less from more, but not more from less. This being so, if we have an idea that is greater than ourselves, then we could not have produced it. God is such an idea, for we as finite beings could not have conceived of the infinite; imperfect man could never have thought of the idea of a perfect being.

Descartes goes on to argue that the only being capable of producing the idea of God in our minds is God himself. He concludes, therefore, that God must exist. From the fact that we know of God, yet could not have conceived of that being by ourselves, we must accept the existence of a God who implanted the idea of himself within us.

Unfortunately, this argument has serious flaws as well. It seems as though the lesser can produce the greater, as in an avalanche caused by a snowball, an acorn that produces an oak tree, or a nuclear explosion that results from a split atom. Now it could be argued that the effect is produced by a combination of causes, for example, the snowball plus additional snow, rocks, and trees. But whether or not less can produce more in the physical realm, in the realm of thought human beings can conceive of things far greater than themselves. Through the power of imagination we can envision creatures with much greater strength, intelligence, or perception than our own, yet these creatures do not necessarily exist. Using Descartes' argument, we could even "prove" the existence of devils, extra-terrestrials, and Superman.

A second classic argument, the *cosmological* proof, is generally attributed to Saint Thomas Aquinas. It concerns the idea of cause and effect, and in its more sophisticated versions, change and gradation, contingency and necessity. The argument goes as follows:

The world is arranged in a network of cause-and-effect such that every event has a cause. Whatever occurs, we can legitimately ask what caused it. The tree crashed against the house because it was blown down by the wind; the old man died because his heart failed; the glass shattered because it fell on the stone floor. We can even trace a series of causes and effects backwards in time to see the factors that precipitated earlier and still earlier events. The flower grew because of the rich soil, but the soil was deposited by the weathering of rock, and the rock weathered because of the action of wind, water, and ice, which was caused by a changing climate, and so on.

However, the proponents say, this process of finding more and more ultimate causes cannot go on indefinitely; we cannot have an "infinite regress." Something must be shown to be the first cause, responsible for all succeeding links in the chain. There must be a beginning to the series, a *primum mobile* behind everything that occurs, and this first cause can only be God.

This argument seems natural and plausible, and it even occurs to children when they wonder where things came from. Nevertheless, it has been criticized on various grounds by numerous thinkers. First, there does not seem to be any logical reason for claiming that an infinite regress is impossible. Just as there may not be a last effect (or a last number), there may not be a first cause; in a circular system, for example, the final event becomes the initial one (which is why the ring is a symbol of eternity).

Second, even if a first cause is necessary, that cause may not be God. A natural rather than a supernatural force may be responsible for the beginning. For instance, the creation of the universe could be due to the explosion of the primal atom, something that astronomers refer to as the "big bang." The background noise of that explosion has, in fact, been detected, along with an unevenness in the radiation, which would have allowed energy to form into clusters of stars and planets.

Third, if the argument begins with the assumption that everything has a cause, then presumably God has a cause as well; he cannot be regarded as an uncaused cause. If on the other hand, God is an exception to the rule, then there might well be other exceptions. The universe itself might be uncaused, in which case there would be no necessity for postulating a God who started it.

Sometimes the advocates of the cosmological argument find themselves arguing in a circle. They claim that everything must have a beginning and that God is that beginning, but when asked how God began, they assert that

God did not begin at all; he has always been. When the logical point is raised that perhaps the universe also has always been, they object that everything must have a beginning.

The more sophisticated versions, also presented by Saint Thomas, state that the fact of change in the world implies the existence of that which is unchanging, and that the contingency of all things implies that something must exist necessarily. By contingent is meant "dependent upon something else for its existence," as distinct from that which is self-existent, or carrying the reason for this existence within itself. These iterations, however, suffer from the same problems as the simple version of cause and effect.

The *teleological* argument is a third justification that has traditionally been offered for belief in God, and, like the cosmological argument, it is part of Saint Thomas' "Five Ways." This argument turns on the fact of nature's structure, regularity, harmony, and complexity. It claims that, rather than randomness and chaos, there is evidence of order everywhere and if there is order, there must be an intelligent mind behind it. If the earth is a work of art there must be a cosmic artist; if we can see a plan there must be a planner; in short, the design of nature implies a designer, and that can only be God.

For example, the temperature and composition of the earth's atmosphere is ideal for maintaining life; if the chemical mixture changed, or the earth were closer or farther away from the sun, life would be impossible. All organisms need water to live, and we have an envelope of moisture surrounding the earth as well as bodies of water. We need edible plants and animals to survive, and they have been provided. In addition, there is a symbiotic relationship between insects, plants, and animals, so that the organisms within the biosphere are mutually supportive.

Furthermore, each species has exactly what it requires in order to live: the porcupine has been equipped with quills, the bird with wings, the tiger with sharp teeth and claws, the turtle with an armored shell, the zebra with camouflage, the snake with venom, and so forth. In fact, every class of creature has been given the ideal characteristics to meet the demands of the environment. Animals have exactly the muscles, organs, and skeletal structure and the circulatory, digestive, reproductive, nervous, and respiratory systems that they require. Even the eye, ear, and other senses are marvelous mechanisms, perfectly suited to their functions, as are, the fin, the paw, and the hand. Human beings in particular, who have a superior brain, have been positioned at the top of the animal hierarchy. In short, nature provides ample evidence of rational organization in all of its manifestations, which means a cosmic intelligence must exist.

The teleological argument is extremely persuasive also, and even when philosophers criticize it, they respect its power and common sense appeal. However, it does have serious weaknesses that make it problematic as a proof of God's existence. For one thing, the design of the world is far from perfect and the imperfections that abound raise questions about the goodness of a God who created such a system. Not only is there chaos as well as order, but parts of the design involve pain and suffering for animals on earth, including human beings. Natural catastrophes (e.g., floods earthquakes), genetic defects (e.g., blindness, Down's syndrome), illnesses and disabilities (e.g., leukemia, cerebral palsy), inhospitable environments (e.g., jungles, deserts), and the overwhelming fact of death, make us doubt the goodness of the plan. We wonder why a benevolent, almighty God would adopt a design of this kind.

This leads to a second criticism, namely, that the order that exists could have come about naturally, not supernaturally. That is, another explanation for the regularity and orderliness in nature, besides that of an intelligent designer, is the scientific one offered by Darwin. According to the theory of evolution, those creatures that had the characteristics called for by the environment were able to survive. They then produced offspring with those same characteristics. Those that did not have the requisite skills, attributes, or capabilities perished in the struggle for survival, and their genetic line died out. Through this process of "natural selection," only the fittest species survived, so it is not at all surprising that the species that exist on earth are fit for survival; if they weren't, they would not exist.

To be surprised that animals are well adapted to their environment would be like finding it uncanny that all Olympic winners are good athletes; if they weren't good athletes, they would not have won the Olympics. Or to use another parallel, one should not be amazed that so many major cities have navigable rivers; if the rivers had not been navigable, they would never have become major cities.

A third criticism that has been offered is that even if the teleological argument were valid, it would not prove a creator of the universe but only a cosmic architect who arranged the materials. Both the cosmological and the teleological arguments would have to be sound in order to establish a God who both created and organized the world. What is more, by analogy with human constructions, a number of designers would have been involved in the project. Polytheism, then, might be established, but not monotheism.

Now if the ontological, cosmological, and teleological arguments are invalid, does that prove that God does not exist? Not necessarily. To disprove an argument for the existence of God is not to disprove God's existence. Rather, we are left with an open question. Should we believe in God until it is disproven, or not believe until it is proven?

B. THE PROBLEM OF EVIL: IF GOD IS GOOD, WHY DO PEOPLE SUFFER?

According to the Judeo-Christian concept, God is a personal being who is infinitely loving, wise, and powerful, a deity who has existed for all eternity, and who created man and the world out of the void. Given this description, however, certain logical questions arise as to why he included natural evil as part of his creation. If God is a loving father, why would he allow his children to suffer? If he is omniscient he knows of the suffering, and if he is omnipotent he could prevent it. Why then are there natural evils such as hurricanes, volcanic eruptions, avalanches, tidal waves, earthquakes, and floods? Why should there be lions, sharks, and cobras, in fact, carnivorous creatures of any kind rather than herbivores. Why have arctic wastes, swamps, and barren deserts, three fifths of the earth water and create humans without gills? Why have the entire catalog of diseases, sickness, and death? In short, if God is good, why is man's earthly home filled with so much pain and suffering?

This is the problem of evil that has puzzled philosophers and plagued theologians for several hundred years. The suffering that people inflict upon each other in wars or violent crimes might be explained within a theological system. But the suffering that human beings experience because of the natural environment is more difficult to justify. With regard to man's inhumanity to man, it can be argued that God wants human beings to possess free will, and that entails the ability to perform good or evil actions. Since free will is an important element in human life (and a necessary ingredient for moral responsibility), a good God would want people to have freedom of choice—even though they could choose cruelty and destructiveness. Therefore man was created "sufficient to have stood, though free to fall" as Milton writes in *Paradise Lost*. But why would a God of perfect love permit natural disasters to occur and, above all, allow children to suffer the pain of awful diseases and terrible genetic deformities?

If one does not believe in God's existence, of course, the problem of evil does not arise. Then all natural events, whether helpful or harmful to man, are thought to happen accidentally, without any reason or ultimate purpose behind them. We can offer explanations in terms of laws governing the behavior of energy and matter but there is no meaning to events, no ultimate purpose. Catastrophes are not meant to occur; they simply happen as part of the natural order of things, and no one is responsible for the human misery that results.

In the same way, if God is thought to exist but to be limited with regard to power, wisdom, and love, then the problem of evil is easily solved. For God could then lack the ability to prevent evil from happening, or the knowledge that it is occurring, or to be less than wholly loving.

Both alternatives, however, have been unacceptable to most theologians who view omnipotence, omniscience, and absolute love as essential characteristics of God. Hence the existence of evil remains a problem for the believer. As the philosopher David Hume writes, paraphrasing Epicurus, "Is [God] willing to prevent evil, but not able? then he is impotent. Is he able, but not willing? then is he malevolent. Is he both able and willing? whence then is evil?

Various answers have been offered to this question within the field of *theodicy*—an area of theology devoted to defending God's relationship to man. One recurring explanation is the claim that evil functions to *punish* people for their sinfulness. In order for the universe to operate fairly, it is argued, people must be punished for their sins just as they must be rewarded for their virtues. For the sake of justice, therefore, God makes the wicked suffer by visiting natural evils upon them, not only in hell but on earth as well. This is the explanation offered in scripture for the Fall of Adam and Eve, the destruction of Sodom and Gomorrah, and for the Flood that drowned everyone on earth except for the virtuous Noah and his family. Humankind was being punished for their sins. It is also the explanation that is often invoked when disasters occur in everyday life, for people frequently ask themselves what they have done to deserve such punishment, thereby assuming that all suffering is brought down on their heads by wrongdoing.

Although this kind of "retributive" thinking may be natural and prevalent, a moment's reflection will show that it cannot be a valid explanation for natural evil. For good people seem to experience as many natural calamities as awful people. Sinners alone do not suffer. When an earthquake devastates a region, good and bad alike are buried beneath the wreckage, and when ships capsize in hurricanes, it is not just the wicked who are drowned. Patients in hospitals are not all depraved people, and those with fine characters are not spared the misery of illness. In short, the human misery that exists as a result of natural evil cannot be correlated with the sinfulness of individuals. Not only is the distribution of evils askew, but the degree of suffering is often grossly out of proportion to the guilt or innocence of the sufferer. This is most evident in the case of children who may barely have had time to sin before they are afflicted with poliomyelitis or leukemia.

Quite obviously, then, this explanation for natural evil is not justified by the facts. Most theologians find it as unacceptable as Job did in the Old Testament when he protested against the suffering he underwent even though he was "blameless and upright." Job finally declared, "I call aloud, but there is no justice." Or as Robert Frost remarked, "People do not necessarily get what they deserve."

Another solution that has been proposed to the problem of evil centers around the idea that *contrasts are necessary for appreciation.* That is, unless we experienced evil we would be unable to appreciate the good in life. God therefore allows a variety of painful events to occur so that we can appreciate his blessings. The discomfort of sickness enables us to enjoy good health; storms and cold temperatures make us value balmy weather; and hunger enables us to relish the joy of eating well. In other words, God permits natural evil in order to provide human beings with a comparison; in that way they can appreciate the pleasures of the earth. It is sometimes added to this argument that unless the world were somewhat hellish, people would lack the incentive to strive for heaven.

Upon analysis, however, the logic of this proposal is also questionable. It is not certain that contrasts are necessary for appreciation An infant seems to enjoy milk immediately, and a child might enjoy the taste of strawberries without ever having tasted castor oil. Furthermore, even if contrasts are necessary, opposites certainly are not. That is, we may need partly sunny days to appreciate brilliant ones, but we do not need blizzards or rainstorms—snows that cause avalanches or torrential rain that precipitate floods. And contrasts can occur between various shades of good; there is no necessity for the bad. The presence of something good might help us to appreciate the better and best, and the least good does not become the bad; it is simply less good. A fine meal is not as good as an exquisite one, but it is not bad. The natural evils that occur, therefore, are not necessary for appreciation; degrees of good can accomplish the same end.[1]

---

[1] It has been argued that our blessings are appreciated more when disasters have been experienced, but this argument stresses only the greater degree of appreciation; it tacitly assumes that opposites per se are not needed for appreciation. Furthermore, most people would happily settle for less appreciation if the sufferings due to natural evil could be eliminated.

Still another alleged solution claims that both good and evil must exist so that we can have *genuine choice*. If good were the only option in the world, our freedom would be rendered meaningless. Real choice occurs only when there are alternative possibilities, so both evil and good must be present.

But the argument is something of a straw man. Not only are natural evils compounded far beyond what is required to provide options, but in most cases, natural evils do not permit any choices to be made. The avalanche or tidal wave overwhelm people; the shark or poisonous snake strikes down its victim without providing alternatives. People do not choose cancer over good health. The relatives of those who die of cancer may have the option of contributing to cancer research but we cannot applaud a scheme that secures freedom of choice for some by the suffering and death of others. God, with all possibilities at his disposal, could devise a more humane system.

A somewhat more persuasive argument is that natural evil is justified because it *builds character*. The claim is that people who undergo severe or prolonged suffering develop dimensions to their personality that individuals living in continual comfort can never hope to attain. Pain is purifying and disciplining, tempering people with fire to make them stronger. It refines the people's sensitivity, stiffens their will, and encourages a more reflective attitude of mind. Soft conditions, on the other hand, tend to produce soft people, those who are complacent, smug, and self-satisfied. The race as a whole has progressed by overcoming adversity—winter cold, predatory animals, plagues and pestilences—and throughout history civilization has thrived in environments that were harsh. Languishing in Tennyson's "Land of the Lotus Eaters" we would never have developed our potentialities, individually or collectively. Just as athletes and artists can only achieve success by prolonged and painful effort, human achievement as a whole must always be preceded by struggle. God, in his wisdom, has provided us with the necessary challenges in our environment so that by surmounting obstacles, we can refine our characters and the species as a whole can improve.

However, many victims of hurricanes, tornadoes, volcanic eruptions, and so on, never survive to have their characters improved; babies that die of disease have no chance to develop any character. Furthermore, even though some individuals may find severe hardship a stimulus to development and creativity, most people are demeaned by suffering. For every Helen Keller or Lance Armstrong, there are hundreds of similarly afflicted individuals who lead miserable lives. In addition, many great leaders in history seem to have developed outstanding characters without having endured great suffering, for example Churchill and Kennedy. This implies that experiencing natural evil is not a necessary condition for building character.

Faced with all of these difficulties, some theologians have declared that we simply must *have faith* in God's greatness. Perhaps the evil we see is only apparent, not real; in the overall scheme of things it may well be good. The symphony may be richer for the dissonance. With our finite understanding we are unable to comprehend the true purpose of human suffering, but in the infinitude of God's wisdom it may have a necessary place.

But if we are unable to know these matters, then we are unable to know, and no conclusion is possible. We cannot invalidate our ability to make judgments then judge that evil has a purpose and God is good.

Furthermore, blind faith is a poor substitute for lucid reasons, and the appeal to faith cannot simply ignore damaging arguments. That would be like kicking over the chess board when one's opponent says "check mate." Genuine faith does not fly in the face of reason but must be based on understanding. The world does contain suffering from natural causes, and the believer must either reconcile this fact with God's goodness or change his or her belief system. Robert Browning wrote when "God's in His heaven, all's right with the world," which suggests that when all's not right with the world, perhaps God's not in His heaven. At least before we accept the claims of religion we can expect some justification for human suffering in a world governed by a loving God.

The first selection by St. Thomas Aquinas presents several of the classic arguments for the existence of God, and C. S. Lewis then proposes a solution to the problem of evil—that the earth is not a place of happiness but of soul-making.

The film *Contact* dramatizes the conflict between religion and science, specifically whether a mystical experience is more trustworthy than the logic of Occam's razor. In *Diary of a Country Priest* the question of a Christian ministry is explored, and *The Devil's Advocate* shows the temptations that are thrown in the path of a moral life. From the standpoint of the philosophy of religion, the question is why a loving God would allow the devil to torment people this way.

A. Philosophic Concepts

Summa Theologica
St. Thomas Aquinas

St. Thomas Aquinas (1225–1274), the Italian philosopher and theologian, is considered to be the most important figure in the development of Christian thought. He produced some eighty works during his lifetime, most notably Summa Theologica *(Summary Treatise of Theology) and* Summa Contra Gentiles *(On the Truth of the Catholic Faith). His fellow students labeled him the Dumb Ox, but during the Middle Ages he became more influential than any other theologian and was subsequently referred to as the Prince of Scholastics.*

Historically, Aquinas is important for reconciling the conflict between Greek and Arab thought, and between the Augustinians and Averroists. These doctrinal disputes are not important for our purposes. What is significant is that Aquinas championed the ability of reason to support faith and to achieve genuine knowledge of God. To Aquinas, faith and reason were harmonious and philosophy and religion formed a unity.

In the following excerpt from Summa Theologica, *sometimes known as the "Five Ways," Aquinas presents rational arguments for the existence of God. To his mind, these demonstrations showed that the head as well as the heart could prove God's reality.*

First Article: Whether the Existence of God is Self-Evident?

We proceed thus to the First Article:—

Objection 1. It seems that the existence of God is self-evident. For those things are said to be self-evident to us the knowledge of which exists naturally in us, as we can see in regard to first principles. But as Damascene says, *the knowledge of God is naturally implanted in all*. Therefore the existence of God is self-evident.

Objection 2. Further, those things are said to be self-evident which are known as soon as the terms are known, which the Philosopher says is true of the first principles of demonstration. Thus, when the nature of a whole and of a part is known, it is at once recognized that every whole is greater than its part. But as soon as the signification of the word *God* is understood, it is at once seen that God exists. For by this name is signified that thing than which nothing greater can be conceived. But that which exists actually and mentally is greater than that which exists only mentally. Therefore, since as soon as the name *God* is understood it exists mentally, it also follows that it exists actually. Therefore the proposition *God exists* is self-evident.

Objection 3. Further, the existence of truth is self-evident. For whoever denies the existence of truth grants that truth does not exist: and, if truth does not exist, then the proposition *Truth does not exist* is true: and if there is anything true, there must be truth. But God is truth itself: *I am the way, the truth, and the life* (John 14:6) Therefore *God exists* is self-evident.

On the contrary, No one can mentally admit the opposite of what is self-evident; as the Philosopher (Metaph. iv, lect. vi) states concerning the first principles of demonstration. But the opposite of the proposition *God is* can be mentally admitted: *The fool said in his heart, There is no God* (Psalm 52:1). Therefore, that God exists is not self-evident.

I answer that, A thing can be self-evident in either of two ways: on the one hand, self-evident in itself, though not to us; on the other, self-evident in itself, and to us. A proposition is self-evident because the predicate is included in the essence of the subject: *e.g., Man is an animal*, for animal is contained in the essence of man. If, therefore the essence of the predicate and subject be known to all, the proposition will be self-evident to all; as is clear with regard to the first principles of demonstration, the terms of which are common things that no one is ignorant of, such as being and non-being, whole and part, and such like. If, however, there are some to whom the essence of the predicate and subject is unknown, the proposition will be self-evident in itself, but not to those who do not know the meaning of the predicate and subject of the proposition. Therefore, it happens, as Boethius says (Hebdom., the title of which is: "Whether all that is, is good"), "that there are some mental concepts self-evident only to the learned, as that incorporeal substances are not in space." Therefore I say that this proposition, *God exists*, of itself is self-evident, for the predicate is the same as the subject, because God is His own existence as will be hereafter shown (3, 4). Now because we do not know the essence of God, the proposition is not self-evident to us; but needs to be demonstrated by things that are more known to us, though less known in their nature—namely, by effects.

Reply to Objection 1. To know that God exists in a general and confused way is implanted in us by nature, inasmuch as God is man's beatitude. For man naturally desires happiness, and what is naturally desired by man must be naturally known to him. This, however, is not to know absolutely that God exists; just as to know that someone is approaching is not the same as to know that Peter is approaching, even though it is Peter who is approaching; for many there are who imagine that man's perfect good which is happiness, consists in riches, and others in pleasures, and others in something else.

Reply to Objection 2. Perhaps not everyone who hears this word *God* understands it to signify something than which nothing greater can be thought, seeing that some have believed God to be a body. Yet, granted that everyone understands that by this word *God* is signified something than which nothing greater can be thought, nevertheless, it does not therefore follow that he understands that what the word signifies exists actually, but only that it exists mentally. Nor can it be argued that it actually exists, unless it be admitted that there actually exists something than which nothing greater can be thought; and this precisely is not admitted by those who hold that God does not exist.

Reply to Objection 3. The existence of truth in general is self-evident but the existence of a Primal Truth is not self-evident to us.

Second Article: Whether It Can Be Demonstrated that God Exists

We proceed thus to the Second Article:—

Objection 1. It seems that the existence of God cannot be demonstrated. For it is an article of faith that God exists. But what is of faith cannot be demonstrated, because a demonstration produces scientific knowledge; whereas faith is of the unseen (*Hebrews* 11:1). Therefore it cannot be demonstrated that God exists.

Objection 2. Further, the essence is the middle term of demonstration. But we cannot know in what God's essence consists, but solely in what it does not consist; as Damascene says. Therefore we cannot demonstrate that God exists.

Objection 3. Further, if the existence of God were demonstrated, this could only be from His effects. But His effects are not proportionate to

Him, since He is infinite and His effects are finite; and between the finite and infinite there is no proportion. Therefore, since a cause cannot be demonstrated by an effect not proportionate to it, it seems that the existence of God cannot be demonstrated.

On the contrary, The Apostle says: *The invisible things of Him are clearly seen, being understood by the things that are made* (*Romans* 1:20). But this would not be unless the existence of God could be demonstrated through the things that are made; for the first thing we must know of anything is whether it exists.

I answer that, Demonstration can be made in two ways: One is through the cause, and is called *propter quid,* and this is to argue from what is prior absolutely. The other is through the effect, and is called a demonstration *quia*; this is to argue from what is prior relatively only to us. When an effect is better known to us than its cause, from the effect we proceed to the knowledge of the cause. And from every effect the existence of its proper cause can be demonstrated, so long as its effects are better known to us; because since every effect depends upon its cause, if the effect exists, the cause must pre-exist. Hence the existence of God, in so far as it is not self-evident to us, can be demonstrated from those of His effects which are known to us.

Reply to Objection 1. The existence of God and other like truths about God, which can be known by natural reason, are not articles of faith, but are preambles to the articles; for faith presupposes natural knowledge, even as grace presupposes nature, and perfection supposes something that can be perfected. Nevertheless, there is nothing to prevent a man, who cannot grasp a proof, accepting, as a matter of faith, something which in itself is capable of being scientifically known and demonstrated.

Reply to Objection 2. When the existence of a cause is demonstrated from an effect, this effect takes the place of the definition of the cause in proof of the cause's existence. This is especially the case in regard to God, because, in order to prove the existence of anything, it is necessary to accept as a middle term the meaning of the word, and not its essence, for the question of its essence follows on the question of its existence. Now the names given to God are derived from His effects. ... Consequently, in demonstrating the existence of God from His effects, we may take for the middle term the meaning of the word *God*.

Reply to Objection 3. From effects not proportionate to the cause no perfect knowledge of that cause can be obtained. Yet from every effect the existence of the cause can be clearly demonstrated, and so we can demonstrate the existence of God from His effects; though from them we cannot perfectly know God as He is in His essence.

Third Article: Whether God Exists?

We proceed thus to the Third Article:—

Objection 1. It seems that God does not exist; because if one of two contraries be infinite, the other would be altogether destroyed. But the word *God* means that He is infinite goodness. If, therefore, God existed, there would be no evil discoverable; but there is evil in the world. Therefore God does not exist.

Objection 2. Further, it is superfluous to suppose that what can be accounted for by a few principles has been produced by many. But it seems that everything we see in the world can be accounted for by other principles, supposing God did not exist. For all natural things can be reduced to one principle which is nature; and all voluntary things can be reduced to one principle which is human reason, or will. Therefore there is no need to suppose God's existence.

On the contrary, It is said in the person of God: *I am Who I am.* (*Exodus* 3:14)

I answer that, The existence of God can be proved in five ways.

The first and more manifest way is the argument from motion. It is certain, and evident to our senses, that in the world some things are in motion. Now whatever is in motion is put in motion by another, for nothing can be in motion except it is in potentiality to that towards which it is in motion; whereas a thing moves inasmuch as it is in act. For motion is nothing else than the reduction of something from potentiality to actuality. But nothing can be reduced from potentiality to actuality, except by something in a state of actuality. Thus that which is actually hot, as fire, makes wood, which is potentially hot, to be actually hot, and thereby moves and changes it. Now it is not possible that the same thing should be at once in actuality and potentiality in the same respect, but only in different respects. For what is actually hot cannot simultaneously be potentially hot; but it is simultaneously potentially cold. It is therefore impossible that in the same respect and in the same way a thing should be both mover and moved, *i.e.* that it should move itself. Therefore, whatever is in motion must be put in motion by another. If that by which it is put in motion be itself put in motion, then this also must needs be put in motion by another, and that by another again. But this cannot go on to infinity, because then there would be no first mover, and, consequently, no other mover; seeing that subsequent movers move only inasmuch as they are put in motion by the first mover; as the staff moves only because it is put in motion by the hand. Therefore it is necessary to arrive at a first mover, put in motion by no other; and this everyone understands to be God.

The second way is from the nature of the efficient cause. In the world of sense we find there is an order of efficient causes. There is no case known (neither is it, indeed, possible) in which a thing is found to be the efficient cause of itself; for so it would be prior to itself, which is impossible. Now in efficient causes it is not possible to go on to infinity, because in all efficient causes following in order, the first is the cause of the intermediate cause, and the intermediate is the cause of the ultimate cause, whether the intermediate cause be several, or only one. Now to take away the cause is to take away the effect. Therefore, if there be no first cause among efficient causes, there will be no ultimate, nor any intermediate cause. But if in efficient causes it is possible to go on to infinity, there will be no first efficient cause, neither will there be an ultimate effect, nor any intermediate efficient causes; all of which is plainly false. Therefore it is necessary to admit a first efficient cause, to which everyone gives the name of God.

The third way is taken from possibility and necessity, and runs thus. We find in nature things that are possible to be and not to be, since they are found to be generated, and to corrupt, and consequently, they are possible to be and not to be. But it is impossible for these always to exist, for that which is possible not to be at some time is not. Therefore, if everything is possible not to be, then at one time there could have been nothing in existence. Now if this were true, even now there would be nothing in existence, because that which does not exist only begins to exist by something already existing. Therefore, if at one time nothing was in existence, it would have been impossible for anything to have begun to exist; and thus even now nothing would be in existence—which is absurd. Therefore, not all beings are merely possible, but there must exist something the existence of which is necessary. But every necessary thing either has its necessity caused by another, or not. Now it is impossible to go on to infinity in necessary things which have their necessity caused by another, as has been already proved in regard to efficient causes. Therefore we cannot but postulate the existence of some being having of itself its own necessity, and not receiving it from another, but rather causing in others their necessity. This all men speak of as God.

The fourth way is taken from the gradation to be found in things. Among beings there are some more and some less good, true, noble and the like. But *more* and *less* are predicated of different things, according as they resemble in their different ways something which is the maximum, as a thing is said to be hotter according as it more nearly resembles that which is hottest; so that there is something which is truest, something best, something noblest and, consequently, something which is uttermost being; for those things that are greatest in truth are greatest in being, as it is written in *Metaph.* ii. Now the maximum in any genus is the cause of all in that genus; as fire, which is the maximum heat, is the cause of all hot things. Therefore there must also be something which is to all beings the cause of their being, goodness, and every other perfection; and this we call God.

The fifth way is taken from the governance of the world. We see that things which lack intelligence, such as natural bodies, act for an end, and this is evident from their acting always, or nearly always, in the same way, so as to obtain the best result. Hence it is plain that not fortuitously, but designedly, do they achieve their end. Now whatever lacks intelligence cannot move towards an end, unless it be directed by some being endowed with knowledge and intelligence; as the arrow is shot to its mark by the archer. Therefore some intelligent being exists by whom all natural things are directed to their end; and this being we call God.

Reply to Objection 1. As Augustine says (*Enchiridion* xi): *Since God is the highest good, He would not allow any evil to exist in His works, unless His omnipotence and goodness were such as to bring good even out of evil.* This is part of the infinite goodness of God, that He should allow evil to exist, and out of it produce good.

Reply to Objection 2. Since nature works for a determinate end under the direction of a higher agent, whatever is done by nature must needs be traced back to God, as to its first cause. So also whatever is done voluntarily must also be traced back to some higher cause other than human reason or will, since these can change or fail; for all things that are changeable and capable of defect must be traced back to an immovable and self-necessary first principle, as has been shown.

STUDY QUESTIONS

1. What does Aquinas mean when he says that the existence of God is self-evident?

2. Does Aquinas believe that the existence of God can be proven ("demonstrated"), or does he think it is a matter of faith, not reason?

3. Explain the argument from motion which says "whatever is moved is moved by another... but this cannot go on to infinity... Therefore it is necessary to arrive at a first mover... this everyone understands to be God."

4. Explain Aquinas' argument from possibility and necessity.

5. Can you detect any flaws in any of the "Five Ways" of establishing God's existence?

238

The Problem of Pain
C.S. Lewis

C.S. Lewis (1898-1963) was a medieval scholar and critic who taught at both Oxford and Cambridge University as well as being a popular novelist, poet, and a writer of children's literature. All of his writings are infused with a commitment to Christianity following his conversion experience that he describes in Surprised by Joy *and his other autobiographical work* Pilgrim's Regress.

Lewis' most important works of literary criticism include The Discarded Image, *and* Allegory of Love, *but he is best known for his literary works, especially the Perelandra trilogy that includes* Out of the Silent Planet. *His didactic works in defense of faith include* Beyond Personality, Miracles, Mere Christianity, The Four Loves, *and his celebrated* Screwtape Letters. *Lewis is also well known for a series of children's books called the Chronicles of Narnia, especially* The Lion, the Witch and the Wardrobe.

In The Problem of Pain *Lewis addresses the question of why a benevolent God would allow humankind to suffer. His answer is that a loving father would not want his son just to have a good time but would "use his authority to make the son into the sort of human being he... wants him to be." The earth is a place where character is formed through overcoming adversity, and it is therefore compatible with God's goodness toward man. God wants the best for us, and that is only possible by creating conditions that ennoble our souls.*

I. INTRODUCTORY

Not many years ago when I was an atheist, if anyone had asked me, 'Why do you not believe in God?' my reply would have run something like this: 'Look at the universe we live in. By far the greatest part of it consists of empty space, completely dark and unimaginably cold. The bodies which move in this space are so few and so small in comparison with the space itself that even if every one of them were known to be crowded as full as it could hold with perfectly happy creatures, it would still be difficult to believe that life and happiness were more than a byproduct to the power that made the universe. As it is, however, the scientists think it likely that very few of the suns of space—perhaps none of them except our own—have any planets;[1] and in our own system it is improbable that any planet except the Earth sustains life. And Earth herself existed without life for millions of years and may exist for millions more when life has left her. And what is it like while it lasts? It is so arranged that all the forms of it can live only by preying upon one another. In the lower forms this process entails only death, but in the higher there appears a new quality called consciousness which enables it to be attended with pain. The creatures cause pain by being born, and live by inflicting pain, and in pain they mostly die. In the most complex of all the creatures, Man, yet another quality appears, which we call reason, whereby he is enabled to foresee his own pain which henceforth is preceded with acute mental suffering, and to foresee his own death while keenly desiring permanence. It also enables men by a hundred ingenious contrivances to inflict a great deal more pain than they otherwise could have done on one another and on the irrational creatures. This power they have exploited to the full. Their history is largely a record of crime, war, disease, and terror, with just sufficient happiness interposed to give them, while it lasts, an agonised apprehension of losing it, and, when it is lost, the poignant misery of remembering. Every now and then they improve their condition a little and what we call a civilization appears. But all civilizations pass away and, even while they remain, inflict peculiar sufferings of their own probably sufficient to outweigh what alleviations they may have brought to the normal pains of man. That our own civilization has done so, no one will dispute; that it will pass away like all its predecessors is surely probable. Even if it should not, what then? The race is doomed. Every race that comes into being in any part of the universe is doomed; for the universe, they tell us, is running down, and will sometime be a uniform infinity of homogeneous matter at a low temperature. All stories will come to nothing: all life will turn out in the end to have been a transitory and senseless contortion upon the idiotic face of infinite matter. If you ask me to believe that this is the work of a benevolent and omnipotent spirit, I reply that all the evidence points in the opposite

---

[1]Astronomers now know that in our Milky Way galaxy alone billions of planets are orbiting other stars. Furthermore, traces of life have been discovered on the Moon (Ed.).

direction. Either there is no spirit behind the universe, or else a spirit indifferent to good and evil, or else an evil spirit.'

There was one question which I never dreamed of raising. I never noticed that the very strength and facility of the pessimists' case at once poses us a problem. If the universe is so bad, or even half so bad, how on earth did human beings ever come to attribute it to the activity of a wise and good Creator? Men are fools, perhaps; but hardly so foolish as that. The direct inference from black to white, from evil flower to virtuous root, from senseless work to a workman infinitely wise, staggers belief. The spectacle of the universe as revealed by experience can never have been the grounds of religion: it must always have been something in spite of which religion, acquired from a different source, was held.

It would be an error to reply that our ancestors were ignorant and therefore entertained pleasing illusions about nature which the progress of science has since dispelled. For centuries, during which all men believed, the nightmare size and emptiness of the universe was already known. You will read in some books that the men of the Middle Ages thought the Earth flat and the stars near, but that is a lie. Ptolemy had told them that the Earth was a mathematical point without size in relation to the distance of the fixed stars—a distance which one medieval popular text estimates as a hundred and seventeen million miles. And in times yet earlier, even from the beginnings, men must have got the same sense of hostile immensity from a more obvious source. To prehistoric man the neighboring forest must have been infinite enough, and the utterly alien and infest which we have to fetch from the thought of cosmic rays and cooling suns, came snuffing and howling nightly to his very doors. Certainly at all periods the pain and waste of human life was equally obvious. Our own religion begins among the Jews, a people squeezed between great warlike empires, continually defeated and led captive, familiar as Poland or Armenia with the tragic story of the conquered. It is mere nonsense to put pain among the discoveries of science. Lay down this book and reflect for five minutes on the fact that all the great religions were first preached, and long practiced, in a world without chloroform.

At all times, then, an inference from the course of events in this world to the goodness and wisdom of the Creator would have been equally preposterous; and it was never made.[2] Religion has a different origin.

---

[2] Lewis speculates on the origin of religion, in such sources as a sense of the holy, then returns to a discussion of pain as an empediment to faith (Ed.).

II. DIVINE OMNIPOTENCE

"If God were good, He would wish to make His creatures perfectly happy, and if God were almighty He would be able to do what He wished. But the creatures are not happy. Therefore God lacks either goodness, or power, or both." This is the problem of pain, in its simplest form. The possibility of answer it depends on showing that the terms "good" and "almighty," and perhaps also the term "happy" are equivocal; for it must be admitted from the outset that if the popular meanings attached to these words are the best, or the only possible meanings, then the argument is unanswerable. In this chapter I shall make some comments on the idea of Omnipotence, and, in the following, some on the idea of Goodness.

   Omnipotence means "power to do all, or everything."[3] And we are told in Scripture that "with God all things are possible." It is common enough, in argument with an unbeliever, to be told that God, if He existed and were good, would do this or that; and then, if we point out that the proposed action is impossible, to be met with the retort, "But I thought God was supposed to be able to do anything." This raises the whole question of impossibility.

   In ordinary usage the word *impossible* generally implies a suppressed clause beginning with the word *unless*. Thus it is impossible for me to see the street from where I sit writing at this moment; that is, it is impossible *unless* I go to the top floor where I shall be high enough to overlook the intervening building. If I had broken my leg I should say "But it is impossible to go to the top floor"—meaning, however, that it is impossible *unless* some friends show up who will carry me. Now let us advance to a different plane of impossibility, by saying "It is, at any rate, impossible to see the street *so long as* I remain where I am and the intervening building remains where it is." Someone might add "unless the nature of space, or of vision, were different from what it is." I don't know what the best philosophers and scientists would say to this, but I should have to reply "I don't know whether space and vision *could possibly* have been of such a nature as you suggest." Now it is clear that the words *could possibly* here refer to some absolute kind of possibility or impossibility which is different from the relative possibilities and impossibilities we have been considering. I cannot say whether seeing round corners is, in this new sense, possible or not, because I do not know whether it is self-contradictory or not. But I know very well that if it is self-contradictory it is absolutely impossible. The absolutely im-

---

[3]The original meaning in Latin may have been "power *over* or *in* all." I give what I take to be current sense.

possible may also be called the intrinsically impossible because it carries its impossibility within itself, instead of borrowing it from other impossibilities which in their turn depend upon others. It has no *unless* clause attached to it. It is impossible under all conditions and in all worlds and for all agents.

"All agents" here includes God Himself. His Omnipotence means power to do all that is intrinsically possible, not to do the intrinsically impossible. You may attribute miracles to Him, but not nonsense. This is no limit to His power. If you choose to say "God can give a creature free will and at the same time withhold free will from it, "you have not succeeded in saying *anything* about God: meaningless combinations of words do not suddenly acquire meaning simply because we prefix to them the two other words "God can." It remains true that all *things* are possible with God: the intrinsic impossibilities are not things but nonentities. It is no more possible for God than for the weakest of His creatures to carry out both of two mutually exclusive alternatives; not because His power meets an obstacle, but because nonsense remains nonsense even when we talk it about God....

By the goodness of God we mean nowadays almost exclusively His lovingness; and in this we may be right. And by Love, in this context, most of us mean kindness—the desire to see others than the self happy; not happy in this way or in that, but just happy. What would really satisfy us would be a God who said of anything we happened to like doing, "What does it matter so long as they are contented?" We want, in fact, not so much a Father in Heaven as a grandfather in heaven—a senile benevolence who, as they say, "liked to see young people enjoying themselves," and whose plan for the universe was simply that it might be truly said at the end of each day, "a good time was had by all." Not many people, I admit, would formulate a theology in precisely those terms: but a conception not very different lurks at the back of many minds. I do not claim to be an exception: I should very much like to live in a universe which was governed on such lines. But since it is abundantly clear that I don't, and since I have reason to believe, nevertheless, that God is Love, I conclude that my conception of love needs correction.

I might, indeed, have learned, even from the poets, that Love is something more stern and splendid than mere kindness: that: even the love between the sexes is, as in Dante, "a lord of terrible aspect." There is kindness in Love: but Love and kindness are not coterminous, and when kindness (in the sense given above) is separated from the other elements of Love, it involves a certain fundamental indifference to its object, and even something like contempt of it. Kindness consents very readily to the removal of its object—we have all met people whose kindness to animals is constantly leading them to kill animals lest they should suffer. Kindness, merely as such, cares not whether its object becomes good or bad, provided only that it escapes suffering. As Scripture points out, it is bastards who are spoiled: the legitimate sons, who are to carry on the family tradition, are punished.[4] It is for people whom we care nothing about that we demand happiness on any terms: with our friends, our lovers, our children, we are exacting and would rather see them suffer much than be happy in contemptible and estranging modes. If God is Love, He is, by definition, something more than mere kindness. And it appears, from all the records, that though He has often rebuked us and condemned us, He has never regarded us with contempt. He has paid us the intolerable compliment of loving us, in the deepest, most tragic, most inexorable sense.

The relation between Creator and creature is, of course, unique, and cannot be paralleled by any relations between one creature and another. God is both further from us, and nearer to us, than any other being. He is further from us because the sheer difference between that which has Its principle of being in Itself and that to which being is communicated is one compared with which the difference between an archangel and a worm is quite insignificant. He makes, we are made: He is original, we derivative. But at the same time, and for the same reason, the intimacy between God and even the meanest creature is closer than any that creatures can attain with one another. Our life is, at every moment, supplied by Him: our tiny, miraculous power of free will only operates on bodies which His continual energy keeps in existence—our very power to think is His power communicated to us. Such a unique relation can be apprehended only by analogies: from the various types of love known among creatures we reach an inadequate, but useful, conception of God's love for man.

The lowest type, and one which is "love" at all only by an extension of the word, is that which an artist feels for an artefact. God's relation to man is pictured thus in Jeremiah's vision of the potter and the clay,[5] or when St. Peter speaks of the whole Church as a building on which God is at work, and of the individual members as stones.[6] The limitation of such an analogy is, of course, that in the symbol the patient is not sentient, and that certain questions of justice and mercy which arise when the "stones" are really "living" therefore remain unrepresented. But it is an important analogy so

---

[4]Heb, vii, 8.
[5]Jer., xviii.
[6]Pet. ii, 5.

far as it goes. We are, not metaphorically but in very truth, a Divine work of art, something that God is making, and therefore something with which He will not be satisfied until it has a certain character. Here again we come up against what I have called the "intolerable compliment." Over a sketch made idly to amuse a child, an artist may not take much trouble: he may be content to let it go even though it is not exactly as he meant it to be. But over the great picture of his life—the work which he loves, though in a different fashion, as intensely as a man loves a woman or a mother a child—he will take endless trouble—and would doubtless, thereby give endless trouble to the picture if it were sentient. One can imagine a sentient picture, after being rubbed and scraped and re-commenced for the tenth time, wishing that it were only a thumb-nail sketch whose making was over in a minute. In the same way, it is natural for us to wish that God had designed for us a less glorious and less arduous destiny; but then we are wishing not for more love but for less.

Another type is the love of a man for a beast—a relation constantly used in Scripture to symbolise the relation between God and men; "we are his people and the sheep of his pasture." This is in some ways a better analogy than the preceding, because the inferior party is sentient and yet unmistakably inferior: but it is less good in so far as man has not made the beast and does not fully understand it. Its great merit lies in the fact that the association of (say) man and dog is primarily for the man's sake: he tames the dog primarily that he may love it, not that it may love him, and that it may serve him, not that he may serve it. Yet at the same time, the dog's interests are not sacrificed to the man's. The one end (that he may love it) cannot be fully attained unless it also, in its fashion, loves him, nor can it serve him unless he, in a different fashion, serves it. Now just because the dog is by human standards one of the "best" of irrational creatures, and a proper object for a man to love—of course, with that degree and kind of love which is proper to such an object, and not with silly anthropomorphic exaggerations—man interferes with the dog and makes it more lovable than it was in mere nature. In its state of nature it has a smell, and habits, which frustrate man's love: he washes it, house-trains it, teaches it not to steal, and is so enabled to love it completely. To the puppy the whole proceeding would seem, if it were a theologian, to cast grave doubts on the "goodness" of man: but the full-grown and full-trained dog, larger, healthier, and longer-lived than the wild dog, and admitted, as it were by Grace, to a whole world of affections, loyalties, interests, and comforts entirely beyond its animal destiny, would have no such doubts. It will be noted that the man (I am speaking throughout of the good man) takes all these pains with the dog, and gives all these pains to the dog, only because it is an animal high in the scale—because it is so nearly lovable that it is worth his while to make it fully lovable. He does not house-train the earwig or give baths to centipedes. We may wish, indeed, that we were of so little account to God that He left us alone to follow our natural impulses—that He would give over trying to train us into something so unlike our natural selves: but once again, we are asking not for more Love, but for less.

A nobler analogy, sanctioned by the constant tenor of Our Lord's teaching, is that between God's love for man and a father's love for a son. Whenever this is used, however (that is, whenever we pray the Lord's Prayer), it must be remembered that the Saviour used it in a time and place where paternal authority stood much higher than it does in modern England. A father half apologetic for having brought his son into the world, afraid to restrain him lest he should create inhibitions or even to instruct him lest he should interfere with his independence of mind, is a most misleading symbol of the Divine Fatherhood. I am not here discussing whether the authority of fathers, in its ancient extent, was a good thing or a bad thing: I am only explaining what the conception of Fatherhood would have meant to Our Lord's first hearers, and indeed to their successors for many centuries. And it will become even plainer if we consider how Our Lord (though, in our belief, one with His Father and co-eternal with Him as no earthly son is with an earthly father) regards His own Sonship, surrendering His will wholly to the paternal will and not even allowing Himself to be called "good" because Good is the name of the Father. Love between father and son, in this symbol, means essentially authoritative love on the one side, and obedient love on the other. The father uses his authority to make the son into the sort of human being he, rightly, and in his superior wisdom, wants him to be. Even in our own days, though a man might say, he could mean nothing by saying, "I love my son but don't care how great a blackguard he is provided he has a good time."…

The problem of reconciling human suffering with the existence of a God who loves, is only insoluble so long as we attach a trivial meaning to the word "love," and look on things as if man were the centre of them. Man is not the centre. God does not exist for the sake of man. Man does not exist for his own sake. "Thou hast created all things, and for thy pleasure they are and were created."[7] We were made not primarily that we may love God

---

[7]Rev. iv, II.

(though we were made for that too) but that God may love us, that we may become objects in which the Divine love may rest "well pleased." To ask that God's love should be content with us as we are is to ask that God should cease to be God: because He is what He is, His love must, in the nature of things, be impeded and repelled by certain stains in our present character, and because He already loves us He must labour to make us lovable. We cannot even wish, in our better moments, that He could reconcile Himself to our present impurities—no more than the beggar maid could wish that King Cophetua should be content with her rags and dirt, or a dog, once having learned to love man, could wish that man were such as to tolerate in his house the snapping, verminous, polluting creature of the wild pack. What we would here and now call our "happiness" is not the end God chiefly has in view: but then we are such as He can love without impediment, we shall in fact be happy.

STUDY QUESTIONS

1. On what grounds did C. S. Lewis formerly reject the existence of God?

2. How would you answer Lewis' question: "If the universe is so bad... how on earth did human beings ever come to attribute it to the activity of a wise and good Creator?"

3. What is the distinction Lewis makes between the intrinsically possible (which God can do) and the intrinsically impossible (which God cannot do)?

4. What is Lewis' solution to the problem of evil, that is, reconciling God's love with human suffering?

5. Evaluate the soundness of Lewis' answer. What is your own reasoned conclusion?

B. Expression in Film

Contact

Director: Robert Zemeckis

Screenplay: Jim Hart, Michael Goldenberg, Carl Sagan, Ann Druyan, et al.

Robert Zemeckis (1952–), a prominent, contemporary filmmaker, has directed, produced, or written screenplays for some sixteen films to date. His best known works are Romancing the Stone, *about a female novelist trying to rescue her sister in* South America; Back to the Future *(I, II, and III) that portrays the adventures of a teenager who travels back in time;* Who Framed Roger Rabbit, *a groundbreaking popular hit combining live action and animation;* Forrest Gump, *a film dealing with a retarded man's involvement in world events; and* Cast Away, *the story of a castaway's suffering, both on his deserted island and when he tries to resume his former relationship. He also directed* I Wanna Hold Your Hand *(his debut film),* Death Becomes Her, *and* Used Cars, *and he acted as executive producer for* The Frighteners, The Public Eye, *and* Trespass. *Most recently Zemeckis has directed* The Polar Express *and* Beowulf. *His films have grossed over two billion dollars worldwide.*

Zemeckis won an Oscar as best director for Forrest Gump, *which was also named Best Picture, and several of his films have won Academy Awards for visual effects, sound effects, editing, and screenplay. In his film* Contact, *based on the book by Carl Sagan, his theme is the search for extraterrestrial intelligence in the universe.*

SYNOPSIS

The search for intelligent life on other planets is not just the stuff of science fiction but of serious scientific interest as well. Beginning in 1960, astronomers have been searching for alien signals using arrays of telescopes at various places on Earth. These SETI projects (Search for Extraterrestrial

Intelligence) have ranged from the pioneering Project Ozma in West Virginia, to the mammoth Arecibo dish in Puerto Rico, to the Allen Telescope constructed in California in 2006.

In addition, the spacecrafts Pioneer 10 and 11, the first to leave the solar system, both carried six-by-nine-inch plaques with drawings of human beings and the location of Earth in the cosmos; Carl Sagan and Frank Drake co-designed the plaque. Pioneer 10 is still transmitting signals from 6.6 billion miles away, but no response has been received from any civilizations in deep space. A further message was sent from the Arecibo Observatory describing our chemical makeup, our planetary system, and so forth; it will reach its destination in M13 globular cluster in 25,000 years. What's more, the spacecrafts Voyager I and II carried a gold-plated phonograph record with information about our planet and its life forms. The Interstellar Recording contains animal noises, including the sounds of humpback whales, music from a variety of human cultures, and the electrical activity of a person's body over a one-hour period. The recording will last for 1 billion years.

The scientific community supports these projects because of the high probability that intelligent life does exist on other planets. An estimated 400 billion stars make up our Milky Way galaxy alone, half of which have orbiting planets that might sustain life, and there are approximately 100 billion galaxies in the universe. Astronomers can calculate the odds of receiving signals from an alien civilization using a formula called the "Drake Equation":

$$N = R^* \times f_p \times n_e \times f_l \times f_i \times f_c \times L$$

Where,

N = The number of civilizations in The Milky Way Galaxy whose radio emissions are detectable.

R^* = The rate of formation of stars suitable for the development of intelligent life.

f_p = The fraction of those stars with planetary systems.

N_e = The number of planets, per solar system, with an environment suitable for life.

f_l = The fraction of suitable planets on which life actually appears.

f_i = The fraction of life-bearing planets on which intelligent life emerges.

f_c = The fraction of civilizations that develop a technology that releases detectable signals of their existence into space

L = The length of time such civilizations release detectable signals into space.

Using this formula, the astronomers involved in SETI support the possibility of communication with some form of extraterrestrial intelligence, however they dismiss the idea of UFO sightings and abductions by alien creatures. Such reports, coming mainly from the rural southwest, are treated as misinterpretations of ordinary events or as signs of emotional problems. The reason for the skepticism is that no scientific proof exists that we have ever been visited by extraterrestrials. Personal accounts abound but verifiable evidence is lacking.

Furthermore, the enormous dimensions of space and time make interstellar travel impossible. Astronomers measure cosmic distances in light years, which is the space traversed by a ray of light over one year traveling at a rate of 186,281 miles per second. Aside from the sun, our nearest star is over 4 light years away or about 24 trillion (24,000,000,000,000) miles. Given the capabilities of rocketry and the absolte limit of the speed of light, that means it would take 300,000 years for aliens from the closest star system to reach the Earth. Any travel from a further star among the billions in the Milky Way would take millions of years.[1]

Nevertheless, the likelihood is that we are not alone. As Frank Drake has stated , "Everything we've learned about the universe has pointed in one direction: we are not so very special. Planets are commonplace, and... life is not a rare occurrence at all, but is as natural throughout the universe as the formation of planets and stars. ... It seems only reasonable to conclude that intelligent life will also be widespread." Carl Sagan also remarked, "There may be millions of worlds in the Milky Way Galaxy which are at this moment inhabited by other intelligent beings."

Although we may never be able to meet these beings, one of our radio telescopes may someday receive a signal from space, either as incidental sound waves released into space or as a message deliberately beamed to Earth. If and when that day happens, we will have to reassess our place in the universe as well as our religious beliefs about the relation between God and man. If we were not unique, would that make our species less valuable? Would it raise doubts about God's existence or, on the contrary, show his creation as even grander that we imagined?

Within this context, the film *Contact* portrays the search for extraterrestrial intelligence and the implications, political and social, when an alien

---

[1]This is the answer given to Fermi's Paradox, which is usually stated as follows: Most of the stars in the galaxy are more than a billion years older than the sun. If intelligent life and civilizations exist throughout the galaxy, then they should have colonized other planets long ago. Where are they? The answer of most astronomers is not that aliens are here in flying saucers but that physical limitations make interstellar space travel impossible.

signal is received. Furthermore, it deals with the role played by faith and revelation and by science and rationality in our understanding. As a personal dimension, the film also contains a live story between an astronomer, Ellie Arroway (Jodie Foster) and a theologian, Palmer Joss (Matthew McConaughey), which manages to transcend the differences in their outlooks.[2] Their passionate discussions on how truth is revealed form the philosophic structure of the plot. The film begins with a visual tour of the stars and planets, beginning on Earth and taking us to the edge of the universe, 8 billion light years away. The camera then zooms back from the macrocosm to the microcosm so that the blackness of space resolves itself into the eye of a young Ellie Arroway.

We see Ellie turning the dial of a short-wave radio under the gentle guidance of her father, Ted Arroway (David Morse) and tuning in Pensacola, Florida. She is enthralled at hearing a voice materialize out of the air from miles away, and draws a scene of a Florida beach. She asks her father "Could we hear to China?…Could we hear to the moon? Her father answers quietly "Big enough radio. I don't see why not." She then asks "Could we hear God? "to which her father replies "Hmm, that's a good one. Maybe his echo…" Conceivably this is an allusion to the sound of Big Bang, the explosion of the primal atom that produced our universe. Because of the enormous distances and the eons of time entailed, astronomers have just now detected that sound.

When Ellie asks whether he thinks there are people on other planets her father answers "Well let's see… the Universe is a pretty big place… And the one thing I know about nature is it hates to waste anything. So I guess I'd say if it is just us, seems like an awful waste of space."

Ted Arroway dies of a heart attack when Ellie is 9 years old, leaving her orphaned and with an acute feeling of abandonment and loss. The film suggests that this trauma may be driving her subsequent search for brothers and sisters in space, and her receptivity to a father in the universe. In fact, one of her professors asks " What is it that makes you so lonely, Miss Arroway? What is it that compels you to search the heavens for life…?"

Ellie subsequently studies astronomy at Cal Tech, receiving her degree *magna cum laude*. In graduate school she receives financial support through her mentor, Professor Drumlin (Tom Skerrit), for a research project at the Arecibo disk in Puerto Rico. She remains at Arecibo for some time, trying to detect radio signals from space. However, when Drumlin becomes

---

[2]The "arrow way" could represent the direct way to a target; a "joss" is an idol or cult image.

head of the National Science Foundation, he withdraws her funds, deciding that taxpayers' money should be spent on more practical and profitable projects. He calls her quest "professional suicide," and Ellie herself wonders whether she ought to be jeopardizing her chances at publishing and, in effect, risking her entire career by searching for "little green men."

Before Ellie leaves Arecibo she begins a relationship with a religious scholar, Palmer Joss, who later becomes a significant figure in her life. They spend one night together, and although Ellie feels drawn to him, she inexplicably throws his telephone number away. Perhaps she fears the conflict that their differences will engender. In one significant conversation Palmer describes a mystical experience that is the source of his faith.

> PALMER: [I was] looking at the sky and then I felt something. All I know is that I wasn't alone, and for the first time in my life I wasn't afraid of nothing, not even dying. It was God.
>
> ELLIE: There's no chance that you had this experience because some part of you needed to have it?
>
> PALMER: I mean, I'm a reasonably intelligent guy, but this, no this... . My intellect, it couldn't even touch this.

Eventually Ellie obtains private backing from a philanthropist, S. R. Hadden (John Hurt) that enables her to rent time at the Very Large Array (VLA) telescope in New Mexico—31 linked dishes that allow more of the sky to be searched in a day than she could formerly do in a year.[3]

Ellie works at the facility for four years, listening almost continuously at the radio telescope and living in a painted cinderblock room; her team refers to her as the High Priestess of the Desert. However, her search proves fruitless, yielding no appreciable results, so once again her funding is cancelled.

At this point the whole enterprise seems lost, but just before the deadline on the grant expires, Ellie hears a deep pulsing signal that her team traces to the star Vega, 26 light years away. The signal takes the form of prime numbers—59, 61, 67, 71, and so forth, indicating a deliberate trans-

---

[3]Ellie's methodology follows that of Project Phoenix in New South Wales, Australia, a targeted search of individual stars. However, rather than listening with earphones as Ellie Arroway does, computers scan for signals, examining 28 million channels simultaneously, and when unusual sounds appear they alert the astronomers. Interestingly, Project Phoenix has a blind astronomer like Kent Clark (William Fichtner) in the film, and a woman astronomer, Jill Tarter, heads it. She is a leading astronomer in the search for extraterrestrial life. Dr. Tarter declared in an interview, however, that although Ellie does what she does, the film is not based on her.

mission from an intelligent source. She quickly informs David Drumlin who is now Science Advisor to the President, and sends out a request to telescope facilities around the world to corroborate her findings; 44 stations confirm the signal.

After a brief meeting with officials at White Sands Air Force Base, a command center is set up at the VLA to pursue the communication. The periodic frequency of the signal appears to be a complex code, so a cryptographer is brought in to decipher the message. As the team watches transfixed, the prime numbers are translated into images—moving pictures of Hitler at the 1936 Olympic Games. This seems bizarre until David Drumlin explains, "this was the first television transmission of any power that went into space. That they recorded it and sent it back is simply a way of saying 'Hello, we heard you.'" However, Michael Kitz (James Wood), the National Security Advisor who is present, warns that it could mean "Sieg Heil! You're our kind of people."

During the succeeding months Kitz continuously presses for the project to be "militarized," citing national security interests. Kitz, along with Drumlin, functions as the villain of the piece. He suspects the "Vegans" of having hostile intentions, and he fears that such an advanced civilization will have alarming destructive power. This theme persists throughout the film, often supported by religious leaders who view the aliens as spawn of the devil, with science as his pawn.

Soon after the discovery, President Clinton calls a press conference, announcing to the world that American scientists have detected a radio signal from space. Ellie Arroway should then have presented an explanation of the SETI project and the significance of the results, but she is upstaged by Drumlin. In effect, he takes credit for the achievement, leaving Ellie shaken and hurt. Through his political manipulation, she is here marginalized and almost loses control of the project.

Now that the extraterrestrial contact is public knowledge, vans, buses, cars, and recreation vehicles jam the roads to the New Mexico facility. A tent city is set up with campfires and barbeques. Elvis impersonators appear, Indians perform tribal dances, and con men sell abduction insurance. News reporters gather in a media frenzy, and New Age gurus preach to crowds of people in an atmosphere resembling Woodstock. One memorable preacher named Joseph declares "The millennium is upon us. God has fulfilled his promise, sending us this herald to warn the faithless—the scientists who tell us He doesn't even exist—and to promise us, the faithful, we will be saved."

Meanwhile, additional data has been received, encrypted pages of text interlaced in frames of Hitler's image. Page after page of complex geometric patterns begin to appear on the screen, and these "hieroglyphics" amount to 63,000 pages of data before the transmission ends. Furthermore, the message starts to repeat itself with no key or 'primer' at the end. Ellie begins to work on the code herself, when suddenly someone hacks into the secured system, inviting her to see him. He promises to reveal a secret, presumably about the hieroglyphics.

The man is her benefactor, S. R. Hadden, and Ellie meets with him aboard a transport plane that is his home, outfitted as a high-tech laboratory with state-of- the-art computers and banks of monitors. Hadden had access to the VLA data and has cracked the code. Using the primer, he shows Ellie that the signal contains a set of instructions for building a highly sophisticated transport. He offers Ellie a deal: he wants to construct the machine in exchange for which he will disclose the decryption primer. He understands the politics and knows "the powers that be are falling all over themselves to play the game of the millennium. Maybe I can help deal you back in the game."

Ellie accepts, agreeing to promote his cause as long as it remains consistent with the best interests of science. Hadden then shows her how, when viewed three dimensionally, the hieroglyphics emerge as engineering schematics for a machine—a transporter designed to carry a single human occupant into space.

Following their discussion, Ellie meets Palmer Joss again, first seeing him at a high-level meeting as spiritual advisor to the President, then at a Washington cocktail party. Their conversation invariably turns to religion and science.

Ellie quotes from Joss' book in which he depreciates science: "Ironically, the thing that people are most hungry for, meaning, is the one thing science has not been able to give them." She then refers to Occam's Razor, the rule of thought that says the simplest explanation is best, implying that the God hypothesis is complicated and therefore dubious.

> ELLIE: So what's more likely, an all-powerful, mysterious God created the universe and decided not to give any proof of his existence, or that he simply does not exist at all and we created him so we wouldn't have to feel so small and alone?
>
> PALMER: I don't know. I couldn't image living in a world in which God didn't exist. I wouldn't want to.

ELLIE: How do you know you aren't deluding yourself?

The theme of possible self-delusion recurs throughout the film.

When the world governments learn that the signal contains plans for a transporter, they decide to collaborate in building it, with the United States providing most of the quarter-trillion-dollar cost; Hadden is the chief contractor. Gradually the machine takes shape as a gigantic crucible, powered by crystals in unearthly fractal patterns. Three concentric rings rotate in different directions at enormous speed, with a metal ball at the center that can encapsulate a person—a compartment referred to as an IPV.

A group of international dignitaries is assembled including Palmer Joss to determine who should be that emissary from Earth, and Ellie and Drumlin are among the 10 candidates the panel considers, probing their political, philosophical, and religious views. Ellie is especially anxious to be chosen, despite the obvious danger, for as she tells Palmer, "For as long as I can remember I've been searching for something, some reason why we're here. What are we doing, who are we? If this is a chance to find out even a little part of that answer, I think that's worth a human life." Palmer embraces her, realizing they are both on a quest for truth in their separate ways.

At the hearing it looks as though Ellie will be selected because the panel is most impressed with her replies. For example, when asked what questions she might ask the Vegans she answers, "How did you evolve, how did you survive this technological adolescence without destroying yourselves?" However, just as her confirmation seems assured, Palmer Joss asks whether she believes in God, and when it becomes clear she is an atheist, David Drumlin is chosen above her. Drumlin claims to be a believer, which is what the group wants to hear, and that affirmation of faith prevails over honesty. Ellie, of course, views Palmer's question as sabotage, but as he explains, the person should represent the mainstream views of humanity. His deeper reason, as he later confesses, is that he was afraid of losing her.

As it turns out, Drumlin is killed when the religious fanatic Joseph blows up the transporter in a suicide bombing, and Ellie is given the chance to travel into space in a duplicate machine that Hadden has constructed.

At this point, the story becomes ambiguous. When the transporter is launched Ellie experiences herself being propelled into space, traveling through translucent, electro-magnetic fields. She sees explosions, whorls of light, and feels herself shot through wormholes in space. When the motion stops, she floats down to a beautiful beach like the one she drew of Florida as a child and, mysteriously, her father is there. He tells her that the beach and perhaps his form had been created to make it easier for her, but he offers no proof of its reality because "that's the way it has always been done." He also says, "The only thing we've found that makes the emptiness bearable is each other."

Immediately afterward Ellie finds herself back at the launch site where people tell her she did not go anywhere. The IPV had dropped straight through the rings and she had been rescued. Only a few seconds had elapsed.

At a subsequent investigation headed by Michael Kitz, her experience is treated as a hallucination, and the entire episode, from receipt of the signal to the space machine, as an elaborate hoax by S. R. Hadden. Kitz challenges Ellie to offer any evidence of her space travel because all that the monitors recorded was static. Using her own weapons against her, he reasons that according to Occam's Razor, the simplest explanation is that she was deluded. Ellie cannot refute the logic but she declares,

> I had an experience. I can't prove it, I can't even explain it, but everything that I know as a human being, everything I am tells me it was real. I was given something wonderful, something that changed me forever, a vision of the universe that tells me undeniably how tiny and insignificant and how rare and precious we all are, a vision that tells us we belong to something that is greater than ourselves, that we are not, that none of use are alone.

Her speech is a parallel to that of Palmer Joss when he described his religious experience at their first meeting. The implication is that faith is a matter of individual, private revelation. It transcends the bounds of evidence and reason, utterly convincing the person who has had the revelation and transforming their lives.

This might be the ultimate message of the film, except for a scene toward the end of the film that throws matters into confusion. Rachel Constantine points out to Michael Kitz that the video did record only static but there were 18 hours of it whereas she has been in the module for only a few minutes. Hard evidence therefore seems to verify Ellie's account, and we need not trust in faith alone to authenticate our personal experience.

Contact obviously poses the question of whether intelligent life exists on other planets, but it also explores the question of God's existence and how belief is proven. Palmer Joss functions as a counterpoint to Ellie Arroway's scientific viewpoint, balancing her demand for proof with the perspective of faith, and her strict rationality with personal feelings. In the end, the two manage to find common ground in a mystical experience so that their ideologies no longer divide them. Nevertheless, we are left uncertain as to whether Ellie really passed through a spiritual doorway to another dimension. If there had not been 18 hours of static as scientific proof, would a subjective impression be enough to support religious belief? Don't people make mistakes all the time about what they think they've seen or heard, especially when placed in extraordinary conditions?

Contact suggests that, beginning from opposite starting points, there is compatibility between science and religion, that both support belief in God. However, the film contains enough ambivalence to leave the matter a mystery.

STUDY QUESTIONS

1. Is it probably or improbable that intelligent life exists somewhere in the universe? If such life exists, would that indicate the presence of a God who created it?

2. In what ways do Ellie and Palmer represent the approaches of science and religion?

3. What drives Ellie to explore the possibility of extraterrestrial life? Is her quest in any way religious?

4. Do you think Ellie contacted some supernatural dimension or imagined the entire episode?

5. In what way to you think religious belief can be established? What would have to happen for people to reject belief in God?

Diary of a Country Priest

Director: Robert Bresson

Based on the Novel by George Bernanos

Robert Bresson (1901–1999) was a celebrated filmmaker of the mid-twentieth century with 13 feature films to his credit over a 40 year career. He is usually ranked among the great directors for movies such as Pickpocket, Mouchette, *and* Beware Balthazar *(Au hasard Balthazar), as well as his most successful* A Man Escaped *(Un condemné à mort s'est échappé).*

All of his films have literary roots in Dostoevsky, Bernanos, Tolstoy, and Diderot, and his most formative influences seem to come from Catholicism and his experience as a prisoner-of-war; all of his characters, in fact, seem imprisoned, if not physically then spiritually. Three of his films have explicit religious subjects: The Angels of Sin *(Les ange des péchés),* The Trial of Joan of Arc *(Le Procés de Jeanne d'Arc), and* Diary of a Country Priest *(Journal d'un curé de compagne).*

The last is typical of his themes and of his filmmaking method, using non-professional actors almost entirely and concentrating on their appearance; he referred to them, in fact, as "models." Paradoxically enough, how the actors look, in long shots of their faces, reveals their inner spirit, and that is Bresson's main purpose. Diary of a Country Priest *is based on the book by Georges Bernanos, and it is generally regarded as superior to the novel.*

SYNOPSIS

Diary of a Country Priest functions as a Christian allegory of sin and redemption, grace, suffering, and, arguably, salvation. A young, sickly priest (Claude Laydu), naïve and pious, arrives in the northern French village of Ambricourt where the people resist his ministry and reject him personally.

He is awkward and they are unwelcoming. The villagers are portrayed as typical in their small-minded malice, and the priest suffers on both a physical and a mental level, trying to infuse their lives with compassion. He seems pathetic but also a fool for Christ. In the end he is defeated, evil overcoming good, but he has some small triumphs along the way and he keeps the faith despite his crises. That is his victory, and the viewer is left to wonder if it is enough.

Because the film tells the story of inner torment, which is difficult to present visually, diary entries are used as a cinematic device for revealing the priest's thoughts. Action and events can show interior states, of course, but the voice-over of the diary and the accompanying narration express his emotions more overtly. Of the diary the priest says he intends to write "with absolute frankness...the simplest and most insignificant secrets of life actually without a trace of mystery." That may be disingenuous because the simplicity masks an emotional complexity.

At the same time, the meaning of the film is revealed more through silence and absence, by the stark and empty farmland, and by sounds whose source is never shown. A train is heard but not seen; an unknown dog barks; carts pass and a hunt takes place off-screen. This only emphasizes the priest's isolation. When he stares out of the rectory window we do not know what he sees; when he suffers through a terrible night, we do not know why; and he is often shown from a distance, as a solitary figure in a vast landscape. The emptiness is introduced from the beginning when we see the priest on a bicycle next to a high gate that looks forbidding. The film is shot in black and white, of course, and true to the minimalist approach, what is significant is only suggested or carefully hidden; absence often carries the meaning.

Two demonic girls lead the persecution of the priest: a blonde schoolgirl named Séraphita (Martine Lemaire) and an older brunette, Chantal (Nicole Ladmiral), daughter of the Countess. As is customary, the dark-haired girl is the more malicious, while the fair-haired girl, although teasing the priest about his beautiful eyes, saves him when he faints in the forest.

Chantal is vindictiveness itself, spreading rumors about the priest, especially that he brought about her mother's death by his severe treatment. At one point she asks the priest what he thinks of her, saying "You have eyes and ears and make use of them like everyone else." He replies, "They would tell me nothing about you...You're always restless, hoping to conceal the truth of your soul or perhaps to forget it." Chantal resents such insights, and is angry at the priest (and her mother) for being ineffectual; they cannot do anything about her father's affair with her governess. Like the devil's instrument, she delights in tormenting him, as when she says "I will sin for sin's sake." When the priest takes her confession, the background fades away leaving only her face surrounded by blackness.

The death of the Countess (Marie-Monique Arkell) is the centerpiece of the film, and her redemption before she dies is the only success the priest experiences. She had been bitter toward God for the death of her young son, so that when the priest says "God will break you," she replies "He has already broken me." But he helps her come to terms with the boy's death, grants her absolution, and in the end reconciles her with the church. (During this scene the gardener outside the window rakes the leaves as if he were gathering souls.) The countess dies at peace, and the priest feels a sense of pride that he brought the woman back to the fold. In her final letter to him, she writes that she is happy.

With this letter the priest could have acquitted himself of Chantal's charges but he chooses not to do so, which suggests a drive toward self-destruction. Like Christ, he must atone for the sins of humankind through pain, and he registers his own failures and uncertainties as an overwhelming burden of guilt. Rather than fighting back, he practices resignation, which only incites the blood-lust of his predators. "Where have I gone wrong?" he asks. If people are not moved by example, then returning good for evil only reinforces their awful behavior.

Of course the priest's actions are not entirely generous; they bring him a good deal of satisfaction, which could be part of his motivation. He sets himself up for rejection, thereby confirming his view of man as permeated with original sin, and when he berates himself as a vile and worthless creature there is something voluptuous about his suffering. Rather than eating sensibly, his meals consist of wine-soaked bread and sugar, which is an offering of penance; the bread and wine, of course, are highly symbolic. He indulges his desire for a life of privation, and allows himself only a moment of pleasure, riding on the back of a motorcycle, a broad smile on his face.

From a psychological standpoint, self-sacrifice can be viewed as masochism, just as positive thinking can be denial. The priest's defeat only reinforces his assumptions about the world, and to that extent is inwardly gratifying.

The priest's friends are not much use. Dr. Delbende (Antoine Balpêtré), whose motto is "Face up to it," dies of a self-inflicted gunshot wound, and an elderly priest from the village of Torcy mearby (André Guibert) can only offer the melancholy advice, "keep order all day long, knowing full well disorder will win out tomorrow."

Morbidity and death also seem omnipresent motifs. A quarrelsome character named Fabregard argues with the priest over funeral costs; the Countess's son has died and, despite her acceptance of God's will, she commits suicide; and a seminary friend Dufréty (Bernard Hubrenne) appears as a macabre, skeletal figure. The priest himself, with his white face and black robes, is suggestive of death, and he vomits blood, collapses, and loses consciousness. He seems bent on suicide, both in his relations with his parish and in neglecting his stomach pains, which turn out to be cancer. The priest's physical illness, of course, corresponds to the sickness of his spirit.

In its dark vision, *Diary of a Country Priest* is sometimes viewed as a "Jansenist" film—the sect that believes people are born evil and cannot be saved except by God's grace. We never deserve that grace but it is freely given and should be lovingly received. Ultimate salvation, they believed, is a mystery. In his foreknowledge, God knew that human beings would choose to sin, and if it was predestined then his justice is not of this world.

In the conclusion the priest dies in Dufréty's flat, and the priest of Torcy reads about it in a letter. An image of a cross appears on the screen, and presumably life in Ambricourt and the world at large proceeds as before. The priest is never given a name, which suggests he is everyman who follows a religious calling and sacrifices himself for God and humanity.

Diary of a Country Priest is obviously Christian in its themes of grace, atonement, and redemption, but it contains anti-Christian elements as well. For the villagers undermine the priest's ministry and resist all his efforts to bring about their redemption, which reduces him to a state of despair. He only saves the Countess, and even that is ambiguous, but the rest of the parishioners remain implacable. The gospel he preaches does not improve people, and if the village is a microcosm of human relationships then the outcome suggests that Christianity does not work. To the priest, his rejection and humiliation are "the dark night of the soul," a test of his faith, but his failure could be an indictment of the religion itself.

On the other hand, perhaps the resistance is a confirmation of the Christian vision of humanity as cursed with original sin. The villagers are spiteful and perverse by nature, making the priest's life miserable, and the cross the priest must bear entails both physical and spiritual suffering. In fact, his ministry echoes that of Christ in being denied, humiliated, and persecuted by an uncomprehending people.

Although Bresson identified himself as an agnostic, he also believed in one "essential soul" and declared "there are no real atheists." In "Diary of a Country Priest" that ambivalence comes through, as in a scene where the priest rises from his bed "with the feeling, the certitude that I had heard someone calling me." But when he goes to the window no one is there, and he thinks "Yet I knew I would not find anyone."

STUDY QUESTIONS

1. Would you judge the priest as generous or self-serving? Does he take pride in his pain; does it bring him satisfaction?

2. Do you think that to be a genuine Christian one must undergo humiliation, persecution, and suffering?

3. Is the priest rejected by the community because of his manner or his message? Would they find any priest acceptable?

4. Do you regard the film as Christian or anti-Christian in nature? Why?

5. Would you agree with the Jansenists that everything that we do is pre-ordained, and that we cannot lead a successful life by our own efforts?

The Devil's Advocate

Director: Taylor Hackford

Screenplay: Jonathan Lemkin and Tony Gilroy

Based on the book by Andrew Neiderman

Taylor Hackford (1945–), an American director and producer, is known for his fast-paced, high-energy films charged with sexuality. His critically acclaimed The Idolmakers *about rock and roll, was followed by the box office success* An Officer and a Gentleman, *a love story set at a naval flight school. He then directed* Against All Odds, *a remake of a film noir classic, and* White Nights, *a cold war drama about dancers in Moscow. This was followed by the documentary* Chuck Berry Hail! Hail! Rock 'n' Roll. *More recently he has directed and/or produced* Bound By Honor, Dolores Claiborne, *and* Proof of Life, *all of which have enhanced his reputation as a filmmaker.*

In The Devil's Advocate, *Hackford presents a supernatural thriller about a lawyer who is seduced into serving the devil. Choosing a law firm as the setting for a morality play is an astute choice, for attorneys can become easy prey for "Satan" if they emphasize winning over the pursuit of justice.*

In terms of the problem of evil, the reader must ask why God would allow the devil to tempt people to sin, dangling the forbidden fruit. Furthermore, the outcome must be known by God since he is all-knowing, which includes foreknowledge, so it is hardly a test of faith.

The Devil's Advocate *does not depict natural evil, that is, the suffering people undergo from natural causes, but the evil perpetrated by Satan. The underlying question, then, is why God would allow the devil to operate, bringing pain to human beings. In his omnipotence, he could have prevented it, so why doesn't he do so? The same question can be asked with regard to the suffering caused by wars and other forms of violence, including the terrorist attacks of September 11th. Should we thank God for those who were saved or wonder why he allowed so many to be lost?*

SYNOPSIS

The theme of a devil's bargain has been presented in numerous literary works, most notably the Dr. Faust tales of Johann Wolfgang von Goethe, Christopher Marlowe, and, to a lesser extent, Stephen Vincent Benet. A man makes a pact with the devil in order to get something he desperately desires—so desperately that he is willing to forfeit his soul to obtain it. In the Faust legends it is unearthly knowledge that is sought, reminiscent of the forbidden fruit in the Garden of Eden. Adam succumbed to the temptations of the serpent (and the woman), thereby losing paradise for himself and all his descendants. In the literary versions, Faust is ultimately saved, for despite the fact that he violates the realm of sacred knowledge, he does so as a seeker after truth. In Goethe's tale, Faust's soul is borne upwards by angels chanting "Lo! Rescued is this noble one/From evil machinations;/Who e'er aspiring struggles on,/For him there is salvation."

The Devil's Advocate explores this same terrain but updated to the contemporary practice of law. In our adversarial system, defense attorneys mount the strongest possible case for their clients, including those they believe are guilty, just as prosecuting attorneys will sometime try cases even when they are convinced the accused is innocent. Furthermore, the trial lawyers' reputation, wealth, power, and status depend on their victories in court. Such circumstances can tempt attorneys to use deceitful practices, rhetorical devices, legal technicalities, and so forth to win the case. They remain within the law but outside the bounds of ethics. In this way the lawyer may become the instrument of Satan, selling his soul for the rewards of success.

Kevin Lomax (Keanu Reeves) practices law in Gainesville, Florida, and his win/loss record is uncanny: 64 convictions as county prosecutor, no losses as a defense attorney. When the film begins, he is defending a schoolteacher named Geddes who is accused of molesting a young student. Although Lomax thinks the man is guilty as sin, he plants a doubt in the jury's mind about the girl's truthfulness, and the teacher is subsequently acquitted. He has a minor crisis of conscience in the washroom but his pride induces him to continue the defense, aided by the (diabolical) prompting of a reporter.

At the celebration party Lomax is offered a position in the prestigious New York law firm of Milton, Chadwick, and Waters, initially to help in jury selection—something he seems able to do with unnatural skill. The terms are so generous and the career prospects so promising, that he accepts the offer despite the objections of his mother Alice Lomax (Judith Ivey). As a fundamentalist, evangelical Christian, his mother, has "bad feelings" about the move, regarding New York as "Babylon... the dwelling place of demons." However, his wife, Mary Ann (Charlize Theron), supports his decision, remarking that the mother just needs grandkids.

In New York, after successfully assisting in jury selection (the jury deliberated only 38 minutes before finding the defendant not guilty), Lomax is invited to meet the senior partner of the firm, John Milton (Al Pacino). The name is an obvious reference to the English poet Milton who wrote "Paradise Lost," a poem in which Mephistopheles (inadvertently?) becomes the hero. Milton's famous line "Better to rule in hell than serve in heaven" is actually incorporated into the ending of the film. The viewer is thus given a hint at the outset that Satan heads the law firm.

Lomax confesses during the interview that he used to listen to juries deliberate through a hole in the wall, which of course pleases Milton; it shows a vulnerability to corruption. Milton asks him whether he can summon his powers at will, whether he can sleep well at night, which sound more like theological questions than legal ones. Notably, the meeting between Milton and Lomax takes place on a penthouse roof with all of Manhattan at their feet. The two men talk on a perilous walkway, suggesting the possibility of a fall, and a thin layer of water spills over the edges of the building creating a sense of a deep descent. Apparently, this modern setting parallels the temptations in the wilderness.

Lomax is subsequently given a luxurious condominium in uptown Manhattan with paneled walls and inlaid floor; it even has an extra bedroom for the baby his wife wants. He is also assigned a court case as a test of his abilities. A man names Moyez (Delroy Lindao) is charged with violating public health codes because he slaughtered a goat in a voodoo ceremony. In a clever defense, Lomax refers to other religious practices that are accepted even though they are bizarre; the circumcision of infants, water being transformed into blood during communion, fakirs who walk on burning coals, cults that handle poisonous snakes. By citing such precedents, which is standard procedure in law, sacrificing a goat is made to appear reasonable. In a comic note, Moyez causes the prosecutor to have a coughing fit, presumably by invoking magical powers.

By winning this case Lomax becomes further enmeshed in the life of the law office, riding on his victories and feeling a part of the wealth and power surrounding him; his time is billed at $400 an hour. He is also responsive to the attractive Christabella Andreoli (Connie Nielsen), a femme fatale at the firm, who eagerly leads him astray; as the plot unfolds, she turns out to be his half sister. Milton orchestrates her moves, including the invitation to a bisexual orgy, because she is critical to his master plan. Christabella does not actually seduce Lomax, but when he makes love to his wife Mary Ann, trying to conceive a child, the images in his mind are of her. In this way he sins in thought, which in scripture is equivalent to the deed, and their love-making to conceive a child is subverted into sexual lust.

Sex, of course, is one of the devil's principal snares, and Christianity has always viewed it with suspicion, mixed with fear. Woman may be regarded as the epitome of purity like Mary, but usually she is thought of as the temptress Eve, a Jezebel, a Mary Magdalen. According to Catholic doctrine, the function of sex is procreation, not pleasure or even the expression of love. Virginity and celibacy are highly prized. To subdue the desires of the body, monks will lash themselves with knouts, seeking the mortification of the flesh for the purification of the soul. It would be natural, therefore, for sex to play a prominent role in Lomax's fall.

At one point Milton does warn Lomax to remain discrete and unobtrusive in all that he does. This is Milton's own approach, so that he has been "underestimated from day one." He tells Lomax, "They don't see me coming," and wouldn't think "I was the master of the universe." This would be Satan's way of functioning; at one point he comments, "Subways—the only way I travel."

In another significant speech, delivered after Milton arranges the murder of Eddie Barzoon (Jeffrey Jones), an associate at the firm, he reflects on humanity, saying

> God's creature, God's special creature... You sharpen the human appetite to the point where it can split atoms with its desire. You build egos the size of cathedrals, fiber optically connect the world to every eager impulse, grease even the dullest dream with these dollar green, gold-plated fantasies until every human becomes an aspiring emperor, his own God. And where can you go from there? And as for scrabbling from one deal to the next, who's got his eye on the planet as the air thickens, the water sours, even the bee's honey takes on the metallic taste of radioactivity. And it just keeps on coming faster and faster. There's no chance to think or prepare to buy futures or sell futures where there is no Future. We got a runaway train.

Al Pacino received high praise for his performance as John Milton/Satan, and this scene and the climax of the film show him at his gleeful, boorish, wicked, lusty best.

As the firm consumes more and more of Lomax's time, Mary Ann is neglected. She becomes second to his career, even an impediment, especially when he is assigned a high-profile case. He is asked to defend Alexander Cullen (Craig T. Nelson), a major real estate developer accused of murdering his wife, stepson, and maid. The evidence against Cullen looks damning; his fingerprints are on the murder weapon, blood was splattered on the wall and on his clothes, and he was the one who telephoned the police saying he had discovered the crime.

Despite the difficulties and Lomax's relative inexperience, Milton insists that he handle the defense. In retrospect we see that Milton anticipates that the case will alienate Lomax from his wife, and that he will persuade a jury once more to acquit a guilty man. Perhaps then, when love is destroyed and evil triumphs, he will belong to Satan completely.

Milton succeeds in his first aim. The love relationship is destroyed, not only because Mary Ann is neglected but because she is driven insane. She begins to hear voices, to see faces reverting to ghoulish forms, and she wakes up one day to find a baby playing with human tissue. She realizes it is her own ovaries, and that she will never have children. Her breakdown is ultimately precipitated when she is seduced then slashed and raped by Milton.

The events are real, of course, not visions, and she truly recognizes that Milton and the firm are actualized hell. However, in our age we do not accept evil but only violence; we believe in guilt perhaps but not shame or sin. Therefore Lomax thinks she is hallucinating and has her sent to the psychiatric unit of a hospital. Here she commits suicide, declaring her love with her last breath.

As for the court case, Cullen's main defense is that at the time of the murder he was having an affair with his assistant Melissa Black (Laura Harrington). The woman verifies the alibi, but it quickly becomes clear that she is lying.

Lomax faces the critical choice of whether to put her on the stand, knowing that she will lie and that a guilty client might be acquitted. He calls her as a witness, thereby choosing to win the case over his integrity.

The action proceeds quickly from this point. A member of the Justice Department, Mitch Weaver (Vyto Ruginis), warns Lomax that the law firm is involved in arms brokering, illegal disposal of chemical waste, and money laundering. Just before being killed by a car, he also informs him that the schoolteacher Geddes, whom Lomax successfully defended in Gainesville, was found with the body of a 10-year-old girl in the trunk of his car. In a further devastating disclosure, his mother reveals the identity of his father. Thirty years previously she had come to New York with the Baptist

Endeavor Youth Crusade, and, out of loneliness, had made love to a waiter. When she saw Milton, she recognized him as that man. The devil took advantage of her neediness just as he did Mary Ann, and Kevin was produced from that loveless union, the child of Satan.

The remainder of the film and its denouement consists of the confrontation between Milton and Lomax, the devil and his progeny. Throughout the scene a fire blazes in the fireplace (appropriately), and the figures in the low relief sculptures come alive as the background begins to swirl. The supernatural effects form a fitting background to the metaphysical debate that follows.

In this climactic scene Lomax accuses Milton of causing Mary Ann's insanity and suicide, and even tries to shoot him, but the devil remains unharmed and unimpressed.

> MILTON: I'm no puppeteer, Kevin. I don't make things happen. It doesn't work like that. Free will. I only set the stage; you pull the strings.... Never lost a case. Why? Because you're so fucking good? But why?
>
> LOMAX: Because you're my father?
>
> MILTON: I'm a little more than that, Kevin. Awfully hot in the courtroom, wasn't it? What's the game plan, Kevin? Was a nice run, kid. Had to close out someday. Nobody wins them all.
>
> LOMAX: What are you?
>
> MILTON: Oh, I have so many names.
>
> LOMAX: Satan?
>
> MILTON: Call me dad.
>
> LOMAX: Mary Ann, she knew it. She knew it. She knew it so you destroyed her.
>
> MILTON: You blaming me for Mary Ann. Oh, I hope you're kidding. You could have saved her any time you liked. All she wanted was love. Heh, you were too busy.
>
> LOMAX: That's a lie.
>
> MILTON: Mary Ann in New York? Face it, you started looking to better-deal her the minute you got here.

LOMAX: That's not true. You don't know what we had. You're a liar. You don't know anything about it.

MILTON: Hey, I'm on your side. Kevin, there's nothing out there for you. Don't be such a fucking chump. Stop deluding yourself. I told you to take care of your wife. What did I say? The world would understand. Didn't I say that? What did you do? [In Kevin's voice] 'You know what scares me, John? I leave the case, she gets better, then I hate her for it.' Remember?

LOMAX: I know what you did. You set me up.

MILTON: Who told you to pull out all the stops on Mr. Geddes? Who made that choice?

LOMAX: It's entrapment. You set me up.

MILTON: And more yet, the direction you took popes, swamis, snake handlers, all feeding at the same trough. Whose ideas were those?

LOMAX: You played me. It was a test, your test.

MILTON: And Cullen, knowing he was guilty, seeing those pictures, what did you do? You put that lying bitch on the stand.

LOMAX: You brought me in. You put me there. You made her lie.

MILTON: I don't do that, Kevin. That day on the subway, what did I say to you? What were my words to you? Maybe it was your time to lose. You didn't think so.

LOMAX: Lose? I don't lose. I win! I win! I'm a lawyer, that's my job, that's what I do.

MILTON: I rest my case. Vanity is definitely my favorite sin. Kevin, it's so basic, self-love, the all-natural opiate. You know it's not that you didn't care for Mary Ann, Kevin, it's just that you were a little more involved with someone else, yourself.

LOMAX: You're right. I did it all. I let her go.

MILTON: Ah, don't be too hard on yourself, Kevin. You wanted something more, believe me.

LOMAX: I left her behind and just kept going.

MILTON: You can't keep punishing yourself, Kevin. It's awesome how far you've come. I didn't make it easy. Couldn't. Not for you, or your sister. Half-sister to be exact.

[*Christabella Andreoli appears*] Surprise.

MILTON: Some scene, eh, Kevin?

CHRISTABELLA: Don't let him scare you.

MILTON: I've had so many children. I've had so many disappointments. Mistake after mistake. And then there's you, the two of you.

LOMAX: What do you want from me?

MILTON: I want you to be yourself. You know, I tell you boy, guilt is like a bag of fucking bricks. All you have to do is set it down.

CHRISTABELLA: Heh, I know what you're going through. I've been there. Just come here. Let it go.

LOMAX: I can't do that.

MILTON: Who are you carrying those bricks for anyway? For God? Is that it, God? Well, I'll tell you. Let me give you some inside information. God is a prankster. He likes to watch. He gives man instincts, he gives you this extraordinary gift and then what does he do? I swear, for his own amusement, for his own private, cosmic gag-reel, he sets the rules in opposition. It's the goof of all time. Look but don't touch. Touch but don't taste. Taste, don't swallow. And while you're jumping from one foot to the next, what's he doing? He's laughing his sick fucking ass off. He's a tight-ass, he's a sadist, he's an absentee landlord. Worship that? Never!

LOMAX: Better to reign in hell than serve in heaven, is that it?

Milton then proposes that Kevin and Christabella have an incestuous relationship and "take over the firm," making the earth a new hell with their child as the Antichrist. He offers Kevin "instant bliss," "that first line of cocaine, that walk into a strange girl's bedroom," pleasure without guilt. When Kevin points out that in the Bible the devil loses, Milton replies "we're going to write our own Book, chapter 1, right here, this altar, this moment."

In response, Kevin shoots himself, exercising his free will. By opting out of the devil's bargain he saves his soul, and the scene suddenly shifts back to the courthouse in Gainesville when Lomax made his fateful decision to defend Geddes. This time, however, he chooses the high road and withdraws from the case, even though he could ruin his career by doing so.

The film might have ended there. Lomax's wife is returned to him and his integrity is restored, but the devil never sleeps. A reporter asks to interview Lomax for a news story about his honesty, and he agrees. After Lomax leaves the courthouse the reporter's face changes to that of Milton who says "Vanity. Definitely my favorite sin."

In essence, *The Devil's Advocate* is a cautionary tale, a Christian parable complete with the seven deadly sins of pride, avarice, lust, anger, gluttony, envy, and sloth, and some opposing virtues of prudence, fortitude, temperance, and justice. It shows in dramatic form the way in which otherwise decent people can be lured by worldly success into betraying their principles and those they love. The devil here does not use crude instruments such as pitchforks, fire, and brimstone, but operates through the more subtle method of temptation. The problem of evil, of course, is why would a benevolent God allow the devil that much power and not offer his children greater protection.

STUDY QUESTIONS

1. What lures does Satan use to entice Kevin Lomax to do the devil's work?

2. Is a lawyer the devil's advocate if he or she defends a client believed to be guilty? On the other hand, does a lawyer have the right to prejudge guilt or innocence or is that for the courts to decide?

3. To what extent is Kevin responsible for Mary Ann's disintegration, insanity, and suicide?

4. Do you think people are free to be saints or sinners as Milton argues, or does the devil compel people to do evil things?

5. Why would a wholly loving God allow the devil to entice people to hell and not protect them more from him and from themselves?

Bibliography of Philosophy, Literature, and Films
IV. Foundations of Belief: The Philosophy of Religion

Philosophy

African Religions and Philosophy	John Mbiti
The City of God	St. Augustine
The Concept of Dread	Soren Kierkegaard
Contact	Robert Zemeckis
The Cosmological Argument	Richard Swinburne
The Courage to Be, Dynamics of Faith	Paul Tillich
Dialogues Concerning Natural Religion	David Hume
The Divine and the Human	Nicholas Berdyaev
Does God Exist?	A. E. Taylor
Euthrphro, Phaedo	Plato
Evil and the Christian Faith	Nels Ferre
The Existence of God	Richard Winburne
Faith and Logic	Basil Mitchell
Fear and Trembling	Soren Kierkegaard
The Female Nature of God	Rosemary R. Reuther
God Has Many Names	John Hick
Good and Evil	Martin Buber
Guide for the Perplexed	Moses Maimonides
I and Thou	Martin Buber
The Immortality of the Soul	Jacques Maritain
Lectures on the Philosophy of Religion	G. W. F. Hegel
Miracles	C. S. Lewis
Moral Man and Immoral Society	Reinhold Niebuhr
Mysticism and Logic	Bertrand Russell
Natural Theology	Wiliam Paley
Nature, Man, and God	William Temple
The Nature of God	Edward Wierenga
New Essays in Philosophical Theology	Anthony Flew
The Ontological Argument	Alvin Plantinga
Philosohpical Theology	F. R. Tenant
The Problem of Pain	C. S. Lewis
Proslogion	St. Anselm
Religion Within the Boundaries of Pure Reason	Immanuel Kant

The Religious Aspect of Philosophy	Josiah Royce
Saints and Postmodernism	Edith Wyschogrod
Summa Theologica	St. Thomas Aquinas
The Theodicy	G. W. Liebniz
Thoughts	Blaise Pascal
Three Essays on Religion	John Stuart Mill
Why Women Need the Goddess	Carol Christ
The Will to Believe	William James

Literature

Anna Karenina, War and Peace	Leo Tolstoy
Adam the Creator	Karel and Josef Capek
The Betrothal	Alessandro Manzoni
The Bridge of San Luis Rey	Thornton Wilder
The Brothers Karamazov	Fedor Dostoevsky
Canterbury Tales	Geoffrey Chaucer
Doctor Faustus	Thomas Mann
The Father, The Spook Sonata	August Strindberg
Growth of the Soil	Knut Hamsun
The Hunchback of Notre Dame	Victor Hugo
The Idiot	Fedor Dostoevsky
Joy	George Bernanos
The Lower Depths	Maxim Gorky
The Man Who Was Thursday	G. K. Chesterton
The Masque of Reason	Robert Frost
The Metamorphoses	Ovid
Moby Dick	Herman Melville
The Plumed Serpent	D. H. Lawrence
Saint Joan	George Bernard Shaw
The Screwtape Letters	C. S. Lewis
Siddhartha	Herman Hesse
The Tragical History of Dr. Faustus	Christopher Marlowe

Films

L'Age d'Or	Luis Bunuel
Agnes of God	Norman Jewison
Aguirre, The Wrath of God	Luis Bunuel
The Apostle	Werner Herzog
Babette's Feast	Gabriel Axel

Ben-Hur	Ramon Novarro
Black Robe	Bruce Beresford
Christ Confounds His Critics	Herbert Dawley
The Communicants	Ingmar Bergman
Contact	Robert Zemeckis
Day of Wrath	Carl Dreyer
Dead Man Walking	Tim Robbins
Der Apfel Ist Ab	Helmut Kautner
The Devil's Advocate	Taylor Hackford
Diary of a Country Priest	Robert Bresson
The Exterminating Angel	Luis Bunuel
The Flowers of St. Francis	Roberto Rosselini
Gandhi	Richard Attenborough
The Garden of Allah	Richard Boleslawski
The Gospel According to St. Matthew	Pier Paolo Pasolini
The Gospel According to Vic	Charles Gormley
Green Pastures	William Keighley
Hail Mary	Charles-Luc Godard
Haxan	Benjamin Christensen
Jacob's Ladder	Adrian Lyne
Joan of Arc	Victor Fleming
Keys of the Kingdom	John Stahl
The King of Kings	Cecil de Mille
The Last Temptation of Christ	Martin Scorsese
The Life of Brian	Terry Gillian
The Meaning of Life	Terry Gillian
The Messiah	Roberto Rosselini
The Miracle	Roberto Rosselini
Monty Python and the Holy Grail	Terry Gillian
Nazarin	Luis Bunuel
Oh God	Carl Reiner
Order	Carl Dreyer
The Passion of Joan of Arc	Carl Dreyer
The Rapture	Michael Tolkin
The Robe	Henry Koster
The Seventh Seal	Ingmar Bergman
The Shoes of the Fisherman	Michael Anderson
The Silence	Ingmar Bergman
Simon of the Desert	Luis Bunuel
The Song of Bernadette	Henry King
Stigmata	Robert Wainwright

The Ten Commandments	Cecil de Mille
Therese	Alain Cavalier
Through a Glass Darkly	Ingmar Bergman
Ticket to Heaven	Ralph Thomas
Viridiana	Luis Bunuel
Wings of Desire	Wim Wenders
Winter Light	Ingmar Bergman

V. The Individual and Society: Political Philosophy

Just as the philosophy of religion is critical thinking about religion, political philosophy is concerned with fundamental issues within the field of politics. Having studied the nature of philosophy, we are in a position to understand what those issues might be.

Specifically, political philosophy looks at the foundation of the state, meaning by "state" the political organization of the society that includes the government, legal system, and social institutions. We want to determine the basis for the state, the relation of its power and authority to individual freedom, rights, and social justice. What control can the state legitimately exercise over its citizens, and what allegiance does the individual owe to the state? For example, what gives the government the right to compel men to risk their lives in war? Does the state have the authority to incarcerate people or execute them for committing crimes, taking away their freedom or even their lives? Do people possess property rights, and can one's property be legitimately taxed or appropriated? Can the state limit a woman's reproductive freedom by prohibiting or requiring an abortion, or by limiting the number of children a couple can have (as in China's rule of 1 child per family)? How much can the state curtail individual freedom for the greater good?

The answer to such questions depends in turn upon one's view of the nature of the state. That is, some political philosophers argue that an implicit *social contract* exists whereby the citizens agree to obey laws in return for the protection and benefits of society. Having received the advantages, they thereby incur the obligations. Others argue that the state is an *organic* entity with the people existing as limbs or even cells within the organism. On this view, citizens are not free and independent beings but parts of the body politic, members of the family or community. The individual can no more refuse the rules imposed by the state that the hand can rebel against the body. Still others argue that the state exists to safeguard the rights of its citizens. If those rights are violated, then armed rebellion is justified.

The political philosopher also tries to evaluate the worth of various types of states, governments, and political structures to determine the best conditions for human flourishing. In trying to reach some conclusion, he or she will analyze the different views of human nature and relate them to the various ideals of the state. For instance, if human beings are considered evil, cursed with original sin or naturally depraved, violent, or selfish, then a strong central government is needed to ensure that everyone is protected from everyone else. On the other hand, if human beings are considered good at heart, then they can be trusted to behave decently without very extensive government control.

A. THE INDIVIDUAL AND SOCIETY: FREEDOM AND EQUALITY

An important part of political philosophy, therefore, concerns the relation that should pertain between the citizen and the state, especially with regard to conflicts over personal independence and the welfare of society. How can we achieve individual liberty and the well being of all?

To begin with the value of *freedom*, this has been a dominant theme in our society since its inception. Most societies, in fact, treat freedom as a social value, but differences arise over what that freedom means. One distinction that is often made is between *freedom from* and *freedom to*, and both are considered important.

If people are oppressed by war, disease, poverty, insecurity, and so forth they want the ability to escape from such things, so that "freedom from" means protection against harmful events. For example, as Americans we do not want taxation without representation, imprisonment without a trial, or unreasonable searches and seizures, any more than we want polluted environments, unsafe neighborhoods, prejudice or discrimination . In war-torn countries people want freedom from the threat of violence, from hunger, displacement, and the fear of death.

In terms of "freedom to," here the emphasis is on having a choice between alternatives that are positive in nature. In the United States and other democratic countries we want to raise our children as we choose, to vote for government representatives, to have access to work, housing, and education, and to enjoy the civil liberties of assembly, press, religion, movement, speech, and so forth. We want freedom from fear and the freedom to be happy.

But once we have made this important distinction, questions can be raised about the worth of freedom altogether. On what basis can we say it is an important value?

In the history of political philosophy, two principal theories have emerged. One school of thought declares freedom to be one of the *natural rights* to which people are entitled. According to this doctrine, which originated in ancient Greece and flourished in the eighteenth century, there are certain universal rights to which all people are entitled. As Aristotle put it referring to justice, "A rule of justice is natural that has the same validity everywhere, and does not depend on our accepting it or not." "Natural rights" are often considered part of a higher law that is embodied in human nature. According to religious views, these natural rights are provided by God and transmitted through revelation, while secular thinkers see them as grounded in the universe itself. Whatever the source, this view maintains that natural rights are guaranteed to citizens of every state.

In a characteristic expression of this concept, Thomas Jefferson wrote in the Declaration of Independence, "We hold these truths to be self-evident; that all men are created equal, that they are endowed by their Creator with certain *inalienable* rights; that among these are life, liberty, and the pursuit of happiness [italics mine]." To Jefferson, rights inhere in persons and no state has the right of depriving its citizens of them. In arguing this way, Jefferson is endorsing the ideas of the seventeenth-century English philosopher John Locke, and this belief was embodied in our founding documents. It had also permeated our national psyche, so that most Americans believe we have an inherent right to freedom.

The natural rights doctrine has had a stormy history, mainly because people disagree over which rights should be included, or even whether any rights are obvious to everyone; the phrase "self-evident" might only mean "evident to oneself." Arguments have been made for slave-owning as a natural right and for wives as the natural property of their husbands. Furthermore, natural rights were identified with St. Thomas Aquinas who maintained that God's rational guidance gave us the Eternal law, but as society grew increasingly secular this became less and less convincing. In the end, many philosophers judge natural rights to be neither provable nor useful.

In the nineteenth century, an alternative theory arose of *utilitarianism*—a theory we have already encountered in ethics. It claimed that rights such as freedom are not innate but conferred by the states for the purpose of maximizing the well being of its citizens. If a right has social utility then it is justified, but if it ceases to further the public good then it must be abandoned.

Values such as *freedom*, therefore, are only contingent not absolute, and are wholly dependent on their utility. Society alone judges whether something is valuable in terms of its needs at the time. This implies that if freedom is a hindrance rather than a help in meeting social goals, the state should curtail the freedom of its citizens. As we have seen, this was done extensively by totalitarian regimes, and in the U.S. the Patriot Act was passed in the light of terrorist threats.

Nevertheless, the assumption that values are not absolute does not mean they can be easily dismissed. John Stuart Mill, for example, presented a very strong case for freedom on utilitarian grounds. In his famous essay "On Liberty," he argued that freedom enhances human happiness, and society is justified in interfering with citizens only to keep them from harming one another, not from harming themselves. In our context, this means we should make murder illegal but not suicide, stealing but not doing drugs, assault but not driving without a seatbelt.

With regard to freedom of speech, Mill argued that society should not suppress any opinion, no matter how unpopular, sacrilegious, offensive, or unpatriotic. For the opinion that is expressed could be true, and by suppressing it we lose the chance to exchange error for truth. On utilitarian grounds, therefore, freedom of speech can be justified for the well-being of society.

Mill, of course, asserts an extreme liberal position, and we wonder today whether we should allow hate speech, anti-gay demonstrations, Nazi parades in Jewish neighborhoods, or rallies by the Klu Klux Klan against blacks. Clearly, speech must be suppressed if it incites riots, endangers the health of minors, discloses national secrets to an enemy power, and so forth, but we are not always sure where the line should be drawn. According to the utilitarian view, the exercise of our freedom depends on the circumstances rather than being an absolute right of citizens.

In recent years both theories have been further developed, the utilitarian theory through John Austin's positivist view of law, and the natural rights theory in Catholic writings on natural law. In war crimes tribunals such as the Hague following World War II and more recently to try Serbian, Cambodian, and Rwandan leaders, a higher law has been cited as legitimizing the authority of the court. The Universal Declaration of Human Rights by the United Nations is certainly based on basic values that apply to all peoples, regardless of national boundaries.

Our decisions on questions of *equality* also depend on whether we accept a natural rights or utilitarian viewpoint, but the issues here are different and usually turn on matters of economics. We could discuss equal opportunity, equal treatment under the laws, equal pay for equal work, and so forth, but political philosophers tend to focus on the fair distribution of wealth, especially property. What would be a just basis for the allocation of wealth? How should we divide the resources of the earth so that we achieve equality in societies?

Our first thoughts might be that wealth should be distributed evenly so that everyone has an equal share. For one human being to have more than another seems unjust since everyone has an equal right to the earth's goods. If we level wealth, that would respect the "equal worth" doctrine, or in religious terms, the view that all souls are equally precious.

The notion that wealth should be leveled is consistent with the principle of "declining marginal utility" in economics. If a man owns a house, that usually brings him pleasure, but if he should purchase a second home that may increase his pleasure but it does not double it. On the other hand, if two men each own houses, that will double the sum total of pleasure in society as a whole. In other words, successive additions to one's wealth produce progressively less pleasure, so to maximize social well being wealth should be distributed evenly; everyone should own a house as well as having sufficient food, clothing, and other belongings.

But what if leveling wealth meant that no one would have a decent standard of living, or worse, that all people would be below the poverty line? This is the point of lifeboat examples. Suppose that a lifeboat were overloaded such that if all those in the water were taken on board the lifeboat would be swamped, everyone would drown. Some people argue that this is the case in the world today. Two-thirds of the world's population is malnourished, mainly in the Third World, where the birth rate is at least twice that of developed nations. Therefore, distributing wealth equally to everyone on earth could mean mass starvation. If only some can survive, what criterion should be used in deciding who to save? This is the dilemma we also face in allocating scarce medical resources such as drugs, machines, specialists, and facilities. Who shall live when not everyone can live?

One possibility is to leave matters to chance. We could say draw straws, hold a lottery, or say "first come, first served," and those who win would have greater wealth than others. This partly explains the present situation in the world where some nations happen to have developed first or have greater resources and therefore enjoy a larger share of the wealth. Within nations some people are born into prosperous families and others into poor ones; it is just the luck of the draw.

But is it fair for those who got there first or have greater opportunities at the start to receive a larger share of the pie? Should an accident of birth determine the distribution of wealth? This has led to the suggestion that all personal inheritances should be prohibited; in that way people will start even.

Because luck can be unfair, another possibility is to distribute wealth in terms of people's merits. Some people are more deserving than others. They have worked hard, taken advantage of opportunities, used their skills effectively, and so forth and so they have the right to a higher income. Those who inherit a fortune may not be admirable people while others with the ability and education deserve to be at the top; their good character has earned them that position. Perhaps, then, it would be just to distribute wealth on the basis of merit, rejecting both the leveling-of-wealth and the good-luck criteria. Perhaps wealth should not be distributed evenly or randomly but equitably according to worth.

Suppose we were to say, then, that the wealthiest people should be the most deserving, the poor the least deserving. People would be distributed on the economic hierarchy strictly according to the principle of just deserts, with nothing for the *un*deserving; they should fall by the wayside because everyone is required to earn a living.

In business organizations, for example, whether someone is hired or fired, promoted or given an increment depends on his or her qualifications and performance. The company does not reward its employees randomly or even equally but in terms of their contribution to the success of the business. In the same way, shouldn't society distribute wealth according to merit? No one could complain that the system is unjust since all would receive what they deserve.

This is the presumption underlying capitalism. It is assumed that those who are bright and industrious, with energy and drive are successful in the marketplace and receive the highest salaries. The poorly paid workers do not have the intelligence or determination to succeed, so they deserve their lower income.

However, problems can arise with this criterion, beginning with conflicts within the system itself. Should we allocate the greatest wealth to those who work the hardest even though they contribute little; to those who contribute the most even though they do not expend much effort, or to those who have the best qualifications in terms of education, skills, or degrees? If we use the last, those qualifications maybe the result of a privileged back-grounds with access to fine schools, a cultured home, family contacts, and so forth so that it was easier for them to succeed than someone from the slum. And should those who are born brighter be given greater wealth while the handicapped are doomed to live in poverty? Is one group more deserv-ing and another less because of an accident of birth?

As for capitalism, sometimes the marketplace rewards those who do not deserve it in terms of the social benefit they provide. We question the appro-priateness of million-dollar salaries for athletes and celebrities while nurses and teachers can hardly make a living. Should CEOs of tobacco companies be millionaires? In this Darwinian world we have survival of the fittest but not necessarily the best.

Still another option for bringing about economic justice is not to distrib-ute wealth according to merit but in terms of need. Regardless of how unde-serving a person might be, his or her needs may be great, and to ignore that would be inhumane. The physically handicapped person, for example, should receive assistance, and a family of six should be allocated more money than a bachelor—irrespective of whether they merit that income. Everyone should work as conscientiously as they can, but their income should not depend upon their contribution. Thus the Marxist principle: from each according to his ability; to each according to his needs.

The flaw here, of course, is that such a system could encourage laziness and inefficiency. This is what happened in several communist countries and led to their collapse. People lacked the incentive to be productive since their income depended solely on their needs. Capitalism, based on self-interest, has been more successful, which might be an indictment of human nature. Competition and the profit motive has not always been paramount in hu-man history but in our materialistic age it seems the primary driving force.

As this brief survey shows, the question of economic justice is not easily answered and we agonize over specific issues in society today that depend upon the conclusions we reach. For example, should an unwed mother of six addicted to crack cocaine be given welfare to the extent of her needs? In case of a military draft, should we use a lottery system, giving everyone an equal chance of being chosen, or should we establish criteria for selection and give certain groups of people exemptions? Should student loans and scholarships be merit-based or, as is usually the case today, need-based? Should we have taxes that affect everyone equally such as a state sales tax, or a graduated income tax with a higher percentage exacted from the wealthy? Should we abandon the inheritance tax (which opponents call a "death tax"), and should the rich be given a tax break to stimulate job growth in a trickle down system. As the courts have ruled, the power to tax is the power to redistribute wealth.

The issue of equality is therefore quite complex, but at this point we must leave the matter unresolved. However, we do know some of the considerations that apply, and with that understanding we can begin to reach our own well-reasoned conclusion.

B. THE IDEAL STATE: WHAT IS THE BEST FORM OF GOVERNMENT?

Aside from issues of freedom and equality, the larger question in political philosophy is what would be an ideal state. That is, what type of government, legal structure, civil organization and so forth would be best for promoting human well being? As Aristotle wrote "a state exists for the sake of a good life, and not for the sake of life only."

All of the major political philosophers have proposed theories of the ideal state from the first speculations of Plato in the *Republic* to Thomas Hobbes in *The Leviathan*, Jean Jacques Rousseau in *The Social Contract*, and Karl Marx in *The Communist Manifesto*. Aristotle in his *Politics* maintains that any one of several states can be best depending on the circumstances, and his typology of governmental forms is a useful springboard for discussion.

1. *Monarchies* are arguably the oldest form of government. One person is designated as the sovereign, having the right to rule as head of state throughout his or her lifetime. In Europe during the Middle Ages monarchies were the accepted political structure, supported by the "divine right of kings." According to this doctrine, monarchs are appointed by God as his representatives for civil government on earth, and they are responsible only to the Lord not to the will of the people. The monarch is the final authority on all secular matters, and in Protestant countries after the Reformation, on religious matters as well. In some Asian and Eastern nations such as ancient Egypt and Japan, the king himself was regarded as divine.

In most cases, monarchies were dynastic with power transferred from the king to his eldest son, and these inherited monarchies were supported by nobles or by financial interests that wanted a monolithic government. If the king rules by the will of God, and he maintains order, protects the nation, ensures prosperity, and keeps the peace, this can be a popular and effective political system.

In defense of monarchy Thomas Hobbes wrote in *The Leviathan,* "In a state of nature with no intervening authority people quarrel and engage in perpetual warfare of "omnium contra omnes" (all against all). Therefore the life of man is "solitary, poore, nasty, brutish, and short." For this reason people willingly accept the restraint of a sovereign in "the foresight of their own preservation, and of a more contented life thereby."

In the fifteenth and sixteenth centuries, King Henry VIII and King Louis XIV ruled as absolute monarchs, but by the seventeenth and eighteenth centuries the power of kings began to be limited, sometimes as a result of revolutions. The dissatisfaction came about mainly because of the abuse of power. A benevolent, well-informed monarch who rules by the dictates of God may be desirable but if he is self-serving and corrupt, then his authority is undermined. This is the degeneration that Aristotle describes. Monarchy can be an excellent form of government, preserving wealth, property, and power but it tends to become a tyranny in which the monarch functions only for his self-interest.

2. In *aristocracy* a small number of individuals are given governmental authority rather than having power vested in a single individual. These few people are considered the most capable of ruling by virtue of their intelligence, nobility, education, character, or other qualifications. *Aristos* means best, *kratos* is power, so aristocracy translates as governmental power exercised by the best of the state's citizens. In its classic form it is not based on birth but power is conferred upon the most meritorious individuals in a society.

Aristocracies existed in Athens from the fifth to the third centuries B.C.E., in Rome from the sixth to the first centuries B.C.E., and perhaps in England from the seventeenth to the nineteenth centuries. Plato, of course, presented the most famous justification for aristocracy in *The Republic*, basing his political philosophy on his metaphysics.

As we saw in Chapter I, Plato maintained that the basic reality consists of the world of Ideas which is accessible through rational thought. Philosophers are the ones best suited to understand these Ideas because they have logical, reflective, and inquiring minds, and for this reason they should become the rulers. The philosopher is especially qualified for governance because he tries to comprehend the Idea of justice, and using that model, strives to create a just society on earth.

Plato therefore advocates an intellectual aristocracy as the ideal form of government. He recognized that philosophers have no power besides their intellect, and most people do not respect the life of the mind. Therefore they would not rule very long—if they got to rule at all. Furthermore, the military would revolt against them using their forces, the masses would attack them using their numerical superiority, and the rich would oppose them using the leverage of their wealth. That is, an intelligentsia would be vulnerable to coups and revolts, but if the people had enough restraint to let philosophers rule, the result would be a just state.

In analyzing aristocracy in the *Politics*, Aristotle feared that it would degenerate into oligarchy in which a dominant class or clique, especially the wealthy, would seize control. However, Plato's system had safeguards against this. He specified that the rulers' lives would be extremely austere and not at all luxurious, so it would attract only those dedicated to the welfare of society. Nonetheless, the idea of entrusting government to a group of superior people makes many uncomfortable, especially in our contemporary world.

3. Referring again to Aristotle's scheme, *democracy* is another possible form of government, and it can be desirable or undesirable. In the form of constitutional democracy in which the majority of the people exercise power within the framework of constitutional restraints, it can produce an excellent result. In general, the people as a whole can be trusted more than the select few, provided that justice is done in accordance with law and legislation. Aristotle writes "The many ... may very likely be better than the few good, if regarded not individually but collectively, just as a feast to which many contribute is better than a dinner provided out of a single purse."

However, democracy can impede human development if the poor, needy, and lower class are in the majority and they use their numbers to ensure their own good rather than the common interests of society. A popular democracy of this kind means a tyranny of the majority. This is why we need a constitutional democracy in which the best interests of both the state and its citizens are legally protected. Ideal democracy is lawful rule by the majority, but in popular democracy we have what Plato called mob rule.

Democracy was instituted in Greek city-states for a brief period but it flowered in the nineteenth and twentieth centuries in Europe and the United States. The Magna Carta (along with the Declaration of Independence and the French Declaration of the Rights of Man) established the foundation for democracy, while the Enlightenment and the American and French revolutions provided the catalysts for establishing democratic governments. Most of these became representative democracies in which citizens exercise their rights through chosen representatives rather than by direct vote. In this way, the people's voice is heard while the leaders are still able to use independent judgment. Ultimately, the representatives are accountable to the people through regular elections, and in order to limit power most democracies have a system of checks and balances. In the United States this equilibrium is established between the executive, legislative, and judicial branches of government. As Aristotle put it, in this way there is "coincidence of interest between the rulers and the ruled."

One inherent tension in any form of democracy is whether the will of the people should be followed or whether rights should be respected above the general will. If the two coincide then there is harmony but if the majority denies rights to the minority then there is a conflict. In Nazi Germany, for example, Hitler was democratically elected and then instituted a program to exterminate the Jews. Assuming the majority supported such a program, should they be given what they want or should we respect principles? This is when constitutions are important, based on universal rights.

In any case, Aristotle judged the worth of a state, whether a monarchy, aristocracy, or democracy according to the extent to which it served the public interest. This varied from nation to nation, depending on the temperament of the people. Sometimes it meant one ruler, sometimes a few, and at other times government by the majority of citizens.

In the twentieth century additional forms of government have arisen, most notably totalitarianism—a form of centralized government that exercised control over people's freedom, will, and thoughts; it depended on strong rulers willing to crush dissent. We have seen the rise of the totalitarian governments of fascism and of communism, and each has been rejected after terrible wars of resistance that cost millions of lives. Fascism is a right-wing, militaristic movement that asserts the absolute primacy of the nation-state and the submission of the individual. The major examples are Nazi Germany and Mussolini's Italy. In communism, an authoritarian government is needed to establish and maintain a centralized economic system. A self-perpetuating political party and a dominant leader establishes rigid control over the state, as occurred in Russia, China, and Cuba. More recently, the Islamic governments in the Middle East have been classified as fascist because of their rigid, theocratic structure.

Is Aristotle right in thinking that different governments can be right for different societies or is there an ideal form of government for all people that will enable human beings to thrive? Is the cynic right in saying that we have a choice between the corrupt few or the ignorant many? In the United States we often assume that democracy is best for every nation, but democracy require an educated electorate and not all countries have even a literate one.

As we can see, determining what constitutes a good state is extremely difficult, in fact the most difficult issue in political philosophy. Obviously, neither philosophy nor the nations of the world have settled the question.

In the selection from the *Politics* that follows, Aristotle presents his theory of the ideal forms of the state, while John Locke in his *Second Treatise of Government* discusses matters of freedom and justice, especially the right to property. According to Locke, human beings in a "state of nature" are free, equal, and independent, but since the natural state is insecure they join in civil society for the mutual protection of their lives and property.

The film *Born on the Fourth of July* portrays a crisis in American democracy when a substantial number of citizens, mainly the young, disagree with the government's decision to fight in Viet Nam. *Schindler's List* shows the Nazi program for the extermination of Jews during World War II, and the attempts by Oskar Schindler to rescue as many as he can from the Holocaust. The last film, *To Kill a Mockingbird*, is an American classic concerning racism in the Deep South during the 1930s and the lessons in justice taught to the children.

A. Philosophic Concepts

The Politics[1]
Aristotle

Aristotle (384–322 B.C.) along with Plato is considered among the fore-most philosophers of ancient Greece. He profoundly influenced St. Thomas Aquinas in building his foundations of Christian theology as well as contributing to theories of language, rules of validity in logic, astronomy, biology, poetry, literary criticism, ethics, and political philosophy. Almost all of Aristotle's early writings for the general public have been lost, but we do have his later work in the form of lecture notes that were preserved and arranged by subsequent scholars. Because this body of work is technical and fragmented, Aristotle's writings are sometimes regarded as dry and dogmatic. In fact, he willingly recognized problems in his theories and continually revised his work, taking into account the thought of his predecessors and the common opinions of his time.

Aristotle's theory of science is contained in his Physics, *and his concept of the nature and structure of reality appears in the* Metaphysics, *including his concept of God as "prime mover." The* Nicomachean Ethics, *dedicated to his son Nicomachus, contains his ethical theory; with the doctrine of the "golden mean" and its various applications, it is almost a handbook of morality. Every investigation of aesthetics begins with Aristotle's* Poetics, *and his* Politics *is a basic reference point in the study of political philosophy.*

Aristotle argues in the Politics *that, contrary to the Utopia described by Plato in* The Republic, *no ideal government can be found. Rather, various types of governments exist, and the circumstances of the society should dictate which one should be adopted. Factors such as the customs, education, ideals, laws, and so forth will determine which government is best for a particular society, but there is no one perfect form for all societies.*

---

[1]Translated by B. Jowett.)

...We have next to consider how many forms of government there are, and what they are; and in the first place what are the true forms, for when they are determined the perversions of them will at once be apparent. The words constitution and government have the same meaning, and the government, which is the supreme authority in states, must be in the hands of one, or of a few, or of many. The true forms of government, therefore, are those in which the one, or the few, or the many, govern with a view to the common interest; but governments which rule with a view to the private interest, whether of the one or of the few, or of the many, are perversions.[2] For the members of a state, if they are truly citizens, ought to participate in its advantages. Of forms of government in which one rules, we call that which regards the common interests, kingship or royalty; that in which more than one, but not many, rule, aristocracy; and it is so called, either because the rulers are the best men, or because they have at heart the best interests of the state and of the citizens. But when the citizens at large administer the state for the common interest, the government is called by the generic name—a constitution. And there is a reason for this use of language. One man or a few may excel in virtue; but as the number increases it becomes more difficult for them to attain perfection in every kind of virtue, though they may in military virtue, for this is found in the masses. Hence in a constitutional government the fighting-men have the supreme power, and those who possess arms are the citizens.

Of the above-mentioned forms, the perversions are as follows: of royalty, tyranny; of aristocracy, oligarchy; of constitutional government, democracy. For tyranny is a kind of monarchy which has in view the interest of the monarch only; oligarchy has in view the interest of the wealthy; democracy, of the needy: none of them the common good of all.

But there are difficulties about these forms of government, and it will therefore be necessary to state a little more at length the nature of each of them. For he who would make a philosophical study of the various sciences, and does not regard practice only, ought not to overlook or omit anything, but to set forth the truth in every particular. Tyranny, as I was saying, is monarchy exercising the rule of a master over the political society; oligarchy is when men of property have the government in their hands; democracy, the opposite, when the indigent, and not the men of property, are the rulers. And here arises the first of our difficulties, and it relates to the distinction drawn. For democracy is said to be the government of the many.

---

[2]Cp. Eth. Viii. 10.

But what if the many are men of property and have the power in their hands? In like manner oligarchy is said to be the government of the few; but what if the poor are fewer than the rich, and have the power in their hands because they are stronger? In these cases the distinction which we have drawn between these different forms of government would no longer hold good.

Suppose, once more, that we add wealth to the few and poverty to the many, and name the governments accordingly—an oligarchy is said to be that in which the few and the wealthy, and a democracy that in which the many and the poor are the rulers—here will still be a difficulty. For, if the only forms of government are the ones already mentioned, how shall we describe those other governments also just mentioned by us, in which the rich are the more numerous and the poor are the fewer, and both govern in their respective states?

The argument seems to show that, whether in oligarchies or in democracies, the number of the governing body, whether the greater number, as in a democracy, or the smaller number, as in an oligarchy, is an accident due to the fact that the rich everywhere are few, and the poor numerous. But if so, there is a misapprehension of the causes of the difference between them. For the real difference between democracy and oligarchy is poverty and wealth. Wherever men rule by reason of their wealth, whether they be few or many, that is an oligarchy, and where the poor rule, that is a democracy. But as a fact the rich are few and the poor many; for few are well-to-do, whereas freedom is enjoyed by all, and wealth and freedom are the grounds on which the oligarchical and democratical parties respectively claim power in the state...

But a state exists for the sake of a good life, and not for the sake of life only: if life only were the object, slaves and brute animals might form a state, but they cannot, for they have no share in happiness or in a life of free choice. Nor does a state exist for the sake of alliance and security from injustice,[3] nor yet for the sake of exchange and mutual intercourse; for then the Tyrrhenians and the Carthaginians, and all who have commercial treaties with one another, would be the citizens of one state. True, they have agreements about imports, and engagements that they will do no wrong to one another, and written articles of alliance. But there are no magistrates common to the contracting parties who will enforce their engagements; different states have each their own magistracies. Nor does one state take care that the citizens of the other are such as they ought to be, nor see that those

---

[3]Cp. c. I. section 4.

who come under the terms of the treaty do no wrong or wickedness at all, but only that they do no injustice to one another. Whereas, those who care for good government take into consideration [the larger question of] virtue and vice in states. Whence it may be further inferred that virtue must be the care of a state which is truly so called, and not merely enjoys the name: for [without this ethical end] the community becomes a mere alliance which differs only in place from alliances of which the members live apart; and law is only a convention, 'a surety to one another of justice,' as the sophist Lycophron says, and has no real power to make the citizens good and just... It is clear then that a state is not a mere society, having a common place, established for the prevention of mutual crime and for the sake of exchange. These are conditions without which a state cannot exist; but all of them together do not constitute a state, which is a community of families and aggregations of families in well-being, for the sake of a perfect and self-sufficing life. Such a community can only be established among those who live in the same place and intermarry. Hence arise in cities family connections, brotherhoods, common sacrifices, amusements which draw men together. But these are created by friendship, for the will to live together is friendship. The end of the state is the good life, and these are the means towards it. And the state is the union of families and villages in a perfect and self-sufficing life, by which we mean a happy and honorable life.[4]

Our conclusion, then, is that political society exists for the sake of noble actions, and not of mere companionship. Hence they who contribute most to such a society have a greater share in it than those who have the same or a greater freedom or nobility of birth but are inferior to them in political virtue; or than those who exceed them in wealth but are surpassed by them in virtue.

From what has been said it will be clearly seen that all the partisans of different forms of government speak of a part of justice only.

There is also a doubt as to what is to be the supreme power in the state: Is it the multitude? Or the wealthy? Or the good? Or the one best man? Or a tyrant? Any of these alternatives seems to involve disagreeable consequences. If the poor, for example, because they are more in number, divide among themselves the property of the rich—is not this unjust? No, by heaven (will be the reply), for the supreme authority [i.e., the people] justly willed it. But if this is not injustice, pray what is? Again, when in the first division all has been taken, and the majority divide anew the property of the

---

[4]Cp. i.2. section 8; N. Erth. I.7. section 6.

minority, is it not evident, if this goes on, that they will ruin the state? Yet surely, virtue is not the ruin of those who possess her, nor is justice destructive of a state;[5] and therefore this law of confiscation clearly cannot be just. If it were, all the acts of a tyrant must of necessity be just; for he only coerces other men by superior power, just as the multitude coerce the rich. But is it just then that the few and the wealthy should be the rulers? And what if they, in like manner, rob and plunder the people—is this just? If so, the other case [i.e., the case of the majority plundering the minority] will likewise be just. But there can be no doubt that all these things are wrong and unjust.

Then ought the good to rule and have supreme power? But in that case everybody else, being excluded from power, will be dishonored. For the offices of a state are posts of honor; and if one set of men always holds them, the rest must be deprived of them. Then will it be well that the one best man should rule? Nay, that is still more oligarchical, for the number of those who are dishonored is thereby increased. Some one may say that it is bad in any case for a man, subject as he is to all the accidents of human passion, to have the supreme power, rather than the law. But what if the law itself be democratical or oligarchical, how will that help us out of our difficulties?[6] Not at all; the same consequences will follow.

Most of these questions may be reserved for another occasion. The principle that the multitude ought to be supreme rather than the few best is one that is maintained, and, though not free from difficulty, yet seems to contain an element of truth. For the many, of whom each individual is but an ordinary person, when they meet together may very likely be better than the few good, if regarded not individually but collectively, just as a feast to which many contribute is better than a dinner provided out of a single purse. For each individual among the many has a share of virtue and prudence, and when they meet together, they become in a manner one man, who has many feet, and hands, and senses; that is a figure of their mind and disposition. Hence the many are better judges than a single man of music and poetry; for some understand one part, and some another, and among them they understand the whole. There is a similar combination of qualities in good men, who differ from any individual of the many, as the beautiful are said to differ from those who are not beautiful, and works of art from realities, because in them the scattered elements are combined, although, if taken separately, the eye of one person or some other feature in another person

---

[5] Cp. Plato Rep. i. 351, 352.)
[6] Cp. C. II. section 20.[7]C. 4–6.

would be fairer than in the picture. Whether this principle can apply to every democracy, and to all bodies of men, is not clear…

…Let us begin by determining (1)[7] how many varieties of constitution there are (since of democracy and oligarchy there are several): (2)[8] what constitution is the most generally acceptable, and what is eligible in the next degree after the perfect or any other aristocratical and well-constituted ,form of government—if any other there be—which is at the same time adapted to states in general[9]; (3)[10] of the other forms of government to whom each is suited. For democracy may meet the needs of some better than oligarchy, and conversely. In the next place (4)[11] we have to consider in what manner a man ought to proceed who desires to establish some one among these various forms, whether of democracy or of oligarchy; and lastly, (5)[12] having briefly discussed these subjects to the best of our power, we will endeavor to ascertain the modes of ruin and preservation both of constitutions generally and of each separately, and to what causes they are to be attributed.

The reason why there are many forms of government is that every state contains many elements. In the first place we see that all states are made up of families, and in the multitude of citizen there must be some rich and some poor, and some in a middle condition; the rich are heavy-armed, and the poor not.[13] Of the common people, some are husbandmen, and some traders, and some artisans. There are also among the notables differences of wealth and property- for example, in the number of horses which they keep, for they cannot afford to keep them unless they are rich. And therefore in old times the cities whose strength lay in their cavalry were oligarchies, and they used cavalry in wars[14] against their neighbors; as was the practice of the Eretrians and Chalcidians, and also of the Magnesians on the river Maeander, and of other peoples in Asia. Besides differences of wealth there are differences of rank and merit, and there are some other elements which were mentioned by us when in treating of aristocracy we enumerated the essentials of a state.[15] Of these elements, sometimes all, sometimes the lesser and sometimes the greater number, have a share in the government. It is evi-

---

[7]C. 4–6

[8]C. 7–9 and 11.

[9]Or: 'after the perfect state; and besides this what other there is which is aristocratical and well constituted, and at the same time adapted to states in general.'

[10]C. 12.

[11]Book vi.

[12]Book v.

[13]Or: 'andf again both of rich and poor some are armed and some are unarmed.'

[14]Reading either πολεμους with v. tr. (Moerbek and Bekk. 2nd edit., or πολεμιους with the Greek MSS; cp. c. 13. section 10; vi. c. 7. section 1.

[15]Not in what has preceded, but cp. vii. 8.

dent then that there must be many forms of government, differing in kind, since the parts of which they are composed differ from each other in kind. For a constitution is an organization of offices, which all the citizens distribute among themselves, according to the power which different classes possess, for example the rich or the poor, or according to some principle of equality which includes both. There must therefore be as many forms of government as there are modes of arranging the offices, according to the superiorities and differences of the parts of the state.

There are generally thought to be two principal forms: as men say of the winds that there are but two- north and south, and that the rest of them are only variations of these, so of governments there are said to be only two forms- democracy and oligarchy. For aristocracy is considered to be a kind of oligarchy, as being the rule of a few, and the so-called constitutional government to be really a democracy, just as among the winds we make the west a variation of the north, and the east of the south wind. Similarly of musical modes there are said to be two kinds, the Dorian and the Phrygian; the other arrangements of the scale are comprehended under one or other of these two. About forms of government this is a very favorite notion. But in either case the better and more exact way is to distinguish, as I have done, the one or two which are true forms, and to regard the others as perversions, whether of the most perfectly attempered mode or of the best form of government: we may compare the oligarchical forms to the severer and more overpowering modes, and the democratic to the more relaxed and gentler ones.

STUDY QUESTIONS

1. How does Aristotle define a tyranny, and in what way is it a deterioration of royalty?

2. How does Aristotle define an aristocracy, and how is oligarchy a perversion of it?

3. Democracy is described as a form of government in which the many and the poor are rulers. Why does Aristotle consider this to be a bad thing? What would be an advantageous form?

4. What is the purpose of the state or political society?

5. Would you agree that different governments suit different societies, or do you think there is an ideal form of government for human beings in general?

Second Treatise of Government
John Locke

John Locke (1632–1704) was an English philosopher who is usually cred-
ited with founding the school of empiricism. He began his career as an aca-
demic at Oxford but then held a series of government posts, moving
between England, France, and Holland as the political climate dictated.
Most of his writing was done toward the latter part of his life, including his
most important works. These include Essay Concerning Human Understanding *in which he expounds his epistemology, and* Two Treatises of Government *which contains his political philosophy. Among his other books*
are Some Thoughts Concerning Education *and* The Reasonableness of
Christianity.

In Locke's Two Treatises of Government, *he attacked the political phi-*
losophy of his contemporary Thomas Hobbes, especially the doctrine of the
divine right of kings. Locke maintained that the sovereignty of a king is not
the same as the authority of a father over his children. Rather, the people
had ultimate political control, provided it was exercised within the bounds
of civil and natural law. The state held power in trust for the good of society,
and if that trust is violated then revolution is justified.

Like most political philosophers of the time, Locke begins by speculating
on the state of Nature—that original condition of humankind before the or-
ganization of civil society. He then describes the "social contract" with the
state, and he concludes by specifying the conditions under which power
could revert to society. Political theory in the United States embodies many
of Locke's ideas, particularly his views on property, the right of revolt, and
natural rights that are based on universally valid, higher laws.

ON THE STATE OF NATURE

Sec. 4. To understand political power right, and derive it from its original, we must consider, what state all men are naturally in, and that is, a state
of perfect freedom to order their actions, and dispose of their possessions

and persons, as they think fit, within the bounds of the law of Nature, without asking leave, or depending upon the will of any other man.

A state also of equality, wherein all the power and jurisdiction is reciprocal, no one having more than another; there being nothing more evident, than that creatures of the same species and rank, promiscuously born to all the same advantages of nature, and the use of the same faculties, should also be equal one amongst another without subordination or subjection, unless the lord and master of them all should, by any manifest declaration of his will, set one above another, and confer on him, by an evident and clear appointment, an undoubted right to dominion and sovereignty.

***

Sec. 6. But though this be a state of liberty, yet it is not a state of licence: though man in that state have an uncontroulable liberty to dispose of his person or possessions, yet he has not liberty to destroy himself, or so much as any creature in his possession, but where some nobler use than its bare preservation calls for it. The state of Nature has a law of Nature to govern it, which obliges every one: and reason, which is that law, teaches all mankind, who will but consult it, that being all equal and independent, no one ought to harm another in his life, health, liberty, or possessions: for men being all the workmanship of one omnipotent, and infinitely wise maker; all the servants of one sovereign master, sent into the world by his order, and about his business; they are his property, whose workmanship they are, made to last during his, not one another's pleasure: and being furnished with like faculties, sharing all in one community of nature, there cannot be supposed any such subordination among us, that may authorize us to destroy one another, as if we were made for one another's uses, as the inferior ranks of creatures are for ours. Everyone, as he is bound to preserve himself, and not to quit his station willfully, so by the like reason, when his own preservation comes not in competition, ought he, as much as he can, to preserve the rest of mankind, and may not, unless it be to do justice on an offender, take away, or impair the life, or what tends to the preservation of the life, the liberty, health, limb, or goods of another.

Sec. 7. And that all men may be restrained from invading others rights, and from doing hurt to one another, and the law of Nature be observed, which willeth the peace and preservation of all mankind, the execution of the law of Nature is, in that state, put into every man's hands, whereby every one has a right to punish the transgressors of that law to such a degree, as may hinder its violation: for the law of Nature would, as all other laws that concern men in this world, be in vain, if there were no body that in the state of Nature had a power to execute that law, and thereby preserve the innocent and restrain offenders. And if any one in the state of Nature may punish another for any evil he has done, every one may do so: for in that state of perfect equality, where naturally there is no superiority or jurisdiction of one over another, what any may do in prosecution of that law, every one must needs have a right to do.

Sec. 8. And thus, in the state of Nature, one man comes by a power over another; but yet no absolute or arbitrary power, to use a criminal, when he has got him in his hands, according to the passionate heats, or boundless extravagancy of his own will; but only to retribute to him, so far as calm reason and conscience dictate, what is proportionate to his transgression, which is so much as may serve for reparation and restraint: for these two are the only reasons, why one man may lawfully do harm to another, which is that we call punishment. In transgressing the law of Nature, the offender declares himself to live by another rule than that of reason and common equity, which is that measure God has set to the actions of men, for their mutual security; and so he becomes dangerous to mankind, the tye, which is to secure them from injury and violence, being slighted and broken by him. Which being a trespass against the whole species, and the peace and safety of it, provided for by the law of Nature, every man upon this score, by the right he hath to preserve mankind in general, may restrain, or where it is necessary, destroy things noxious to them, and so may bring such evil on anyone, who hath transgressed that law, as may make him repent the doing of it, and thereby deter him, and by his example others, from doing the like mischief. And in the case, and upon this ground, every man hath a right to punish the offender, and be executioner of the law of Nature.

***

Sec. 10. Besides the crime which consists in violating the law, and varying from the right rule of reason, whereby a man so far becomes degenerate, and declares himself to quit the principles of human nature, and to be a noxious creature, there is commonly injury done to some person or other, and some other man receives damage by his transgression: in which case he who hath received any damage, has, besides the right of punishment common to him with other men, a particular right to seek reparation from him that has done it: and any other person, who finds it just, may also join with him that is injured, and assist him in recovering from the offender so much as may make satisfaction for the harm he has suffered.

***

Sec. 13. To this strange doctrine, viz. That in the state of Nature every one has the executive power of the law of Nature, I doubt not but it will be objected, that it is unreasonable for men to be judges in their own cases, that selflove will make men partial to themselves and their friends: and on the other side, that ill nature, passion and revenge will carry them too far in punishing others; and hence nothing but confusion and disorder will follow, and that therefore God hath certainly appointed government to restrain the partiality and violence of men. I easily grant, that civil government is the proper remedy for the inconveniencies of the state of Nature, which must certainly be great, where men may be judges in their own case, since it is easy to be imagined, that he who was so unjust as to do his brother an injury, will scarce be so just as to condemn himself for it: but I shall desire those who make this objection, to remember, that absolute monarchs are but men; and if government is to be the remedy of those evils, which necessarily follow from men's being judges in their own cases, and the state of Nature is therefore not to be endured, I desire to know what kind of government that is, and how much better it is than the state of Nature, where one man, commanding a multitude, has the liberty to be judge in his own case, and may do to all his subjects whatever he pleases, without the least liberty to anyone to question or control those who execute his pleasure and in whatsoever he doth, whether led by reason, mistake or passion, must be submitted to. Much better it is in the state of Nature, wherein men are not bound to submit to the unjust will of another. And if he that judges, judges amiss in his own, or any other case, he is answerable for it to the rest of mankind.

Sec. 14. It is often asked as a mighty objection, where are, or ever were there any men in such a state of Nature? To which it may suffice as an answer at present, that since all princes and rulers of independent governments all through the world, are in a state of Nature, it is plain the world never was, nor ever will be, without numbers of men in that state. I have named all governors of independent communities, whether they are, or are not, in league with others: for it is not every compact that puts an end to the state of Nature between men, but only this one of agreeing together mutually to enter into one community, and make one body politic; other promises, and compacts, men may make one with another, and yet still be in the state of Nature. The promises and bargains for truck, etc. between the two men in the desert island, mentioned by Garcilasso de la Vega, in his history of Peru; or between a Swiss and an Indian, in the woods of America, are binding to them, though they are perfectly in a state of Nature, in reference to one another: for truth and keeping of faith belongs to men, as men, and not as members of society.

✻✻✻

Of Property

✻✻✻

Sec. 25. God, who hath given the world to men in common, hath also given them reason to make use of it to the best advantage of life, and convenience. The earth, and all that is therein, is given to men for the support and comfort of their being. And tho' all the fruits it naturally produces, and beasts it feeds, belong to mankind in common, as they are produced by the spontaneous hand of Nature; and no body has originally a private dominion, exclusive of the rest of mankind, in any of them, as they are thus in their natural state: yet being given for the use of men, there must of necessity be a means to appropriate them some way or other, before they can be of any use, or at all beneficial to any particular man. The fruit, or venison, which nourishes the wild Indian, who knows no enclosure, and is still a tenant in common, must be his, and so his—i.e. a part of him, that another can no longer have any right to it, before it can do him any good for the support of his life.

Sec. 26. Though the earth, and all inferior creatures, be common to all men, yet every man has a "property" in his own "person": this nobody has any right to but himself. The "labor" of his body, and the "work" of his hands, we may say, are properly his. Whatsoever then he removes out of the state that nature hath provided, and left it in, he hath mixed his labor with, and joined to it something that is his own, and thereby makes it his property. It being by him removed from the common state nature hath placed it in, it hath by this labor something annexed to it, that excludes the common right of other men: for this "labor" being the unquestionable property of the laborer, no man but he can have a right to what that is once joined to, at least where there is enough, and as good, left in common for others.

Sec. 27. He that is nourished by the acorns he picked up under an oak, or the apples he gathered from the trees in the wood, has certainly appropriated them to himself. Nobody can deny but the nourishment is his. I ask, then, when did they begin to be his? When he digested? Or when he ate? Or when he boiled? Or when he brought them home? Or when he picked them up? And it is plain, if the first gathering made them not his, nothing else could. ...

Sec. 30. It will perhaps be objected to this, that if gathering the acorns, or other fruits of the earth, etc. makes a right to them, then anyone may ingross as much as he will. To which I answer, Not so. The same law of Nature, that does by this means give us property, does also bound that property too. "God has given us all things richly." Is the voice of reason confirmed by inspiration. But how far has he given it us "to enjoy?" As much as any one can make use of to any advantage of life before it spoils, so much he may by his labor fix a property in: whatever is beyond this, is more than his share, and belongs to others. Nothing was made by God for man to spoil or destroy. And thus, considering the plenty of natural provisions there was a long time in the world, and the few spenders; and to how small a part of that provision the industry of one man could extend itself, and ingross it to the prejudice of others; especially keeping within the bounds, set by reason, of what might serve for his use; there could be then little room for quarrels or contentions about property so established.

Sec. 31. But the chief matter of property being now not the fruits of the earth, and the beasts that subsist on it, but the earth itself; as that which takes in and carries with it all the rest; I think it is plain, that property in that too is acquired as the former. As much land as a man tills, plants, improves, cultivates, and can use the product of, so much is his property. He by his labor does, as it were, inclose it from the common. ...

Sec. 32. Nor was this appropriation of any parcel of land, by improving it, any prejudice to any other man, since there was still enough and as good left, and more than the yet unprovided could use. So that, in effect, there was never the less left for others because of his enclosure for himself. For he that leaves as much as another can make use of does as good as take nothing at all. Nobody could think himself injured by the drinking of another man, though he took a good draught, who had a whole river of the same water left him to quench his thirst. And the case of land and water, where there is enough of both, is perfectly the same.

***

Sec. 40. Nor is it so strange, as perhaps before consideration it may appear, that the property of labor should be able to over-balance the community of land: for it is labor indeed that puts the difference of value on every thing; and let any one consider what the difference is between an acre of land planted with tobacco or sugar, sown with wheat or barley, and an acre of the same land lying in common, without any husbandry upon it, and he will find, that the improvement of labor makes the far greater part of the value. I think it will be but a very modest computation to say, that of the products of the earth useful to the life of man nine tenths are the effects of labor: nay, if we will rightly estimate things as they come to our use, and cast up the several expences about them, what in them is purely owing to nature, and what to labor, we shall find, that in most of them ninety-nine hundredths are wholly to be put on the account of labor.

***

Sec. 46. The greatest part of things really useful to the life of man, and such as the necessity of subsisting made the first commoners of the world look after, as it doth the Americans now, are generally things of short duration; such as, if they are not consumed by use, will decay and perish of themselves: gold, silver and diamonds, are things that fancy or agreement hath put the value on, more than real use, and the necessary support of life. Now of those good things which nature hath provided in common, every one had a right (as hath been said) to as much as he could use, and property in all that he could effect with his labor; all that his industry could extend to, to alter from the state nature had put it in, was his. He that gathered a hundred bushels of acorns or apples, had thereby a property in them, they were his goods as soon as gathered. He was only to look, that he used them before they spoiled, else he took more than his share, and robbed others. And indeed it was a foolish thing, as well as dishonest, to hoard up more than he could make use of. If he gave away a part to any body else, so that it perished not uselessly in his possession, these he also made use of. And if he also bartered away plums, that would have rotted in a week, for nuts that would last good for his eating a whole year, he did no injury; he wasted not the common stock; destroyed no part of the portion of goods that belonged to others, so long as nothing perished uselessly in his hands. Again, if he would give his nuts for a piece of metal, pleased with its color; or exchange his sheep for shells, or wool for a sparkling pebble or a diamond, and keep those by him all his life he invaded not the right of others, he might heap up as much of these durable things as he pleased; the exceeding of the bounds of his just property not lying in the largeness of his possession, but the perishing of any thing uselessly in it.

Sec. 47. And thus came in the use of money, some lasting thing that men might keep without spoiling, and that by mutual consent men would take in exchange for the truly useful, but perishable supports of life.

Sec. 48. And as different degrees of industry were apt to give men possessions in different proportions, so this invention of money gave them the opportunity to continue and enlarge them: for supposing an island, separate from all possible commerce with the rest of the world, wherein there were but an hundred families, but there were sheep, horses and cows, with other useful animals, wholsome fruits, and land enough for corn for a hundred thousand times as many, but nothing in the island, either because of its commonness, or perishablness, fit to supply the place of money; what reason could any one have there to enlarge his possessions beyond the use of his family, and a plentiful supply to its consumption, either in what their own industry produced, or they could barter for like perishable, useful commodities, with others? Where there is not some thing, both lasting and scarce, and so valuable to be hoarded up, there men will not be apt to enlarge their possessions of land, were it never so rich, never so free for them to take: for I ask, what would a man value ten thousand, or an hundred thousand acres of excellent land, ready cultivated, and well stocked too with cattle, in the middle of the inland parts of America, where he had no hopes of commerce with other parts of the world, to draw money to him by the sale of the product? It would not be worth the enclosing, and we should see him give up again to the wild common of nature, whatever was more than would supply the conveniences of life to be had there for him and his family.

***

Of the Beginning of Political Societies

Sec. 95. Men being, as has been said, by nature, all free, equal, and independent, no one can be put out of this estate, and subjected to the political power of another, without his own consent. The only way whereby any one divests himself of his natural liberty, and puts on the bonds of civil society, is by agreeing with other men to join and unite into a community for their comfortable, safe, and peaceable living one amongst another, in a secure enjoyment of their properties, and a greater security against any, that are not of it. This any number of men may do, because it injures not the freedom of the rest; they are left as they were in the liberty of the state of Nature. When any number of men have so consented to make one community or government, they are thereby presently incorporated, and make one body politic, wherein the majority have a right to act and conclude the rest.

Sec. 96. For when any number of men have, by the consent of every individual, made a community, they have thereby made that community one body, with a power to act as one body, which is only by the will and determination of the majority: for that which acts any community, being only the consent of the individuals of it, and it being necessary to that which is one body to move one way; it is necessary the body should move that way whither the greater force carries it, which is the consent of the majority: or else it is impossible it should act or continue one body, one community, which the consent of every individual that united into it, agreed that it should; and so every one is bound by that consent to be concluded by the majority. And therefore we see, that in assemblies, impowered to act by positive laws, where no number is set by that positive law which impowers them, the act of the majority passes for the act of the whole, and of course determines, as having, by the law of Nature and reason, the power of the whole.

***

Sec. 98. For if the consent of the majority shall not, in reason, be received as the act of the whole, and conclude every individual; nothing but the consent of every individual can make anything to be the act of the whole: but such a consent is next to impossible ever to be had, if we consider the infirmities of health, and avocations of business, which in a number, though much less than that of a common-wealth, will necessarily keep many away from the public assembly. To which if we add the variety of opinions, and contrariety of interests, which unavoidably happen in all collections of men, the coming into society upon such terms would be only like Cato's coming into the theatre, *tantum ut exiret.*[1] Such a constitution as this would make the mighty Leviathan of a shorter duration, than the feeblest creatures, and not let it outlast the day it was born in: which cannot be supposed, till we can think, that rational creatures should desire and constitute societies only to be dissolved: for where the majority cannot conclude the rest, there they cannot act as one body, and consequently will be immediately dissolved again.

***

Sec. 119. Every man being, as has been showed, naturally free, and nothing being able to put him into subjection to any earthly power, but only his own consent; it is to be considered, what shall be understood to be a sufficient declaration of a man's consent, to make him subject to the laws of any government. There is a common distinction of an express and a tacit consent, which will concern our present case. Nobody doubts but an express

---

[1] only to go out again; Cato (234–140 B.C.), the Roman statesman, disapproved of the theater.

consent, of any man entering into any society, makes him a perfect member of that society, a subject of that government. The difficulty is, what ought to be looked upon as a tacit consent, and how far it binds, i.e. how far any one shall be looked on to have consented, and thereby submitted to any government, where he has made no expressions of it at all. And to this I say, that every man, that hath any possessions, or enjoyment, of any part of the dominions of any government, doth thereby give his tacit consent, and is as far forth obliged to obedience to the laws of that government, during such enjoyment, as anyone under it; whether this his possession be of land, to him and his heirs for ever, or a lodging only for a week; or whether it be barely traveling freely on the highway; and in effect, it reaches as far as the very being of any one within the territories of that government.

***

Sec. 122. But submitting to the laws of any country, living quietly, and enjoying privileges and protection under them, makes not a man a member of that society: this is only a local protection and homage due to and from all those, who, not being in a state of war, come within the territories belonging to any government, to all parts whereof the force of its laws extends. But this no more makes a man a member of that society, a perpetual subject of that common-wealth, than it would make a man a subject to another, in whose family he found it convenient to abide for some time; though, whilst he continued in it, he were obliged to comply with the laws, and submit to the government he found there. And thus we see, that foreigners, by living all their lives under another government, and enjoying the privileges and protection of it, though they are bound, even in conscience, to submit to its administration, as far forth as any denizen; yet do not thereby come to be subjects or members of that commonwealth. Nothing can make any man so, but his actually entering into it by positive engagement, and express promise and compact. This is that, which I think, concerning the beginning of political societies, and that consent which makes any one a member of any commonwealth.

Of the Ends of Political Society and Government

Sec. 123. If man in the state of Nature be so free, as has been said; if he be absolute lord of his own person and possessions, equal to the greatest, and subject to no body, why will he part with his freedom? why will he give up this empire, and subject himself to the dominion and controul of any other power? To which it is obvious to answer, that though in the state of Nature he hath such a right, yet the enjoyment of it is very uncertain, and constantly exposed to the invasion of others: for all being kings as much as he, every man his equal, and the greater part no strict observers of equity and justice, the enjoyment of the property he has in this state is very unsafe, very unsecure. This makes him willing to quit a condition, which, however free, is full of fears and continual dangers: and it is not without reason, that he seeks out, and is willing to join in society with others, who are already united, or have a mind to unite, for the mutual preservation of their lives, liberties and estates, which I call by the general name, property.

Sec. 124. The great and chief end, therefore, of men's uniting into commonwealths, and putting themselves under government, is the preservation of their property. To which in the state of Nature there are many things wanting.

First, There wants an established, settled, known law, received and allowed by common consent to be the standard of right and wrong, and the common measure to decide all controversies between them: for though the law of Nature be plain and intelligible to all rational creatures; yet men being biassed by their interest, as well as ignorant for want of study of it, are not apt to allow of it as a law binding to them in the application of it to their particular cases.

Sec. 125. Secondly, In the state of Nature there wants a known and indifferent judge, with authority to determine all differences according to the established law: for every one in that state being both judge and executioner of the law of Nature, men being partial to themselves, passion and revenge is very apt to carry them too far, and with too much heat, in their own cases; as well as negligence, and unconcernedness, to make them too remiss in other men's.

Sec. 126. Thirdly, In the state of Nature there often wants power to back and support the sentence when right, and to give it due execution, They who by any injustice offended, will seldom fail, where they are able, by force to make good their injustice; such resistance many times makes the punishment dangerous, and frequently destructive, to those who attempt it.

***

Sec. 243. To conclude. The power that every individual gave the society, when he entered into it, can never revert to the individuals again, as long as the society lasts, but will always remain in the community; because without this there can be no community, no common-wealth, which is contrary to the original agreement: so also when the society hath placed the legislative in any assembly of men, to continue in them and their successors, with direction and authority for providing such successors, the legislative can never revert to the people whilst that government lasts; because having provided a legislative with power to continue for ever, they have given up their political power to the legislative, and cannot resume it. But if they have set limits to the duration of their legislative, and made this supreme power in any person, or assembly, only temporary; or else, when by the miscarriages of those in authority, it is forfeited; upon the forfeiture, or at the determination of the time set, it reverts to the society, and the people have a right to act as supreme, and continue the legislative in themselves; or erect a new form, or under the old form place it in new hands, as they think good.

STUDY QUESTIONS

1. According to Locke, what is the "state " and the "law of nature?"

2. On what grounds are people entitled to property?

3. According to Locke, do governments require the consent of the governed?

4. Can power revert to the individual once he or she has surrendered it to the community?

5. How much of a person's freedom is the state entitled to take?

B. Expression in Film

Born on the Fourth of July

Director: Oliver Stone

Screenwriters: Ron Kovic and Oliver Stone

Oliver Stone (1946—) is a celebrated director and screenwriter who has pre-sented controversial interpretations of contemporary events in America. He has won three Academy Awards, one for Midnight Express *as best screen-play, and two as best director for* Platoon *and* Born on the Fourth of July. *The latter two films were based on Stone's own experience of combat during the Vietnam War. Stone also wrote the screenplays for* Conan the Barbarian, Scarface, Year of the Dragon, and 8 Million Ways to Die.

Among the more provocative films he directed are Salvador, *that criti-cizes American involvement in Central America, and* JFK, *arguing that the Kennedy assassination was the result of a conspiracy between the govern-ment and intelligence communities.* JFK *provoked a national debate on who was responsible for Kennedy's death and whether Stone had the right to present his theory as a quasi-documentary. His more recent films,* Heaven and Earth, *the third in his Vietnam trilogy, and* Natural Born Killers, *about America's fascination with serial killers, received less attention.*

Born on the Fourth of July *is based on the best-selling autobiography of Ron Kovic, who collaborated with Stone on the screenplay. Like the protag-onist in the film, Kovic came home from Vietnam paralyzed from the chest down, underwent a metamorphosis in his attitude toward the war, was thrown out of the 1972 Republican convention (with his wheelchair), and addressed the Democratic National convention in 1976.*

SYNOPSIS

The question of (1) rebellion and revolution, and (2) dissent and disobedi-ence is one that should be addressed in deciding on the structure of an ideal state. When citizens disagree with their government, are they still obligated to carry out its mandates, even when it means endangering their lives? On what grounds can states require citizens to support the government and to obey laws that are unjust? Can states force their people to fight in wars that they oppose?

(1) The first issue, that of rebellion (open, organized and armed resistance to a government) and revolution (a forcible overthrow and replacement of a government), has arisen at various points in world history. In the United States, we agonized especially over the Revolutionary War, the Civil War, and the Vietnam War. *Born on the Fourth of July* deals with the last, of course—a particularly bitter debate within our society. At that time, between the mid-60s and 70s, dissidents began thinking the unthinkable: the violent overthrow of the United States government.

The broad issue in political philosophy is whether and when citizens can use violence against the state. As mentioned in the introduction, Hobbes argues in *The Leviathan* that the state demands absolute submission to its laws, so that neither rebellion nor revolution is ever justified. When societies were first formed, people surrendered such power to a supreme ruler in exchange for protection from each other's aggression. In a state of nature constant warfare takes place, so people pledge their loyalty to this sovereign who maintains the peace. The sovereign rules in accordance with divine law, as required by man's selfish and violent nature.

His contemporary, John Locke in his *Second Treatise of Government*, takes an opposite position with regard to the state of nature and the foundation of government. To Locke, human beings are naturally peaceable and possess inherent rights. They enter into a social contract to safeguard those rights, especially property and religion. The government they establish exists by the consent of the governed and fosters the people's mutual interests. If that trust in government is broken, then people can legitimately revolt. Ultimately, it is not the state but the people who retain sovereignty, and they can rem ove officials or change the government if their rights are violated.

Whenever nations are in civil turmoil the question arises as to who is correct: Hobbes or Locke. Governments will often suppress revolts in the name of authority, law and order, while the opposition will argue that an uprising is appropriate and necessary for the sake of social justice. In recent history, China put down a demonstration in Tiananmen Square in Beijing, declaring all dissent illegal; about seven thousand people were shot to death. In our own country, the National Guard fired on students at Kent

State University who were protesting the Vietnam War, killing four and wounding nine. At Kent State the numbers were relatively small, but the nation was shocked that U.S. troops had killed college students to quell a demonstration. (In the war itself over fifty-eight thousand Americans were killed.) Can civil protests be allowed, including outright rebellion, opposing the authority of the state?

(2) The related issue of dissent (expressed political differences in doctrine or opinion) and disobedience (refusal to comply with governmental rules) is less severe but equally vexing. The first philosophic discussion of this issue occurs in the *Crito*, a Platonic dialogue in which Socrates discourses about right and wrong, while awaiting execution. Sorcates had been accused of corrupting the youth, unfairly convicted, and sentenced to death by poison (drinking hemlock). One of his followers, Crito, urges Socrates to escape from prison, arguing that he would not want to lose a cherished friend and that people would blame him for not bribing the guards; they would think he did not care for Socrates enough. He also argues that if Socrates allowed himself to be executed he would play into the hands of his enemies. Furthermore, he would be abandoning his children.

Socrates questions Crito, in his customary way, to try to decide whether escaping from prison would be right. By escaping he would be opposing the court's ruling, and he wonders whether citizens have a debt of loyalty to the state, even when they disagree with its decisions. Should we be faithful only when we obtain benefits from the government and not when its laws go against us?

> SOC: Then consider the matter in this way: Imagine that I am about to play truant (you may call the proceeding by any name which you like), and the laws and the government come and interrogate me: "Tell us, Socrates," they say; "what are you about? are you going by an act of yours to overturn us—the laws and the whole State, as far as in you lies? Do you imagine that a State can subsist and not be overthrown, in which the decisions of law have no power, but are set aside and overthrown by individuals?" What will be our answer, Crito, to these and the like words? Anyone, and especially a clever rhetorician, will have a good deal to urge about the evil of setting aside the law which requires a sentence to be carried out; and we might reply, "Yes' but the State has injured us and given an unjust sentence." Suppose I say that?
>
> CR: Very good, Socrates.

SOC. "And was that our agreement with you?" the law would say, "or were you to abide by the sentence of the State?" And if I were to express astonishment at their saying this, the law would probably add: "Answer, Socrates, instead of opening your eyes: you are in the habit of asking and answering questions. Tell us what complaint you have to make against us which justifies you in attempting to destroy us and the State? In the first place did we not bring you into existence? Your father married your mother by our aid and begat you. Say whether you have any objections to urge against those of us who regulate marriage?" None, I should reply, "Or against those of use who regulate the system of nurture and education of children in which you were trained? ... And because we think right to destroy you, do you think that you have any right to destroy us in return, and your country as far as in you lies? And will you, O professor of true virtue, say that you are justified in this? Has a philosopher like you failed to discover that our country is more to be valued and higher and holier far than mother or father or any ancestor, and more to be regarded in the eyes of the gods and of men of understanding? also to be soothed, and gently and reverently entreated when angry, even more than a father, and if not persuaded, obeyed? And when we are punished by her, whether with imprisonment or stripes, the punishment is to be endured in silence; and if she leads us to wounds or death in battle, thither we follow as is right; neither may anyone yield or retreat or leave his rank, but whether in battle or in a course of law, or in any other place, he must do what his city and his country order him; or he must change their view of what is just; and if he may do no violence to his father or mother, much less may he do violence to his country." What answer shall we make to this, Crito? Do the laws speak truly or do they not?

CR. I think that they do.

SOC. Then the laws will say: "Consider, Socrates, if this is true, that in your present attempt you are going to do us wrong. For, after having brought you into the world, and nurtured and educated you, and given you and every other citizen a share in every good that we had to give, we further proclaim and give the right to every Athenian, that if he does not like us when he has come of age and has seen the ways of the city, and made our acquaintance, he may go where he pleases and take his goods with him. Any of you who does not like us and the city, and who wants to go to a colony or to any other city, may go where he likes, and take his goods with him. But he who has experience of the manner in which we order justice and administer the State, and still remains, has entered into an implied contract that he will do as we command him....[1]

Socrates' position may be persuasive but it is also questionable. He opposes escaping and affirms his loyalty to the state based on three arguments: that by not leaving Athens previously he had tacitly promised to obey the state's laws; that he has a debt of gratitude toward the state for the benefits it conferred upon him; and that the consequences would be disastrous if citizens refused to obey the law.

Each of these points can be challenged. In terms of the first argument, that of a tacit promise, the fact that people remain in a country does not mean that its laws are just or that they thereby consent to obey all of them. There can be a loyal opposition that refuses to follow those laws it considers unjust. This is not necessarily traitorous since one should oppose unfair laws and work openly to have them rescinded. "Love it or leave it" is a thoughtless slogan. People may choose to remain in the country they love and work to improve it.

As for the second argument of gratitude, citizens are not necessarily indebted to the state for benefits they receive, and may not be expected to repay them. If someone gives you a gift, that does not always place you under a moral obligation to them. You may never have asked for the gift, it could have been a general benefit to others beside yourself, and it might advance the interests of the giver. You certainly do not have any debt of gratitude if the gift is something to which you have a right. In fact, if you deserve it anyway, it ceases to be a gift and becomes an entitlement.

The privilege of marriage, nurture, and education that Socrates refers to may be rights of citizens along with health, liberty, life, and property. Perhaps the state safeguards such rights rather than conferring them, and people should not be grateful for that which is due to them.

The third argument, that the state would collapse if its citizens disobeyed the laws, is an argument from utility. To allow people to disobey laws, it is argued, would be "the thin edge of the wedge," a first step on "the long slippery slope" toward anarchy. However, Socrates is not fomenting a general revolution, and if *some* people at *some* times oppose *some* laws, that would

---

[1]Translation: Benjamin Jowett

not be a serious threat to the state. In fact, if a country's bad laws are changed in response to protests, that could increase people's satisfaction with the government and strengthen its hand. Furthermore, if citizens protest openly, they are not engaging in criminal actions that undermine the state but using public, democratic methods to stimulate discussion about the merits of a law. Freedom of speech and assembly seems a healthy means for bringing about change.

In the *Apology*, Socrates' compares himself to a gadfly that stings the sluggish horse of society into awareness. Perhaps his metaphor can be used against him in this context. If the horse is sound, the sting will merely stimulate him; at worst, it will be a nuisance. Only the unhealthy horse is threatened by the gadfly—the unsound state that cannot survive criticism.

Based on such considerations, many people throughout history have defied their government's laws, and this issue furnishes the philosophic context for *Born on the Fourth of July*. The setting is the controversial Vietnam War (1965–1975) and its attendant protest movements and civil disobedience in the United States. The war provoked anti-war demonstrations all across the country, and there were equally strong pro-war sentiments by "the silent majority." The nation was divided, bitter, and confused, with sentiments running high both for and against our involvement. The government was determined to win the war, even if that meant deforesting combat zones, using napalm, and giving dubious information to the public about our successes, including body counts.

Meanwhile the American people were growing increasingly uneasy about our warrant for being in Vietnam. Was it really necessary to risk injury or death to our sons in what seemed to be an internal conflict in a foreign country? Was it in our national interest to stop communism in southeast Asia before the "domino effect" brought it to our shores? The cost in human suffering was horrendous, televised for all the nation to see, and people questioned whether the carnage should include civilians, which seemed contrary to American values.

Above all, the country struggled with the question of whether the war was just, and whether opposition to it was disloyal or a higher patriotism. Should young men escape to Canada to avoid the draft? Would that be an act of cowardice and desertion or a courageous act of conscience and good sense? Should we say "my country right or wrong?" or dissociate ourselves from shameful acts of our nation? Where does patriotism end and blind obedience begin? People also wondered how much dissent a democracy can tolerate, and when elected leaders should defer to the will of the electorate.

Born on the Fourth of July tells the particular story of Ron Kovic who fought in Vietnam and returned paralyzed from the chest down; his experiences are recounted in his autobiography, and he collaborated with Oliver Stone in writing the screenplay. However, Kovic and the film functions as a general metaphor for the experience of the country. At first, America was enthusiastic about the war, the way it was about the invasion of Iraq. Then people felt conflicted about it, disillusioned, and in varying degrees, repentant. Although the nation never apologized for the youth it sacrificed, its artists did.

At the start of the film, we see Ron Kovic (Tom Cruise) trying to decide whether to enlist in the Marines and fight in Vietnam. As a teenager, raised in a small town and nourished by values of family, God, and country, he is strongly attracted to the prospect of combat, especially as a marine, the emblem of toughness and masculinity. Like most boys, Ron regards war as the crucible of courage, and he is eager to prove himself a man, establish a mature identity, and come back a celebrated hero. The marine recruiter (Tom Berenger) plays into such feelings and, his parents (Raymond Barry and Caroline Kava) are ambivalent; they encourage him to enlist by default. In his search for guidance, Ron prays to God but even He seems to remain silent.

INT. LIVINGROOM

MOM in the bedroom, DAD watching the news, a newspaper in hand, dozing, exhausted from work. Waking now as RONNIE shuffles in, watching the NEWS CLIP—an Infantry COLONEL is being interviewed at a base camp someplace, TROOPS moving or convoying in the background; shades on his eyes, a green baseball cap over close-cropped hair, a revolver in his shoulder holster, thick forearms:

COLONEL: ... no question 'bout that. The 82nd Airborne and the First Cavalry Division are the newest concepts in mobile warfare. One division is worth about 2 ½ Russian and six Chinese divisions...

NEWSMAN: But how well do you think the individual soldier will hold up in Vietnam, Colonel?

COLONEL: I've never seen anything like it. I been in World War II—in Korea, these boys—they're gung ho, they wanna eat nails—the finest combat troops we've ever had! It's an honor to lead them.

RONNIE has sat down facing his DAD. A pause between them.

RONNIE: What do you think, Dad—about that?

NEWSCASTER: Do you think, Colonel, the war here will be over soon?

DAD: Oh... I don't know—13,000 miles—it's a long way to go to fight a war—

COLONEL: Well, that's a hard question to answer. But without seeming overconfident, I'd say at the outside, yes—about a year—Course it's a guerilla war so you can't force...

RONNIE: But if we give them Vietnam, they'll take the rest. That's the way they are. It's the domino theory, Dad. They'll nibble us up piece by piece. We gotta stop them someplace.

NEWSCASTER: But do you think these people—the Viet Cong— who've fought the Japanese and the French and lived in these caves and tunnels for thirty years—do you really think Colonel...

DAD (sighs): Maybe... I just hope they send you to Europe or Korea or someplace safe...

COLONEL: I think that anything that lives in a tunnel can be weeded out. It takes time and patience, and the support of the people back home—and the support of the press—

RONNIE: They can't Dad! They gotta send me to Vietnam for 13 months, that's the way it is—

NEWSCASTER: Colonel, do you mean... the Press is not...

DAD: Well, maybe they'll put you on garrison duty someplace... an embassy?

RONNIE: Yeah, but they *won't* Dad! Every marine has a tour over there, it's not like the Army (stronger now). What's *wrong* with everybody around here? Don't you remember what President Kennedy said, Dad, we're not gonna have an America anymore unless there's people willing to sacrifice...

MOM has come out into the livingroom.

DAD: I know Ronnie, I know.

COLONEL: I mean that… an important part of the war effort … is the attitude of the home front…

ANOTHER ANGLE—DAD doesn't want to think about it, looks away. RONNIE deeper in frame exasperated—this mute climate, this failure to beat a drum on the home front, this early silence and sadness about the war…

MOM: It's your decision, Ronnie, it's up to you whatever you decide, we're behind you. We'll pray for you Ronnie but you be careful.

NEWSCASTER: We… we all know…

She tries to kiss him on the cheek but RON'S eyes are unsatisfied, on his DAD.

RONNIE: Dad, do you understand what it means to me to be a Marine? Ever since I've been a kid, Dad, I've wanted this, I've wanted to help my country. (pause, the rain) … and I wanna go. I wanna go to Vietnam. I'll *die* if I have to over there…

COLONEL: … remember one thing now. Up in Hanoi they don't allow newspapers and televisions to cast any doubts on the system—the military system.

The silence. Why is life so anti-climactic at moments like this and words mean nothing?

DAD: Not a nice night for the prom…

NEWSCASTER: Well, I…

COLONEL: …and it seems to me sometimes we forget that.

NEWSCASTER: Well, Colonel the basic question is do you think the South Vietnamese government is a viable political entity that can stand up to…

COLONEL: If we didn't think so we wouldn't be here now would we—(Chopper starts coming overhead, drowning out sound)

INT. RON'S BEDROOM / BATH / HALL—NIGHT (1964)

RONNIE is kneeling in front of the MIRROR with the CRUCIFIX in his BEDROOM ("Let the Beauty of Jesus Be Seen In Me").

> RONNIE: …sometimes God I'm so confused, sometimes I think I'd like just to stay right here in Massapequa and never leave … but I gotta go. You gotta help me Jesus … help me to make the right decision … I wanna do the right thing …

THE RAIN lashing against the bedroom window, suggesting a plea to a barbaric god. RONNIE inside on his knees.

After a brief scene at the prom where Ron and his girl Donna (Kyra Sedgwick) slow-dance to a sentimental song, filled with youthful longing and loss, we are suddenly catapulted to a war zone in Vietnam. The shift from an innocent and idyllic American moment to intense physical combat in a foreign country is deliberate and startling. Ron's platoon is deployed outside a fishing village on the South China Sea, poised to attack the Viet Cong from across some rice paddies. As they lie on the dunes, a heavy, monsoon rain is falling, obstructing the view of the activities in the village.

> The fresh-faced LIEUTENANT listens over the radio and barks orders at RON over the wind.
>
> LIEUTENANT: Red Platoon's receiving fire on the northwest edge of the ville. NVA suspects are coming this way …
>
> RON alert, listening now to the imagined sound of distant gunfire …
>
> LIEUTENANT: (points) … set your squad in a line along the dune …
>
> He's very excited, repeating his orders.
>
> LIEUTENANT: I think we got'em, I think we got 'em this time Sargeant?
>
> Their POV—through the rain—the village. Hard to see anything.

A GRAVEYARD.

> In the distance, some movement in the village.
>
> LIEUTENANT (very excited now): You see? Look, they got rifles. Can't you see the rifles?… Can you see them?
>
> RON looking very hard through the rain.

RON: Yes, I see them. I see them.

LIEUTENANT (puts his arm around him): Tell them when I give the order, I wanna light this village up like a fucking Christmas tree—okay!!! Get going!

Turning back to his radio, overly keyed.

KOVIC running down the line, sinking in the sand, his baggy poncho flopping over the gear on his back.

Suddenly, SEVERAL FIGURES break from the huts, running.

As RON runs down the straggled LINE OF MEN, someone starts firing from the end with his M-16. Now the whole line suddenly erupts, pulling their triggers without thinking, emptying everything they have into the huts across the graveyard.

RON yelling, trying to get his men to stop the fire.

Voices screaming in the distance.

RON looking at the LIEUTENANT running up the line yelling across the sand.

LIEUTENANT: What happened! Goddamn it, what happened!…Who gave the order to fire? I wanna know who gave the order to fire!

Everybody is looking at everybody else with that peculiar awkwardness of a platoon without real leadership.

RON: We better get a killer team out there, sir.

LIEUTENANT: All right, all right Sergeant, got out there with Molina and tell me how many we got…

The VOICES continue to scream from the village, an eerie wailing amid the noise of rain.

RON moving to assemble FIVE MEN.

The LIEUTENANT on the radio; there seems to be increased fire from the distance, coming across the radio. Incipient panic building…

RON leading his five men across the dunes into the edges of the village…

…The Voices, the screams continuing… RON knows something is wrong, the rain beating on his face as he moves cautiously to the lip of the hut…

MOLINA is alongside him… They both turn into the hut and see it at the same time…

MOLINA: Oh God! Oh Jesus Christ!

RON's eyes convey the horror.

INT. HUT—DAY—RAIN

The floor of the small hut is covered with CHILDREN, screaming and thrashing their arms back and forth, lying in pools of blood, crying wildly, screaming again and again. They're shot in the face, in the chest, in the legs, moaning and crying…

RON: Oh Jesus…

The LIEUTENANT'S VOICE now blasting in on the radio…

LIEUTENANT: Tango Two, how many you got?

An old, OLD MAN in the corner with his head blown off from his eyes up, his brains hanging out of his head like jelly…

RON keeps looking at the strange sight, he's never seen anything like it before.

A SMALL BOY, next to the old man is still alive, though shot many times. He's crying softly, lying is a large pool of blood. His small foot has been shot off almost completely and hangs by a thread.

LIEUTENANT (*voice*): What's going on? What's going on up there?

MOLINA (*voice*): You better get up here fast, Lieutenant. There's a lot of wounded people up here.

A SMALL GIRL moaning now, shot through the stomach.

RON feels crazy, weak, helpless, staring at them…

The other THREE MARINES are looking, staring down at the floor like it's a nightmare, like it's some kind of dream and it really isn't happening…

Subsequently, in the confusion of a firefight, Ron kills one of his own men and then is badly wounded himself. Little is done for him at the understaffed, overcrowded, vermin-infested hospital where he is sent; in fact, the neglect probably causes him to become a paraplegic, confined to a wheelchair for the rest of his life.

When Ron returns home wearing his uniform with medals on his chest he expects a hero's welcome, but although town officials proudly display him on patriotic occasions, people in the anti-war movement treat him as a criminal, adding to the guilt he already feels for killing innocent civilians. His heroism and sacrifice are not recognized by his family and friends either; they treat him with gentle pity. His father constructs a special bathroom for him and carries him to bed each night.

Ron is still a loyal soldier and feels betrayed and confused by the conflicting attitudes he encounters, unsure whether the war was worth fighting. For example, while sitting in a bar one night, watching couples on the dance floor, he expresses his bitterness and is attacked for it:

> RON: ... It was the wrong fucking war when you gotta come back to a dogshit hospital where they don't give a fuck if... when it was just a waste of fuckin' time, and it was all one big fuckin' mistake right and I'm sorry but you can take your Viet Nam and shove it up your ass...

> MAN #2: Why don't you shove it up *your* ass pal... okay? Just 'cause you're in a fuckin' wheelchair you think everybody's gotta feel sorry for you?

> RON: What?

> MAN #2: You ain't the only Marine here. I was on Iwo Jima. We lost 6,000 the first day. So don't go crying in your fucking beer to me. You served, you lost, and now you gotta live with it. You're a marine, semper fi, they didn't pick you, you picked them so stop moaning and pissing about it!

> RON: ... I think guys like you are assholes that what I think.

> MAN #2: Yeah, I bet you do buddy, you sorry motherfucker... 'cause you know if they win... it's guys like you they're gonna put up against the wall first... 'cause they know you sure as hell can't trust a traitor.

Ron becomes dissolute as he becomes disillusioned, and for a time he joins a group of drunken veterans in Mexico. He also travels to Syracuse University to visit his ex-girlfriend Donna who is now heavily involved in the anti-war movement. He explains to her why he went to war, and here Oliver Stone suggests that a boy's motives for fighting have more to do with his manhood than with his patriotism.

RON: I wanted you to see me at my best, I don't know why that is with people, but... you know it's like... it's never enough... It's like you do something at twelve 'cause you wanna show everybody you can be fifteen, and when you're fifteen you wanna be eighteen, and when you're eighteen you wanna be twenty-one, you really wanna be a man so you go out and join up and you go to... War... and War is like this big secret see—it's something only a few people in this country really know about—and you think if you know what that secret is... then you think ah! Then finally at last. I'll be a man... and when I'm a Man—then I'm gonna have you "Donna"— ... like you're part of a timepiece you know... when I'm twenty-one I'm gonna have Donna and that's just the way it is... and everything... *everything* I ever did, hitting that home run that day you were up in the stands with that stupid guy and that crazy song playing "awalking in the rain... awhoo whooo whoo whoo..." was for you Donna... it was for you. (pause). I wanted to *shine. I really wanted to shine* for you, Donna... 'cause I loved you... goddamnit I really *loved you*... I just never told you... (exhales, a long beat) Jeesus!

Donna comforts him as he cries, but the intervening years and the past difference in their politics make it impossible for them to be together as they once were. The way she and the country have changed is made clearer by a rally at Syracuse that same day. The protest moves Ron further to question the rightness of the war, and we see him gradually becoming radicalized.

The STUDENTS have taken over a BUILDING—waving protest banners and flags from the windows. Starting to trash the place now—desks, papers, file cabinets being thrown out the windows onto the lawns.

CHANTS: FUCK THE PIGS! FUCK THE PIGS! ONE – TWO – THREE – FOUR WE DON'T WANT YOUR FUCKING WAR!! FIVE – SIX – SEVEN – EIGHT – WE DON'T WANT TO ESCALATE!

The COPS are forming at two ends of the quadrangle, emptying out of their vans... LOUDSPEAKERS shouting orders...

...as RON looks on with DONNA and her BOYFRIEND, a tall, lean intellectual young man of pleasant demeanor... "Peace Now" and

"Stop the War" buttons. They are in a LARGE GROUP in the center of the quadrangle listening to one of the SPEAKERS, a young, black Veteran in cut off fatigues, his medals pinned to his chest.

On the platform behind him are OTHER YOUNG VETS mixed with STUDENT LEADERS, the UNIVERSITY REVEREND, and a few TEACHERS...

The SPEAKER is a fiery, moving man, waving a document in the air.

SPEAKER: It says right here People—in the Declaration of Independence, if the Government fucks you over, it's not only your RIGHT but YOUR FUCKIN DUTY, PEOPLE... to BRING IT DOWN!!!

A huge roar from the agitated crowd, sensing the POLICE closing in.

CHANTS: RIGHT ON! POWER TO THE PEOPLE MAN! REMEMBER KENT AND JACKSON STATE!

RON has never heard words like this... his eyes hungrily roving through the crowd...

...to a FEW HIPPIES all painted up, long hair, flowers, one of them breast-feeding a BABY... A tab of acid being passed in a priestly manner.

...guys and girls passing joints... a guy beating a drum...

... a

SPEAKER: ... If Jefferson and Tom Paine and those dudes were here today, d'you think they'd be with Nixon or with us? (ad lib answers "WITH US!") Shit yes, Nixon's the same as King George!

On the loudspeakers, the COPS are advising the STUDENTS to get out of the DORMS...

LOUDSPEAKER: YOU ARE ORDERED TO DISPERSE. YOU HAVE FIVE MINUTES. THIS IS AN UNLAWFUL ASSEMBLY. IF YOU DO NOT DISPERSE, YOU WILL BE ARRESTED.

SPEAKER: First he invades Cambodia and bombs the shit out of it, and then he kills four kids at Kent State 'cause they tried to protest. This guy's gotta go!!! (ROARS—"BURN BABY BURN!") Right on! The people of this country been fucked over cheated and lied to by all of 'em. Truman, Eisenhower, Kennedy, Johnson. The whole war is a big rip off... people are dying over there to make some fat cat capitalist businessman rich, this whole generation's being sold out. People... (MORE) and we GOTTA DO SOMETHING. WE GOTTA GET RID OF THIS GOVERNMENT NOW. (Roars—"BURN BABY BURN! POWER TO THE PEO-PLE!")...

A YOUNG VETERAN walking through the CROWD, spots RON, comes over ... seeing him, RON tries to shrink back as the VET gives him a high-fiver ... the VET seeming to know RON is a vet.

VET: Hey brother, Larry Boyle, what's happening man.

RON: Ron Kovic.

VET: Welcome brother ... to the War at home ... You gotta get up there, man, say a few words to these dudes. Wake 'em up man ...

RON: No. No. Not today. Thanks anyway ...

VET: (looking him right in the eye): Peace, Ron ... and welcome home ...

HE goes ... RON stirred, something in him reluctantly moved by the man ... DONNA noticing it, smiles ...

SPEAKER: We're the ones put our bodies on the line—for people who didn't even care about us when we came home. I loved this country once ...

The SPEAKER now rips the medals from his chest and brandishes them in his hands...

SPEAKER: ... And all this I won over there... The Purple Heart, the Bronze Star, all the Commendation Medals and the rest of this gar-bage... don't mean a thing. FUCK THIS SHIT.

Shaking with emotion, he hurls them into the distance...

RON is shocked. He's never seen or heard something like this. As he catches DONNA'S eyes for a moment.

She has her fist in the air yelling "RIGHT ON, BURN, BABY, BURN!" beautiful yet cruel in her anger, she embodies the revolution. RON looks away.

Stone might have left Ron Kovic an embittered, crippled veteran, taking drugs, paying for prostitutes, and alienating himself from his parents by his drunkenness, obscenity, and violence. That could have been an effective protest against the war. However, Stone chose to present a resolution of the conflict, which is what happened to the real Kovic and Stone himself after they fought in Vietnam.

For a long time Ron struggles to understand whether love of country means protests or loyalty (*semper fidelis*, after all, means always faithful), but eventually he turns against the Vietnam War, for very mixed reasons. On a personal level, the war took away his manhood instead of validating it, and rather than winning Donna he lost her by fighting. Politically, he never really grasped the reasons for the war while feeling duty-bound to enlist, and he gradually comes to doubt the war's justification. The personal and the political, that is, rage at his paralysis and awareness of his greater responsibility, come together to make him an activist. Symbolically, by deciding to be an effective agent for change, he overcomes his paralysis and recovers.

As the film progresses, we see Ron as part of a protest group at the 1972 Republican National Convention, following a procession of ragged young people with pipe and drum whistling, "When Johnny Comes Marching Home Again," Vietnam veterans walk down a boulevard in Miami wearing fatigues and bush hats, long hair and beards, some with medals on their chests, others carrying Viet Cong flags.

> The WOUNDED now appear—blind vets, amputated vets, proudly escorted, parting now onto RON and two other PARAS abreast of him in chairs pushed by FELLOW VETS. RON now has a full mustache and is unshaven, his hair longer than ever ... a banner above their heads: STOP THE WAR—VIETNAM VETERANS AGAINST THE WAR—'hurray! hurrah! Up from the song...
>
> As SPECTATORS watch from the sidewalks or porches ... ANGRY MEN ...CHEERING MEN ... OLD JEWISH LADIES on their verandas ... mostly neutral, curious looks ...
>
> SECRET SERVICE cars trailing ... suits, earplugs, walkie talkies.
>
> COPS in full riot gear filing out of a TRUCK on a quiet street. STATIC of a walkie talkie ... 'proceed to 5th and Cyprus ... cordon off ... contain ... separate ... the hippies ... marijuana busts ... traffic violations ..." ... SOUNDS of the WHISTLING MARCHERS in the distance.

INT. MIAMI CONVENTION CENTER—NIGHT

Into an ocean of thundering SOUND ...

RON and the TWO OTHER PARAS are in the hall, wheeling their way closer to the stage...

with them is a FOURTH MAN, a redheaded guy with a beard, floppy bush hat, jungle fatigues who is pushing RON at the parade. He's inside now, and helping push RON and the TWO OTHERS.

... past the YOUNG REPUBLICANS yelling "FOUR MORE YEARS. FOUR MORE YEARS!!"

... past MEN and WOMEN in summer suits with happy Republican pink faces looking with some concern and possibly apprehension at these three scruffy Vietnam Vets rolling into their midst...

A NEWS CAMERA filming them. RON angling into the camera, playing the crowd looking for people to lisen.

> RON: Do you hear me? Can I break through your complacency? Can I have an inch... a moment of your compassion for the human beings who are suffering in this war... do you hear me when I say this war is a crime... when I say I am not as bitter about my wound as the men who have lied to the people of this country... do you hear me?

But they hear nothing. Deaf, blind, dumb, roaring for their leader as he now appears... the sound waves rolling up the hall...

CLIP—NIXON now coming to the podium. A huge smile. A pause before he stretches out his arms in his famous victory pose. The ROARS pound over RON and THREE COMRADES continuing to wheel closer.

Like assassins, deep in enemy territory; their POV—the hall looming like a jungle far away. The tension in RON—

CLIP—NIXON

> NIXON: Mr. Chairman, delegates to this convention, my fellow Americans...

INTERCUT RON speaking at the same time to a NEWS CAMERA.

> RON: WHY DO THEY WANT TO HIDE US? Why won't they let the veterans of that war speak tonight? Because they don't wanna

know, they don't wanna see, they wanna hide us because they've *lied* and *cheated* us for so long—but we're not gonna run away and hide anymore, we're going to win because we loved it and believed in *everything* it stood for and tonight we're *ashamed* of it, and we've come from all the little towns, thousands of us to get this country *back* again, to make it *whole* again. Truth, honesty, integrity—this is the lost American dream here tonight, and *we're gonna take it back*!

INTERCUT CLIP—NIXON

Talking about Vietnam. The completely counter argument about ideals, patriotism, ideology—the basis of the Cold War. Cogent, coherent, something we've all heard before—and totally false to its core.

INTERCUT RON—to the cameras. He has become a professional 107 orator now, his voice and eyes and overall intensity the same RON but older now, polished, a political leader.

RON: We're never never gonna let the people of the United States forget that war, because the moment we do, there's gonna be another war and another, and another, that's why we're gonna be there for the rest of our lives telling you that the war happened, it wasn't some nightmare, it happened and you're not gonna sweep it under the rug because you didn't like the ratings like some television show... this wheelchair... this steel is your Memorial day on wheels, your Yankee Doodle.

A violent confrontation ensues in which secret service agents surround the veterans, blocking their entry to the convention and attempting to prevent TV cameras from covering the demonstration. As the paraplegics chant "STOP THE BOMBING, STOP THE WAR," and people in the crowd shout "THROW THEM OUT... TRAITORS... COMMUNISTS," the agents pull the veterans into the street in their wheelchairs. Ron is tipped out of his chair and brutally handcuffed, but when the agents try to throw him into a car several veterans converge and pull him away.

Ron and the other veterans then regroup and prepare to fight the police who face them with nightsticks. The police slowly advance, striking the sticks against their leather gloves, as the camera freezes and fades on drifting teargas and pulsing red lights. We are left with the impression that clubbing and beating are imminent.

In a final scene four years later, we see Ron Kovic addressing the 1976 Democratic National Convention in New York City. By his authority and presence we can assume he has become a major figure in the anti-war movement. And from the fact that he is allowed to speak we can assume that the country is now listening to dissenters without regarding them as traitors.

One obvious message of the film is that democracies must be able to tolerate opposition to government policy. Such freedom allows the individual and the nation the opportunity to correct disastrous policy.

> RON: I am the living death. Your Memorial Day on wheels. I am your Yankee Doodle Dandy. Your John Wayne come home. Your Fourth of July firecracker exploding in the grave... Twelve years ago when I was 18 years old, I left Massapequa, Long Island and joined the United States Marines... I wanted to serve my country... I wanted to be a good American... I couldn't wait to fight my first war, and I went with the others like our fathers before us with hope in our hearts and dreams of great victory...

Blending into the MUSIC THEME now... of tragedy overcome. Of life renewed...

STUDY QUESTIONS

1. In what way is Ronnie made to feel that it is his patriotic duty to fight in Vietnam? Do states have the right to compel people to risk their lives for their country?

2. Do you think the attack on the village was necessary? If noncombatants cannot be differentiated from combatants, doesn't that justify treating them as the enemy?

3. Is the anti-war protest legitimate, or do citizens have an obligation to support their government's decision to attack another country? Do the police have the right to disburse the protest as unpatriotic?

4. Does the fact that Ronnie fought in Vietnam and was wounded give him greater authority in condemning the war or does it undermine his protest?

5. What are the limits of free speech in a democracy? Can people be allowed to criticize the government, even if that threatens the stability of the state?

Schindler's List

Director: Steven Spielberg

Screenplay: Steven Zaillian

Based on the book by Thomas Keneally

For information on the director, Steven Spielberg, see the headnote preceding *Saving Private Ryan*.

The film Schindler's List, *a synopsis of which follows, was adapted for the screen from a 1982 biographical novel by Thomas Keneally. The title character, Oskar Schindler, was a real person, and Steven Zaillian's screenplay departs very little from the actual events of his life. Starting as an entrepreneur willing to work with the Nazis as suppliers of Jews for his factory, Schindler develops into a saintly individual who protects hundreds of Jews from extermination. Spielberg tells the story as though we were witnessing history, never intruding in the narrative but allowing the scenes of horror and of triumph to speak for themselves.*

    Schindler's List *won seven Academy Awards including Best Picture, Best Cinematography (Janusz Kaminski), Best Adapted Screenplay, Best Original Score (John Williams), Best Editing (Michael Kahn), and Best Art Direction. Liam Neeson was nominated as Best Actor and Ralph Fiennes as Best Supporting Actor, and the film received nominations for Best Costume Design, Best Sound, and Best Makeup. In addition to the Academy Awards,* Schindler's List *was also honored by the Golden Globes and the New York Film Critics Circle.*

SYNOPSIS

The twentieth century has seen enormous advances, principally in science, technology, and medicine, but the horrors committed against the world's peoples are also part of its legacy. It was a time of unprecedented violence

and atrocities with wars on an enormous scale, rebellions and ethnic geno-
cides, the introduction of tanks, planes, and submarines in combat, the em-
ployment of nuclear, chemical, and biological weapons, and the
displacement, maiming, and starvation of millions of people.

We have seen 12 million people killed by the Nazis in Europe, 4 to 5 million killed in the Soviet Union and another 4 to 7 million peasants starved to
death, 1.7 million killed by the Khymer Rouge in Cambodia, 1.5 million
killed in China's Cultural Revolution, 1.5 million Hindus and Muslims killed
in Pakistan, 1.5 million Armenians and 100,000 Kurds killed in Iraq, 1.3 million killed in the Sudan, 1 million killed in Ethiopia, 1 million Muslims killed
by Serbs in Bosnia, and hundreds of thousands killed in Namibia, Tanzania,
Uganda, Burundi, East Timor, Guatemala, and Rwanda.

The Holocaust is undoubtedly the prime expression and symbol of evil
in the twentieth century. The Nazis deliberately murdered six million Jews
during World War II, not as collateral damage but systematically and for
ideological reasons. According to Nazi theory, Jews were engaged in a financial conspiracy against Germany and Europe at large and had to be
eliminated. Moreover, they were accused of having killed Christ and were
judged as an inferior people like Negroes, homosexuals, Slavs, and gyp-
sies. The Nazis considered themselves the "Aryan" master race, destined to
rule the world, while Jews were thought to be mankind's traditional menace
and not fully human. Consequently, they could be used as slave labor and
ultimately exterminated in a "final solution."

Schindler's List is one of numerous films such as Jan Kadar's *The Shop
on Main Street* and Alan Pakula's *Sophie's Choice*, that have documented
and dramatized the horrors of the Holocaust. However, many critics regard
it as the finest and most powerful film ever made about this atrocity. The
black and white photography enhances the documentary feel of the film,
and augments the realism; blood flowing from a head wound is somehow
more affecting in black while avoiding tastelessness. In addition, the music
selected and composed by John Williams provides a haunting score. Popular Hungarian songs such as "Gloomy Sunday," the German's favorite
march "Erica," and Hebrew songs played by Itzhak Perlman provide a fitting background for the events depicted.

The story begins with Oskar Schindler (Liam Neeson) ingratiating himself to Nazi officers in an art deco cabaret in occupied Poland. It is the beginning of World War II, and Schindler wants to make important contacts
so he can open a factory, using Jewish workers at slave wages. As a failed
businessman in Czechoslovakia (a Sudenten German), he is gambling his

remaining funds on war profiteering, and his charisma enables him to win over those with the power to help him. By the end of the evening, he has joined the tables of the cabaret together in a drunken party, and everyone comes away impressed by his strong, physical presence, expensive clothes, and bon-vivant manner.

Schindler is subsequently appointed Direktor of a plant that manufactures enameled cooking utensils in Krakow for the German army; Emailwarenfabrik. He hires an accountant named Itzhak Stern (Ben Kingsley) to recruit Jews for the work force and later to manage the factory for him. He himself knows nothing about manufacturing cookware; his genius lies in charming people, in this case the Nazi authorities. The Jews are grateful for the job, even at starvation pay, because unless they are employed as "essential workers" contributing to national defense, they will be deported, imprisoned, or executed. Occupations such as teachers and musicians are classified as non-essential while those contributing to the war effort are protected. Schindler, meanwhile, by having low labor costs, begins to amass a fortune.

To maintain his position, Schindler builds strong ties with the Nazi hierarchy through bribery and luxurious gifts; Beluga caviar, Hennesey cognac, Dom Perignon champagne, Cuban cigars, fresh fruit, chocolate, and German cigarettes—all obtained through contacts on the black market. With each box of gifts he encloses a note:

> (*Schindler's voice-over*) It is my distinct pleasure to announce the fully operational status of Deutsche Emailwaren Fabrick—manufacturers of superior enamelware crockery, expressly designed and crafted for military use, utilizing only the most modern equipment. DEF's staff of highly skilled and experienced artisans and journeymen deliver a product of unparalleled quality, enabling me to proffer with absolute confidence and pride, a full line of field and kitchen ware unsurpassable in all respects by my competitors. See attached list and available colors. Anticipating the enclosed bids will meet with your approval, and looking forward to a long and mutually prosperous association, I extend to you, in advance, my sincerest gratitude and very best regards. Oskar Schindler.

Schindler also hires a staff of eighteen women who function as secretaries and hostesses at parties for the Nazi officers; in addition, they serve as an ever-changing stable of his mistresses. Schindler has a photograph taken with him outside the factory, dressed impeccably as usual, wearing a Nazi party pin in his lapel and projecting an air of power and success. His aim in everything is to become rich and live well, and with his parties, women, and gifts as well as the cheap labor in his plant, he manages to accomplish both goals.

When a family is evicted from their luxurious apartment and relocated in a slum dwelling, Schindler takes it over. He stretches out on the bed amidst elegant furnishings, glistening woodwork, and French doors commenting, "It couldn't be better," while the displaced Jewish family comfort themselves by saying, "It could be worse."

When his wife Emilie (Caroline Goodall) comes to visit from Czechoslovakia he tells her that his father at his peak had only fifty employees whereas he has "350 workers on the factory floor with one purpose... to make money—for me." He declares that people back home in Czechoslovakia will say of him

He did something extraordinary. He did something no one else did. He came here with nothing, a suitcase, and built a bankrupt company into a major manufactory. And left with a steamer trunk, two steamer trunks, full of money. All the riches of the world... There's no way I could have known this before, but there was always something missing. In every business I tried, I can see now it wasn't me who was failing. Something was missing. Even if I'd known what it was, there's nothing I could have done about it, because you can't create this sort of thing. And it makes all the difference between success and failure.

EMILIE: Luck

SCHINDLER: War

As the pogroms intensify and people are sent to the death camps for extermination, Schindler's factory becomes a way for Jews to remain alive. Nevertheless, saving Jews is not Schindler's intention but a consequence of their being employed; to his mind, they are merely instruments, expendable and replaceable. If a Jew is shot, that's the loss of a worker, not the death of a person. Gradually, however, the means become the end, and he feels a humane connection to the Jews, individually and collectively, as they suffer and are murdered.

The transformation occurs through a series of incidents, some large-scale, other more personal. After a machinist is brought to his office, to thank him for the opportunity to work, he tells Stern," Don't ever do that to me again. Did you happen to notice that the man had one arm. What use is he?" Later, however, when the man is shoveling snow and is shot by a guard, he regrets the man's death. In similar circumstances, Schindler begins to intervene to save Jews' lives saying, "He's a metal press operator, quite skilled," and in the case of children, "They polish the insides of shell casings."

In another incident, he becomes furious at a woman who asks obsequiously that her parents be transferred from a concentration camp to work in his plant. The woman pleads, "They say that no one dies here. They say your factory's a haven. They say that you are good." Schindler threatens to have her arrested for making such a request, and she runs terrified from his office, but later he has her parents brought to work for him.

Schindler also saves Stern, his accountant/plant manager, from deportation, removing him from a cattle car that is headed to a concentration camp. The clerk and soldier he intimidates into stopping the train say, "It makes no difference to us, you understand. This one, that one. It's the inconvenience to the list. It's the paperwork." To Schindler, however, the Jews are becoming human beings and not a bureaucratic category.

In a chilling scene afterwards, the camera follows the luggage as it is wheeled into a shed off the platform. Here the suitcases are emptied and the contents sorted into piles: paintings, jewelry, photos, watches, precious stones. A pile of teeth is poured out in front of a jeweler so the gold fillings can be extracted.

In perhaps the most horrific scenes in the movie, Schindler sees Jews in the Krakow ghetto being brutally murdered. The incident is shown with graphic realism, and Schindler, overlooking the scene on horseback from a hill, is appalled at the butchery. By contrast, this "liquidation of the ghetto" is regarded as a triumph by the Nazis, for this section of the city that had existed for six centuries and fostered business, science, education, and art is now consigned to the dustbin of history.

As Schindler grows in his moral responses and understanding, we see his opposite in the person of the S.S. Commandant of the Plaszow camp, Amon Goeth (Ralph Fiennes). He helps Schindler establish his factory within the prison camp but only because he receives a cut of the profits. His doctrinaire attitude and extreme sadism makes him the embodiment of Nazi evil. In summary executions, he shoots an engineer for making a suggestion, treating it as arguing, and he kills every other man from a barrack where a worker tried to escape—some twenty-five men at point-blank range. In one incident, he tries to shoot a worker for some infraction, and when his gun jams, he clubs him with the butt end of the rifle, almost casually. In a haunting scene, Goeth shoots several workers from a parapet of his house overlooking the work yard, apparently as sport or for target practice, then sets down the rifle and returns to the woman waiting to make love to him in bed. Like a sociopath, he kills without remorse or regret.

Several chinks do appear in his armor, however. In a half-drunken conversation Goeth tells Schindler that, "They fear us because we have the power to kill arbitrarily," to which Schindler replies, "Power is when we have every justification to kill and we don't." He is trying to influence

Goeth toward being merciful, and his words do have some effect. Goeth pardons two offenses, that of a girl smoking on the job and a stable boy who puts a saddle on the ground, but he quickly reverts to type; he first forgives then shoots a boy for not removing stains on a tub. Doing his duty as camp Commandant seems to mesh with his own temperament; he savors the cruelty needed to make the Nazi machine run efficiently. Goeth believed what he was told about Jews because it suited his nature.

A common practice among oppressors is to label a group subhuman and to reduce them to an animal state; this then justifies their being treated as animals, slaves, or commodities. The opposite process occurs when members of a despised group are suddenly regarded as persons; then one can identify with their suffering and feel compassion for them as fellow creatures.

Goeth's closest approach to humaneness occurs in his relationship with a Jewish servant, Helen Hirsch (Embeth Davidtz). Because of her attractiveness, he picks her out of a lineup to be his maid and, despite himself, feels drawn to her. In one definitive scene, Goeth almost yields to his softer feelings, but in the end his hardness prevails.

> I would like so much to reach out and touch you in your loneliness… What would be wrong with that? … I know that you are not a person in the strict sense of the word. When they compare you to the vermin and a rodent and lice, they make a good point… Is this the hair of a rat, are these the eyes of a rat? Has not a Jew eyes? … No, I don't think so. You Jewish bitch, you nearly talked me into it.

Goeth is obviously conflicted. He is attracted to Helen, probably in love with her, but according to Nazi dogma she is the enemy and beneath consideration. Throughout his speech, Helen says nothing but he blames her for seducing him. Obviously, his own natural feelings made him respond to her as a woman. Goeth then beats her, transferring his guilt to her as scapegoat. He is trying to drive out what he regards as impure feelings, suppressing emotions that he perceives as weakness. If Goeth had been able to express his love, he might have reclaimed his humanity but he cannot act on his emotions and remains a victim of ideology.

Itzhak Stern occupies the other end of the spectrum, a composite figure who functions as the good soul in the film. He and Schindler have a wary respect for each other that grows more authentic through the years, but their relationship always remains unspoken and understated. Their conversation when Schindler first hires Stern is typical of their interaction.

SCHINDLER: There's a company you did the books for on Lipowa Street, made what—pots and pans?

STERN: By law, I have to tell you, sir. I'm a Jew.

SCHINDLER: Well, I'm a German, so there we are. (Schindler pours a shot of cognac into the cap of his flask and offers it to Stern—who declines.) A good company, you think?

STERN: Modestly successful.

SCHINDLER: I know nothing about enamelware, do you?

STERN: I was just the accountant.

SCHINDLER: Simple engineering, though, wouldn't you think? Change the machines around, whatever you do, you could make other things, couldn't you? Field kits, mess kits, army contracts. Once the war ends, forget it, but for now it's great. You could make a fortune, don't you think?

STERN: I think most people right now have other priorities.

SCHINDLER: Like what?

STERN: I'm sure you'll do just fine once you get the contracts. In fact, the worse things get, the better you will do.

At one point, Schindler thanks Stern for managing the factory, saying he could not have done it without him, but Stern does not respond, feeling perhaps too ambivalent about his role to accept praise. When Schindler says "Someday this is all going to end… I was going to say, we'll have a drink then," Stern replies, "I think I'd better have it now."

Throughout their association Stern maintains a steady, quiet presence, disciplined, ascetic, patiently doing his job. He first acts out of self-preservation, then because he realized that the more the factory succeeds, the more lives can be saved.

Aside from the characteristics of Schindler, Goethe, and Stern and the events surrounding them, there are numerous moments in the film that are both numbing and indelible. Ashes that consist of human remains drift down on people like snow from crematorium chimneys; Jewish women use their own blood to rouge their cheeks and give an appearance of health; bodies are stacked on wheelbarrows while fires burn all around; a boy hides in a latrine, waist-deep in excrement. There are quick images of a little girl's red garment at the beginning of the film and at her death at the end—notably one of the few shots in color. We see people summarily shot if they offer any resistance to being dragged from their apartments; a Polish woman gleefully shouting "Goodbye Jews" as trucks of men, women, and children pass on the street; and a boy running his finger across his throat as cattle cars filled with Jews roll along the tracks.

Schindler's apotheosis meanwhile has become complete, and while he must maintain good relations with the Nazis, including Goeth, he actively works to help the Jews. We see this in different ways. For example, at a train station one hot afternoon, when he and some Nazi officers are sipping cold drinks and watching overloaded boxcars with their human freight, he realizes that the people inside are dying of suffocation and thirst. With the help of some soldiers he manages to spray the cars with water from a fire hose, cooling them down and allowing the people to drink the drops. This amuses the Nazis rather than offending them because they know the Jews a re going sent to their deaths in Auschwitz. So does Schindler, of course, but he tries to relieve suffering where and when he can. Oddly enough, Schindler seems jovial when he does this, as though his benevolence is an extension of his spirit and flamboyance.

Schindler's most significant act of compassion occurs when the war is beginning to wane. He spends his entire fortune buying his Jewish workers from Goeth, allegedly in order to use them in his Czech factory as essential workers. In this way he saves over eleven hundred lives, including that of Helen Hirsch whom he wins from Goeth in a bet. Stern, who types Schindler's list, realizes that these Jews are being rescued from extermination. "This list is absolutely good," he says, "The list is life."

When the train carrying the women is mistakenly diverted to Auschwitz, Schindler uses his influence to bring them to Brinnlitz, Czechoslovakia. At this point his motive is wholly humanitarian, and his previous goal of profiting form slave labor has been completely supplanted by compassion.

Later, when he establishes his new factory, his rules include no summary executions and no guards on the shop floor, ostensibly because it might interfere with production. In fact, he wants more humane working conditions and secrecy so that he can miscalibrate the shells; for seven months his factory is "a model of non-production." When the war ends, he saves the workers by telling the guards that they can now leave or else commit wholesale slaughter according to their orders. Predictably, the soldiers choose to go home.

As a whole *Schlindler's List* brings home the horror of the Holocaust and shows the successful efforts of one man to oppose the atrocities. A message on the screen reads that the Jewish population of Poland today stands at four thousand, while there are now six thousand descendants of the Jews that Schindler saved. (Ninety-nine percent of Polish Jewish children were annihilated during the war). At the end of the film we see some of these descendants paying tribute to his memory by laying stones on his grave.

Schindler died penniless in 1974 after trying (and failing) to run a farm in Argentina, and the Schindlerjuden cared for him until his death.

One intriguing aspect of the film has to do with the transformation of Schindler's character. We wonder how a high-living, war-profiteer who begins by exploiting the persecution of Jews in order to enrich himself, ends up spending all his money to rescue Jews from death, at great personal risk. The cynical interpretation is that Schindler simply enjoyed the heroic role and the grand gesture, whether that meant being a devil or a saint, The more customary interpretation is that, because of the barbarism he witnessed, he underwent a fundamental change from an opportunist to a caring human being. The metamorphosis does remain an enigma, however, just as we wonder how decent, cultured Germans could have abandoned the principles of civilization and become Nazi monsters.

Whatever his motivation, Schindler acted while others were uninvolved or paralyzed. Elie Wiesel, who has written extensively on the Holocaust, has called indifference the greatest sin. The Catholic Church in Poland remained silent as did most Poles, and many Germans claimed they did not know what was happening. The political philosopher Hannah Arendt wonders why the Jews themselves were so passive, and filed to their deaths without greater protest. Schindler at least did not stand by but behaved righteously. One survivor wrote as follows:

> We live in a shaky and uncertain world, a world that offers little help in choosing life values. In such a setting, knowledge and awareness about noble and self-sacrificing behavior may help restore some shattered illusions. Indeed, mere awareness that in the midst of ultimate human degradation some people were willing to risk their lives for others denies the inevitable supremacy of evil. (Tec Nechama, *When Light Pierced the Darkness*)

STUDY QUESTIONS

1. Do you think we can generalize about groups of people—races, nations, ethnic or religious groups (such as Jews)? Is it legitimate, for example, to characterize the French as people who love good food, the Japanese as industrious, Americans as friendly? Can we differentiate between generalizations and stereotypes? Should we only make positive generalizations and not negative ones about people such as the Japanese during World War II?

2. What rights were taken away from the Jews in Nazi-occupied countries such as Poland? Is it ever morally justified to deprive people of their rights—convicts, military personnel, the mentally ill, foreign nationals of a hostile country?

3. At the Nuremburg Trials, many Nazis argued that they simply obeyed orders as soldiers should and therefore that they should not be held responsible for the atrocities they committed. Is this a sound argument? Why?

4. If Schindler had been discovered helping Jews, he would have been killed as a traitor for violating the laws of the state. Under what conditions do you think the law should be broken?

5. Should the Polish people have helped the Jews, even at the risk of their own lives? Is that asking too much of people?

To Kill a Mockingbird

Director: Robert Mulligan

Writers: Harper Lee (Novel); Horton Foote (Screenplay)

Born in 1925 in Bronx, New York, Robert Mulligan has been a dependable, journeyman director in both TV and films for over 57 years. *He began his career in CBS with several dramatic series such as* Television Playhouse, Suspense, *and* Studio One, *then moved to feature films with* Fear Strikes Out. *Mulligan then directed or produced some 23 films. including* Up the Down Staircase *and* Summer of '42; *for the latter, he was nominated for a Golden Globe Award.*

To Kill a Mockingbird *was his most successful film, garnering him an Academy Award nomination as Best Director. Based on the Pulitzer Prize winning novel by Harper Lee, the film explores the theme of justice, especially racial justice. It is also a Bildungsroman, a coming-of-age story of three children who achieve a more complex understanding of morality. Mulligan was always drawn to the world of youth and adolescence, to deviants and loners in their attempt to find meaning in the world they move through. The film benefits from his sympathetic understanding of outsiders, as well as from Mulligan's soft, restrained direction. He allows the characters and the story to be presented rather than represented, which enhances the film's authenticity.*

SYNOPSIS

Very few American films have achieved the legendary fame of *To Kill a Mockingbird,* the critically acclaimed winner of three Oscars. Its classic status came about through a blend of extraordinary acting, narrative charm and dramatic force, and the social message of the plot. The book by Harper Lee, on which the film is (faithfully) based, invariably makes the list of Best Novels as selected by teachers and librarians. It is a largely autobiographical novel, and the only book that Lee ever wrote. Translated into 10 languages, it has sold 30 million copies to date.

The story is set in the Old South of 1932, a time of economic depression and racial tension, and revolves around a lawyer Atticus Finch (Gregory Peck) who is called upon to defend a black man accused of raping a white woman. The plot also involves Atticus's two children, Scout (Mary Badham) and Jem (Philip Alford), and their friend "Dill" Harris (John Megna)—the last is based on Harper Lee's childhood neighbor, Truman Capote. These two strands come together in a way that reveals the nature of fairness and unfairness, malice and integrity.

The film is shot in black-and-white at a time when directors were using color, probably to underscore the conflict between the races. This also gives it the feel of an antique photograph and emphasizes the stark moral contrasts. The film was released during the Civil Rights movement in the 1960s.

The place is Macomb, Alabama, a languid southern town, impoverished and Gothic, with a mythic quality to it. There is a strict code of segregation between blacks and whites in all areas of life, especially with regard to sex. White men can take advantage of black women but for a white woman to have sexual relations with a black man is the South's worst nightmare. The stability of the social structure depends upon maintaining this taboo. That is why the alleged rape of a white woman, Mayella Ewell (Collin Wilcox), by a black man, Tom Robinson (Brock Peters), must be categorically punished; it is symbolically important to the power relation between whites and blacks.

But the story is witnessed and told through the eyes of Scout, a six-year-old with the perceptions of a child but adult insight and comprehension. She and her older brother Jem and their friend Dill while away the summer days swinging on a rubber tire, playing in a tree house, and scaring themselves with frightening stories about "Boo" Radley (Robert Duvall), their reclusive, silent neighbor. (They later discover he has been leaving presents for them inside the hollow of a tree.) Although Boo has rarely been glimpsed, Jem is able to describe him: "He eats raw squirrels and all the cats he can catch. There's a long, jagged scar that runs all the way across his face. His teeth are yella and rotten. His eyes are popped. And he drools most of the time." They dare each other to go near the house where he is "chained to a bed," only coming out "at night when you're asleep and it's pitch-dark."

They also spin stories about an elderly neighbor, Mrs. Henry Lafayette Dubose (Ruth White), who sits in a wheelchair on the porch of a nearby house. Jem warns them, "Listen, no matter what she says to you, don't answer her back. There's a Confederate pistol in her lap under her shawl and she'll kill you quick as look at you."

Their father Atticus is able to allay every childish fear, offering an explanation that reflects an even-tempered tolerance. He advises them on how to treat Boo, Mrs. Dubose, and even on using a rifle, as when he says it is a sin to kill a mockingbird, a creature that lives only to sing and bring us pleasure. Atticus is, in fact, an extraordinarily caring parent as well as a forthright lawyer. He may be larger-than-life, his nobility overdone and unrealistic, but he represents an ideal citizen and father, man at his best. He reflects deeply and acts strongly, from shooting a rabid dog to discussing with Scout the way to handle a teacher's unfairness. Although he says we cannot judge a man until we have walked in his shoes, the depiction of his character is so strong we feel as though that we have done just that.

The children are exposed to a serious world of conflict when Atticus is called upon to defend Tom Robinson against a charge of rape. They do not fully understand what is at stake but they know there is opposition to their father taking the case. This comes from much of the town and, of course, from the girl's redneck father, Robert E. Lee "Bob" Ewell (James Anderson). At one point he confronts Atticus and says, "I'm real sorry they picked you to defend that nigger that raped my Mayella. I don't know why I didn't kill him myself instead of goin' to the sheriff. That would have saved you and the sheriff and the taxpayers lots of trouble." Then he adds rather ominously, "What kind of man are you? You got chillun of your own."

When Scout returns to school in the fall she gets into a fight over the trial and asks Atticus, "Do you defend niggers?" He replies, "Don't say 'nigger' Scout." She answers "I didn't say it…Cecil Jacobs did. That's why I had to fight him."

> ATTICUS: There are some things that you're not old enough to understand just yet. There's been some high talk around town to the effect that I shouldn't do much about defending this man.
>
> SCOUT: If you shouldn't be defending him, then why are you doing it?
>
> ATTICUS: For a number of reasons. The main one is that if didn't, I couldn't hold my head up in town. I couldn't even tell you or Jem not to do somethin' again. (He puts his arm around her.) You're gonna hear some ugly talk about this in school. But I want you to promise me one thing…that you won't get into fights over it, no matter what they say to you.

The following summer when the trial is scheduled to begin Tom is brought to the Macomb jail from an adjoining town, and that night Atticus stands watch for fear of vigilante justice. In a vivid image, he leans his chair against the jailhouse door and reads under a lamp brought from home. Contrary to Atticus's wishes, the children come to the jail, arriving at the same time that a lynch mob converges in cars. Atticus attempts to reason with the armed men but without success, until Scout comes forward and speaks to a man she knows in the crowd in a matter of fact, conversational way.

> Don't you remember me, Mr. Cunningham? I'm Jean Louise Finch. You brought us some hickory nuts one early morning, remember? We had a talk. I went and got my daddy to come out and thank you. I go to school with your boy. I go to school with Walter. He's a nice boy. Tell him 'hey' for me, won't you.

Out of embarrassment, the mob disburses.

The trial then proceeds with the children watching from the balcony with the "colored folk" because, as Jem says, "I'm not going to miss the most exciting' thing that ever happened in this town." A series of witnesses are called, beginning with Sheriff Tate who testifies that Bob Ewell reported to him that his daughter had been raped. "She was beaten around the head. There were bruises already comin' on her arms. She had a black eye…It was her right eye, Mr. Finch. Now I remember. She was beaten up on that side of her face…she showed me her neck. There were definite finger marks on her gullet…I'd say they were all around."

Bob Ewell then testifies that he came home to discover his daughter screaming and Tom Robinson on top of her. "I seen him with my Mayella…po' Mayella was layin' on the floor squallin'." Ewell, the antitype of Atticus, embodies the anger, ignorance, and ugliness of the worst type of backwoodsman; he is as malicious as Atticus is morally courteous.

Mayella then testifies that she had asked Tom to break up a chifforobe, but "'fore I know it, he's on me, and I fought and hollered, but he had me around the neck, and he hit me again and again, and the next thing I knew, Papa was in the room, a-standin' over me, hollerin', 'Who done it, who done it?'"

Under cross-examination it becomes obvious that she is lying. Mayella testifies that she cannot recall whether or not Tom hit her, that her father "never touched a hair o' my head in my life" but at the same time he could beat her when he was drinking. Also contradictory is Bob Ewell's's testimony that he saw Tom Robinson raping his daughter, although Mayella reported that he asked her who did it. Most damning is the revelation that Tom's left hand is useless following an accident with a cotton gin but

Mayella's injuries were all to the right side of her face; the finger marks were also "all around."

Despite her perjury, Mayella comes across as a sympathetic character, bullied by her father into lying on the stand and trying to maintain a residue of respectability. The town sees her as "poor white trash," and she has assumed that image. In her speech to the court she is dishonest but also pathetic, and her resentment is palpable at being trapped in a squalid life. During the trial she says to the court,

> I got somethin' to say. And then I ain't gonna say no more. He took advantage of me. An' if you fine, fancy gentlemen ain't gonna do nothin' about it, then you're just a bunch of lousy, yella, stinkin' cowards, the whole bunch of ya, and your fancy airs don't come to nothing'. Your Ma'am'in' and your Miss Mayellarin'—it don't come to nothin'.

When Tom Robinson takes the stand he is extremely frightened, but he declares that Mayella had asked him to do chores for her on several occasions, "chopin' kindlin' and totin' water." He says he did so out of pity, which causes a murmur in the court. The prosecuting attorney responds "You felt sorry for her? A white woman? You felt sorry for her?"

Tom then testifies that on this particular day Mayella grabbed him around his legs while he was standing on a chair getting a box down.

> Mr. Finch, I got down off the chair, and I turned around an'she sorta jumped on me. She hugged me aroun' the waist. She reached up an' kissed me on the face. She said she'd never kissed a grown man before an' she might as well kiss me. She says for me to kiss her back. And I said, Miss Mayella, let me outta here, an' I tried to run. Mr. Ewell cussed at her from the window and said he's gonna kill her.

Obviously, this is a true account of the events, but the all-white jury would have to believe the word of a black defendant over that of white witnesses, including a white woman calling on their chivalry. In the face of the bigoted attitudes of the jury and of the town, Tom stands little chance of acquittal. In his summation Atticus speaks directly to the underlying issue of black-white relations—the racial prejudice that should not be allowed to blind people to the truth. In a moving speech he pleads for social justice:

> I have nothing but pity in my heart for the Chief Witness for the State. She is the victim of cruel poverty and ignorance. But, my pity does not extend so far as to her putting a man's life at stake, which is what she has done in an effort to get rid of her own guilt. Now I say "guilt" gentlemen, because it was guilt that motivated her. She's committed no crime. She has merely broken a rigid and time-honored code of our society, a code so severe that whoever breaks it is hounded from our midst as unfit to live with. She

must destroy the evidence of her offense. But, what was the evidence of her offense? Tom Robinson, a human being. She must put Tom Robinson away from her. Tom Robinson was to her a daily reminder of what she did.

Now what did she do? She tempted a negro. She was white and she tempted a negro. She did something that in our society is unspeakable. She kissed a black man. Not an old uncle, but a strong, young negro man. No code mattered to her before she broke it, but it came crashing down on her afterwards...

And so, a quiet, humble, respectable negro, who has had the unmitigated TEMERITY to feel sorry for a white woman, has had to put his word against two white people. The defendant is not guilty. But somebody in this courtroom is.

Now, gentlemen, in this country the courts are the great levelers. In our courts, all men are created equal. I'm no idealist to believe firmly in the integrity of our courts and of our jury system. That's no ideal to me. That is a living, working reality.

Now I am confident that you gentlemen will review without passion the evidence that you have heard, come to a decision, and restore this man to his family.

In the name of God, do your duty. In the name of God, believe Tom Robinson.

Despite Atticus's eloquence, the jury finds Tom guilty, and there is a memorable scene when the blacks rise as Atticus leaves the courtroom defeated. A Reverend Sykes says to Scout, "Miss Jean Louise, stand up, your father's passin'." Tom is subsequently shot to death, allegedly while trying to escape from custody. "Tom broke loose and ran. The deputy called out to him to stop. Tom didn't stop...[he] just ran like a crazy man."

The coda to the film, which focuses once more on the children, takes place the following fall and weaves the threads into a final fabric. A Halloween pageant is planned with each child representing an agricultural product of the county; Scout is to dress as a ham. On the way home with Jem, the two children are viciously attacked in a dark woods. Scout is thrown to the ground and hears sounds of a struggle, but she can only see confused scenes through the eye holes of the ham costume. She hears Jem shouting "Run, Scout," then suddenly sees the hands of another person fighting with the assailant. After managing to remove her costume, she sees Jem being carried into their house by an unknown man. Jem is unconscious with a badly broken arm but the doctor assures the family that he will recover with bed rest.

The man who protected the children and carried Jem home turns out to be Boo Radley, and the assailant, Bob Ewell, who was killed in the fight. As the Sheriff reports it, "Bob Ewell's lyin' on the ground under that tree down yonder with a kitchen knife stuck up under his ribs...He's not gonna bother these children any more."

Clearly it was Boo who killed him, which means he should be taken into custody and put on trial. However, the Sheriff chooses not to apply the criminal law but a higher mode of justice. He says to Atticus,

> Bob Ewell fell on his knife. He killed himself. There's a black man dead for no reason, and now the man responsible for it is dead. Let the dead bury the dead this time, Mr. Finch. I never heard tell it was against the law for any citizen to do his utmost to prevent a crime from being committed, which is exactly what he did…To my way of thinkin', takin' one man who's done you and this town a big service, and draggin' him, with his shy ways, into the limelight, to me, that's a sin, It's a sin, and I'm not about to have it on my head. I may not be much, Mr. Finch, but I'm still Sheriff of Macomb County, and Bob Ewell fell on his knife.

Scout agrees, saying "Mr. Tate was right." When Atticus asks her what she means she replies "Well, it would be sort of like shooting a mockingbird, wouldn't it?"

The film therefore circles back to the theme of justice, between blacks and whites and fairness on a more personal level. An innocent black man was killed as a result of racial hatred, and one of the perpetrators had been killed in turn. Poetic justice was achieved, carried out by Boo Radley whose nature was as misunderstood as the blacks in the town. The world could then settle back into balance because the scales of justice had been righted.

STUDY QUESTIONS

1. Why did Atticus feel honor-bound to defend Tom Robinson?

2. What were the rules regarding sexual relations between the races? Why did the society at large feel it was important that these rules be maintained?

3. What was the evidence that showed Tom did not rape Mayella?

4. In what ways did Scout grow in moral awareness and understanding?

5. How does the sheriff's decision not to arrest Boo Radley reflect a higher justice? Why would you agree or disagree with this decision?

Bibliography of Philosophy, Literature, and Films

V. The Individual and Society: Political Philosophy

Philosophy

Anarchy, State, and Utopia	Robert Nozick
Abortion, Law, Choice and Morality	Daniel Callahan
Apology, Crito, Republic	Plato
Basic Rights	Henry Shue
Capital	Karl Marx
Capitalism and Freedom	Milton Friedman
"Civil Disobedience"	H. D. Thoreau
Communism, Fascism, and Democracy	Carl Cohen
The Communist Manifesto	Karl Marx
The Enforcement of Morals	Patrick Devlin
Equality and Preferential Treatment	Marshal Cohen
Feminist Politics and Human Nature	Alison Jagger
The Free Society	John Middleton Murray
Freedom of Expression	Fred R. Berger
Justice and Economic Distribution	John Arthur
Law, Legislation, and Liberty	F. A. Hayek
Leviathan	Thomas Hobbes
Libertarianism: A Political Philosophy	John Hospers
Life and Death with Liberty and Justice	Grisez, Germain
Lifeboat Ethics	George R. Lucas
Mortal Questions	Thomas Nagel
The New Atlantis	Francis Bacon
Of Civil Government	John Locke
On Liberty	John Stuart Mill
The Open Society and Its Enemies	Karl Popper
Persons and Masks of the Law	John T. Hoonan
Political Power and Personal Freedom	Sidney Hook
Political Violence and Civil Disobedience	Ernest van den Haag
Politics	Aristotle
Property, Profits, and Economic Justice	Viginia Held
Sex Equality	Jane English
Social Philosophy	Joel Feinberg
The Social Contract	Jean Jacques Rousseau
Socialism	Michael Harrington

To the Finland Station	Edmund Wilson
A Theory of Justice	John Rawls
Second Treatise of Government	John Locke
The Utopia	Thomas More

Literature

Billiards at Half Past Nine	Heinrich Boll
Brave New World	Aldous Huxley
Bread and Wine	Ignazio Silone
Book of Songs	Heinrich Heine
Cancer Ward	Alexander Solzhenitsyn
Clerambault	Romain Rolland
Darkness at Noon	Arthur Koestler
Dirty Hands	Jean-Paul Sartre
Doctor Zhivago	Boris Pasternak
An Enemy of the People	Henrich Ibsen
Erehwon	Samuel Butler
A Farewell to Arms, The Sun Also Rises	Ernest Hemingway
Fathers and Sons	Ivan Turgenev
The Flies	Jean-Paul Sartre
From Here to Eternity	James Jones
A Hero of Our Time	Mikhail Lermontov
Lord of the Flies	William Golding
Man's Estate	Andre Malraux
The Master and Magrita	Mikhail Bulgakov
Mother	Nikolay Gogol
The Naked and the Dead	Norman Mailer
Of Mice and Men	John Steinbeck
"The Overcoat"	Nikolay Gogol
Penguin Island	Anatole France
And Quiet Flows the Don	Mikhail Sholokov
Soldier's Pay	William Faulkner
The Sleepwalkers	Hermann Broch
Things Fall Apart	Achua Achebe
The Time Machine	H. G. Wells
The Tin Drum	Gunter Grass
Walden II	B. F. Skinner

Films

Absolute Beginners	Julian Temple
Advise and Consent	Otto Preminger
Alexander Nevsky, Battleship Potemkin	Sergei Eisenstein
All Quiet on the Western Front	Lewis Milestone
All the King's Men	Robert Rossen
All the President's Men	Alan Pakula
The Angry Silence	Guy Green
Apocalypse Now	Francis Ford Coppola
Birth of a Nation	D. W. Griffith
Blue Collar	Paul Schrader
Boat People	Ann Hui
Born on the Fourth of July	Oliver Stone
The Boys From Brazil	Franklin Schaffner
The Candidate	Michael Ritchie
Citizen Kane	Orson Wells
City Lights	Charlie Chaplin
Closely Observed Trains	Jiri Menzel
The Conformist	Bernardo Bertolucci
The Cranes Are Flying	Mickail Kalatozov
The Deer Hunter	Michael Cimino
Doctor Strangelove	Stanley Kubrick
Easy Rider	Dennis Hopper
Fahrenheit 451	Francois Truffaut
Fury	Fritz Lang
Gallipoli	Peter Weir
Gandhi	Richard Attenborough
The Garden of the Finzi-Continis	Vittorio de Sica
The Grand Illusion	Jean Renoir
Hiroshima Mon Amour	Alain Resnais
The Informer	John Ford
Judgment at Nuremberg	Stanley Kramer
The Killing Fields	Roland Joffe
Kiss of the Spider Woman	Hector Babenco
The Lion in Winter	Anthony Harvey
La Grande Illusion	Jean Renoir
Love and Anarchy	Lina Wertmuller
The Machurian Candidate	John Frankenheimer
Man of Marble	Andrzej Wajda
The Marriage of Maria Braun	Rainer Fassbinder

Nixon	Oliver Stone
El Norte	Gregory Nava
The Official Story	Luis Puenzo
On the Waterfront	Elia Kazan
The Pawnbroker	Sidney Lumet
A Passage to India	David Lean
Paths of Glory	Stanley Kubrick
Platoon	Oliver Stone
A Raisin in the Sun	Daniel Petrie
The Rules of the Game	Jean Renoir
Schindler's List	Steven Spielberg
The Servant	Joseph Losey
The Shop on Main Street	Jan Kadar
Sophie's Choice	Alan Paluka
State of Siege	Constantine Costa-Garvas
Swept Away	Lina Wertmuller
The Thin Red Line	Andrew Marton

Index